AF574230

Disney

PRINCESS

BEYOND THE TIARA

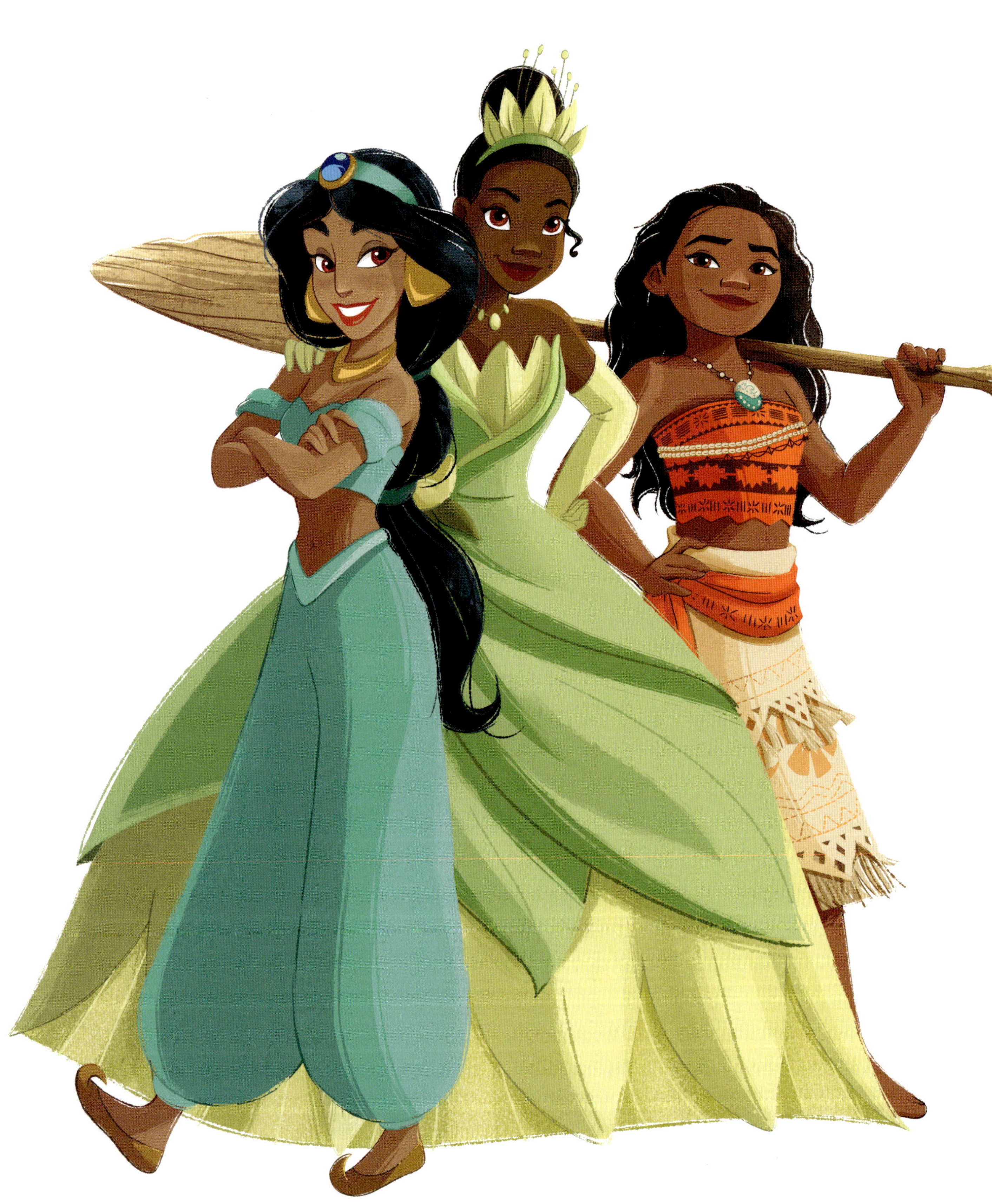

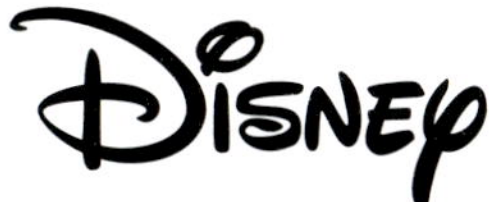

PRINCESS
BEYOND THE TIARA

THE STORIES + THE INFLUENCE + THE LEGACY

EMILY ZEMLER

FOREWORD BY JODI BENSON
VOICE OF ARIEL FROM *THE LITTLE MERMAID*

EPIC INK

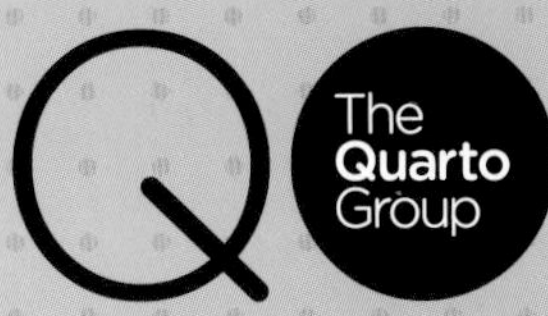

First published in 2022 by Epic Ink,
an imprint of The Quarto Group,
142 West 36th Street, 4th Floor,
New York, NY 10018, USA
T (212) 779-4972 F (212) 779-6058
www.Quarto.com

22 23 24 25 26 5 4 3 2 1

Library of Congress Control Number: 2021950415.

ISBN: 978-0-7603-7362-0

Publisher: Delia Greve
Creative Director: Laura Drew
Managing Editor: Cara Donaldson
Editor: Laura Hitchock
Editorial Assistance: Haley Stocking
Photo Research: Julie Alissi
Layout Design: Kim Winscher

Printed in China

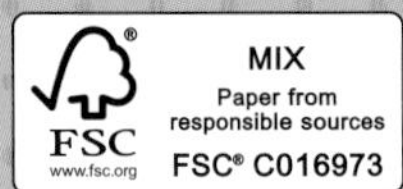

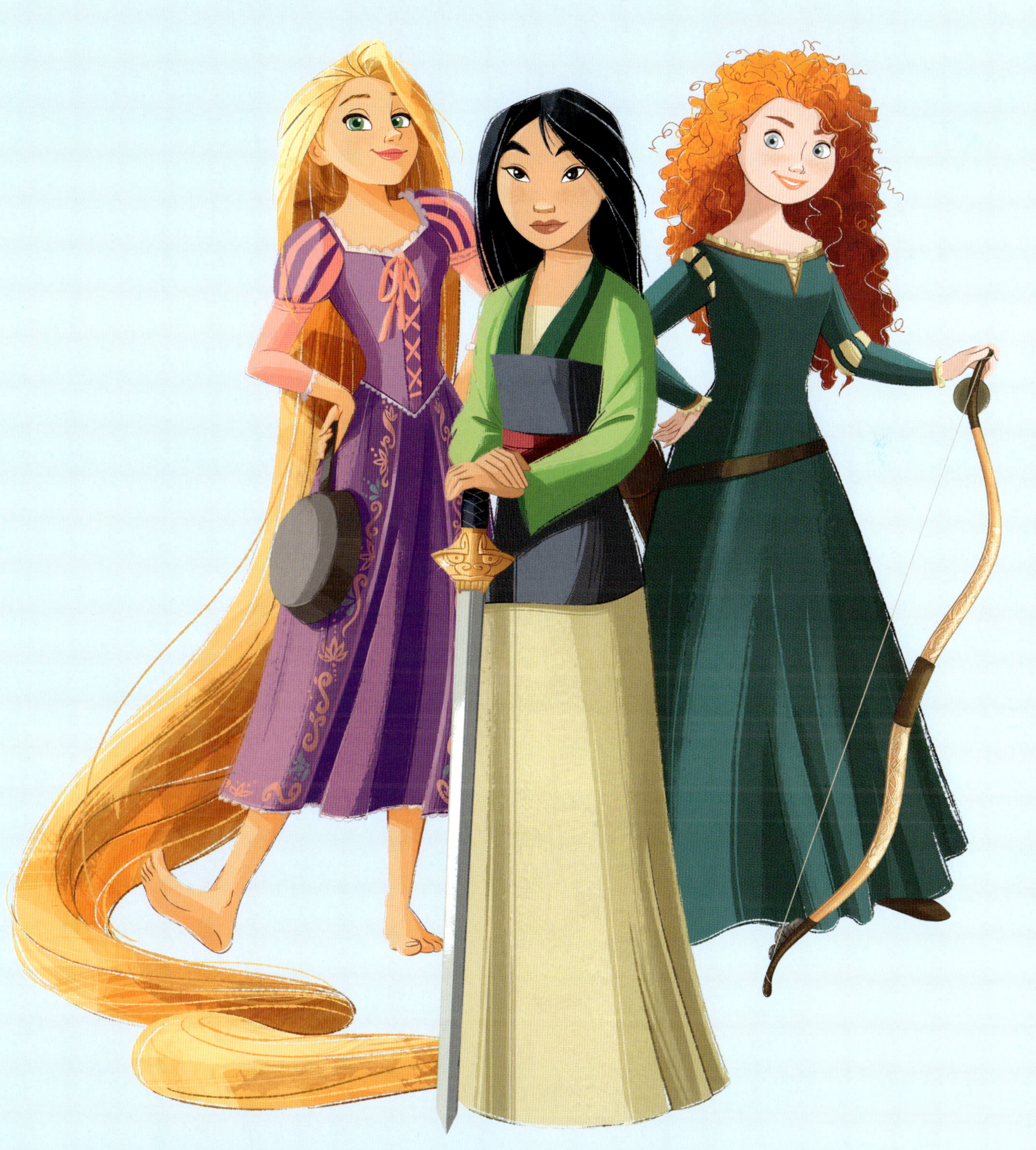

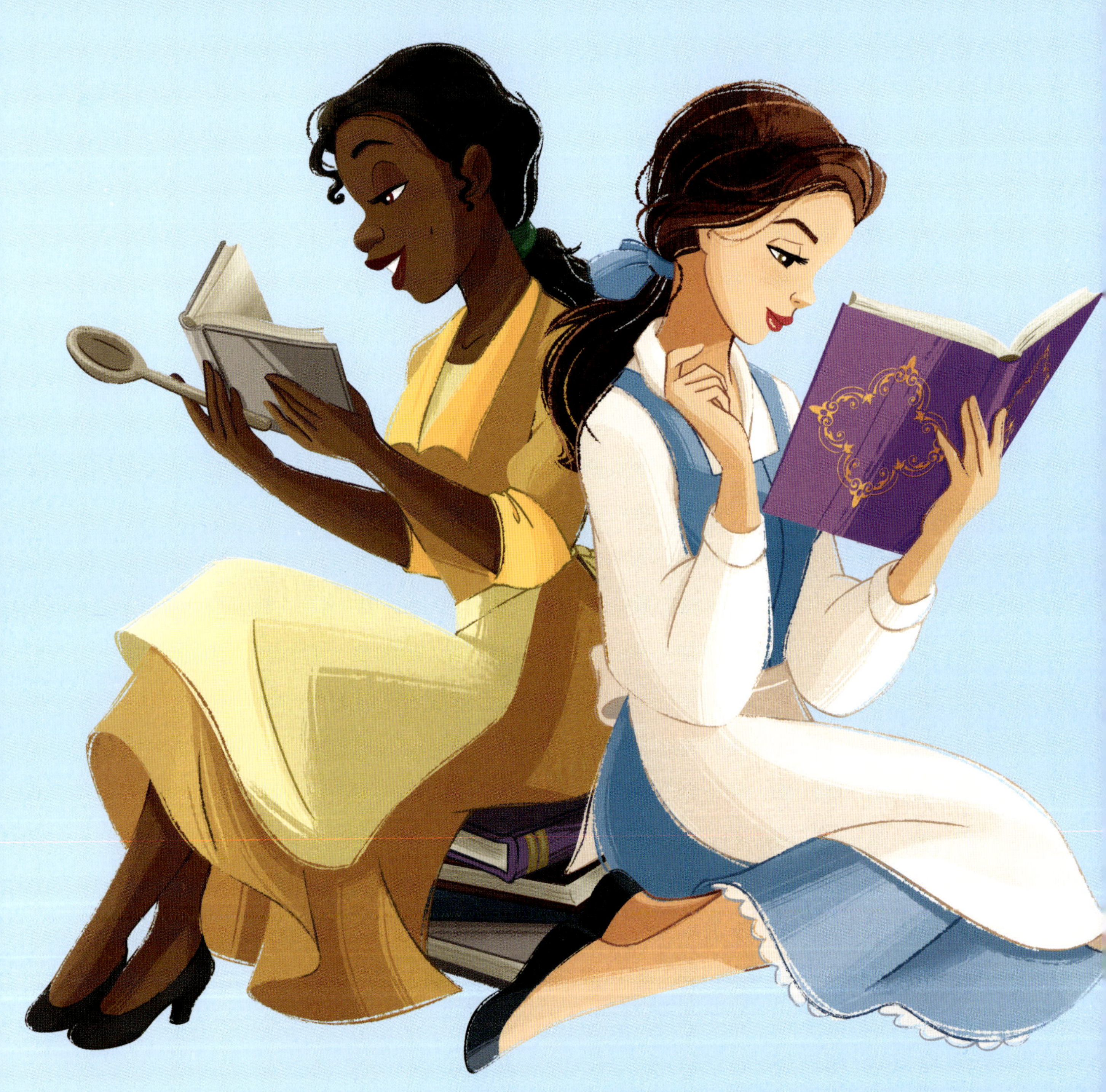

CONTENTS

FOREWORD: By Jodi Benson 8
INTRODUCTION: I'm Wishing 10

CHAPTER ONE
ONCE UPON A DREAM: Origins and Inspirations 12

CHAPTER TWO
A WHOLE NEW WORLD: Reimaginings 54

CHAPTER THREE
PART OF YOUR WORLD: Toys, Collectibles, and Games 72

CHAPTER FOUR
BIBBIDI-BOBBIDI-BOO: Fashion 94

CHAPTER FIVE
WITH A SMILE AND A SONG: Music 114

CHAPTER SIX
BE OUR GUEST: Parks, Resorts, and Cruise Ships 130

CHAPTER SEVEN
REFLECTION: Fandom, Cosplay, and Art 146

CHAPTER EIGHT
HOW FAR I'LL GO: Girl Power 160

AFTERWORD: Keep on Believing 174
ACKNOWLEDGMENTS 176
ABOUT THE AUTHOR 177
TIMELINE 178
SOURCES 180
IMAGE CREDITS 184
INDEX 186

FOREWORD

BY JODI BENSON

It's an incredible honor and a privilege to be a Disney Princess, but I never would have guessed in a million years, that *The Little Mermaid* would become such a huge part of my life.

In 1986, I was doing a Broadway show called *Smile* with Howard Ashman and Marvin Hamlisch. When the show closed, Howard was kind enough to invite a few of us in the show to audition for his next project, an animated film for The Walt Disney Company called *The Little Mermaid*. I auditioned in a Broadway rehearsal studio in New York, and they gave me two pages of Ariel's dialogue and a little cassette tape of Howard singing "Part of Your World." I went to the restroom, made sure no one else was there, and quickly created a voice for a rebellious teenage mermaid. It wasn't until over a year later that I learned I had been cast as Ariel, and started flying back and forth to Los Angeles to record with the filmmakers.

At first, the studio wasn't going to call attention to the voice talents involved with the film. I assumed no one would focus on who was doing the voice of Ariel and that they would just care about Ariel as a character. I figured that voicing Ariel would be a neat experience, but I never expected the lasting impact the role would have on me. But about a month before *The Little Mermaid* was due to arrive in theaters, I received a call and was told they were sending me on a press tour to twenty-two cities in twenty days. It was far beyond what I had anticipated. Suddenly, my voice was directly connected to the character.

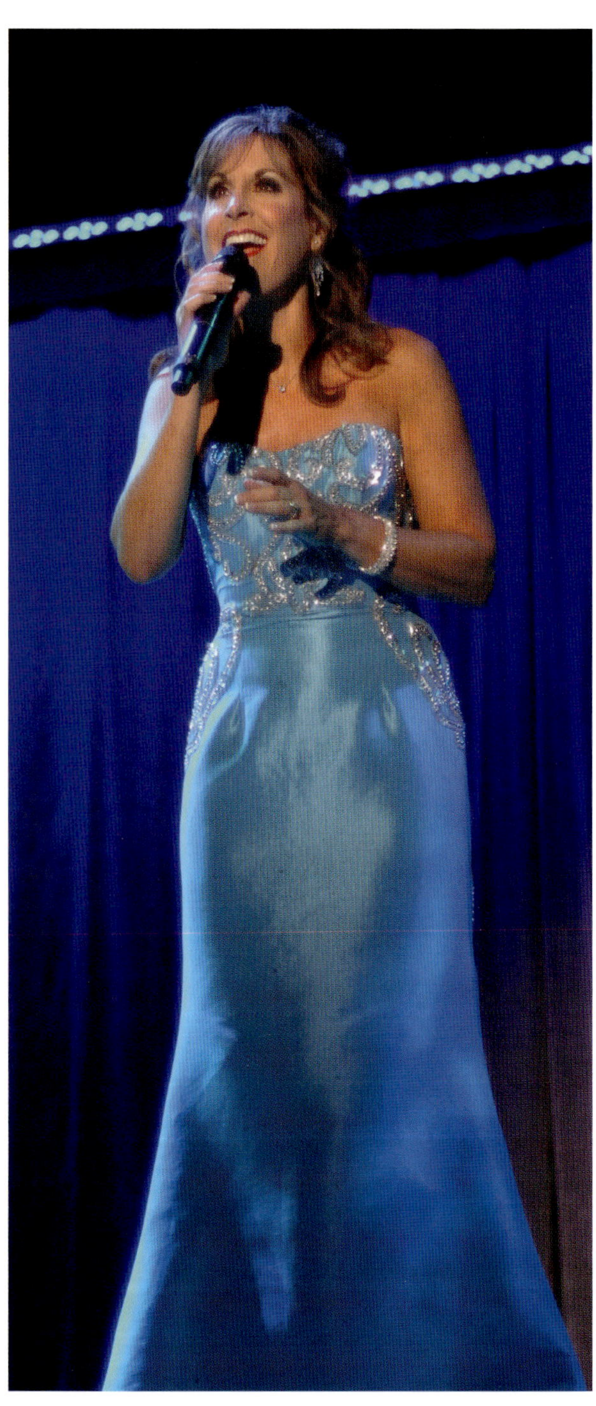

Jodi Benson performs for fans at D23 Expo in 2011 after being officially inducted as a Disney Legend.

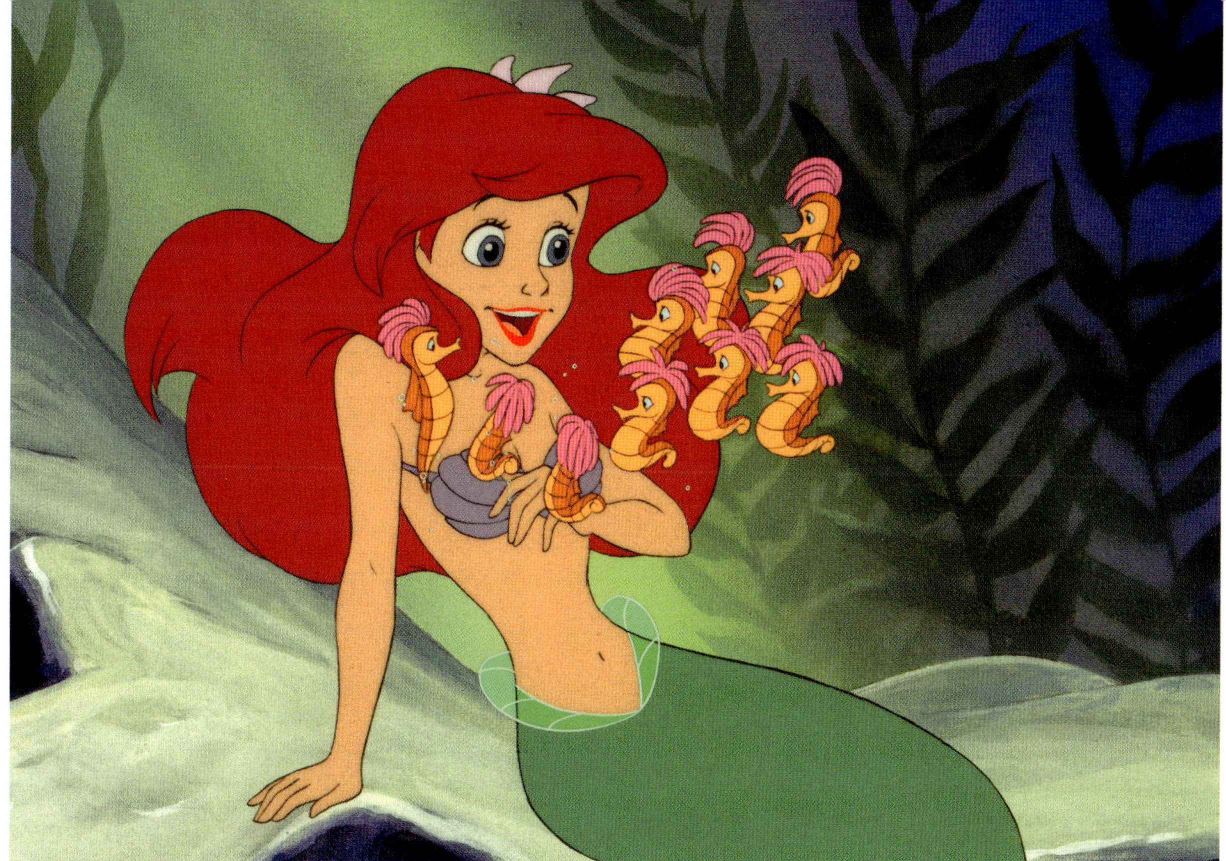

Ariel in the 1989 animated classic *The Little Mermaid.*

The movie came out on November 17, 1989, and by that Christmas, Ariel was everywhere—she was everywhere you looked, in every store, on toys and dolls and merchandise.

Ariel and I are a lot alike. I grew up in a small town that was very conventional, and when I was young, I too dreamed of something more. I myself was a kid from a broken home. My father left when I was eleven, and I had to dream big. I wanted to sing and dance and act on Broadway. So, to take that leap of faith was very much like Ariel. I was able to make that emotional connection with her right away.

Like all of the Disney Princesses, Ariel is an incredible character and so inspiring. I love her curiosity, her independence, and her fiery spirit. I love that she never gives up, even when facing extreme adversity. I love how she sees the good in humans when no one else does. That's something we all can carry with us: how to love others even when they seem to be unlovable. There are so many admirable qualities about Ariel, and I try to convey them through my voice performances.

I've heard hundreds of stories from people all over the world about how Ariel has changed their lives, and it's easy to understand why. The spark of her character has guided them through challenging times and feeling like an outsider who will never truly fit in. It's unbelievable that an animated feature film can touch people's lives like that and actually change them. I'm so honored to be a little piece of their stories.

Since *The Little Mermaid* premiered, I've voiced Ariel in many projects over the years, from sequels to TV series to toys, and continue to do so to this day. She's part of an ongoing legacy of magic and fantasy created by Disney, and all the Disney Princesses are very much connected to that. Seeing characters like Ariel allows children—and adults—to know their own dreams can come true. After all these years, it's really incredible to see that my little mermaid is still flipping her fins and is a part of our world forever.

Jodi Benson

INTRODUCTION

I'M WISHING

Growing up, I wanted to be a princess. I imagined far-off lands filled with magical creatures, sparkling gowns, and an existence where good is always greater than evil. For me, it wasn't about marrying a prince or looking pretty; it was about being the protagonist of my own story. (And, of course, being able to speak with animals.) Because I, like so many others, was raised on the vibrant animated films of Walt Disney, my idea of a princess was a Disney Princess. I waved my hair around in the swimming pool like Ariel, carried books everywhere I went like Belle, and wandered through the woods behind our house like Aurora. These animated heroes were my role models, and their stories allowed me to dream of something beyond my hometown.

What we see onscreen is always a reflection of the time it was made, and each Disney Princess story showcases how we've grown and changed as a culture. Fashion and desires shift from year to year, and from generation to generation. Snow White represents American society in the 1930s, and her resilience resonated with people during the lingering years of the Great Depression. Today, we look to her for inspiration and guidance on how to be kind, empathetic, and caring to those around us—characteristics that are universal and timeless. As society has evolved, so have the Disney Princesses. In the years since *Snow White and the Seven Dwarfs* (1937), each Disney Princess has brought us a new, magical world and taken us on an encouraging, aspirational journey.

"Fairy tales are about the ordinary hero who accomplishes something extraordinary," explains Jennifer Lee, Walt Disney Animation Studios Chief Creative Officer. "Usually, there

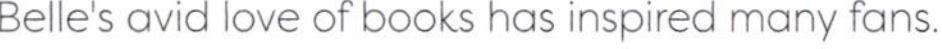

Belle's avid love of books has inspired many fans.

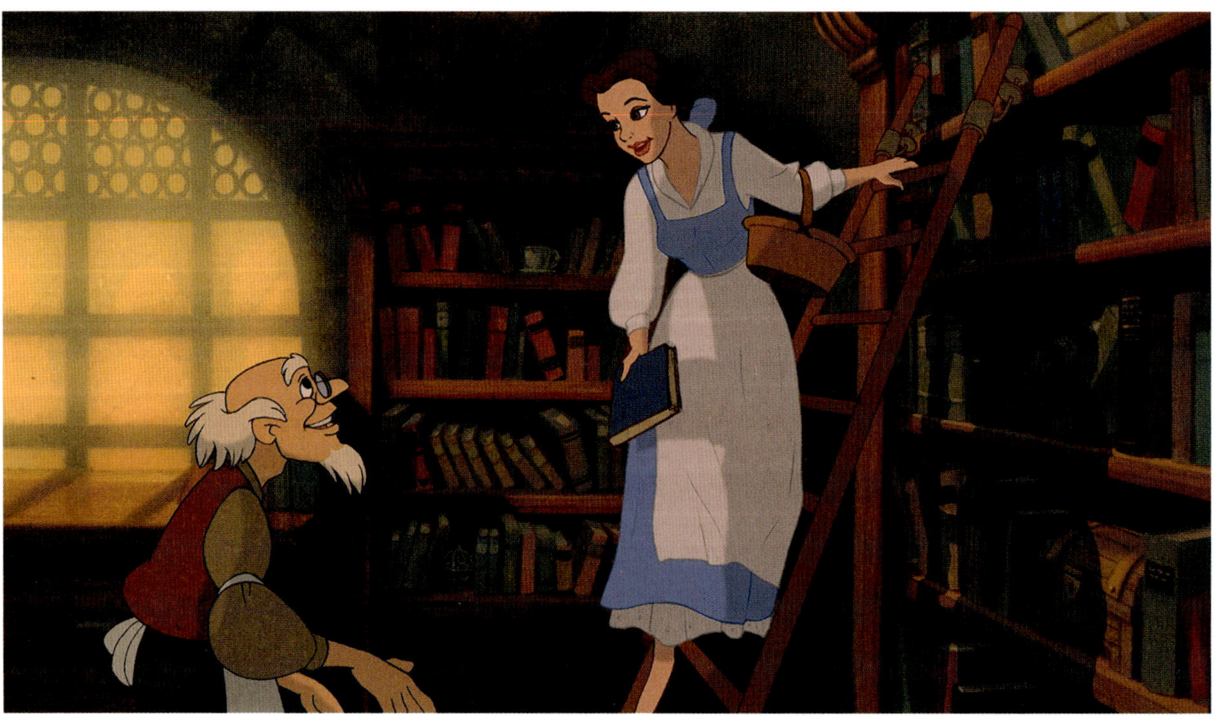

are deeper themes about good versus evil. But they're also about the ability of the human spirit to persevere. When you have female heroes in these stories, what's always interesting is that it depends on the era they were made. Each generation has a different perspective on the most innocent or the most vulnerable person in a society, but seeing the courage in that person resonates with everyone."

The Disney Princess films have been passed down from generation to generation for nearly a century. They leave profound imprints on us as kids, and continue to be impactful as we grow up. The generation that was raised on the films of the late 1980s and 1990s, like *The Little Mermaid* (1989) and *Mulan* (1998), now embraces the nostalgia of those beloved stories in memes, fashion, and music. It's the reason that The Walt Disney Studios' recent live-action reimaginings of the animated classics have been—and will continue to be—such hits. "These fairy tales have stood the test of time because they speak to something very deep in our humanity," notes Sean Bailey, President of Production at The Walt Disney Studios. "They reflect our experiences and our values, and that touches people at a deep level when done well."

It's no mistake that Walt Disney began his journey into feature-length animated films with fairy tales. These long-told stories have captivated people around the world for centuries, and each new version becomes part of its own era. The Disney Princesses are part of a long tradition of storytelling that extends far beyond their specific narratives. We look to these tales for light in the darkness—another reason the Disney films are so compelling.

"We love fairy tales for the same reason you buy a lottery ticket: Your life changes overnight and all your dreams come true," says Edward Kitsis, co-creator of the television series *Once Upon a Time* (2011-2018). "For fairy tales, there's a wish fulfillment that ends with hope. You can feel like Cinderella sweeping up and not going to the ball, but then you get to go. People love stories where, at the end, the person actually comes out the other side feeling better."

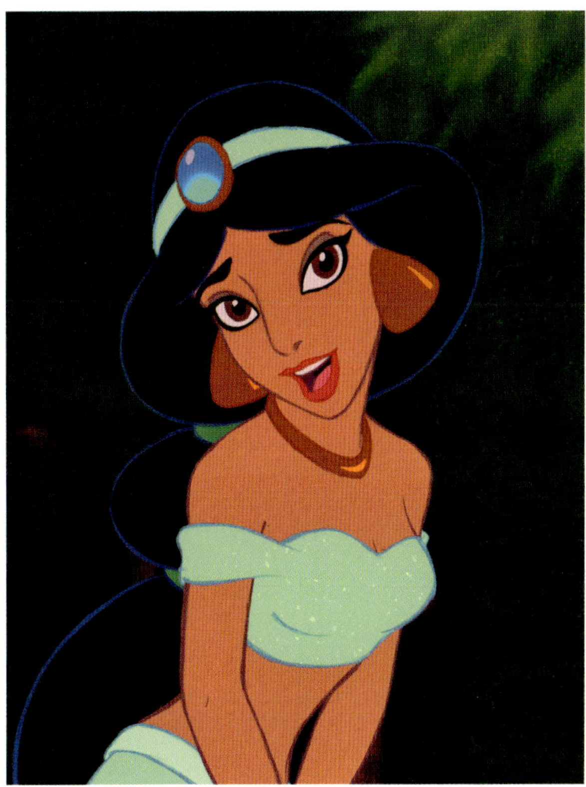

Jasmine was one of several Disney Princesses created during the 1990s.

As I began to pay more attention, I saw the influence of the Disney Princesses everywhere. They have impacted our experiences at the Disney Parks and Resorts, the toys we play with, how we dress for big events, and how we communicate with each other on the Internet. Their influence is greater than any living celebrity, not only because they've endured for so many decades, but because they continue to grow and change along with us. And a Disney Princess is so much more than a character on a screen. As she moves out into the world, embraced by people of all ages, backgrounds, and genders, she becomes an icon. There are a lot of reasons one might want to be a princess, all of them valid and essential. But the most important one is the ability to dream. A true Disney Princess knows she is capable of so much more, if she can only reach for it.

– Emily Zemler

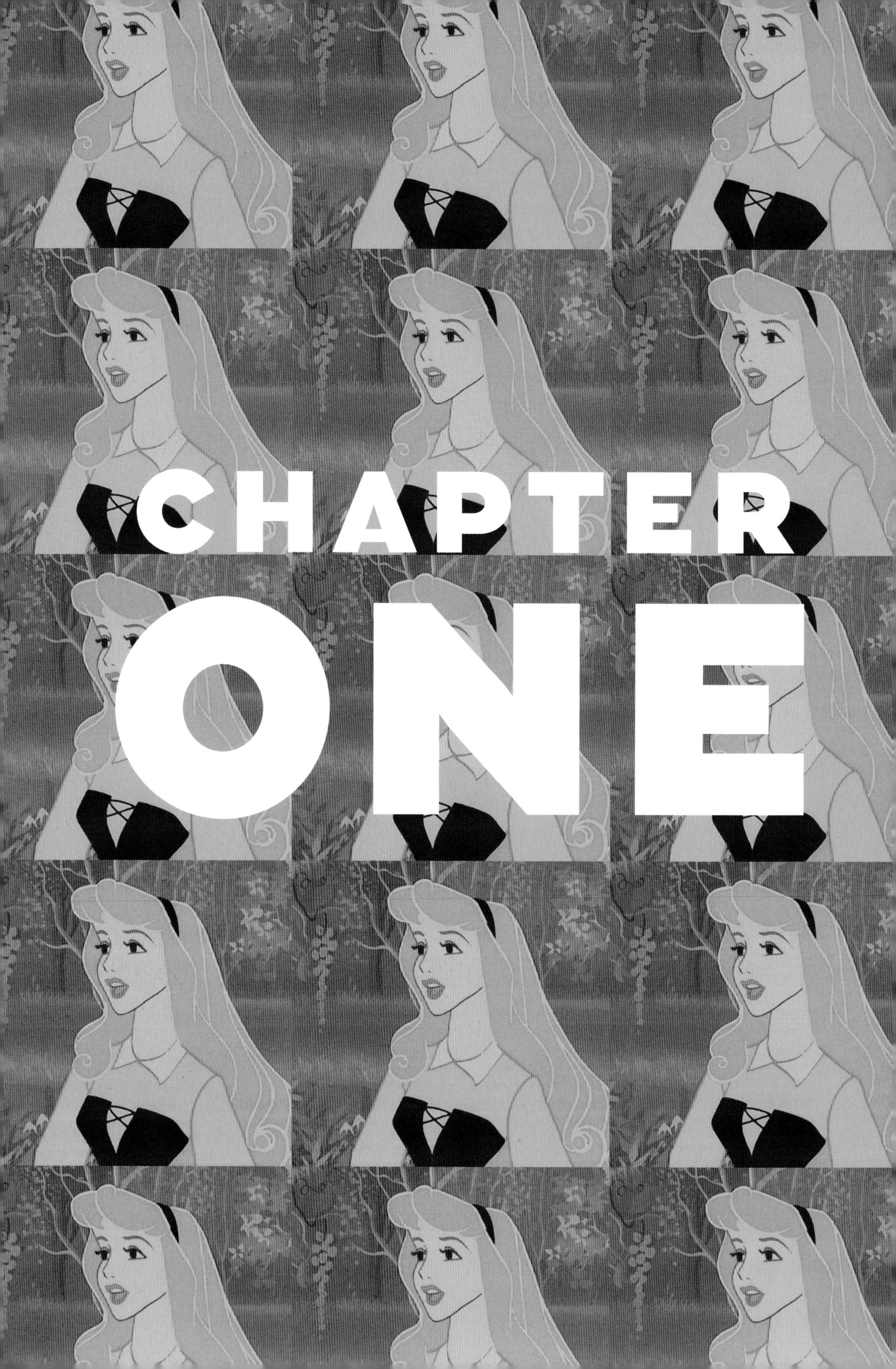

CHAPTER ONE

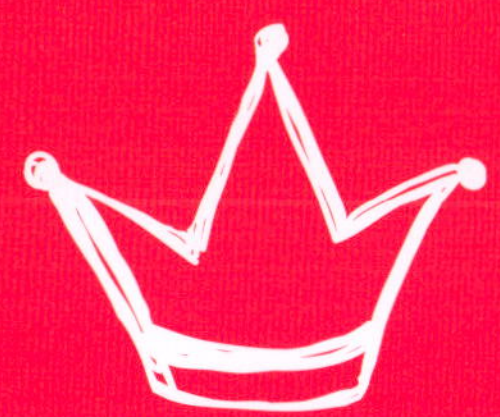

ONCE UPON A DREAM

ORIGINS AND INSPIRATIONS

Walt Disney once said, "Animation can explain whatever the mind of man can conceive." At the time, the filmmaker likely didn't know how much influence his own vibrant, magical animation would have on the public consciousness. But since the late 1930s, Disney animated features have become part of our collective identity, and with them, the Disney Princesses. Each Disney Princess reflects the era in which she was created, but her resulting cultural influence extends far beyond. From *Snow White and the Seven Dwarfs* in 1937 to *Moana* in 2016—and continuing onward—it's clear that each era's collective dreams and values are mirrored in its respective Disney films.

"The mannerisms of the princess and the dreams the princess has are very much guided by what's going on in the world at that particular moment," explains Dr. Tracey Mollet, author of *Once Upon an American Dream: A Cultural History of the Disney Fairy Tale*. "What it is they're dreaming of, how old they are, what it is they're hoping for, what kind of a relief they're wanting from their everyday lives. That very much changes as we go through history. The princesses are vehicles through which this dream and this happily-ever-after journey happens."

The way the Disney Princesses are designed and animated has also evolved over the decades. For many years, the characters were developed by concept artists and animators, who often drew on real-life actors or literary characters as inspiration. Although they were placed in fairy-tale worlds, early heroes like Snow White and Aurora took on the fashions and styles of their creators' era. Live-action footage was also used as reference to help the animators draw realistic movement as early as *Snow White and the Seven Dwarfs*. The actresses who acted out the scenes for the animators had tremendous impact on how the princesses looked and moved.

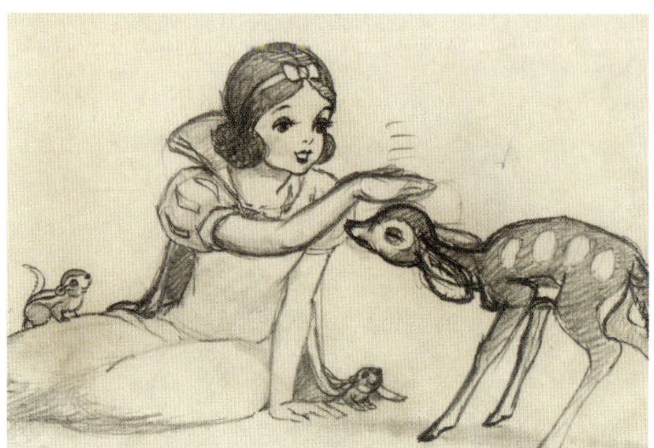

Above: An early studio sketch of Snow White. *Below:* Snow White peers through a window into the Seven Dwarfs' cottage.

There has been an increasing emphasis on cultural and historical research, with Walt Disney Animation Studios embracing diversity and inclusion as key elements of its filmmaking. For example, Disney formed the Oceanic Story Trust, a cultural advisory group, to ensure

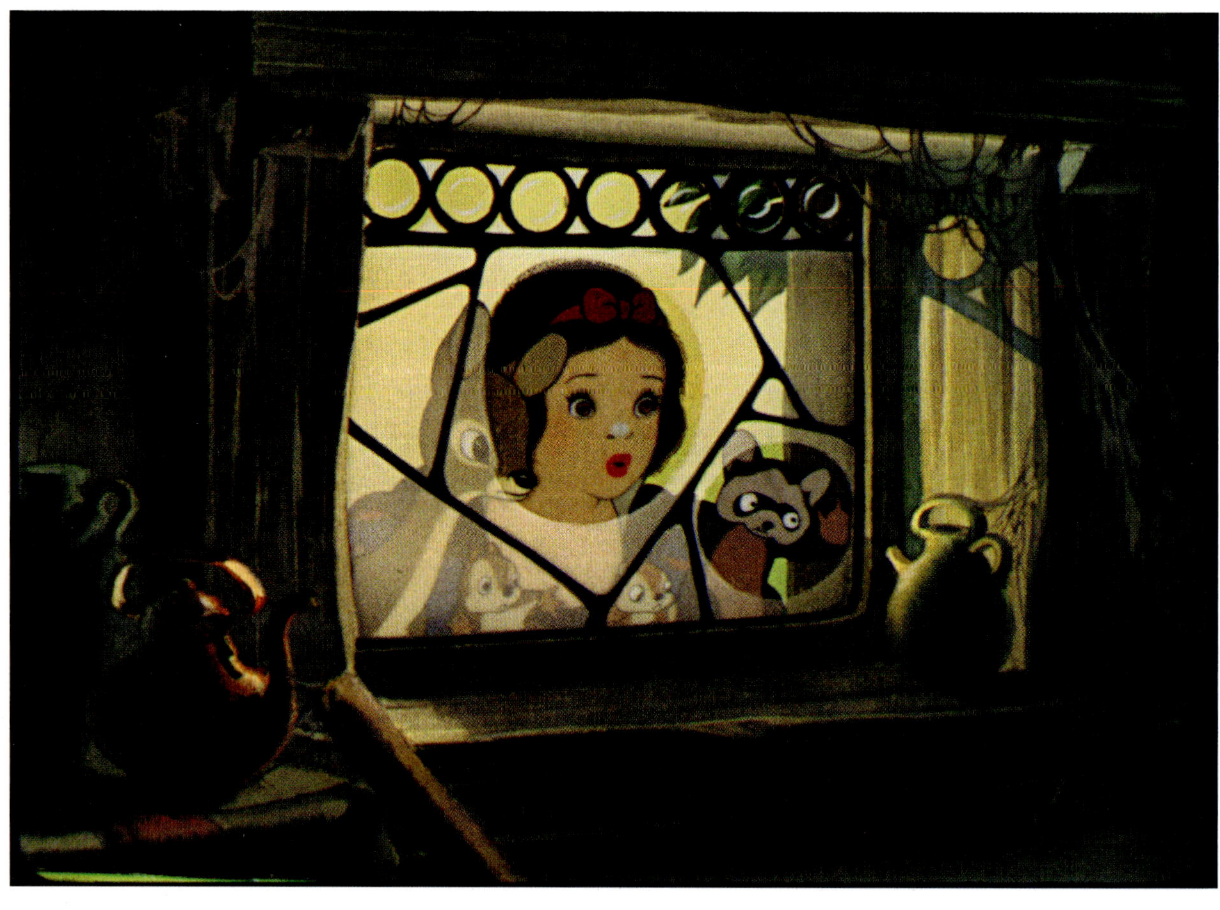

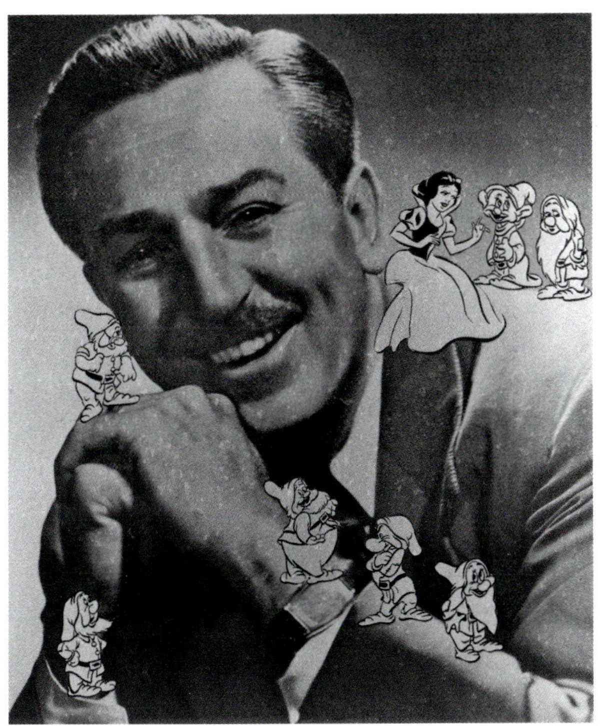

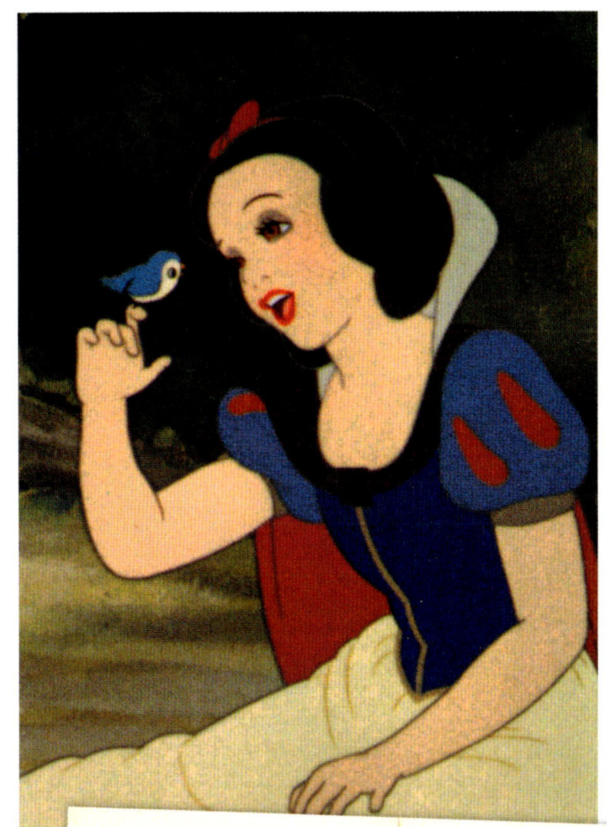

Above: Walt Disney with his animated creations. *Right:* An animation still of Snow White. *Bottom right:* The original theatrical poster for *Snow White and the Seven Dwarfs*.

accuracy in *Moana* (2016). The animators occasionally shoot the live-action reference using themselves as models, rather than bringing in actresses, which means that the filmmakers, their aspirations, and their values can also be inspirations for the characters.

While all of the Disney Princesses showcase qualities audiences can admire, there is a clear progression in the protagonists' proactiveness as time goes on. As women gained more gender equity within society, so did the characters. Ariel, for example, dreamed of a world beyond her own and did whatever it took to get herself there—an aspiration she had long before she laid eyes on Prince Eric. Our onscreen heroes reflect the times in which they were created, and audiences can see the influences of the different time periods on the characters and their actions.

"These are mythic tales that have been around long before Disney," explains *Beauty and the Beast* (1991) screenwriter Linda Woolverton. "The stories come from legends and myths and fairy tales, and have had an impact on people for generations. It's how we

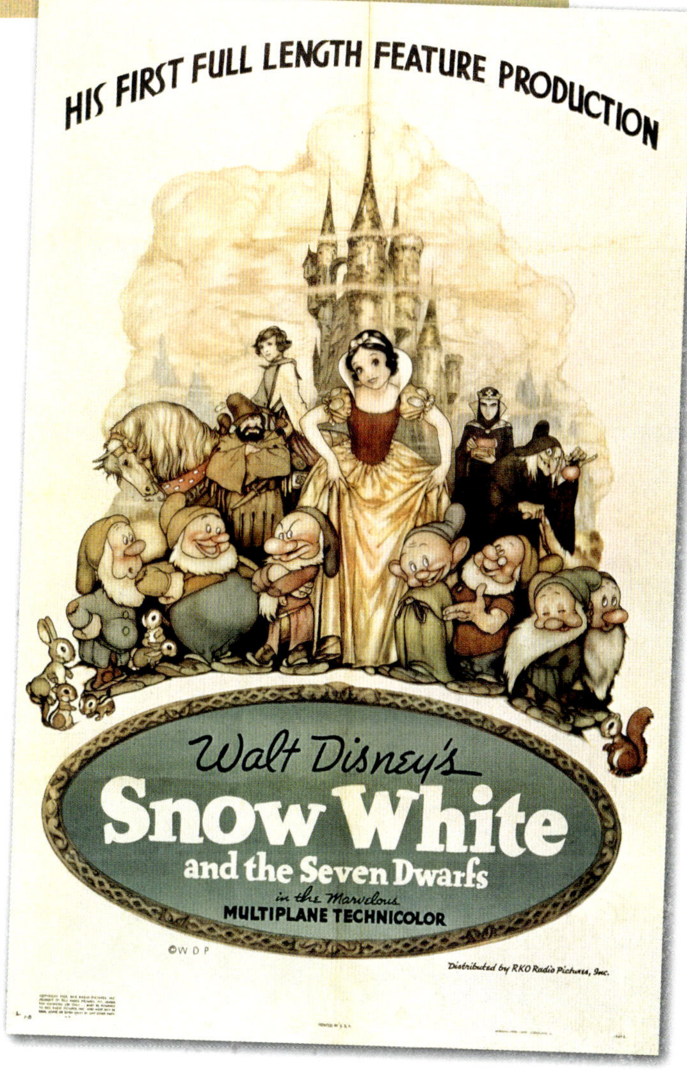

make sense of the world. The stories depict how people go through hardship and come out the other side and what it takes for them to do it. Every single period in our world's history approaches those answers in different ways, especially for women."

ONCE UPON A TIME...

Growing up, Walt Disney was surrounded by stories, including the fairy tales of the Brothers Grimm and Hans Christian Andersen. His grandmother read the beloved tales to him in the evenings, setting Walt off on a lifelong love for the genre. "It was the best time of day for me and the stories and the characters in them seemed quite as real as my schoolmates and our games," Walt once recounted. "Of all the characters in the fairy tales, I loved *Snow White and the Seven Dwarfs* the best." As a teenager in 1917, Walt saw a free showing of Paramount's silent film *Snow White*, starring Marguerite Clark, in his hometown of Kansas City, and the story stayed in the back of his mind as he began pursuing a career in animation.

From the beginning, Walt understood that using established stories was the best way to approach animated shorts. One of his early *Laugh-O-gram* films, from 1922, was a Jazz Age take on *Cinderella*, and he subsequently created a series in the early 1920s known as the *Alice Comedies* (1924-1927), loosely inspired by Lewis Carroll's *Alice's Adventures in Wonderland*. Later, Walt's *Silly Symphony* series included well-known tales like *Three Little Pigs* (1933) and *The Tortoise and the Hare* (1935), as well as the jazz-themed *Music Land* (1935), which featured a princess character. These early shorts, particularly the *Silly Symphony series*, were a great success, and in 1933, Walt had the idea to make a full-length animated feature film.

Several ideas were thrown around for what story to use, including a possible adaptation of the 1923 book *Bambi, a Life in the Woods*, but eventually Walt landed on *Snow White and the Seven Dwarfs*, which he referred to as "the perfect story." In 1935, Walt and Roy Disney, along with their wives Lillian and Edna, embarked on a European tour, through England, France, Germany, and Italy—an opportunity to

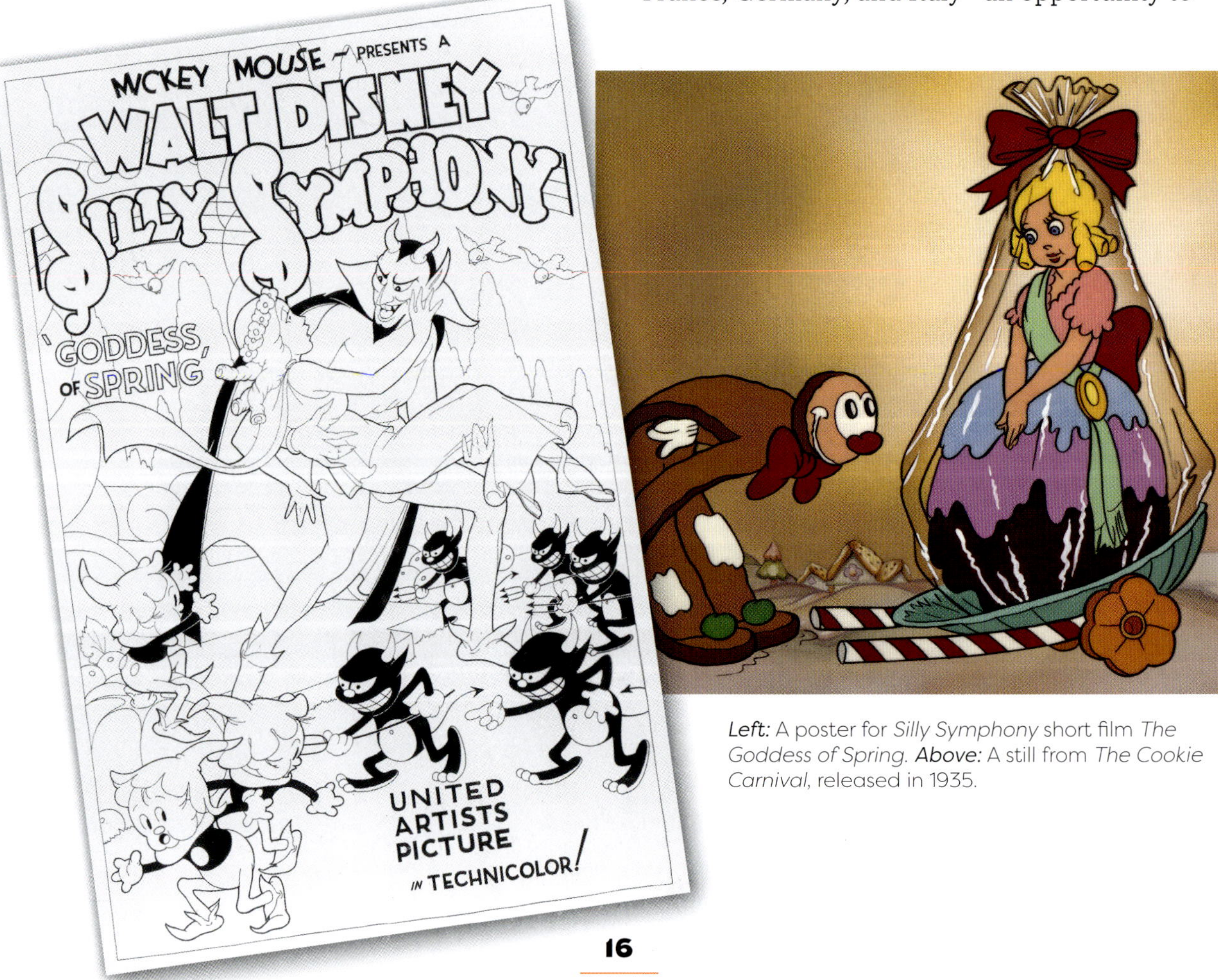

Left: A poster for *Silly Symphony* short film *The Goddess of Spring*. *Above:* A still from *The Cookie Carnival*, released in 1935.

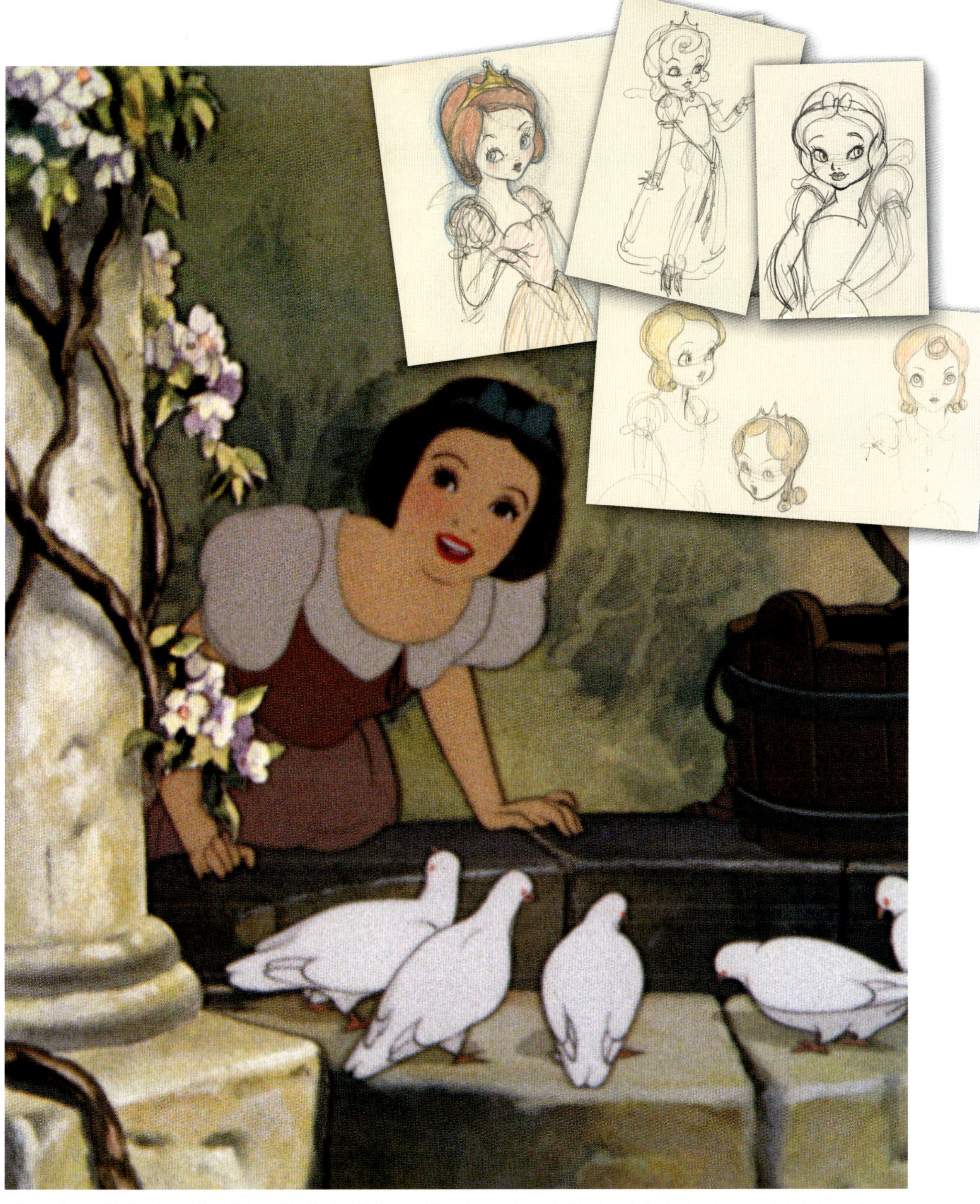

Above: Snow White sings "I'm Wishing" in *Snow White and the Seven Dwarfs*. *Top Inset:* Early development sketches of Snow White.

seek out inspiration for *Snow White* and future films. He returned with a selection of books for the Disney studio library, including copies of the Brothers Grimm fairy tales with illustrations by different artists. While Snow White's origins date back hundreds of years (and perhaps longer), appearing in several cultures, Walt wanted to maintain a fidelity to the Brothers Grimm version, first published in 1812. Still, it was important to brighten up some of the darker aspects of the original tale and to infuse the story with some levity.

Bringing Snow White and her story to life through animation was a massive challenge that

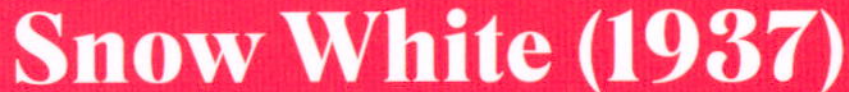

Snow White (1937)

During the creative process, animators are often influenced by celebrities of the era, and Snow White embodies the popular beauty trends of the time. Her narrow eyebrows and pert haircut evoke Jean Harlow, Claudette Colbert, and Marlene Dietrich—all popular actresses of the era. Dancer and Disney Legend Marge Champion acted out scenes from the film as a live-action reference model for Snow White, and her presence can also be seen in the animation. "They never copied [the live-action footage] frame for frame, because it was not cartoon action," Champion explained. "Still, anybody who knows me can see me in Snow White." Early sketches of the character, with a larger head and huge eyes, also reflect animator Grim Natwick's earlier work on Betty Boop.

Voice: *Disney Legend Adriana Caselotti*

Personality traits: *Empathetic, Faces her Fears, Captivating*

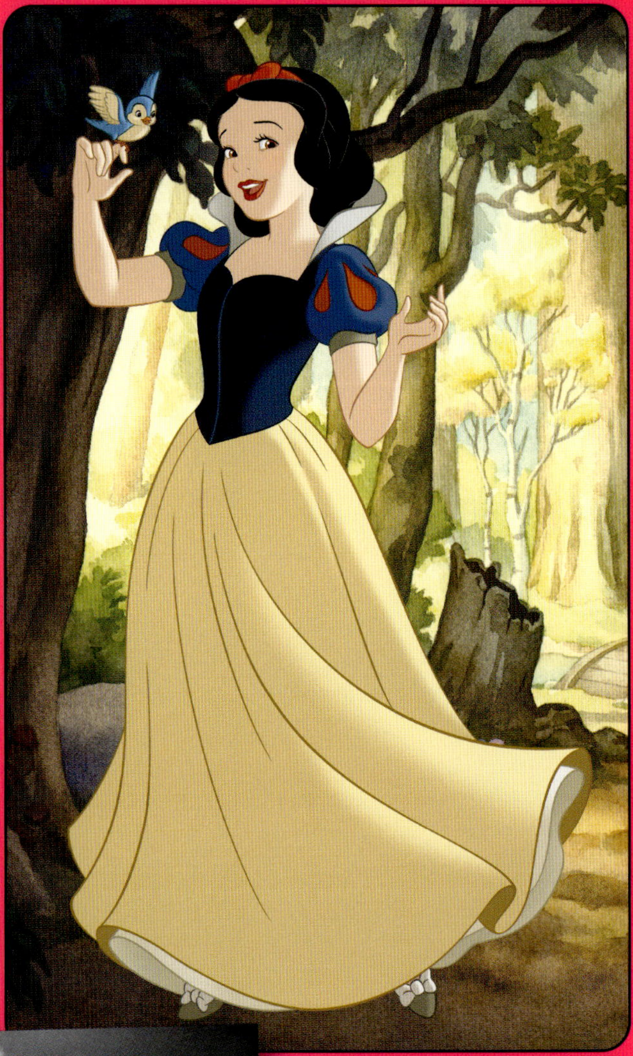

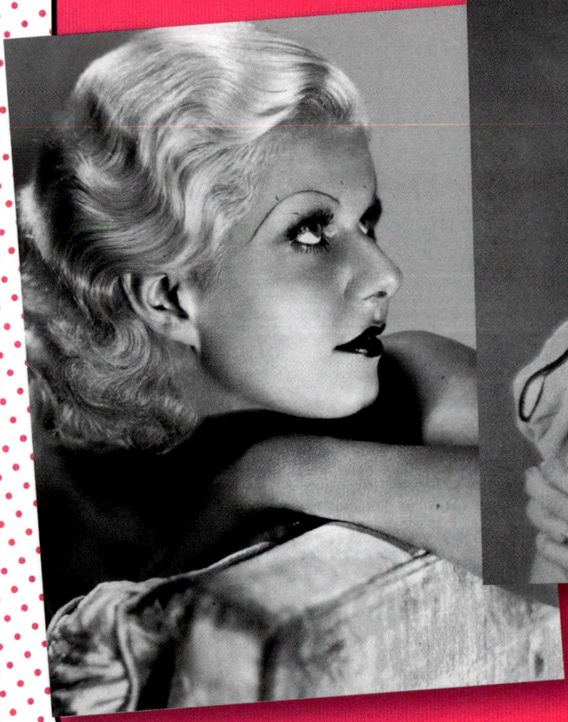

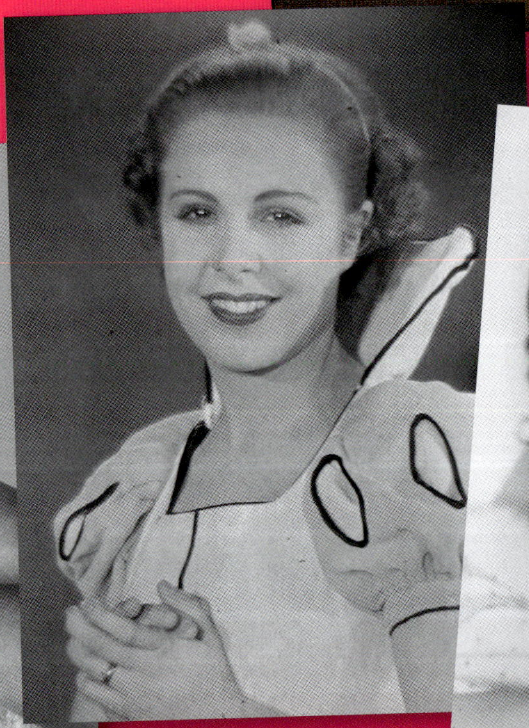

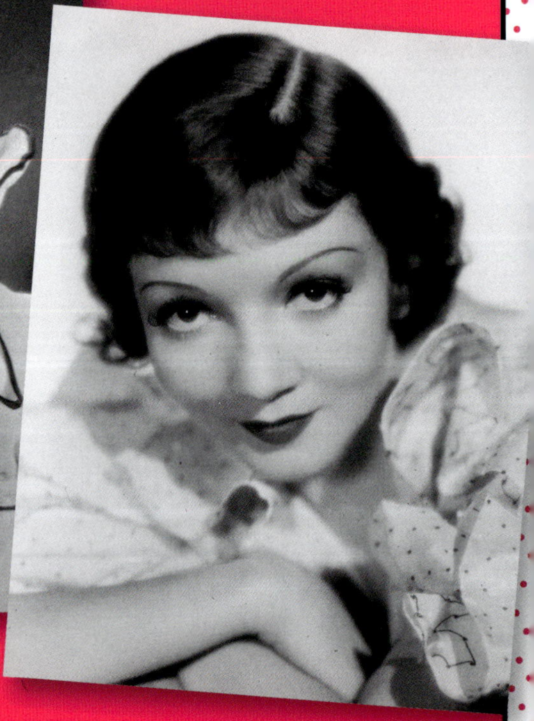

From left: Jean Harlow; Marge Champion; Claudette Colbert

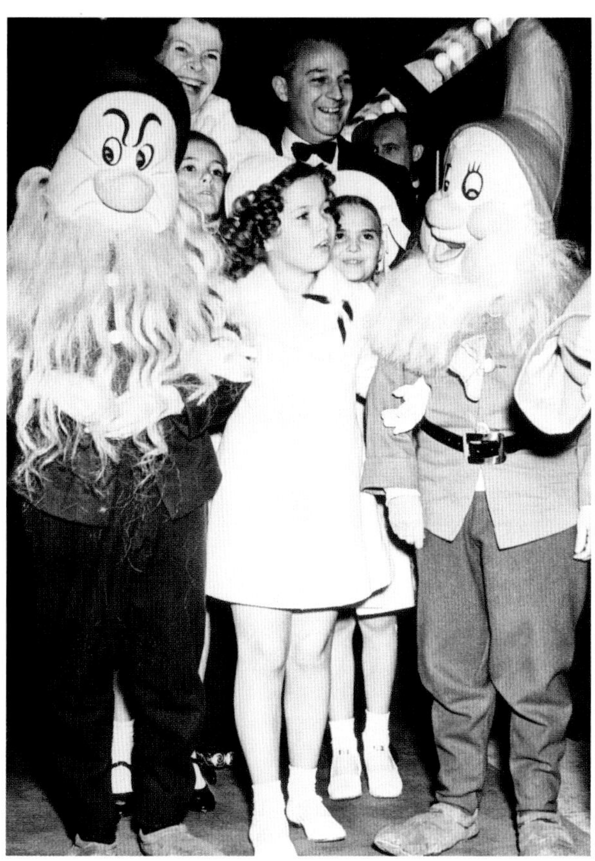

Shirley Temple attends the premiere of *Snow White and the Seven Dwarfs.*

took several years of trial and error. So much so that Hollywood critics referred to the endeavor as "Disney's Folly." But Walt and his animators, undeterred, used the *Silly Symphony* series as a testing ground to create a believable human woman—hints of Snow White's movement and figure are apparent in 1934's *The Goddess of Spring* and 1935's *The Cookie Carnival.* Snow White was primarily designed and animated by two of Disney's best animators, Disney Legend Hamilton Luske and Grim Natwick, the creator of Betty Boop for the Fleischer Studios. The princess's visual aesthetic evolved throughout the animation process—she was going to be blonde at one point—but eventually Snow White developed into the charming, wide-eyed princess we all know and love today.

In many ways, Snow White was a reflection of the mid-1930s, embodying the traits admired in women at the time. Her voice, performed by actress and Disney Legend Adriana Caselotti, was high-pitched and childlike, indicating the princess's innocence. She made the best of terrible circumstances, something audiences of the Great Depression era could appreciate. Most importantly, *Snow White and the Seven Dwarfs* offered audiences a respite from their own lives and reflected the possibility that wishes might come true, no matter how dire the circumstances.

Snow White and the Seven Dwarfs, the first ever American animated feature film in Technicolor, premiered on December 21, 1937, at the Carthay Circle Theatre in Los Angeles, California. It was a glamorous event that was attended by well-known actresses Shirley Temple, Marlene Dietrich, and Claudette Colbert—three possible influences on Snow White—as well as Mickey Mouse and Donald Duck. The Seven Dwarfs also strolled down the red carpet. Response to the film was overwhelming, from critics, audiences, and the movie industry alike. After a run at Radio City Music Hall in January, the film found a wider release on February 4, 1938, and earned $8.5 million, a huge amount back then. More people saw *Snow White and the Seven Dwarfs* during its initial theatrical run than saw *Star Wars: A New Hope* (1977), years later, during its also-famous first run. It was a significant moment in Hollywood history, with *Snow White and the Seven Dwarfs* leaving an indelible mark on pop culture.

It was clear that magic was the way to viewers' hearts. The film's global success encouraged MGM to make *The Wizard of Oz,* another musical fantasy. "With costume dramas and musicals as the most consistently popular genres, it appears that escapism was a key aspect of cinemagoing for most people in the period," film historians Mark Glancy and John Sedgwick noted in an essay titled "Cinemagoing in the United States in the mid-1930s." Following up on the popularity of *Snow White and the Seven Dwarfs,* Walt Disney next produced the films *Pinocchio* and *Fantasia,* both in 1940, but he wouldn't revisit the princess genre for another decade.

RETURNING TO THE FAIRY TALE

During World War II, Disney's output shifted dramatically. As the United States entered the war in 1941, the public was not always in the mood for such whimsical stories. U.S. Army troops requisitioned part of Disney's Burbank studio soon after, and everyone at the studio, including the animators, joined the war effort, creating military training films, educational shorts, and even military insignia. Several animated features did emerge during the war years, including *Bambi* in 1942, but it wasn't until the end of World War II that the studio began considering how to infuse life into another princess.

Walt and his animators began actively developing *Cinderella* (1950) in 1948 as an adaptation of Charles Perrault's French fairy tale, originally published in 1697. The film represented a financial risk for the studio, which desperately needed another hit like *Snow White and the Seven Dwarfs*. "All the things Walt had tried for seven years hadn't really gone over for one reason or another," noted animator Frank Thomas. "He had to go back to something that was as surefire as he could make it: Something like *Snow White*—a pretty young girl in trouble, a fairy tale—and a popular one."

Coming out of World War II, a period of sacrifice and scarcity, there was a marked return to luxury and opulence, as seen in the fashion of the late 1940s. After years of rationing, audiences wanted to return to fantasy worlds, which *Cinderella* represented. Its hero was a classic underdog, whose optimism and kindness allowed her to persevere in the face of wickedness, which was perhaps a parable of World War II. Plus, *Cinderella* is one of the oldest and most

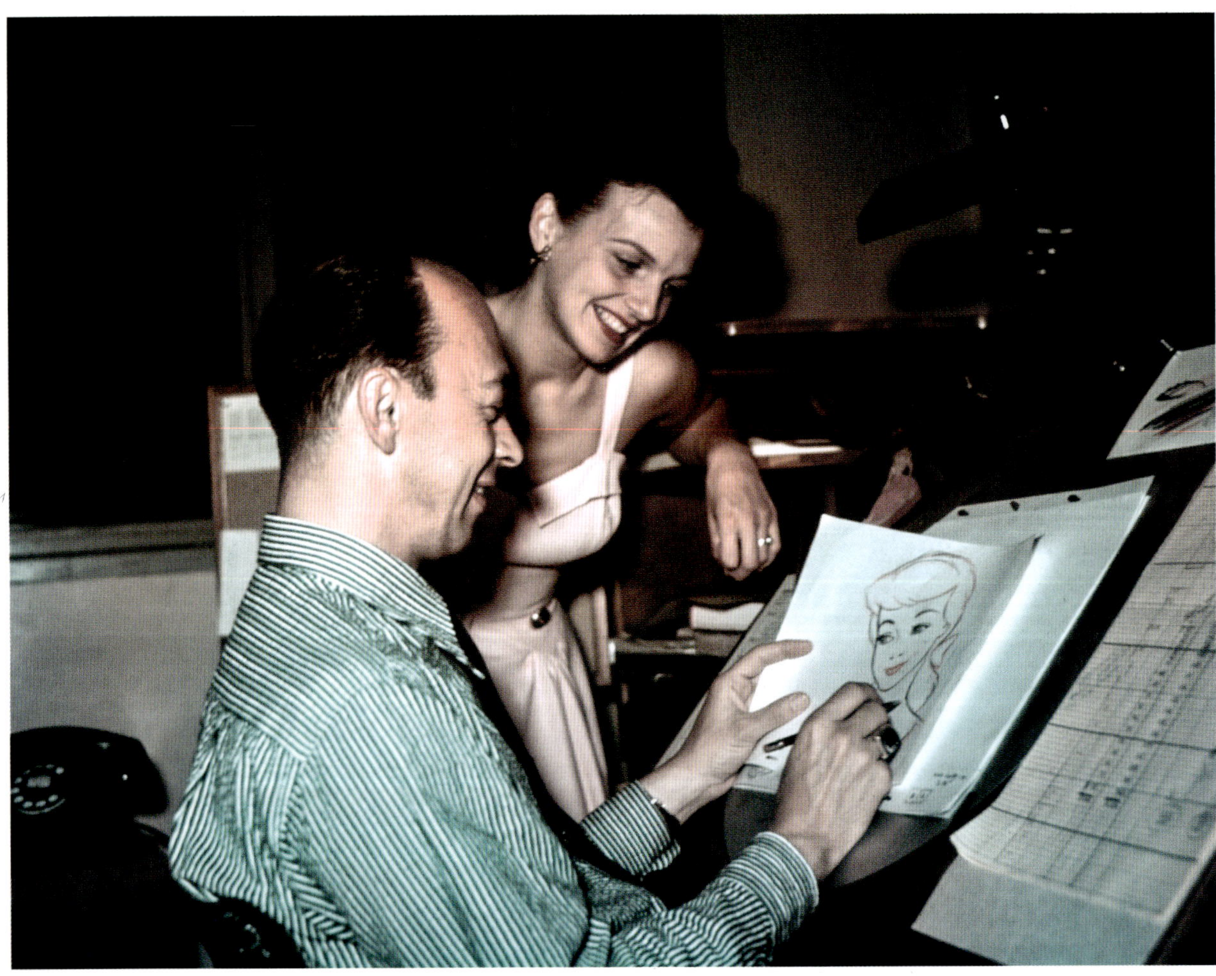

Animator Marc Davis shows Ilene Woods a sketch of Cinderella.

Cinderella (1950)

Cinderella's classic look emphasized what was considered beautiful during the postwar era. Her blonde hair and delicate features suggest actress Grace Kelly, and her iconic ballgown mirrors Dior's "New Look" trend, which became popular during the late 1940s. Actress Helene Stanley filmed live-action reference footage for Cinderella, and her influence can be clearly seen in the character's final appearance. Inspiration was also found in Mary Blair's vibrant concept paintings, which created the look and palette of *Cinderella*. The animation became more sophisticated, too. "Marc Davis had a big influence on Cinderella's appearance, and all the people who worked on her drew a lot better than fifteen years earlier on Snow White," said animator Frank Thomas. "Marc insisted that everything be related mechanically, so for her head to be okay, the chin, the cheeks, all had to be in place."

Voice: *Disney Legend Ilene Woods*

Personality traits: *Hopeful, Realistic, Compassionate*

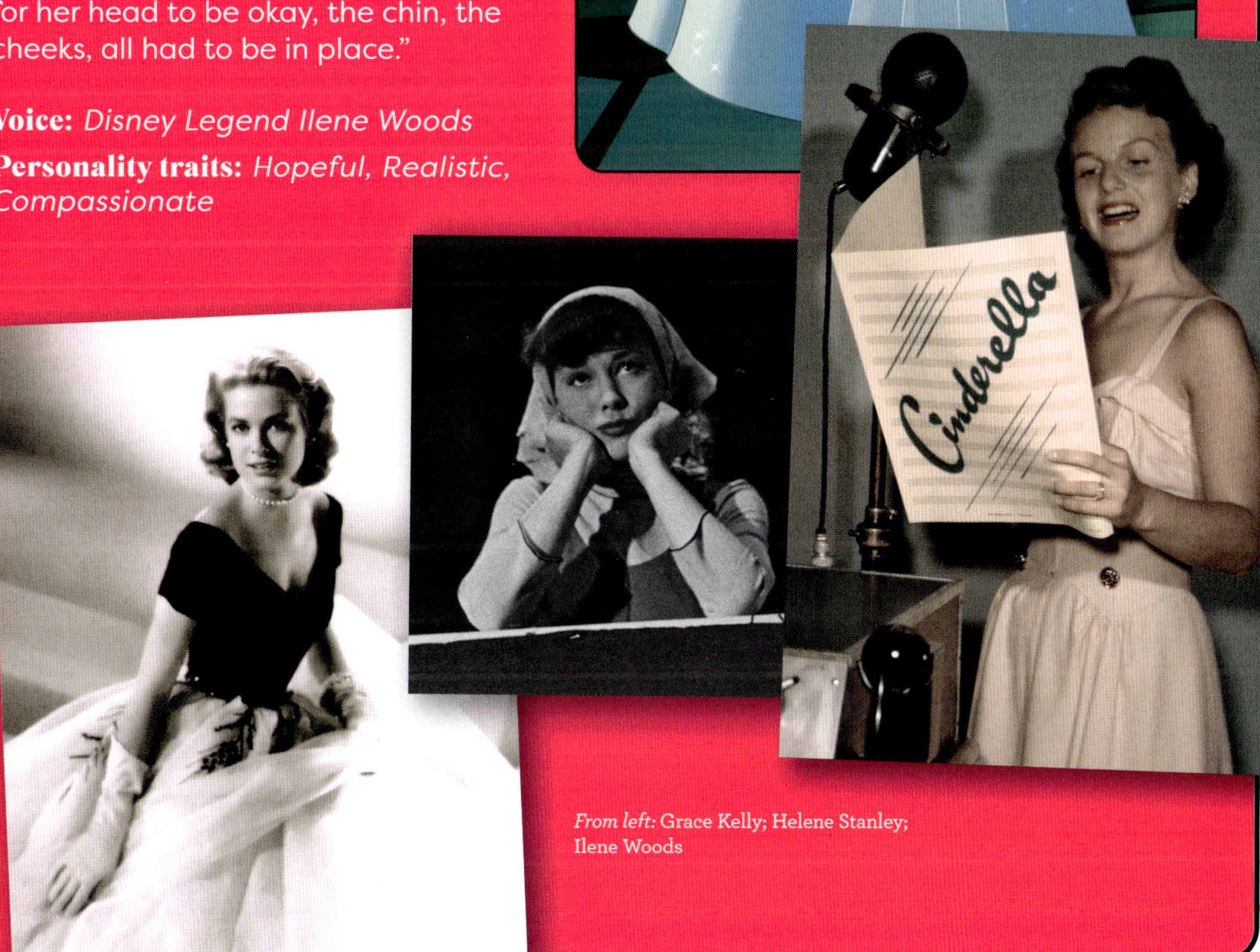

From left: Grace Kelly; Helene Stanley; Ilene Woods

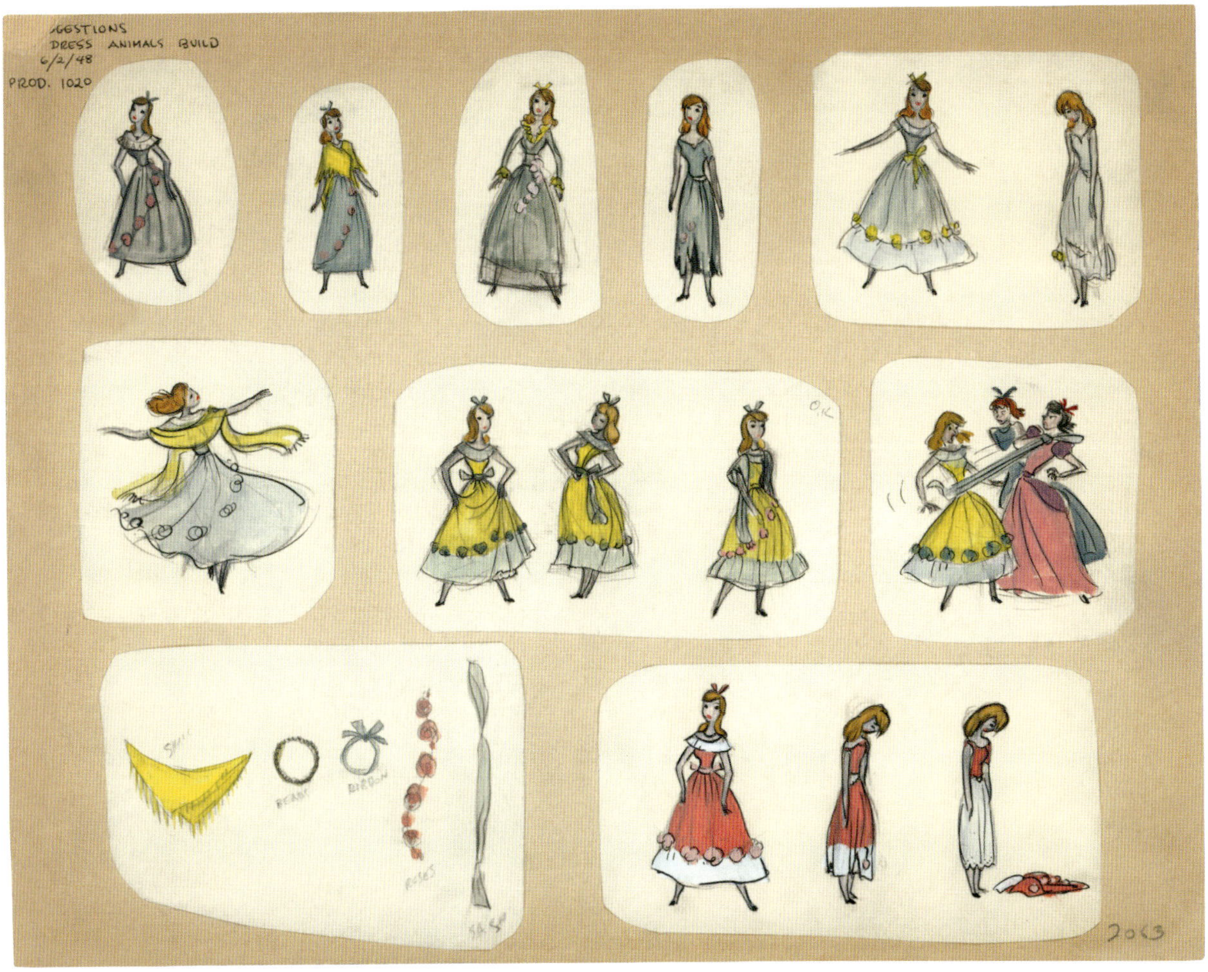

Above: Sketches for a sequence from *Cinderella*. *Below:* *Cinderella* concept art by Mary Blair.

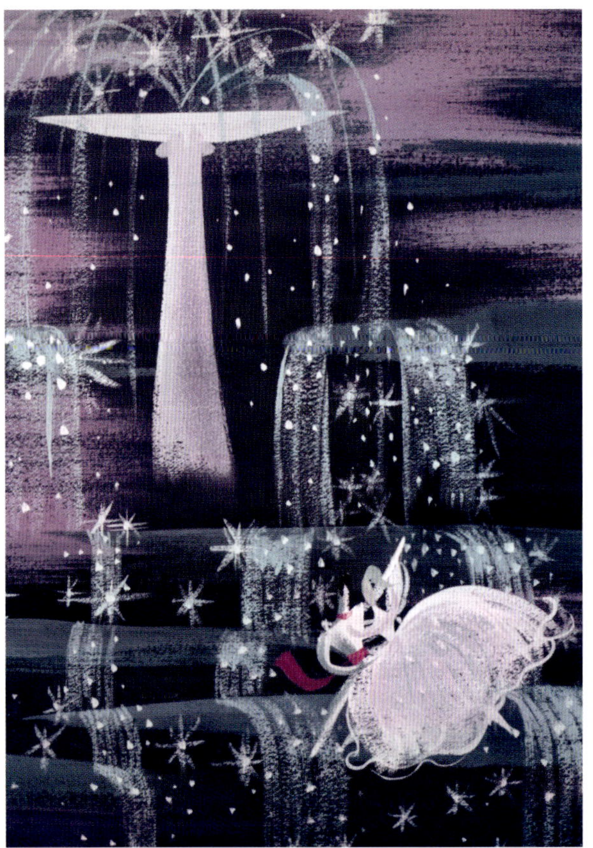

well-known fairy tales in history, which felt like a sure thing for the studio.

Disney Legends Marc Davis and Eric Larson, two of Walt's key animators, and part of a group collectively known as the "Nine Old Men," were primarily responsible for animating Cinderella, although some of the film's aesthetic was inspired by concept art created by Disney Legend Mary Blair, an influential color stylist and concept artist employed by Disney. Cinderella may have needed a little help from the prince to escape her troubles, but she is still the hero of her own story, as Walt himself emphasized when reflecting on his characters a few years later.

"It's always a challenge bringing a great story classic to the screen, giving visual form to characters and places that have only existed in the imagination," Walt explained during an appearance on *The Fred Waring*

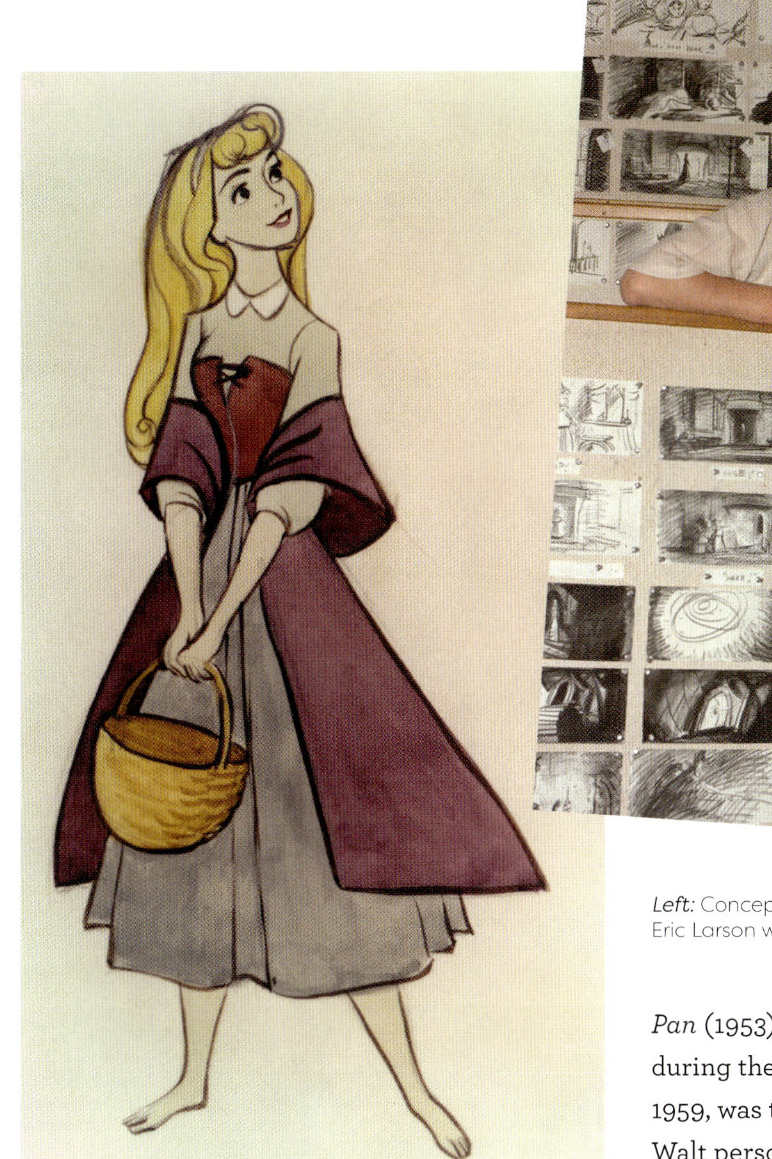

Left: Concept art for *Sleeping Beauty*. **Above:** Animator Eric Larson with voice actress Mary Costa.

Show in 1951 to promote the release of *Alice in Wonderland*. "But it's the kind of challenge we enjoy. As you know, there's been three girls in my professional life: Snow White, Cinderella, and now Alice. And believe me, they're all different. Snow White is a kind, simple little girl who believed in wishing and waiting for her Prince Charming to come along. On the other hand, Cinderella here was more practical. She believed in dreams all right, but she also believed in doing something about them."

Cinderella grossed more than $4 million in its initial release, which helped to stabilize the studio financially. The film's success enabled Walt to pursue other projects, such as live television and theme parks. The studio made several more animated features, including *Peter Pan* (1953) and *Lady and the Tramp* (1955), during the 1950s. *Sleeping Beauty*, released in 1959, was the third and final fairy tale feature Walt personally oversaw. The ornately animated film brought fans a new Disney Princess, Aurora.

Several animators were responsible for Aurora's appearance, including concept artist Tom Oreb, but Marc Davis, who had worked on Snow White and Cinderella, brought her fully to life. As a character, Aurora was more sophisticated than her predecessors, but like Snow White and Cinderella, she embodied kindness and a love for animals. She, too, dreamed of a life beyond her reality. "We were faced with the challenge of finding a girl who was different from Snow White, Cinderella, Alice, and other heroines we had, and yet still a heroine," noted Davis. Ultimately, Aurora was the final princess created before Walt's death in 1966. It wouldn't be until the mid-1980s, when Walt Disney Animation Studios underwent a revitalization, that the Disney Princess would rise again.

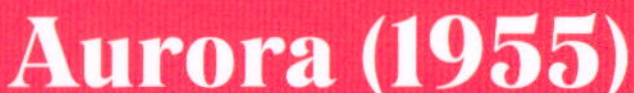

Aurora (1955)

Audrey Hepburn, who had starred in William Wyler's film *Roman Holiday* in 1953, may have had a direct influence on Aurora. The two share a similar facial structure, including expressive eyes and prominent eyebrows, and many of Aurora's costumes feature elements similar to the fashion in Wyler's film. Helene Stanley provided live-action reference for the animators again, and Disney Legend Alice Davis, Marc Davis's wife, designed a costume for Stanley to wear. "Marc told me how he wanted the skirt to flow when she turned and gave me a sketch of the costume," she noted. "I was pleased that I was able to get the material to work the way he wanted."

Voice: *Disney Legend Mary Costa*

Personality traits: *Playful, Imaginative, Passionate*

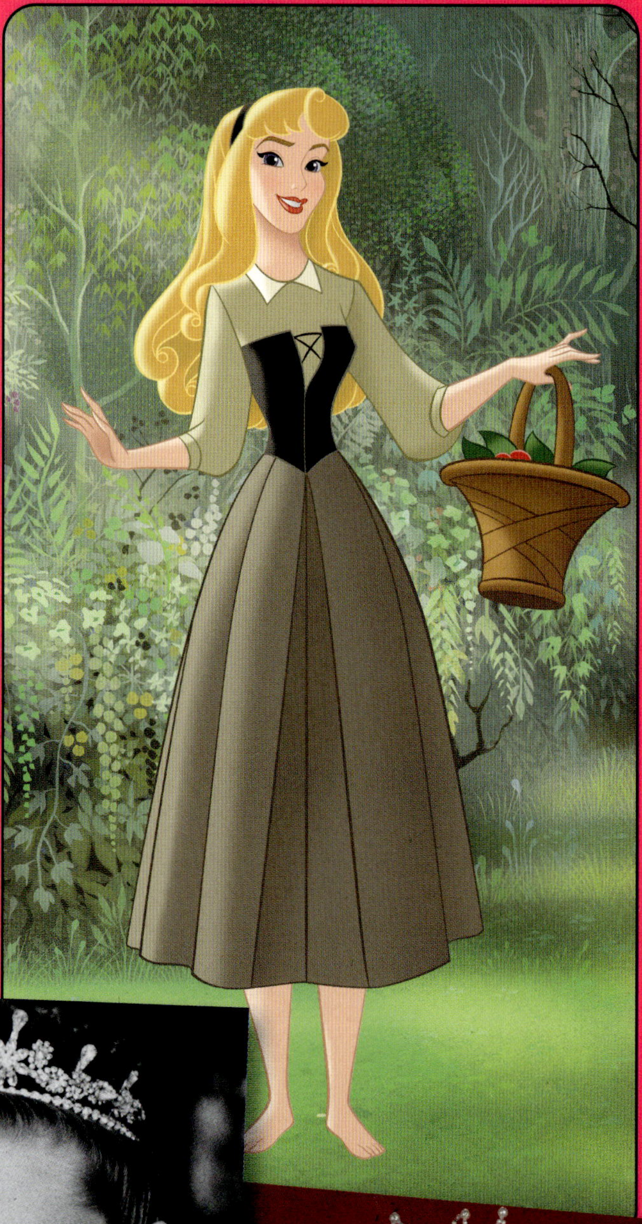

From left: Mary Costa; Audrey Hepburn; Helene Stanley

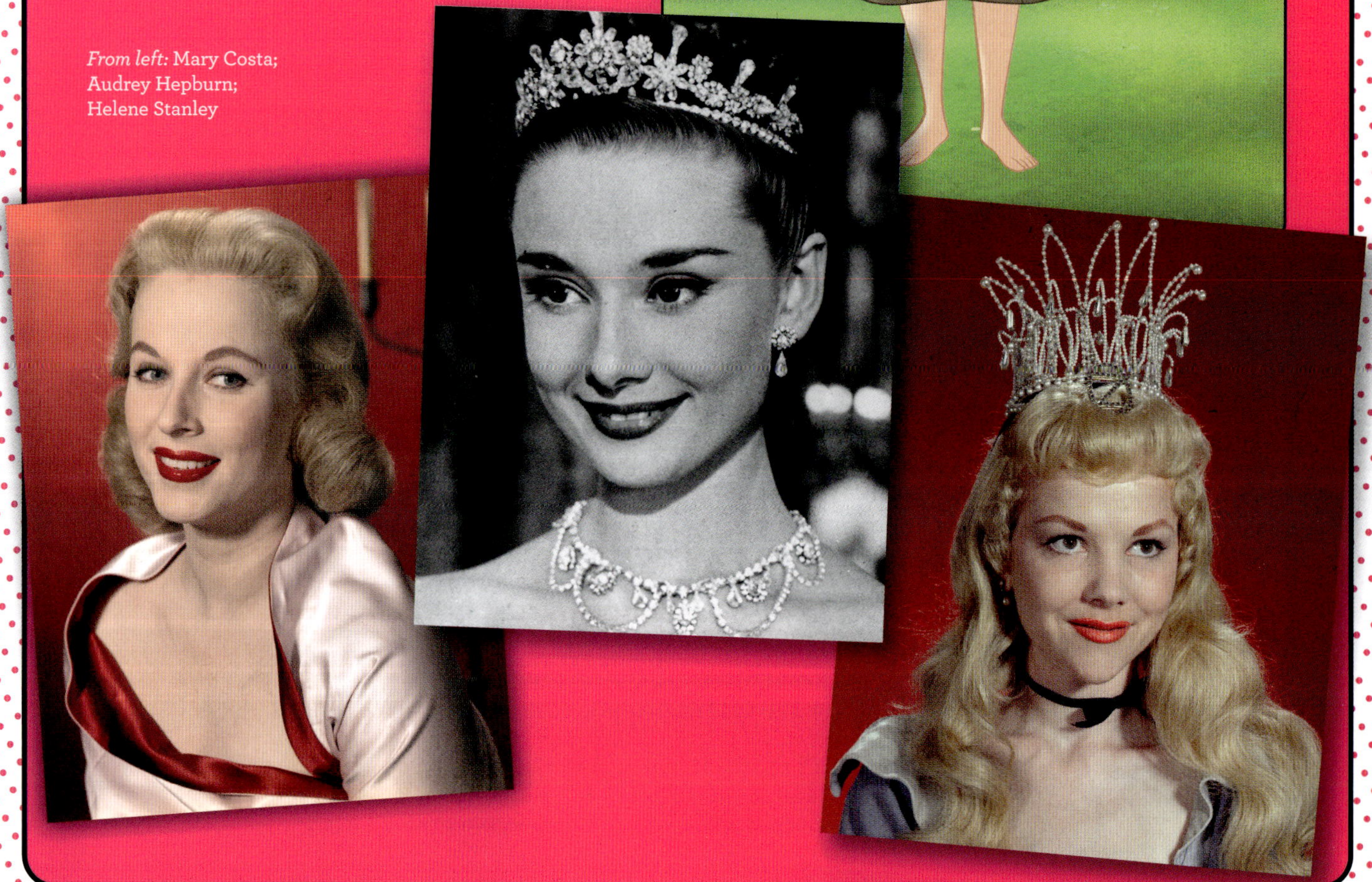

THE ROYAL RENAISSANCE

In the 1950s, Walt's attention shifted away from animation to live-action films, television, and his theme park, Disneyland. Animation started a slow downward spiral, in terms of film success, after Walt died in 1966, but the studio continued producing animated features through the 1970s and 1980s, including *The Jungle Book* (1967), *The Rescuers* (1977), and *The Fox and the Hound* (1981). In 1984, Michael Eisner, Frank Wells, and Jeffrey Katzenberg arrived to run The Walt Disney Company, and one of Katzenberg's priorities was to bring animation back into the spotlight. He famously said, "We've got to wake up Sleeping Beauty." After *Oliver & Company* was released in 1988, the studio decided they would subsequently release a new animated feature each year, and on November 17, 1989, *The Little Mermaid* was released in theaters, ushering in an era that is sometimes identified by fans and film historians as the "Disney Renaissance."

The Little Mermaid had been considered for a feature at Disney for decades. Walt had made *Merbabies* in 1938 as part of his *Silly Symphony* series and in 1940-41 artist Kay Nielsen created dramatic story sketches and concept art for a possible retelling of the fairy tale, originally published by Hans Christian Andersen in 1837, but the idea had been shelved. After co-directing *The Great Mouse Detective* in 1986, however, John Musker and Ron Clements had the idea to create a version of *The Little Mermaid* in the same tradition of Disney's early animated fairy tales, but with a modern flair.

Early sketches of Ariel for *The Little Mermaid*, released in 1989.

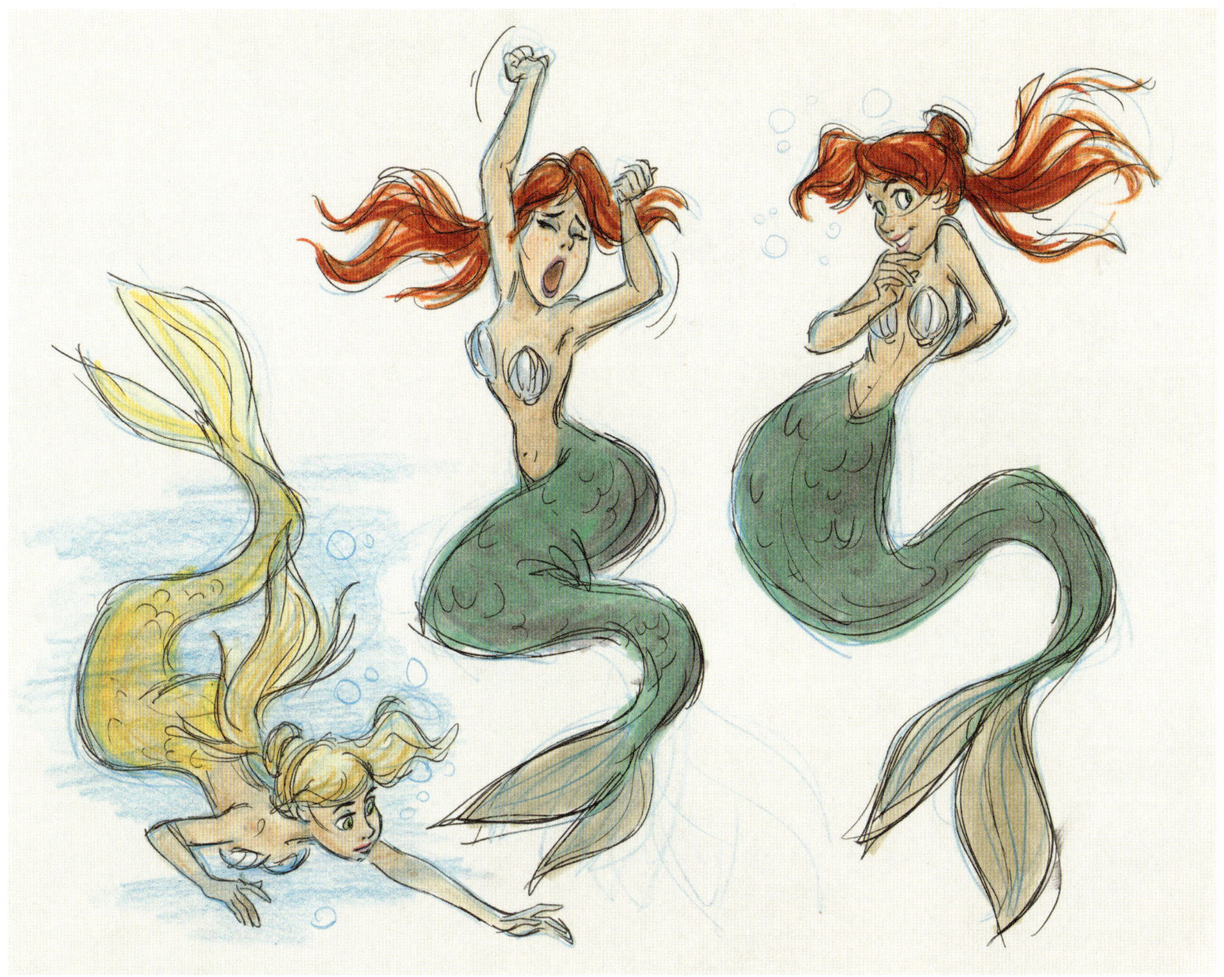

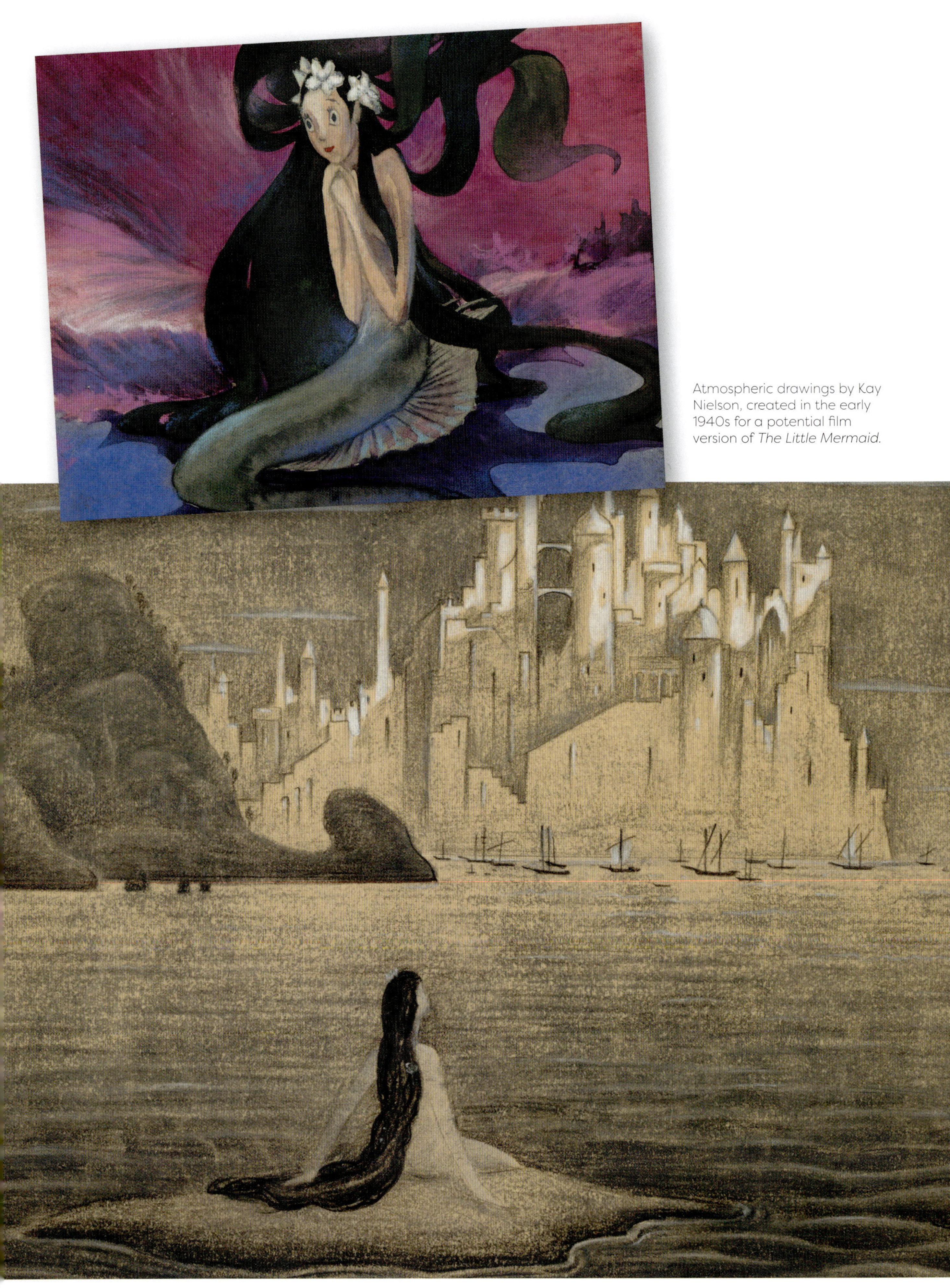

Atmospheric drawings by Kay Nielson, created in the early 1940s for a potential film version of *The Little Mermaid*.

Ariel (1989)

Ariel's look was drawn from popular culture, such as actress Christie Brinkley, and animator Glen Keane also drew personal inspiration from his wife. Live-action actress Sherri Stoner also provided lots of inspiration for the character, particularly in her movement and expression. Ariel—named for Ariel Moore in *Footloose* (1984)—is also a unique interpretation of a fantastical character, hence her red hair and purple shell bikini. Ariel's hair, in particular, helped juxtapose her reality with her desires. "For Ariel, she's this girl underwater and you constantly see this hair floating," Keane recalled in an interview. "It's always a reminder that this girl lives in another world but she wants to be a part of *that* world."

Voice: *Disney Legend Jodi Benson*

Personality traits: *Inquisitive, Fierce, Independent*

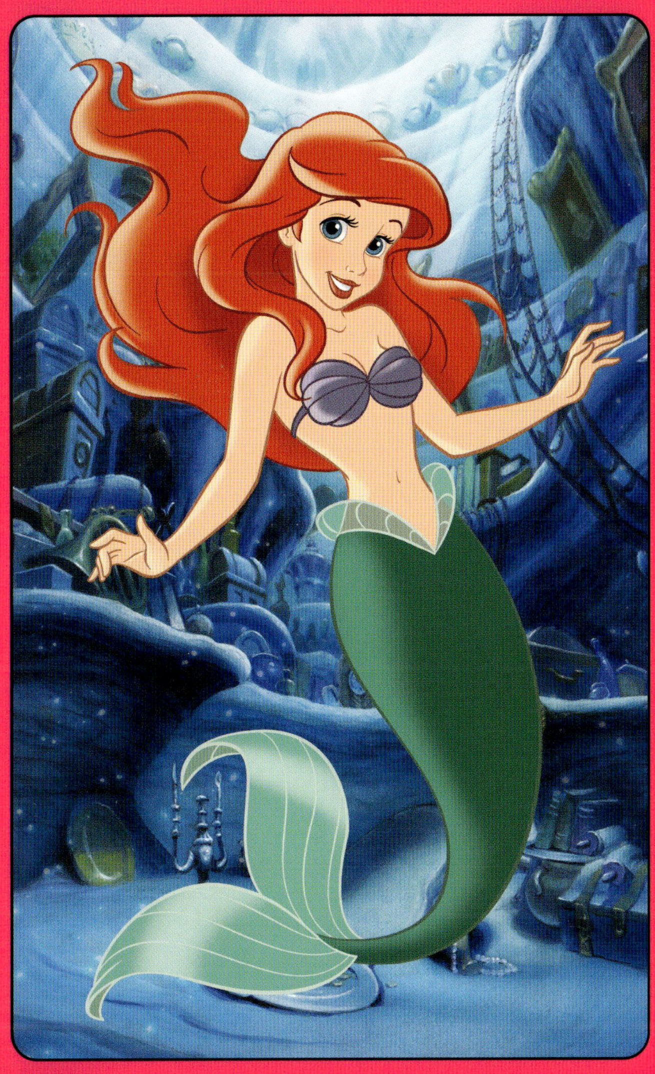

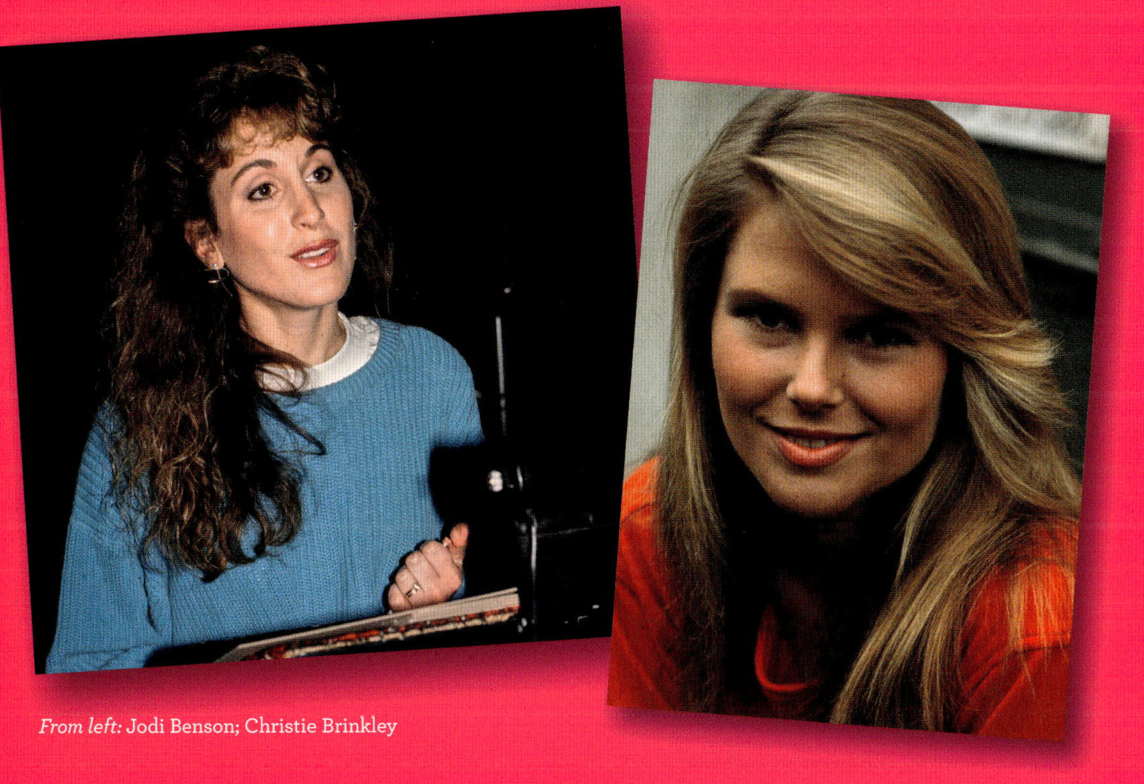

From left: Jodi Benson; Christie Brinkley

The directors worked on the story with songwriting team and Disney Legends Howard Ashman and Alan Menken, who decided to structure *The Little Mermaid* as a Broadway-style musical. Everyone wanted the film's lead character, Ariel, to be spirited, empowered, and aspirational.

"We embarked on [*The*] *Little Mermaid*, knowing that we were doing the first fairy tale in thirty years," Musker recalled. "We wanted [*The*] *Little Mermaid* to be able to stand on a shelf with *Cinderella* and *Snow White* and *Sleeping Beauty*. Yet we didn't want it to seem like the movie was made in 1940. We tried in both the writing and the directing to shape the heroine into somebody we could relate to and the audience could relate to." Ariel was someone who wanted to take charge of her own destiny and make choices, and she was active physically, as well as dramatically. "She swam, she got engaged, she participated in the battle at the climax," Musker noted.

Ariel was originally envisioned as a blonde mermaid, similar to Daryl Hannah's character in *Splash* (1984), but the animators ultimately decided to make her a redhead. Not only would it help her stand out against the blues and greens of the water, but it also signified her rebellious nature. Animator and Disney Legend Glen Keane, who was largely responsible for Ariel's look, took inspiration from his wife, Linda, and the animation team also had a board covered with celebrity photos to help guide them. This included photos of model Christie Brinkley, whose swooping bangs can be clearly seen on Ariel, and Alyssa Milano.

The animation team also used live-action reference footage to help guide the characters' movement, enlisting comedian Sherri Stoner to perform Ariel's scenes in a studio on camera. Stoner acted out key scenes to voice actress and Disney Legend Jodi Benson's voice recordings of the character, going in a few days per month for a year and a half. She even acted out a scene underwater in a tank so the animators could see how Ariel's hair would move. Small physical quirks, like Ariel biting her lip or blowing her bangs out of her eyes, came directly from Stoner's movements.

"I'm not a naturally graceful person at all," Stoner remembers. "The fact that my natural clumsiness and personality was made charming by the artists is a testament to their talent. They were always so delighted with whatever personality I brought to the table, it made me fearless, and safe to be unabashedly myself." She adds, "I know, for instance, me blowing my hair out of my face because my bangs were just too

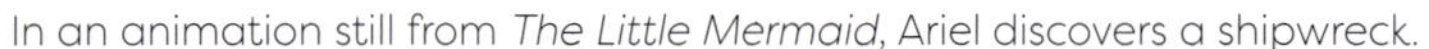

In an animation still from *The Little Mermaid*, Ariel discovers a shipwreck.

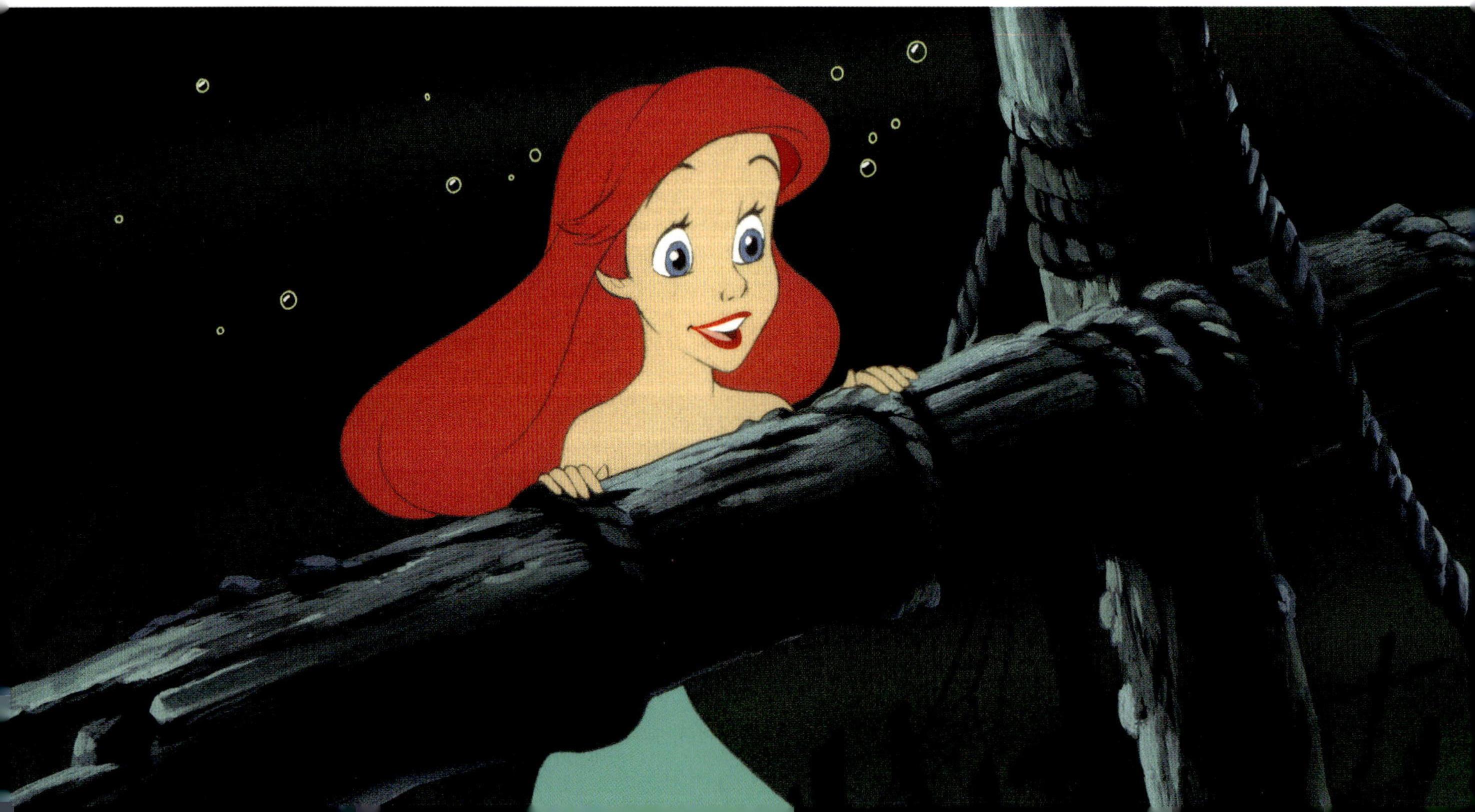

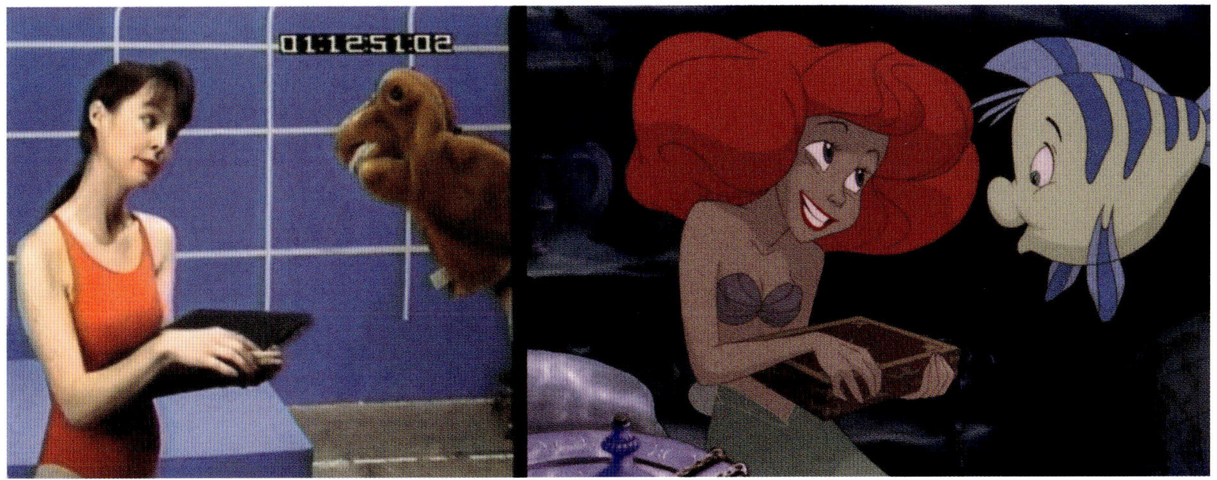

Sherri Stoner acting out a moment from *The Little Mermaid* for animator reference, alongside the final film version of the scene.

long was something they used. It was a thing that just came out of the moment and being frustrated that my hair wouldn't stay out of my face."

The fact that Ariel was a teenage rebel, which reflected the changing role of women in society, made her more relatable to contemporary audiences than the traditional princesses of Walt's time. "Modern filmmaking is about authenticity of emotion: Not an idealized princess, but a real princess," Keane said. "Whenever I had a choice, I chose real. If that meant an awkward little expression, I went with it. You animate how the character is feeling through the muscles of the face. That Ariel had these little flashes of expression surprised people. It felt like a princess suddenly became a real girl."

Benson was similarly attracted to Ariel's relatability. The actress recorded the character's voice over two and a half years, developing her into the adventurous mermaid we know and love today. "I loved her tenacity, her independence, her rebellious spirit, and her thinking outside of the box," Benson says. "She wanted to be part of a whole different world from where she was raised. She was very nonconventional."

Like *Snow White and the Seven Dwarfs, The Little Mermaid* surpassed expectations and became a massive hit. It also brought Disney back into the pop culture zeitgeist, with audiences anticipating more fairy tale adaptations. In the following years, the studio released *Beauty and the Beast* (1991), *Aladdin* (1992), *The Lion King* (1994), *Pocahontas* (1995), *The Hunchback of Notre Dame* (1996), *Hercules* (1997), *Mulan* (1998), and *Tarzan* (1999), in quick succession. The era also gifted fans with five additional Disney Princesses: Ariel, Belle, Jasmine, Pocahontas, and Mulan. There was a sense of regeneration around the possibilities for new animated tales. "*Mermaid* was the one that just awakened people," Menken reflected. "They went, 'Wow, it's back.' It was like this whispering: 'It's back.'"

Because Ariel was an empowered character who took charge of her own destiny, there was a sense that more courageous heroes should follow. When screenwriter Linda Woolverton came onboard to write *Beauty and the Beast*, an adaptation of an eighteenth-century fairy tale by Gabrielle-Suzanne Barbot de Villeneuve, she and songwriter Howard Ashman pushed hard for Belle to be a feminist character. Taking inspiration from Jo March in Louisa May Alcott's *Little Women*, as well as her own upbringing, Woolverton crafted Belle as an intellectual with strong empathy for others. She wanted to create a character who could live in the world of a fairy tale and also embody a contemporary young woman.

"It was essential for both Howard [Ashman] and I to make her a reader, a thinker, and have a curiosity about the world," Woolverton says. "Basic storytelling says you have to see the seeds

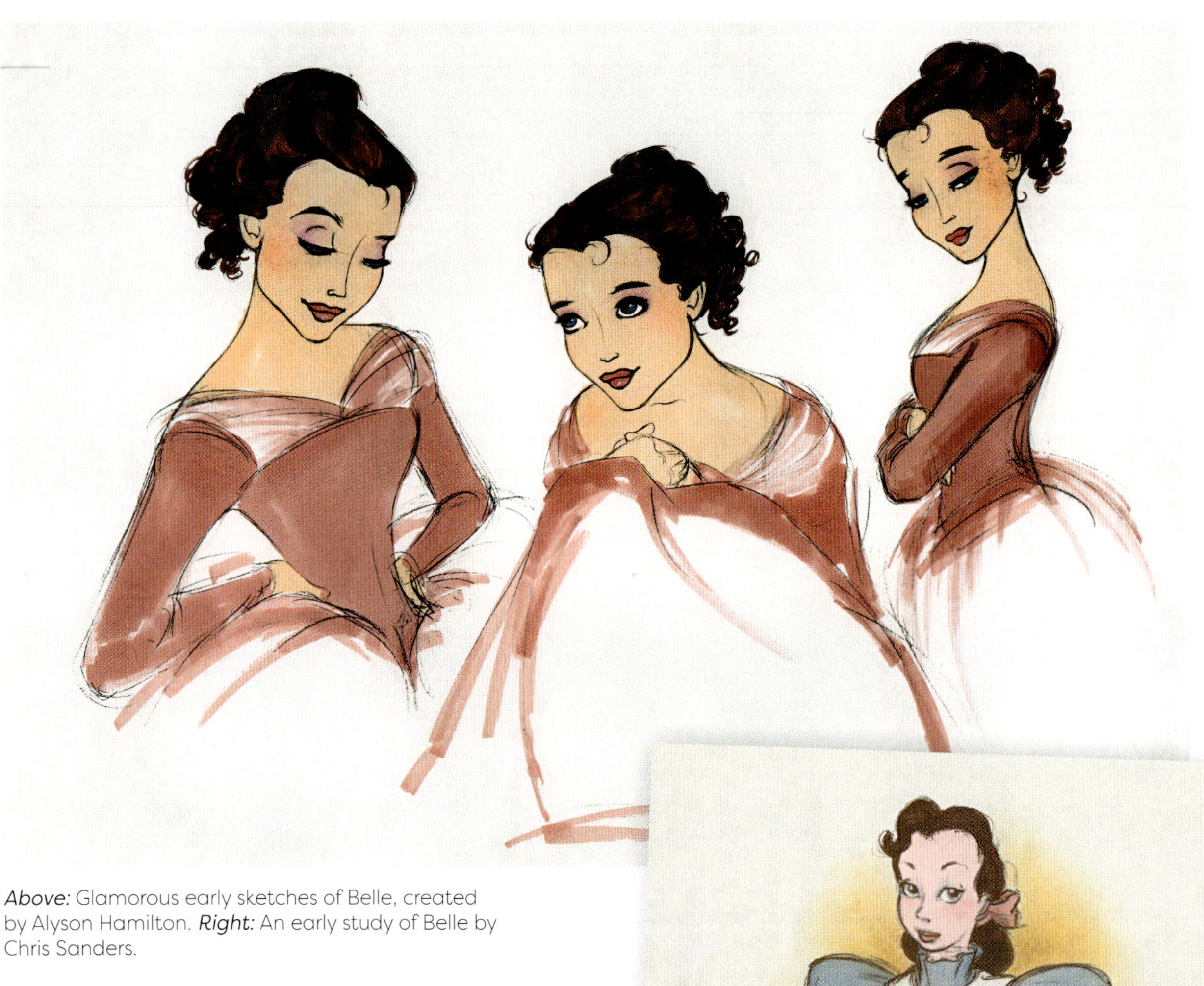

Above: Glamorous early sketches of Belle, created by Alyson Hamilton. *Right:* An early study of Belle by Chris Sanders.

of something in a character. If they're going to do some huge thing later, you have to have planted those seeds. Belle's going to do a huge thing—she's going to trade herself for her father, she's going to take on the Beast, and she's going to transform that entire world. We have to be able to see those elements in her or we won't be able to buy it later."

Belle, designed by a team of animators that included James Baxter and Mark Henn, was a brunette, something audiences gravitated to, and she was notably mature. "Physically, we tried to make her a little bit more European-looking with fuller lips, a little bit darker eyebrows, and slightly smaller eyes than Ariel," Baxter said of Belle. "She's also a few years older than Ariel and a lot more worldly because she's always reading. We tried to make her movements very real, whether she's simply walking or waltzing with the Beast in the ballroom sequence."

Belle (1991)

As with Ariel, the animators kept a board of celebrity photos on the wall, including images of Elizabeth Taylor, Natalie Wood, and Audrey Hepburn, as well as voice actress Paige O'Hara, who had been tapped to voice Belle. "Paige was a big influence," Mark Henn says. "All the voice talents bring something to the table, whether it's in the performance or the personality of the character." Sherri Stoner returned to film live-action reference footage for the character, as well. Belle's signature blue dress stands out from the other townspeople, representing her emotional coolness, while her yellow ballgown, which evoked Baroque and Rococo era fashion, revealed her warming to the Beast.

Voice: *Disney Legend Paige O'Hara*

Personality traits: *Adventurous, Intelligent, Compassionate*

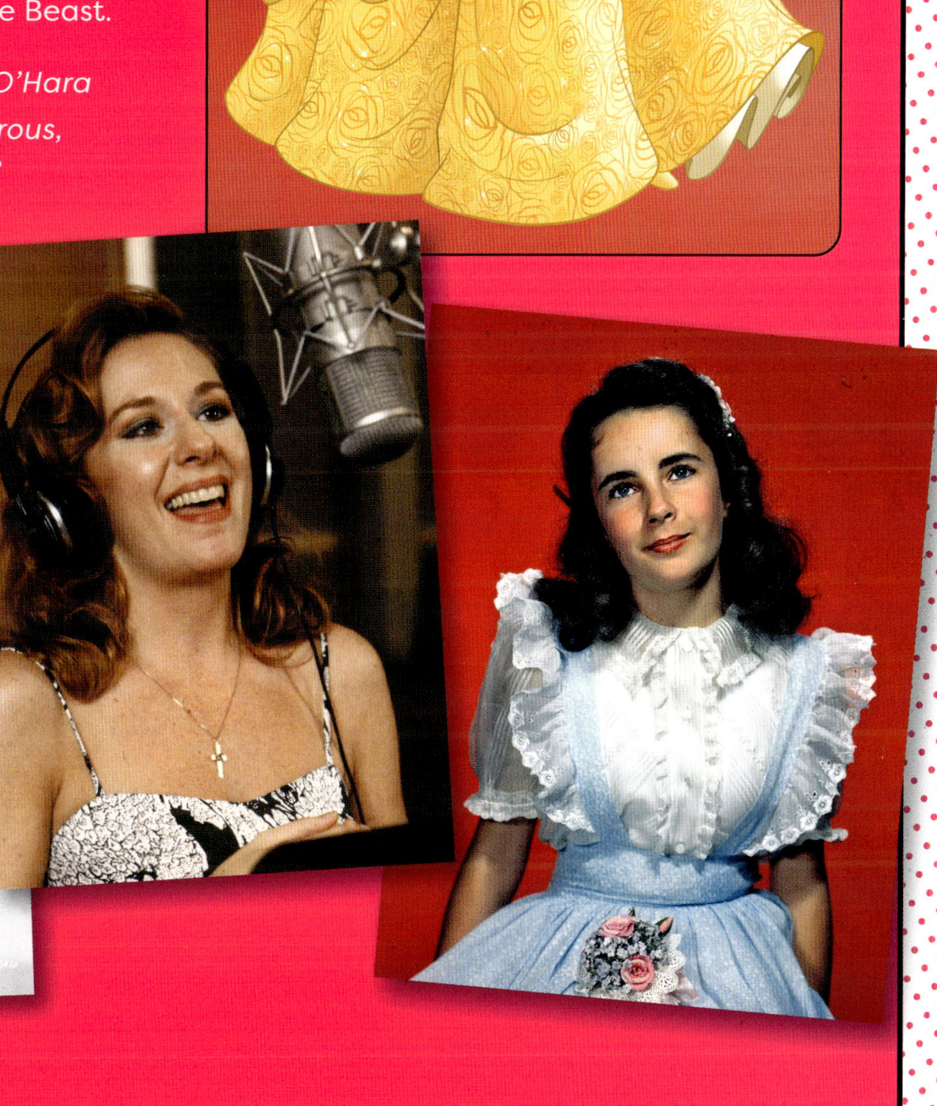

From left: Natalie Wood; Paige O'Hara; Elizabeth Taylor

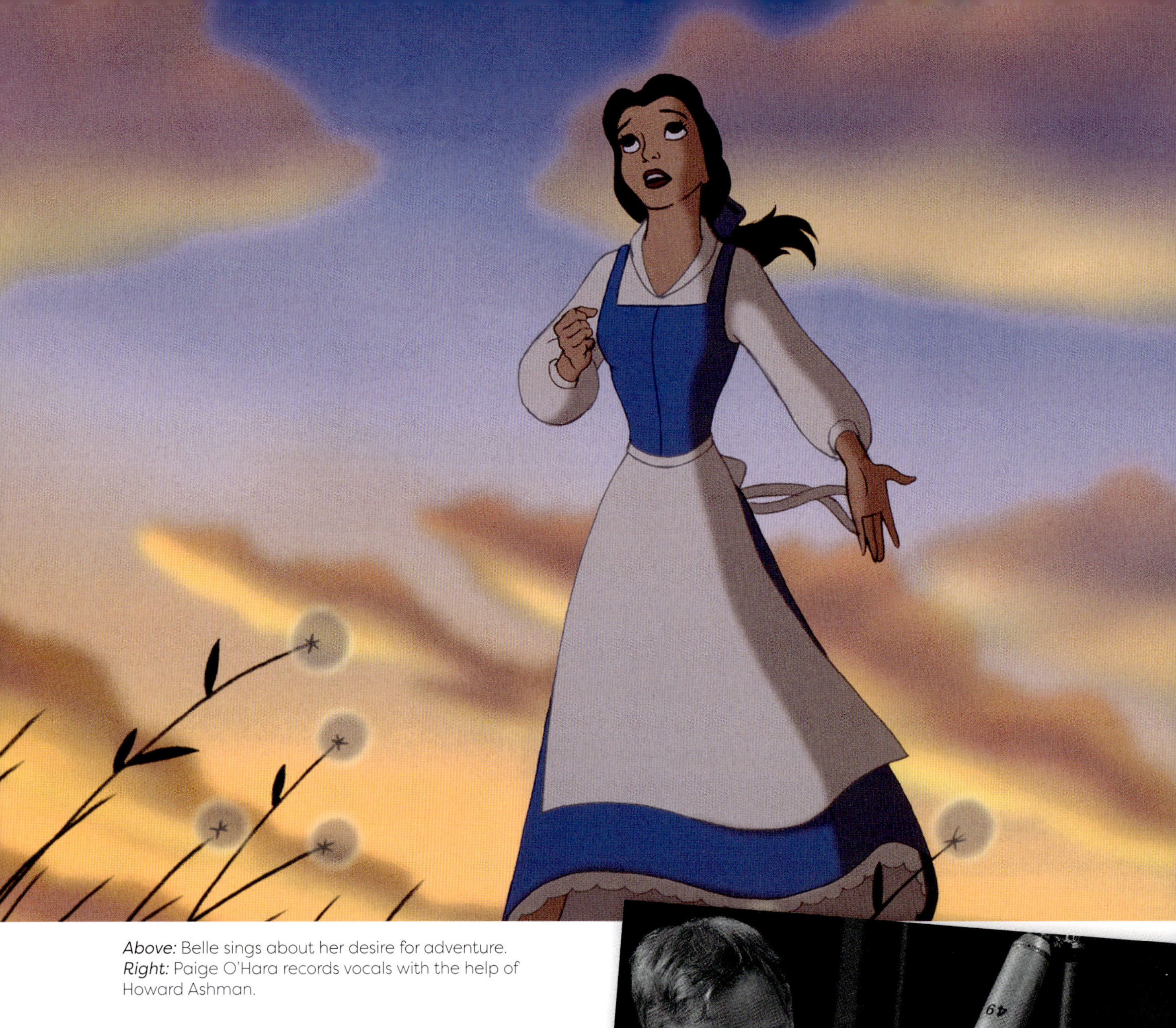

Above: Belle sings about her desire for adventure.
Right: Paige O'Hara records vocals with the help of Howard Ashman.

There was a concerted effort to ensure that Belle, like Ariel, was relatable. Original concept art for Belle shows her as a glamorous woman, but the animators quickly adapted the character's look to ensure viewers could connect to her. "She kind of looked like Angelina Jolie—very beautiful," recalls voice actress and Disney Legend Paige O'Hara, who was also an inspiration for the animators. "I didn't see how anybody would identify with that person. You'd look at her and put her on a pedestal. Mark and James changed the look of her. She was a little too perfect."

She adds, "I knew that this was going to change the view of Disney Princesses. Belle was the first one not looking for a man. She wanted to see the world and all the places she'd read about in books."

The success of *The Little Mermaid* and *Beauty and the Beast* had a ripple effect. It was proof that strong female protagonists would bring audiences to the theaters. That led to changes in the next Walt Disney Animation

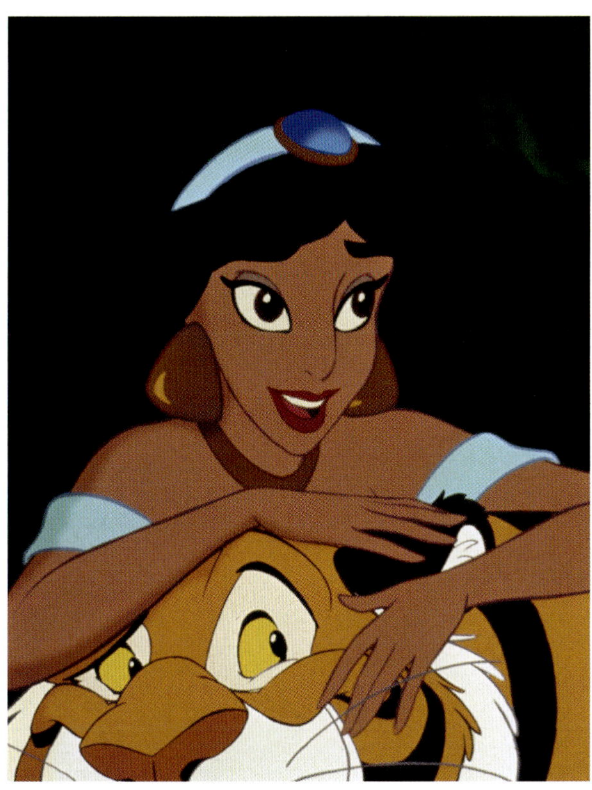

Above: Jasmine with her pet tiger Rajah. *Below:* An early concept sketch for *Aladdin*.

Studios film, *Aladdin*, which introduced the feisty Princess Jasmine. "It was like the flood gates opened," Woolverton remembers. "Jasmine got stronger. And I think Disney female heroes got stronger after Jasmine, as well."

While Jasmine wasn't the protagonist of the new film, her presence in this new adaptation was essential. In *Aladdin*, her character is courageous and outspoken, illustrated by her early declaration that she is "not a prize to be won." Jasmine was the first Disney Princess whose creation was inspired by the Middle East, and she also embraced being a leader of her people.

"From the original script, Jasmine faced her challenges with confidence and courage," remembers voice actress and Disney Legend Linda Larkin. "That was something I really connected to in her because she made things happen in her life. She had this natural sense

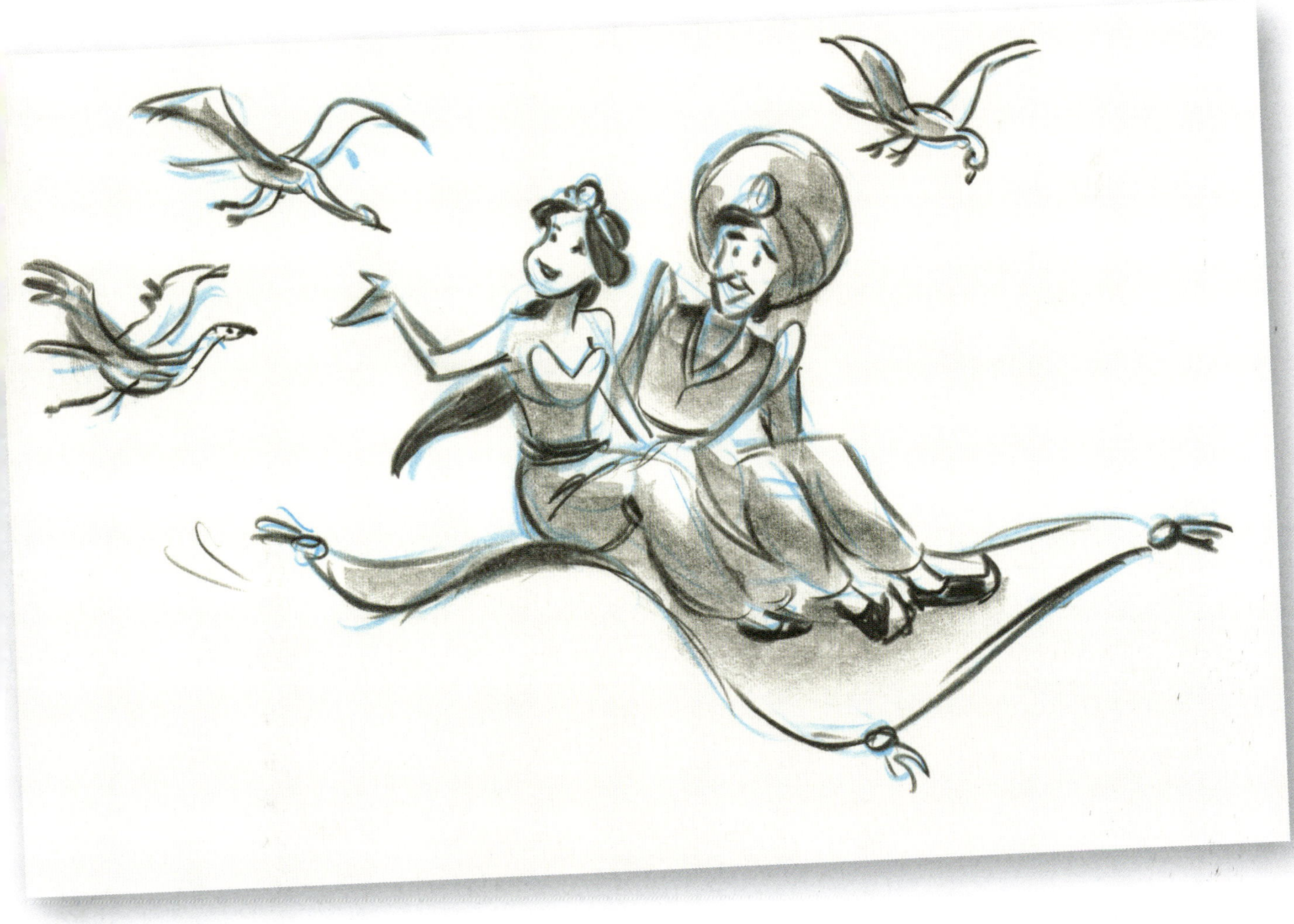

Jasmine (1992)

Overall, *Aladdin* took its cues from the design work of Al Hirschfeld, but Jasmine specifically found her look from an unlikely source: animator Mark Henn's younger sister, Beth. Henn kept a photograph of the dark-haired Beth at her high school graduation above his desk throughout the film, and the animators' designs were also aided by live-action reference footage filmed with actress Robina Ritchie. Using his sister helped Henn find new inspiration. "I had done one, two, three Disney Princesses in a row," Henn remembers. "And when I got to the third one, it was like, 'Oh, I've got to keep doing something new.'"

Voice: *Disney Legend Linda Larkin (speaking) and Disney Legend Lea Salonga (singing)*

Personality traits: *Generous Leader, Stands Up for Herself and Others, Non-Conformist*

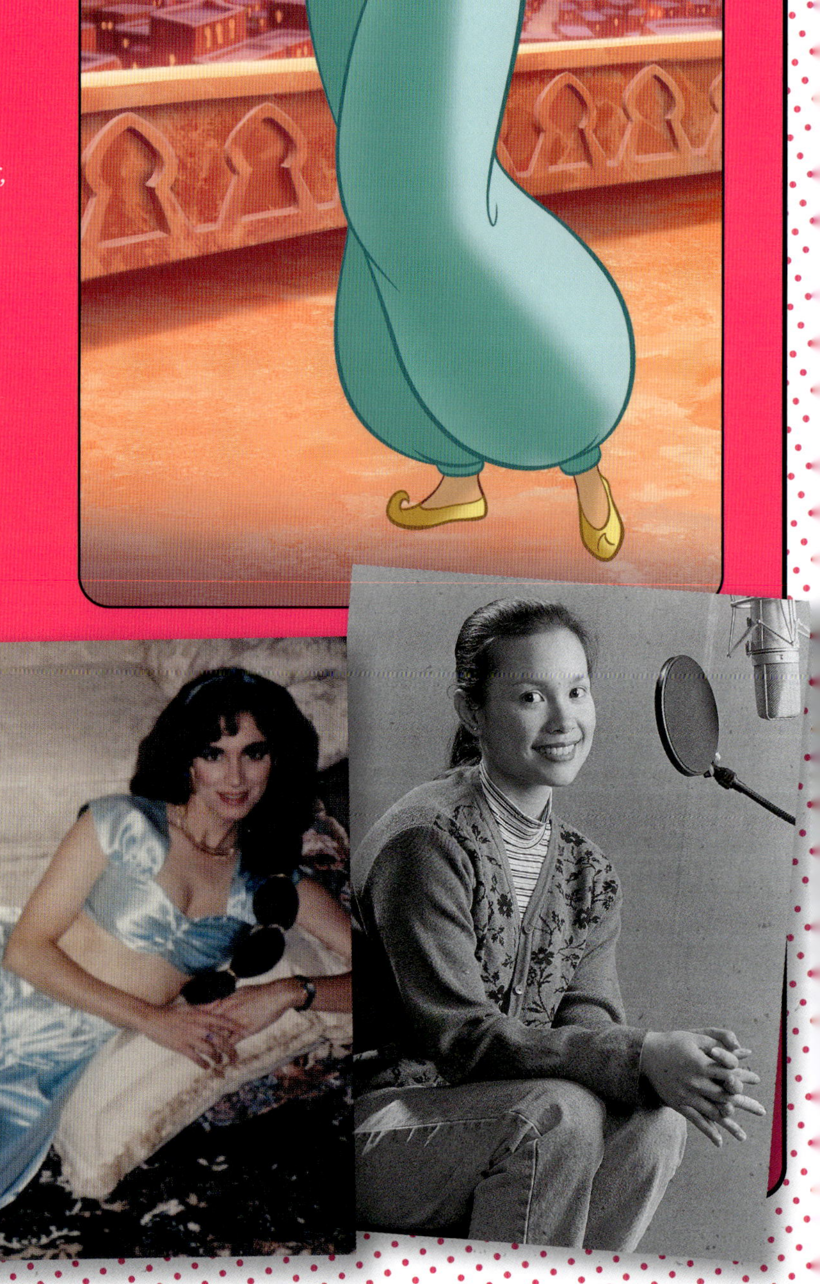

From left: Linda Larkin; Beth Henn dressed as Jasmine; Lea Salonga

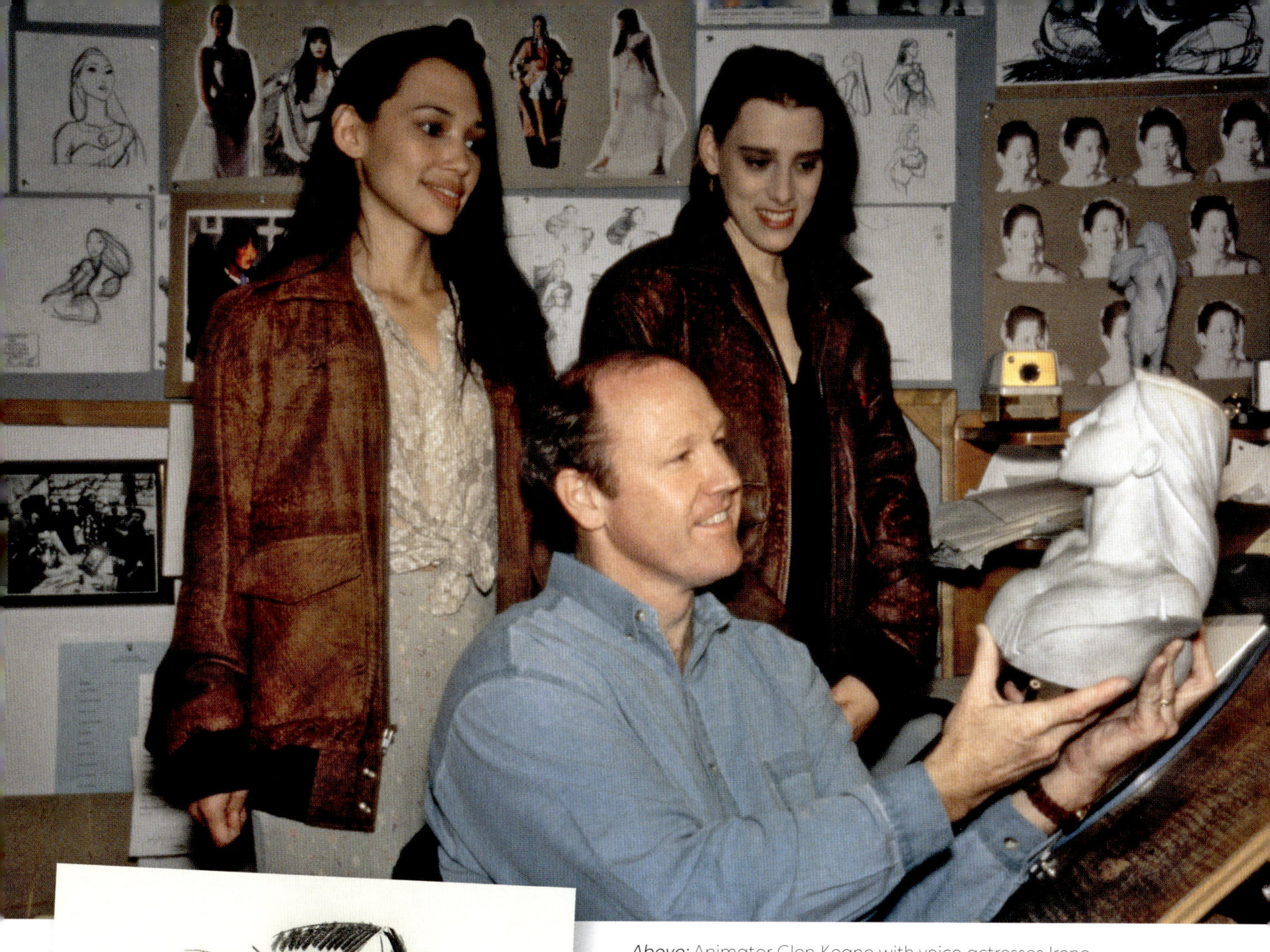

Above: Animator Glen Keane with voice actresses Irene Bedard and Judy Kuhn. *Left:* A development sketch of Pocahontas by Disney artist Jean Gilmore.

of what was important to her: freedom and human connection and love. She risks everything she has—and the comforts and safety of everything she's born into—and has the courage and the heart to go out and seek what's meaningful to her."

Pocahontas, too, represented female strength. The character, the protagonist of 1995's *Pocahontas*, was Disney's first animated female lead to be inspired by a real person. She was courageous, athletic, and deeply empathetic. The film exists as an interpretation of the story, rather than being completely historically accurate. "She had to come from people's understanding of who she was and what she brought to both sides," director Eric Goldberg explained of Pocahontas, "which was peace. That's kind of daunting: It doesn't give you as much flexibility as a character who never existed before the movie."

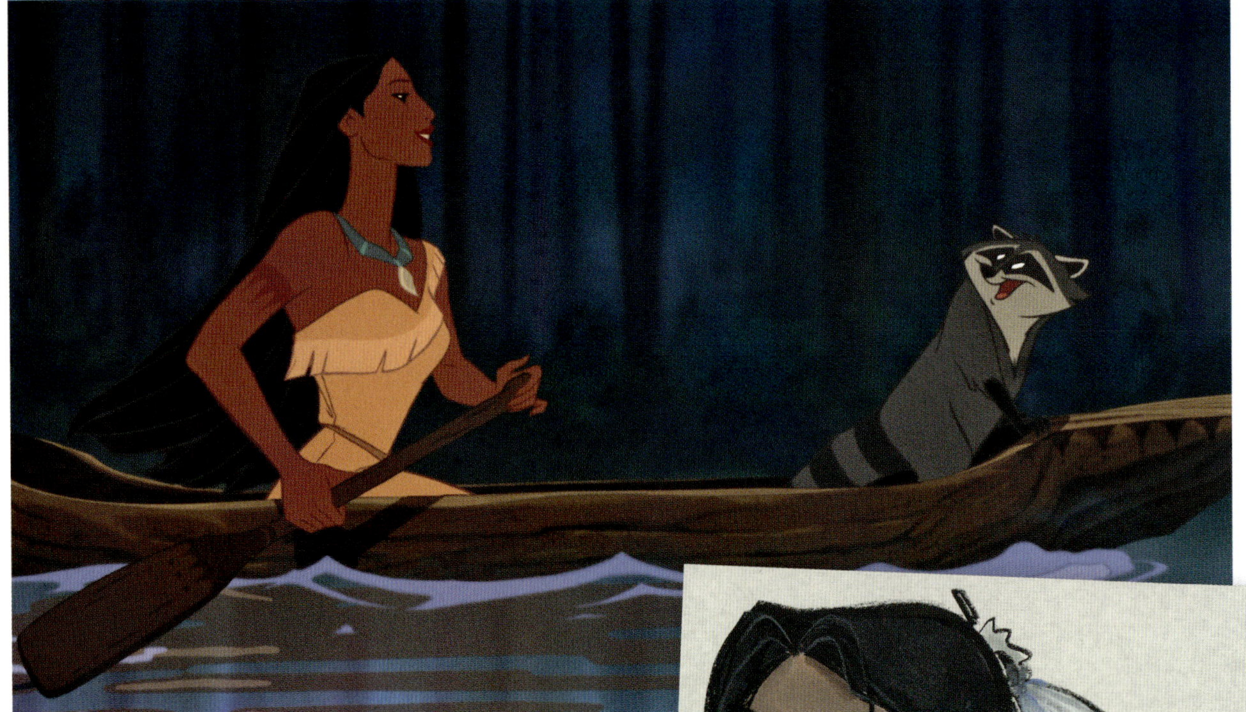

Above: Pocahontas seeks excitement around the river bend. *Right:* Concept art for Pocahontas created by a Disney artist.

Still, *Pocahontas* was an opportunity to convey an important message with a hero who has both conviction and a concern for others. "At Disney, we're always searching for projects set in big mythic arenas," noted former Disney Animation President Peter Schneider. "When [writer and character designer] Mike [Gabriel] made his pitch, we had been thinking about an animated *Romeo and Juliet*, with its clash of two worlds and its especially timely theme of 'If we don't learn to live with one another, we will all destroy ourselves.'"

Voice actress Irene Bedard, who shares Pocahontas's love for sunflowers and hummingbirds, admired the character's resilience and courage. "She wasn't waiting for her prince to come and save her," says Bedard, who is Iñupiat and Cree herself. "She was the one who actually saves John Smith. I felt like I could go into my performance with a lot of strength. And my cultural perspective helped, as well."

By the time *Mulan* was released in 1998, Walt Disney Animation Studios had fully established itself as the studio that knew how to create epic tales with strong women in the lead. Even its non-princess releases, including animated films *The Lion King*, *The Hunchback of Notre Dame*, and *Hercules*, were defined by female characters who were clever, courageous, and outspoken. That stood in welcome contrast to what was happening in Hollywood films in general—the top box office output in 1997 and 1998 was primarily male-led action movies.

Pocahontas (1995)

The animators for *Pocahontas* were inspired by a variety of historical sources, as well as a visit to Jamestown, Virginia. Animator Glen Keane, who designed Pocahontas, specifically looked to Native American sisters Shirley Littledove and Debbie Whitedove. “Shirley stood there very still, looking straight into my eyes with this unnerving presence,” Keane remembered. “Her sister was a vivacious airline stewardess . . . Pocahontas is very spiritual, strong, confident, but at the same time, not afraid to break from tradition and find a direction that is contrary to everything else.”

Voice: *Irene Bedard (speaking) and Judy Kuhn (singing)*

Personality traits: *Intuitive, Protector, Mediator*

From left: Irene Bedard; Judy Kuhn

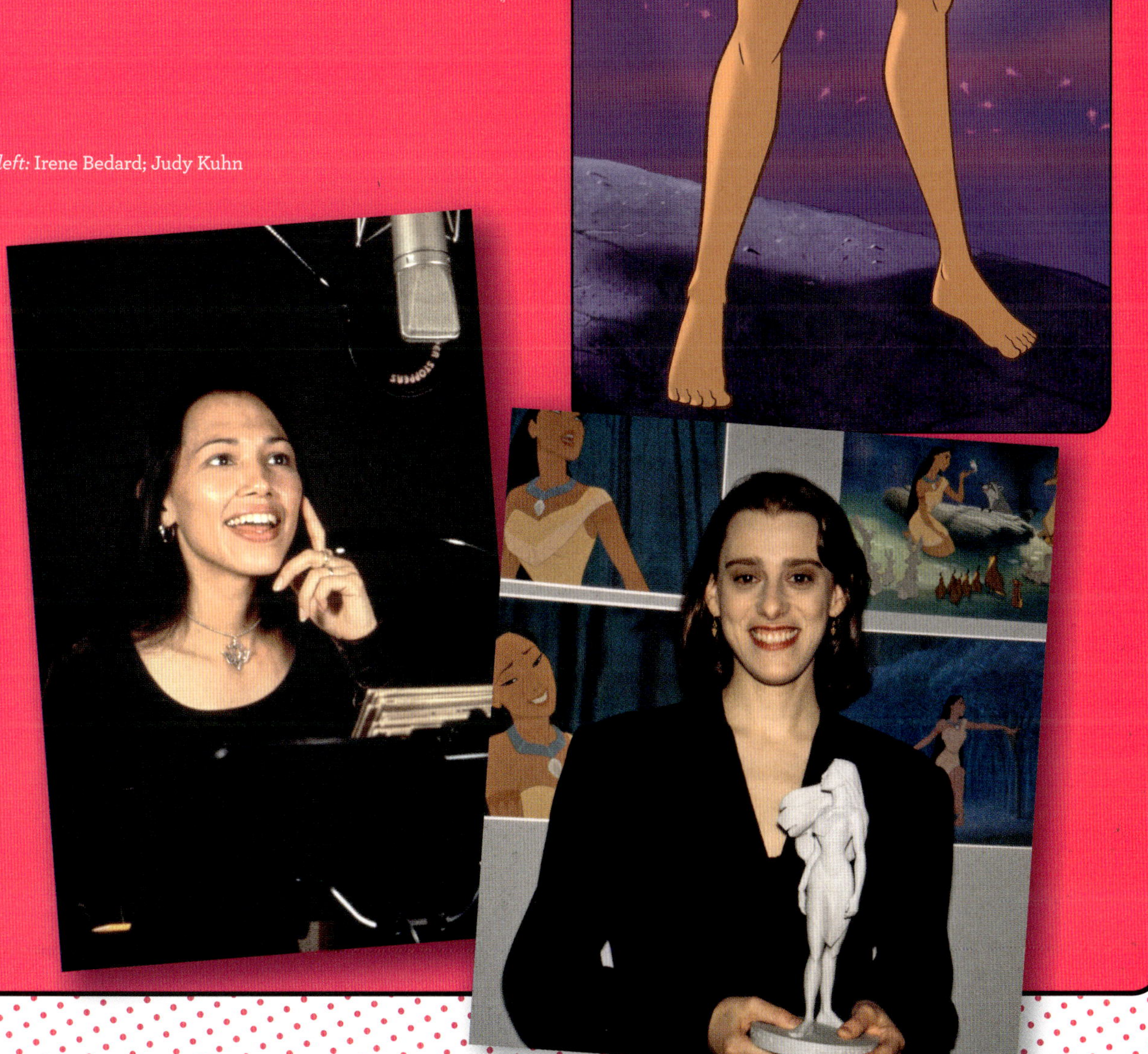

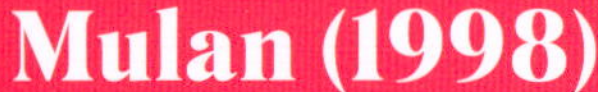

Mulan (1998)

For *Mulan*, the animators looked to history for inspiration when crafting the animated lead character. The filmmakers found most of their artistic influence in the Han dynasty (206 BCE-220 CE) and Tang dynasty (618-906 CE), and also looked to voice actress Ming-Na Wen, who animator Mark Henn says impacted Mulan's final design and personality. Character designer Chen-Yi Chang was responsible for the character's overall look, noting, "My concern as a Chinese artist was that Mulan's look be classical in Chinese terms, but also have a modern quality."

Voice: *Disney Legend Ming-Na Wen (speaking) and Disney Legend Lea Salonga (singing)*

Personality traits: *Courageous, Clever, Adaptable*

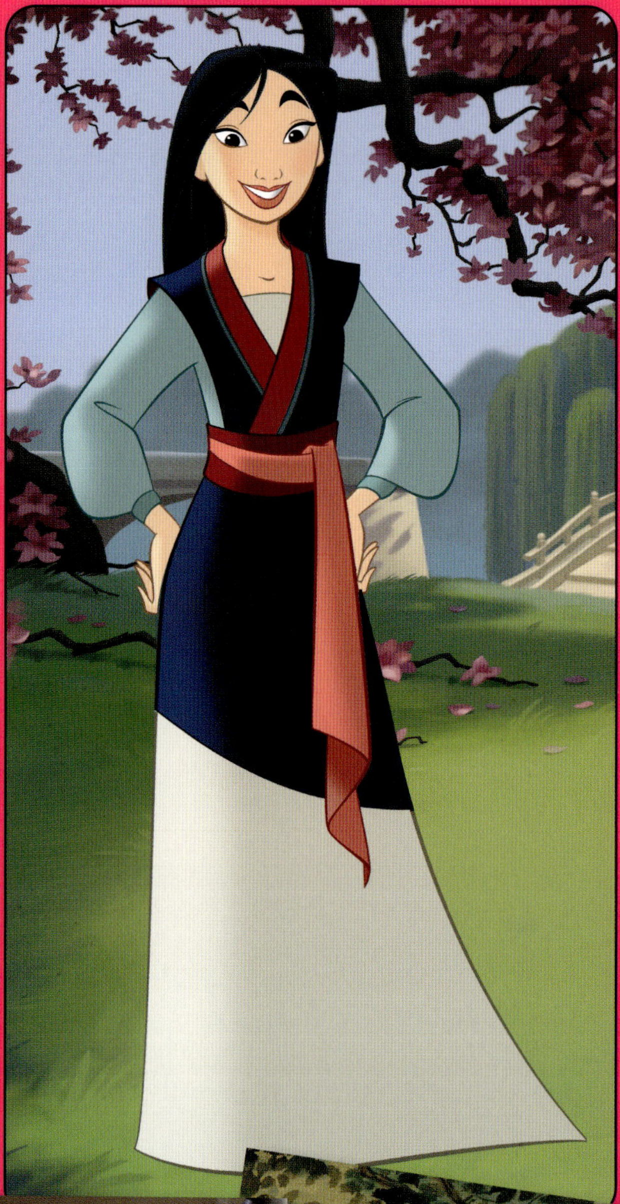

From left: Ming-Na Wen; Lea Salonga; a traditional Chinese depiction of Mulan.

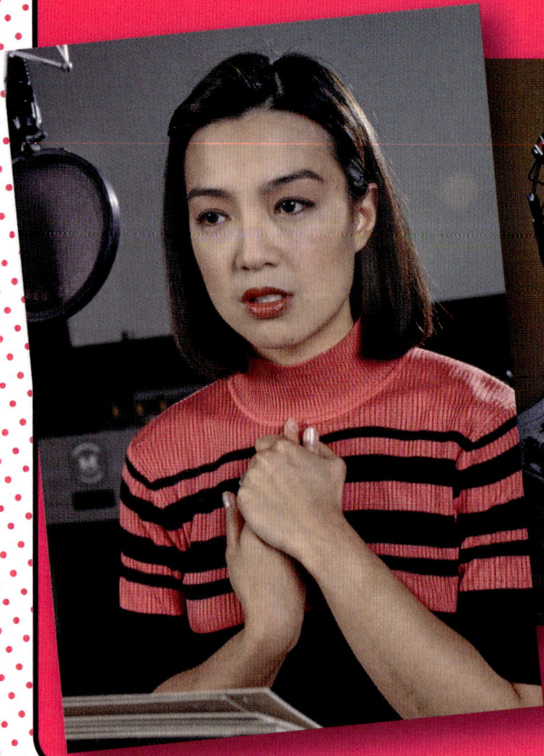

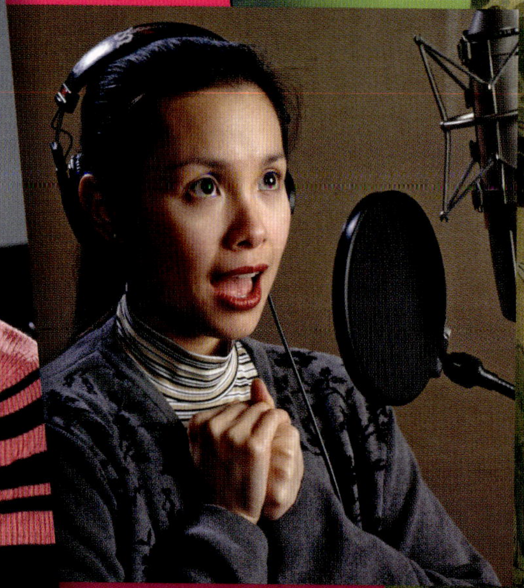

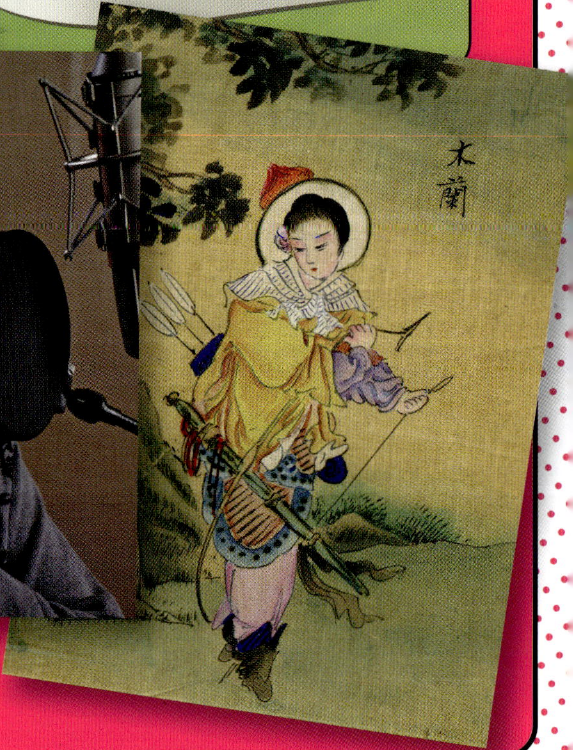

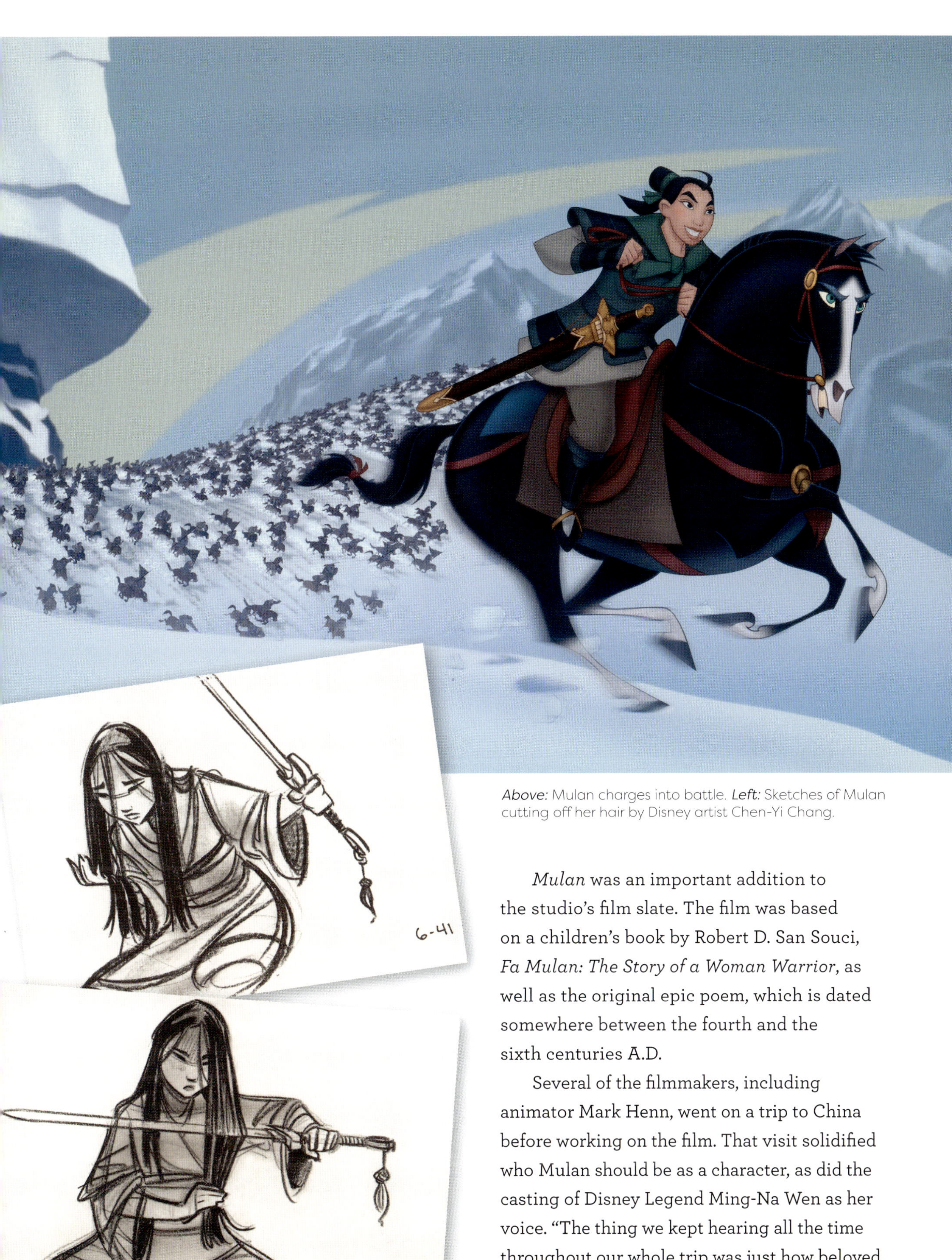

Above: Mulan charges into battle. *Left:* Sketches of Mulan cutting off her hair by Disney artist Chen-Yi Chang.

Mulan was an important addition to the studio's film slate. The film was based on a children's book by Robert D. San Souci, *Fa Mulan: The Story of a Woman Warrior*, as well as the original epic poem, which is dated somewhere between the fourth and the sixth centuries A.D.

Several of the filmmakers, including animator Mark Henn, went on a trip to China before working on the film. That visit solidified who Mulan should be as a character, as did the casting of Disney Legend Ming-Na Wen as her voice. "The thing we kept hearing all the time throughout our whole trip was just how beloved Mulan is in the Chinese history," remembers Henn. "There's some debate about whether she was a real person, but the legend of Mulan and what she represents is still to this day extremely important. And that was something I took in when drawing her."

Like her royal predecessors, Mulan's journey is one of self-discovery. She doesn't start out a warrior; she becomes one. The audience is invited to experience how she overcomes the challenges before her, never deviating from her path. She acts out of duty and loyalty to her family. "Mulan was quite different from our previous leads," noted *Mulan* screenwriter Chris Sanders. "She did not perceive herself to be a misfit, and didn't long for anything beyond her own backyard. Her strength was her selflessness, which was very unusual."

By 1999, Walt Disney Animation Studios had re-established itself as the home of vibrant animated fairy tales. The studio also further redefined who a princess could be. It wasn't necessarily birth or marriage that made one royal; it was one's actions. Ariel opened the door for a new generation of Disney Princesses, although the heroes of the "Disney Renaissance" were only the beginning.

"It was obvious that the world had been hungry for what Disney animation used to be in our culture," says Menken. "So *The Little Mermaid* and all that followed really satisfied that appetite in a big way. It became a natural passing of the torch to a new generation. It was very clear that seeing these characters have strengths and a passionate dream and a commitment to seeing that dream through was really important for our generation and for the next generation."

Animator Mark Henn sketches Mulan.

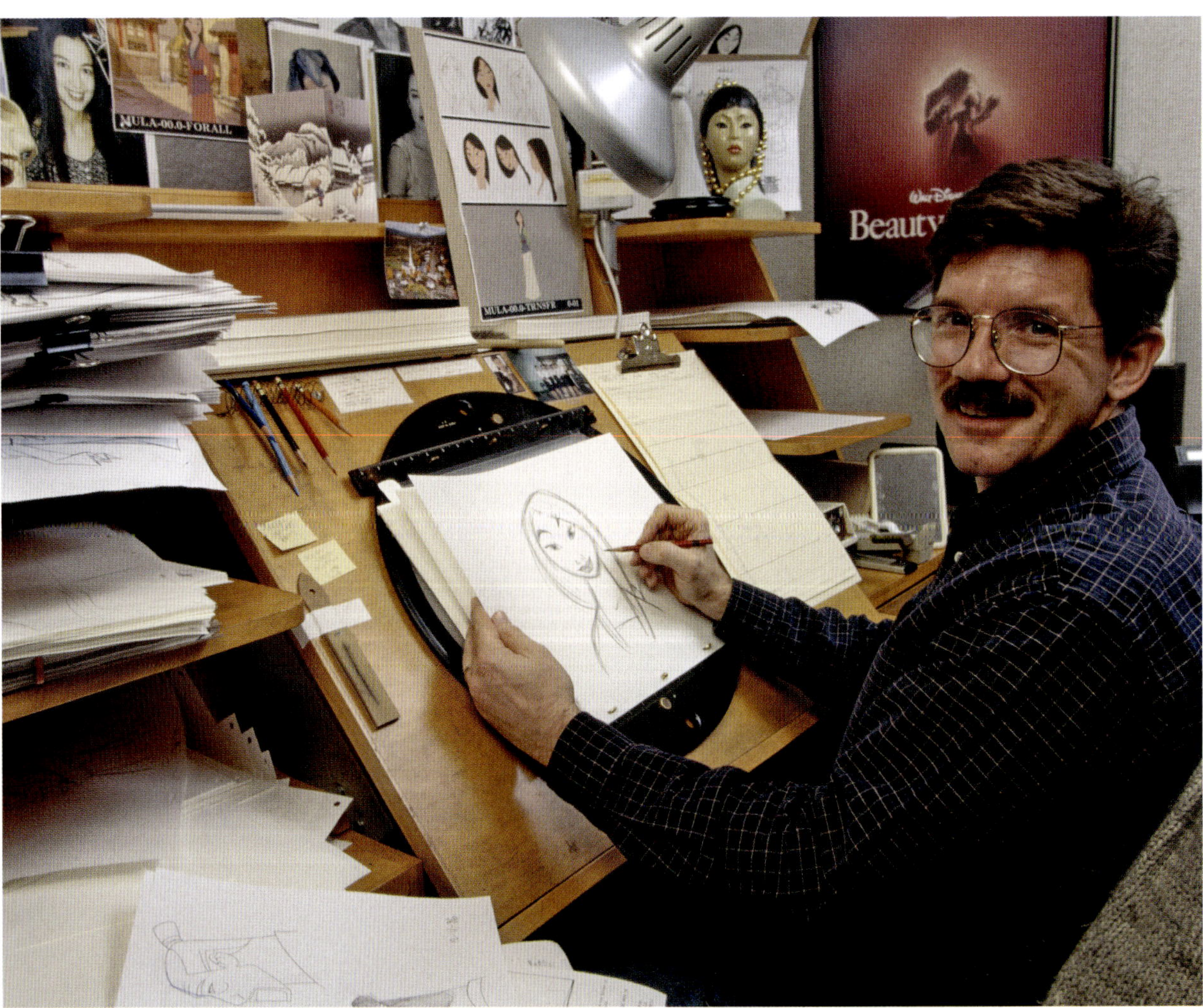

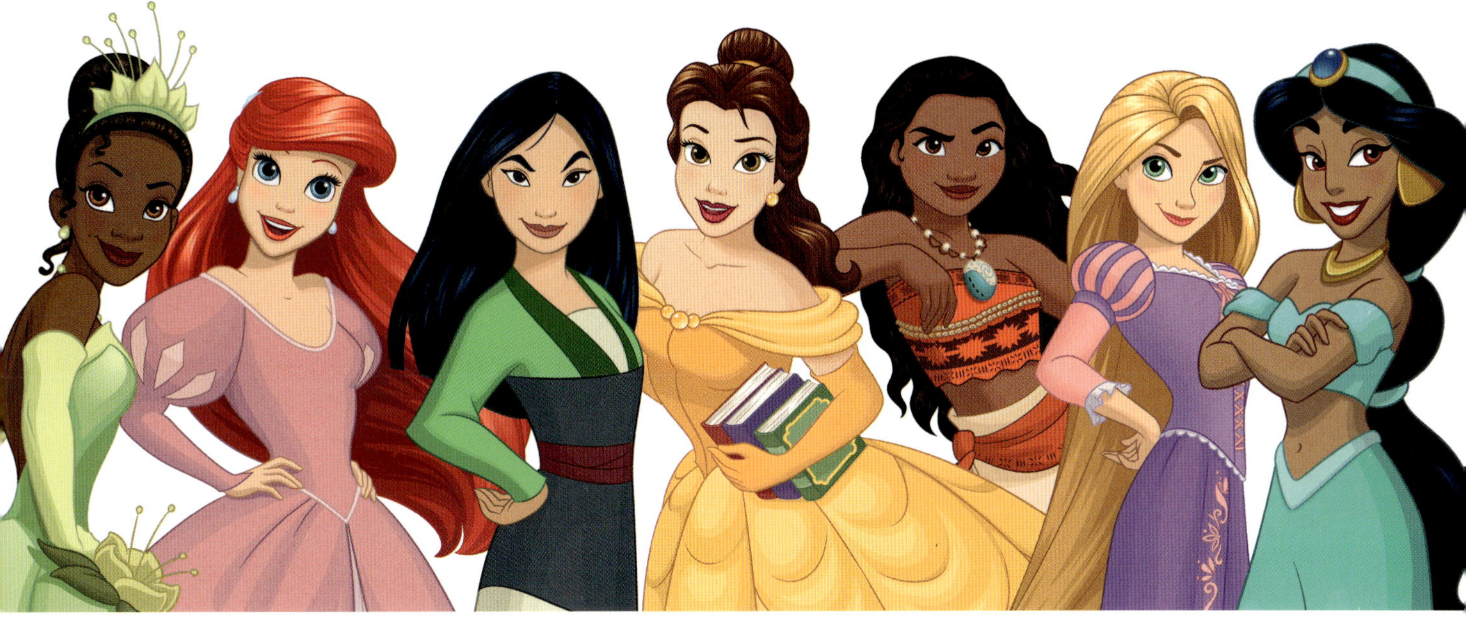

A FRANCHISE IS BORN

As the list of royal heroes on the Disney Animation roster grew over the years, the princesses always appeared separately in books and on products. That is, until Andy Mooney, former chairman of Disney Consumer Products, had a revelation at a Disney On Ice show in 2000. "I was standing in line with mothers and daughters, all dressed head to toe in princess regalia that they had made at home," Mooney said in an interview with *BBC*. "I said to a few of the mums, 'If Disney made official dresses like this, would you buy them?' and they all replied that they'd buy lots. So I rushed back to [Disney headquarters] in Burbank [Los Angeles], and we launched the Disney Princess series pretty quickly."

Mooney realized that Disney was missing a key element in merchandising the characters. He wanted to bring the royal heroes together under one franchise, which was not only a powerful merchandising idea, but also a compelling narrative one. The original Disney Princess lineup featured Snow White, Cinderella, Aurora, Ariel, Belle, Jasmine, Pocahontas, and Mulan. Tinker Bell was included briefly, but she was later given her own franchise, Disney Fairies, in 2005. The production of Disney Princess clothes, toys, games, books, and more quickly ramped up over the years.

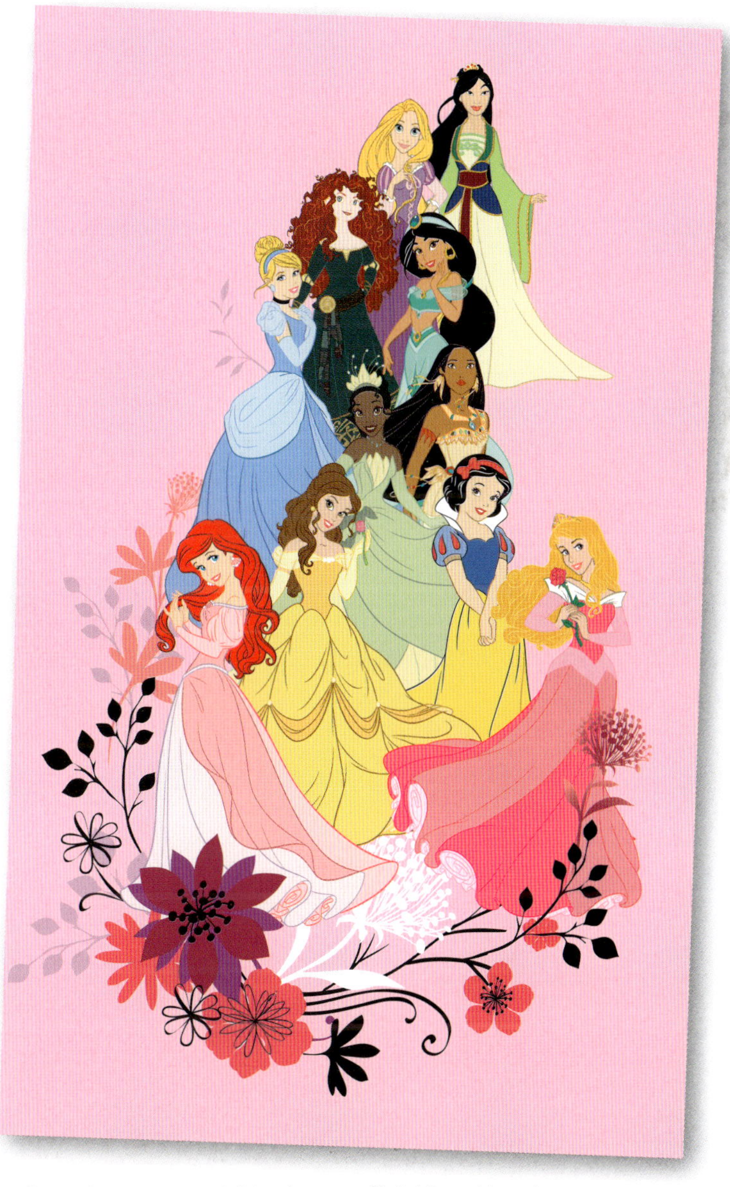

Once they were established as an official franchise, the Disney Princesses could finally be shown together.

On March 14, 2010, Tiana became the first new addition to the Disney Princess lineup with a coronation ceremony at the New York Palace hotel. Rapunzel was added on October 2, 2011, at Kensington Palace in London, while Merida joined as the eleventh member at a ceremony in front of Cinderella Castle at Walt Disney World on May 11, 2013. Moana became a Disney Princess in 2019.

What connects the members of the Disney Princess franchise is that each is an empowered hero who makes her own decisions. Each has a path she sets out for herself and a journey she undertakes with courage and confidence. To be a Disney Princess means being authentic, adventurous, and kind, with each hero embracing those traits in her own way.

A MODERN PRINCESS FOR MODERN DAY

The Princess and the Frog, released in 2009, ushered in another new era for Disney. Sometimes referred to as the "Disney Revival" by fans, the following decade was marked by empowered heroes who represented stories and fairy tales from around the world. These new Disney Princesses, from Tiana to Rapunzel to Merida to Moana, were not defined by romantic relationships.

The Princess and the Frog, Walt Disney Animation Studios' return to hand-drawn animation, had a lot riding on it. Not only was the film vital for the studio because of its artistic aspirations, but it arrived during a time of calls for increased diverse representation in American media (a year prior, Barack Obama had been elected as the first African American President of the United States). Importantly, the film's protagonist, a hard-working, talented young woman named Tiana, would become Disney's first Black Disney Princess.

John Musker and Ron Clements helmed the film, based loosely on *The Frog Prince,* from *Grimm's Fairy Tales.* The filmmakers set the

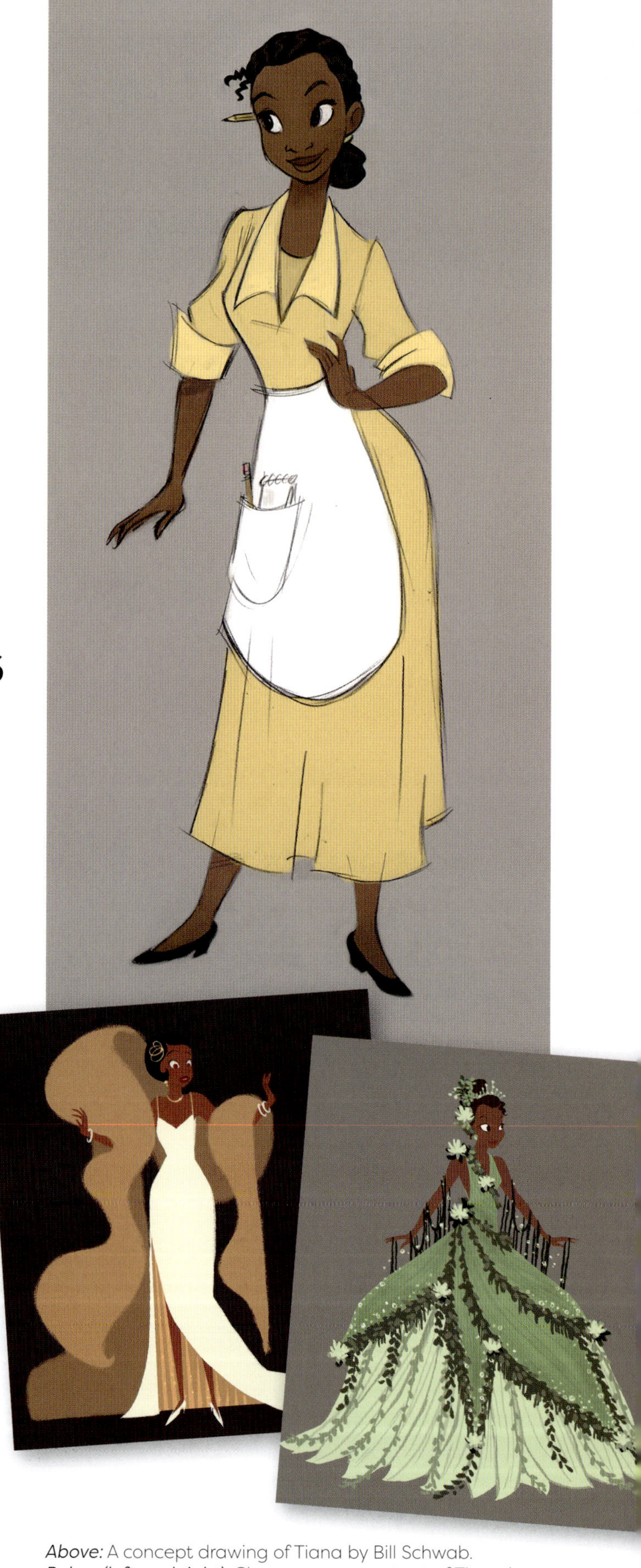

Above: A concept drawing of Tiana by Bill Schwab.
Below (left and right): Glamorous concept art of Tiana by Ian Gooding, and a digital rendering of Tiana's gown by Lorelay Bové.

Tiana (2009)

Leah Chase, who opened Dooky Chase's Restaurant in New Orleans in 1941 and was known as the "Queen of Creole Cuisine," was a major inspiration for Tiana. "The way that food can bring a community together was something we heard about when we read about Leah Chase, the great New Orleans restaurateur, who became kind of a role model for Tiana," noted director John Musker. The filmmakers looked at historical reference of the time period, and even harkened back to Cinderella, such as with the transformation of Tiana's green gown at the end of the film. To ensure Tiana reflected the African American community, the filmmakers met with members of the NAACP and consulted Disney Legend Oprah Winfrey, who voiced Tiana's mother, Eudora.

Voice: *Disney Legend Anika Noni Rose*

Personality traits: *Visionary, Pursues Her Dreams, Graceful*

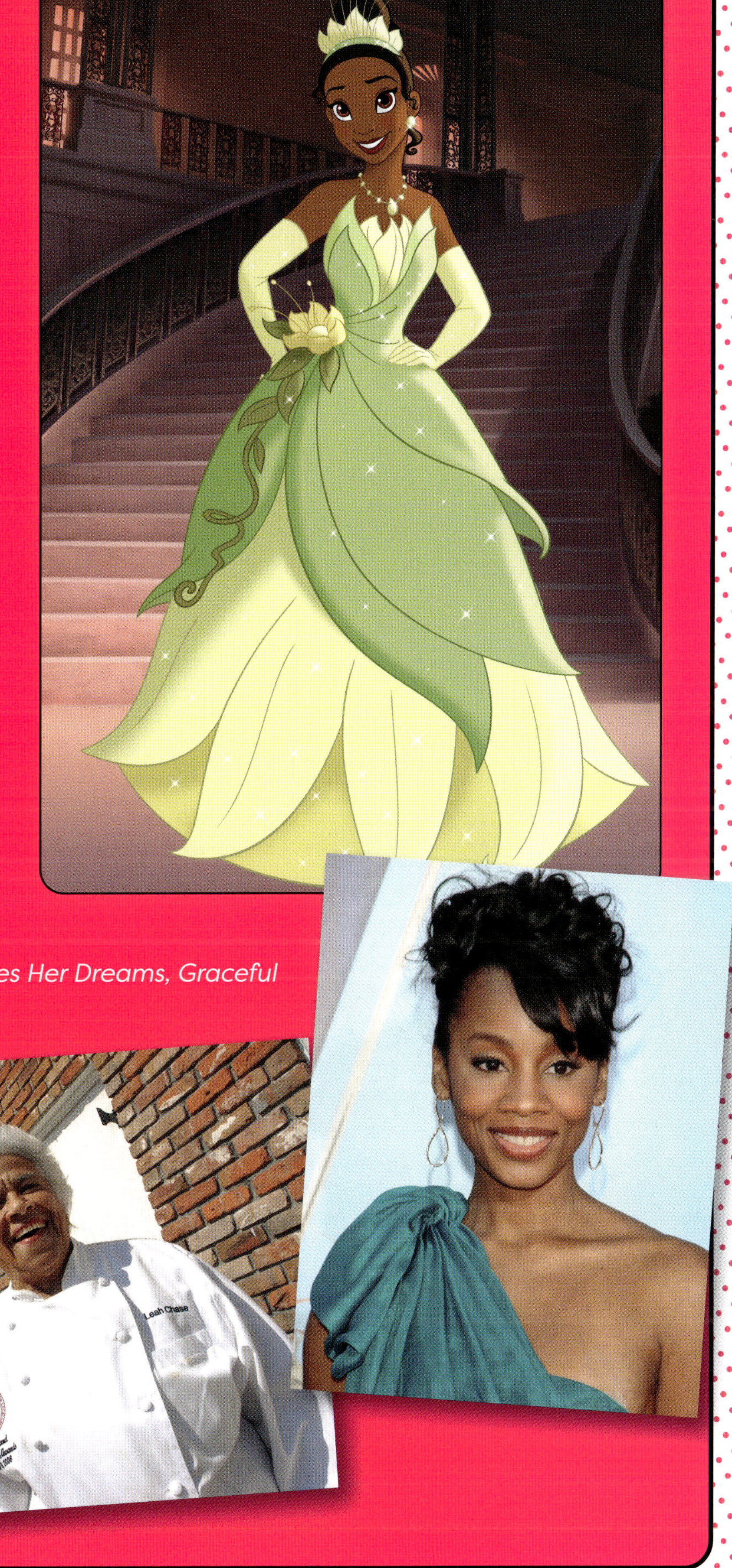

From left:
Leah Chase;
Anika Noni Rose

story in New Orleans in the 1920s, giving it a vibrant, Jazz Age feel, and found inspiration for Tiana in famed restauranteur Leah Chase. "Tiana has had a tough life: We always related her to Cinderella as more of an underdog princess," Clements explained. "And to contrast her with the prince. We were sort of basing things on *It Happened One Night* in reverse. Tiana in some ways was Clark Gable, and the prince was Claudette Colbert. Tiana is like Cinderella: She's got to fight, she's got to struggle. She's a little bit of an anti-princess. [Her best friend] Charlotte represents the princess dream, and Tiana rejects all that. It's the last thing she's interested in."

The animators, led by Mark Henn, wanted to ensure that Tiana reflected real-life African American women. They also took a lot of inspiration from voice actress and Disney Legend Anika Noni Rose, who had been cast as the protagonist, including making Tiana left-handed, like Rose. "In the voice recording sessions watching Anika bring Tiana to life, I noticed her smile and her dimples," Henn recalls. "I went to the directors one day and said 'Can I put dimples in? I see Anika's got these amazing dimples and when she smiles, it just lights up a room.'"

The power of storytelling expands when more people can see themselves onscreen. This was particularly true of *The Princess and the Frog*, which became a historic moment for many. The goal was to make Tiana as unique, interesting, and complex of a character as she could be.

"Being the first Black Disney Princess, that was such a first and it really has changed the way young brown children are looked at in school and fantasy when they are playing," Rose told *Variety*. "It's no longer 'You can't be the princess.' It's expected and normal. And I see children of all different ethnicities wearing their Tiana gear, so what it says is that she speaks to people on so many different levels."

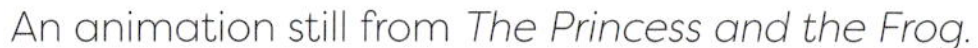

An animation still from *The Princess and the Frog*.

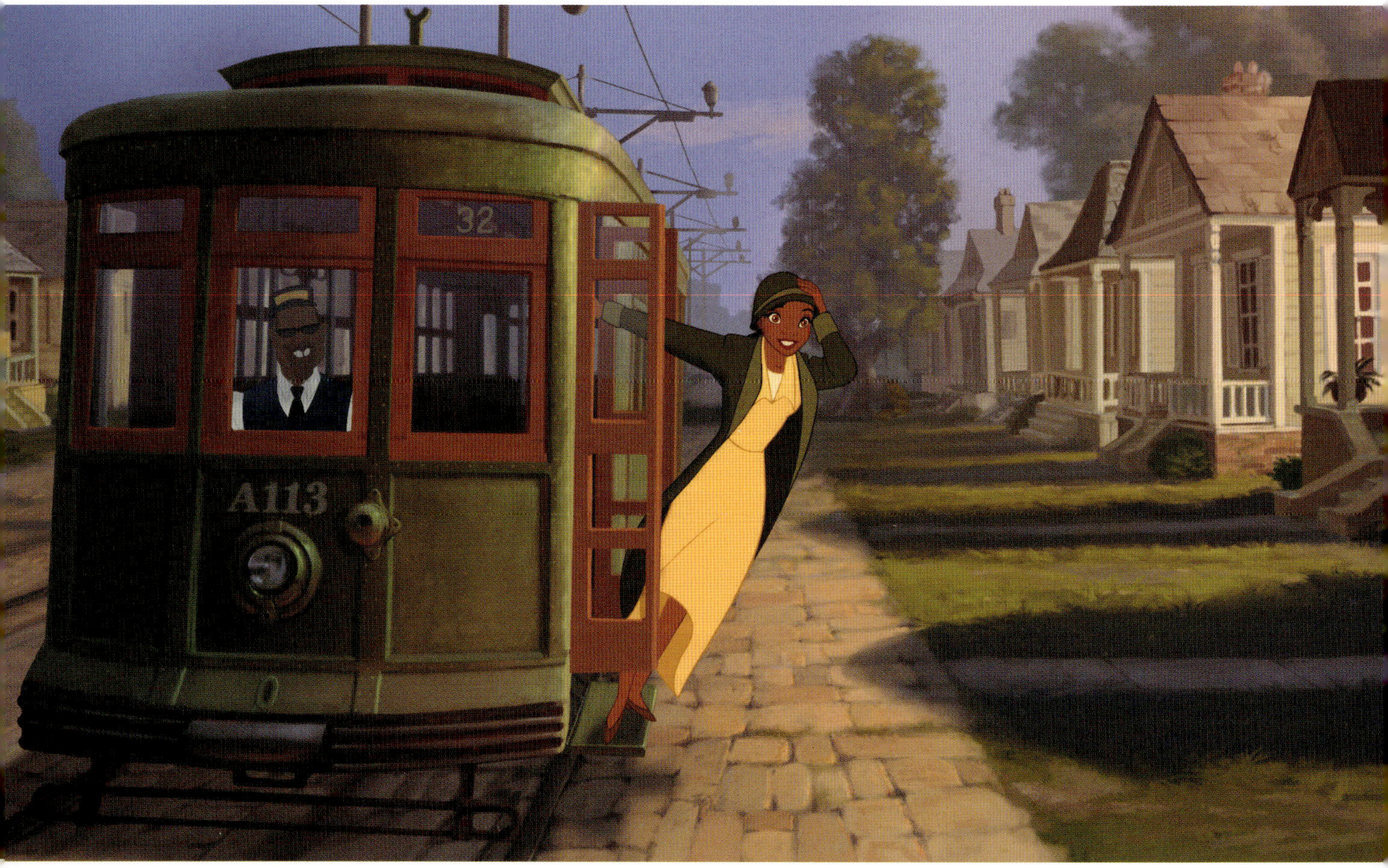

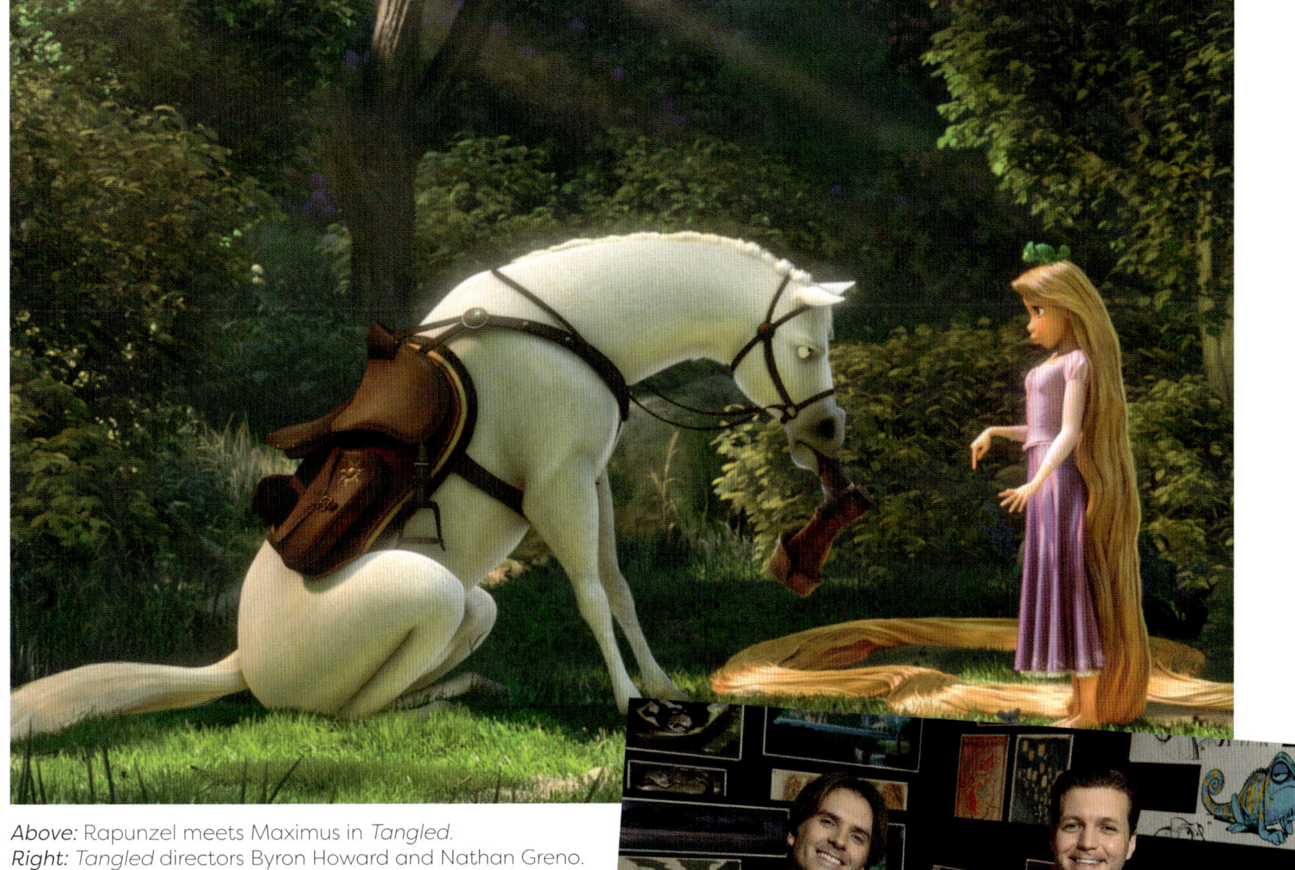

Above: Rapunzel meets Maximus in *Tangled*.
Right: *Tangled* directors Byron Howard and Nathan Greno.

Tangled (2010) marked Disney's 50th animated feature, although Walt had toyed with the idea of making the Rapunzel story into a film back in the 1940s. A new version was first imagined by Glen Keane, who was slated to direct it, but health issues forced him to step back in 2008. Directors Byron Howard and Nathan Greno came onboard with the idea to adapt the dark fairy tale into a more modern, whimsical story that gave equal weight to Rapunzel and to her love interest, Flynn Rider.

"We were looking at redefining the princess," explains producer Roy Conli. "We wanted to make sure she was as strong as Flynn Rider. We wanted to make sure she had a journey of self-awareness. And it was really important for us that fundamentally she chose to get out of that tower herself."

Howard adds, "The most important difference in our Rapunzel is that we did not want her to be a passive participant in her own life. We needed to set a good example for young people in the modern world. She needed to drive her own story."

While Rapunzel, voiced by actress Mandy Moore, may have looked like a traditional princess, with long blonde hair and a sweeping gown, she represented an evolution. Although she's not a warrior, she wields a frying pan with confidence. She's artistic and finds creative ways to express herself. That self-expression, which manifests as murals that she paints, covering the interior walls of her tower, was directly inspired by life in the late 2000s.

"During *Tangled*'s production, social media was growing in a huge way," Howard remembers.

Rapunzel (2010)

Animator Glen Keane was inspired by his daughter, Claire, who worked on the film's visual development and created Rapunzel's tower paintings for the film. Voice actress Mandy Moore also helped give direction to the princess, and Rapunzel's attire draws on European looks from the Medieval period to the early nineteenth century. The guiding light behind Rapunzel's design was what Glen Keane called her "irrepressible spirit." "That manifested itself in the 70 feet of golden hair," notes animator Kira Lehtomaki. "She couldn't be contained in her tower. That worked into how we were animating her. It changed her expressions."

Voice: *Mandy Moore*

Personality traits: *Creative, Inquisitive, Vibrant*

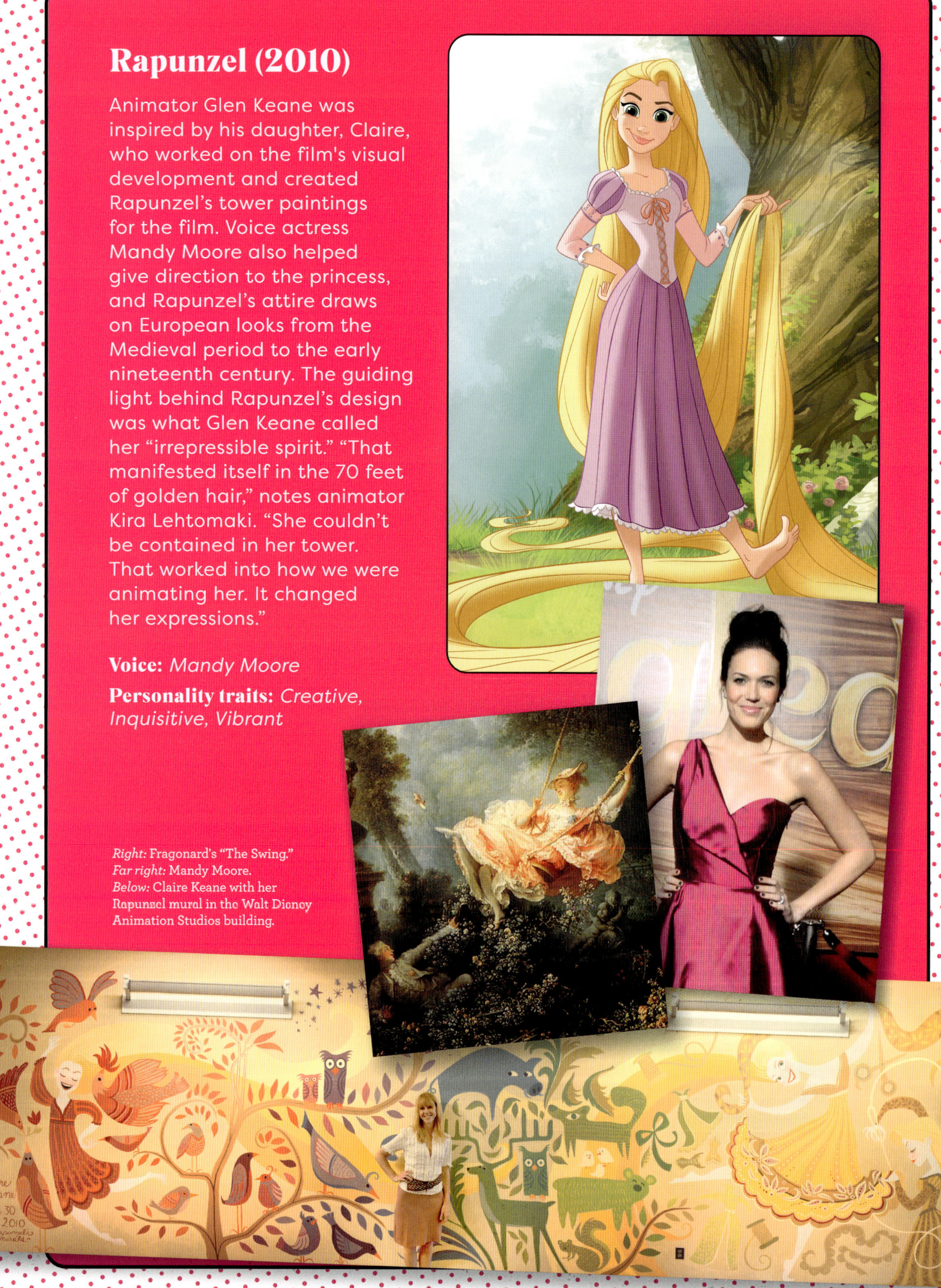

Right: Fragonard's "The Swing."
Far right: Mandy Moore.
Below: Claire Keane with her Rapunzel mural in the Walt Disney Animation Studios building.

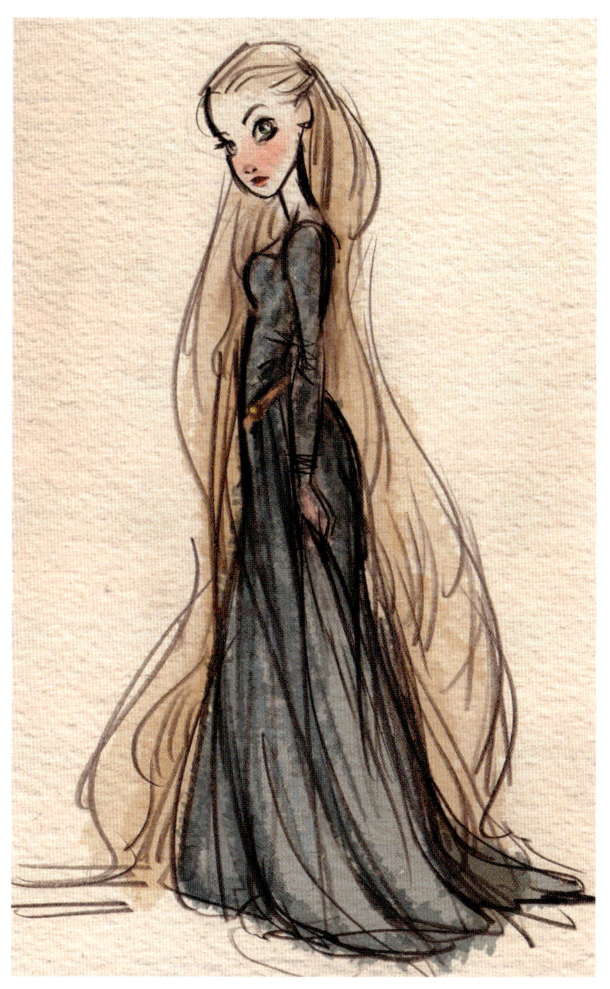

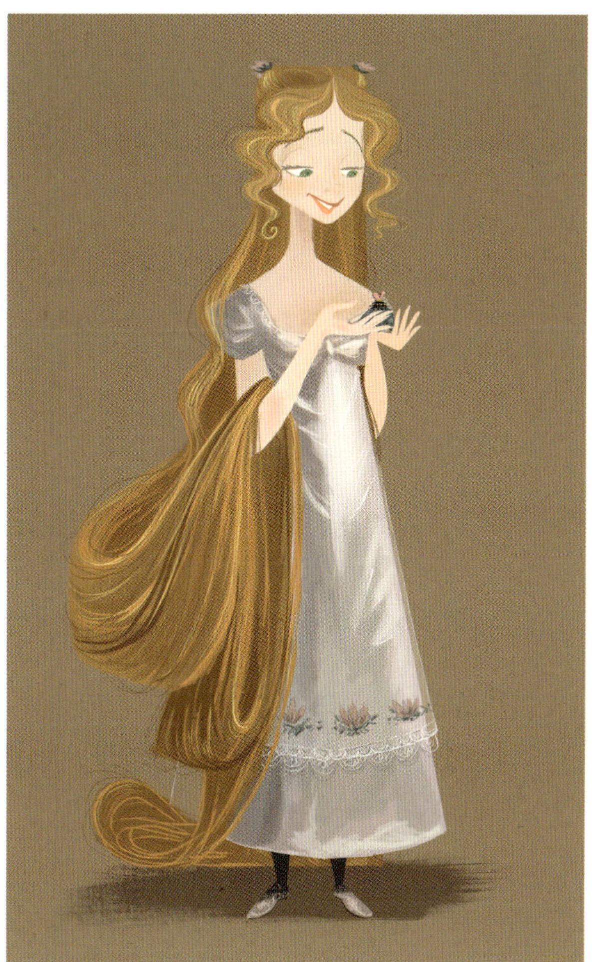

Development sketches of Rapunzel by Claire Keane (*left*) and Lorelay Bové (*right*).

"Facebook, Twitter, and other platforms allowed millions of people to post online and say 'Here's who I am' by sharing interests, hobbies, art, personal opinions, and observations about life. So, in a very real way, I think the Rapunzel character in *Tangled* is a reflection of everyday people expressing themselves and looking for human connection through social media. For Rapunzel, she has used every inch of that tower to show us who she is. She's rapidly running out of wall space, and for her, there's no other option left but to get out of there and into the world."

Ultimately, *Tangled* underscored the idea that rescue can come from within, rather than always from others. "When we set out to make this film, we were not looking to box any young person into a situation where they would think they needed to be saved by anyone," Conli says. "The great thing about Disney storytelling is that there is always a goal of imparting a positive message of strength and self-reliance in any of the characters we do. And certainly with Rapunzel in *Tangled* we wanted to make sure that power was something women would be proud of."

The same sense of self-reliance found in Rapunzel was also apparent in Merida, the hero of *Brave* who was voiced by Kelly Macdonald. The film, released in 2012, was Disney and Pixar Animation Studios' first foray into the fairy tale princess genre, but its filmmakers wanted it to be an unconventional interpretation. Merida was a confident hero who would rather shoot her bow and arrow in a field than attend a ball.

"The main thing that inspired *Brave* was my relationship with my daughter, our love and our battle of wills," co-director and writer Brenda Chapman said. "I wanted to create an

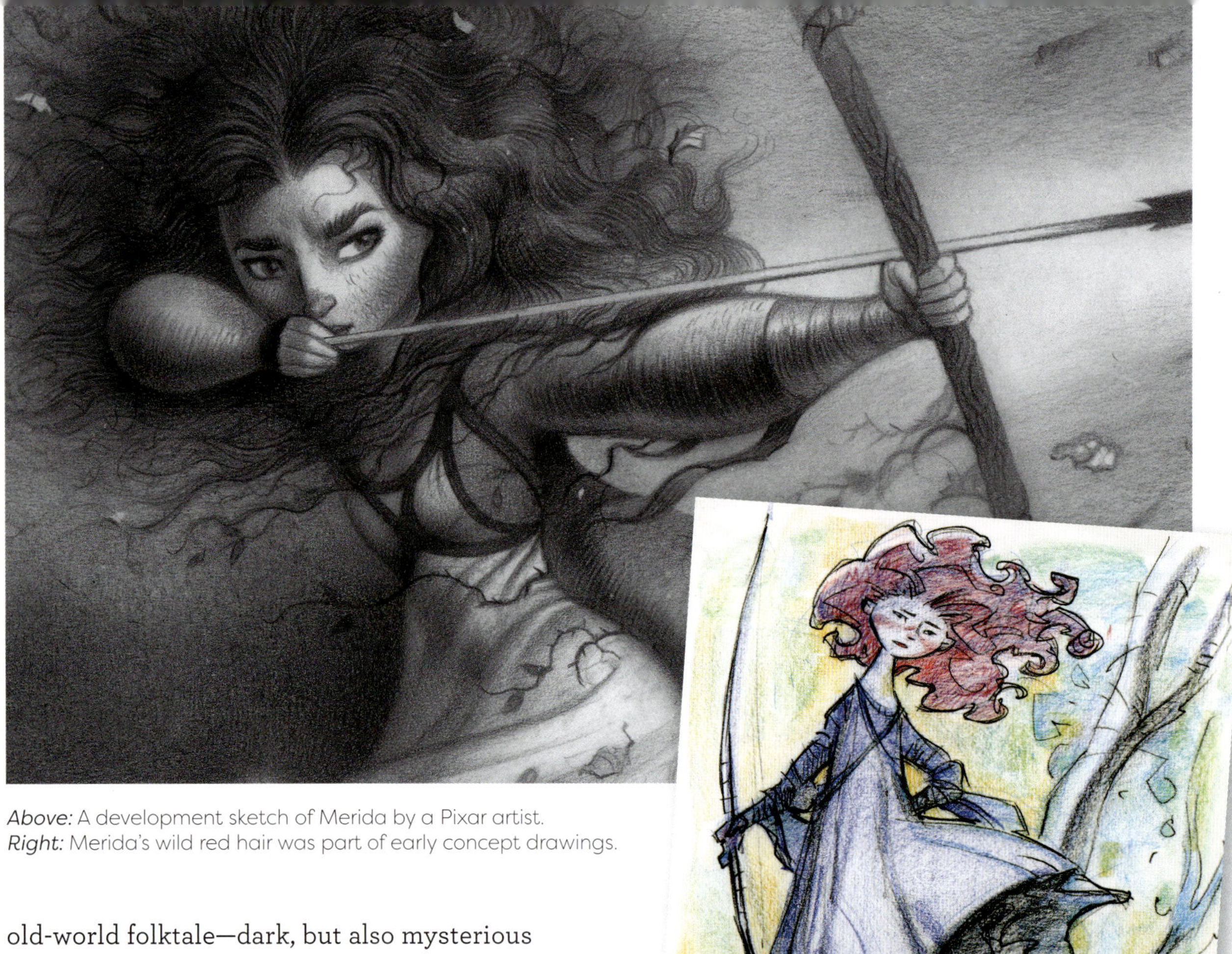

Above: A development sketch of Merida by a Pixar artist.
Right: Merida's wild red hair was part of early concept drawings.

old-world folktale—dark, but also mysterious and magical, where the magic is almost a mystery. I purposely didn't want to have a love story, I didn't want to have a prince. We've seen that, and I'd done that before. I love *Cinderella* and *Sleeping Beauty*, and I loved working on *Beauty and the Beast*, but I really wanted to do something different."

While Merida's parents urge her to marry, the core relationship in *Brave* is between the hero and her mom. Chapman has referred to the film as a "love story between a mother and her daughter," and, along with co-director Mark Andrews, built a world where women didn't have to be defined by their connection to a man—a very contemporary idea. While Merida embraced her physicality and strength, she didn't deny her feminine side. She also never tried to escape her duty as a royal. Overall, it was important for the filmmakers to portray the character as complex and with flaws, just like a modern-day woman.

"With Merida, one thing Brenda really understood was how easy it could be to tip Merida over into a tomboy," said story artist Emma Coats. "But it's not that she wants to be a boy. She's a girl, she likes being a girl—she just doesn't like some of the things that come with being a girl in that time. Her temperament is more like her father's than her mother's. That doesn't mean that she doesn't like dresses, for example. I initially played her more tomboyish, but then I started digging down through layers and I saw that she's a really three-dimensional person. There's the person she shows people, and then there's who she really is, and she's always doing a balancing act between them."

Each animated Disney feature continues to expand the definition of a princess. While *Brave* evoked a more traditional European fairy tale setting, 2016's *Moana* revealed how other cultures might perceive the role of a leader. The film's protagonist, the daughter

Merida (2012)

The filmmakers looked at several of John William Waterhouse's paintings when designing Merida and her dresses, including "The Lady Clare," "Ophelia," and "The Tempest." Co-director and writer Brenda Chapman, who was inspired by her own daughter, also brought a specific stature to Merida. "I wanted a strong, physical heroine because of the story I was creating," she said. "There were no athletic princesses except Pocahontas. Also, I wanted her to be physically more relatable. I wanted to give her more of an athlete's body, with some meat on her bones, and not make her waist the size of her wrist."

Voice: *Kelly Macdonald*

Personality traits: *Confident, Defies Expectations, Rebellious*

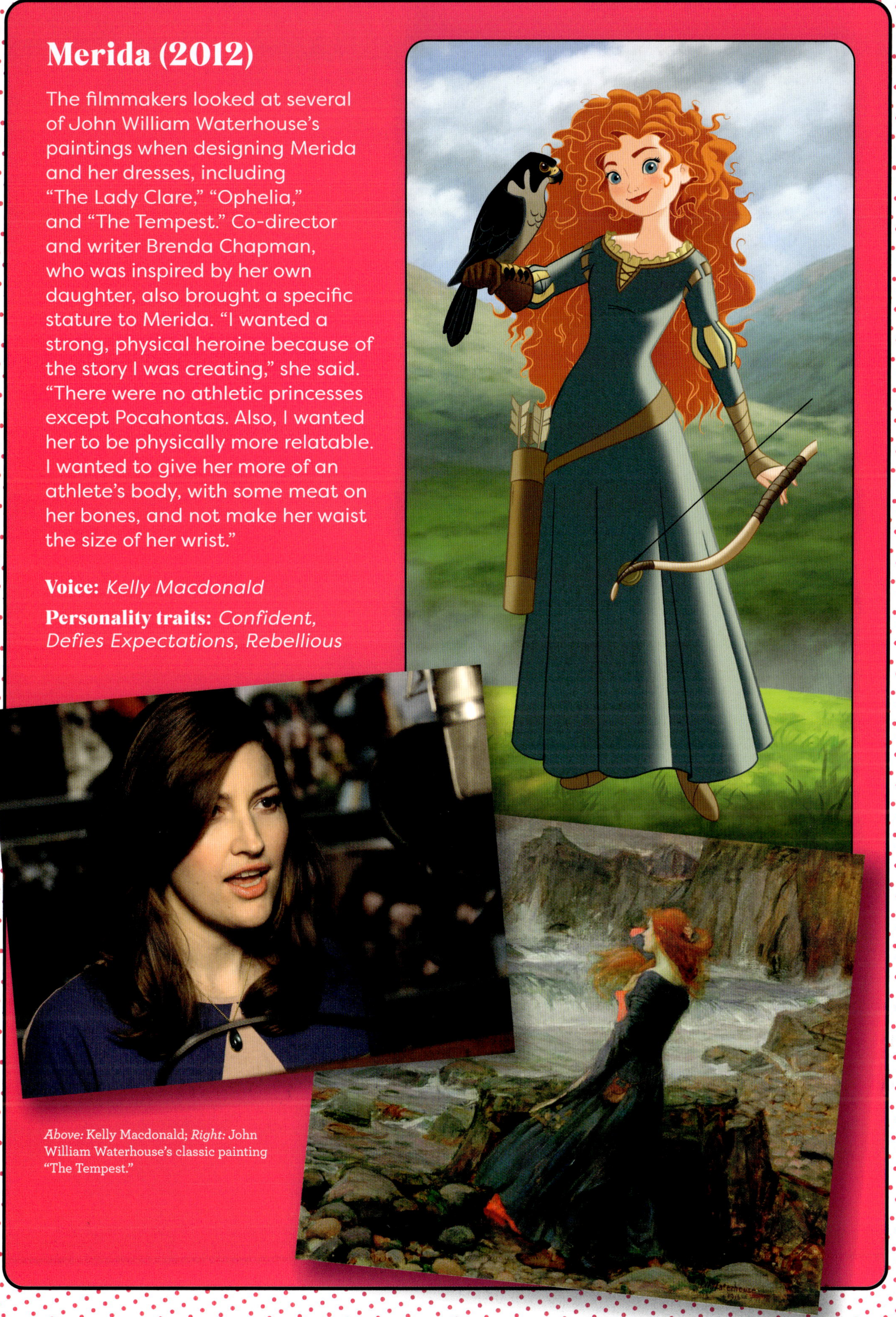

Above: Kelly Macdonald; *Right:* John William Waterhouse's classic painting "The Tempest."

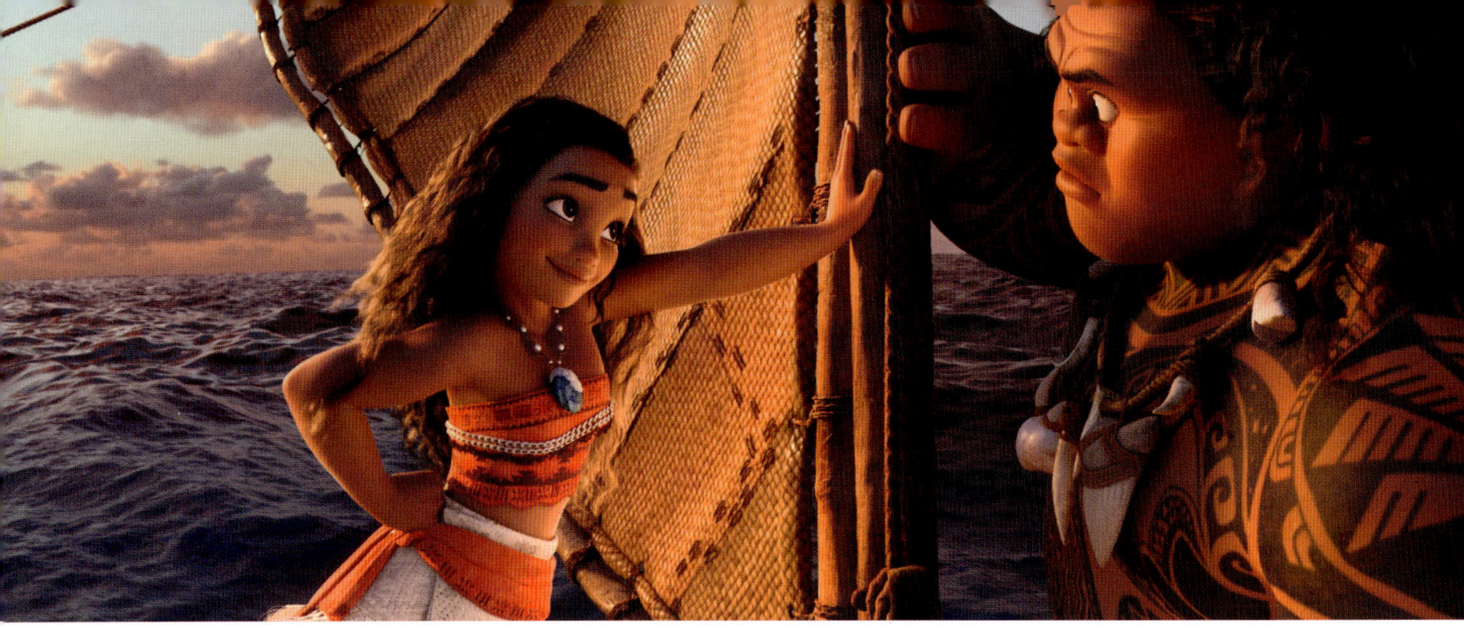

Moana and the demigod Maui set sail on the Pacific Ocean.

of a Pacific Island chief, embarks on a classic hero's journey, both across the literal ocean and within herself. The filmmakers decided to make Moana a chief's daughter because it added to her sense of responsibility. She's courageous, determined, and she has a sense of humor, and, most importantly, Moana's challenges aren't due to her gender. She's accepted as the next rightful leader, and she wants to prove that.

"Moana is a fearless, tenacious, intelligent young woman," explained director John Musker. "She yearns to be something that she doesn't yet have a name for, something that doesn't seem to be a possibility in her world."

Moana, whose name means "ocean" in several Polynesian cultures, wasn't inspired by a celebrity or a live-action reference model. Instead, the filmmakers drew inspiration from the real-life young women they met in the Pacific Islands during their research trips. Moana is also the first Disney Princess to have a visibly muscular build. "We wanted a character who could fight," says Osnat Shurer, the film's producer. "She needs to have ankles, she needs to have legs, she needs to be capable. So as we designed her, we thought about her being very athletic and strong, and showing that can also be very, very beautiful."

Voice actress Auli'i Cravalho, who grew up in Hawai'i and was cast while attending traditional Hawaiian high school Kamehameha, felt a kinship with Moana before she even began recording the character's voice. The actress grew up playing water sports, paddleboarding, and swimming, and had knowledge of Polynesian voyaging society. Cravalho, who was a big inspiration for the animators, was excited to see her own heritage and values on the screen.

"Moana influences me because she has a strong backbone and the willpower to make this world better than how she found it," says Cravalho, who thought of the character as a best friend while recording. "That, I love. And even if she gets into disputes with a demigod or a giant crab, she knows in her heart that her family and her grandmother, specifically, are with her always. That, too, I understand. No matter what, I'm always representing my family."

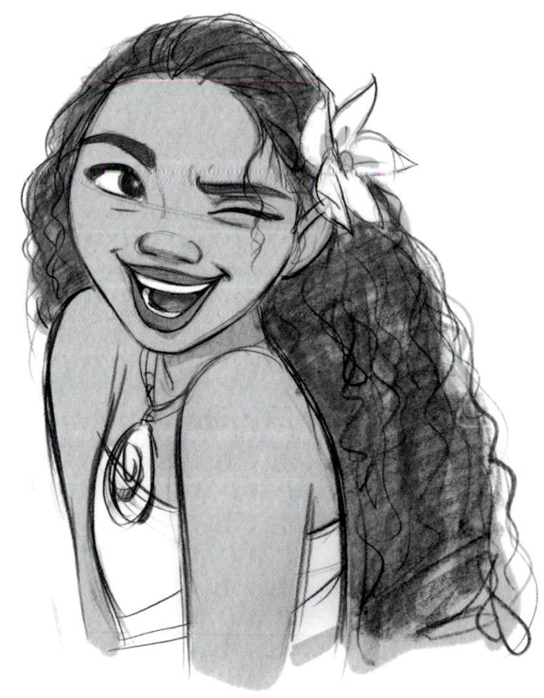

Moana (2016)

While making *Moana*, Disney Animation created the Oceanic Story Trust, a group of experts whose goal was to ensure the people and cultures of the Pacific Islands were accurately portrayed. The filmmakers were inspired by the many people they met on the islands, as well as by voice actress Auli'i Cravalho, who discussed the character with filmmakers while at the studio during voice recording sessions. While the hero's costumes are based largely on historical research, they're also practical. "When we were designing Moana, I knew that we were going to want her to be very athletic," said Amy Smeed, head of animation. "Maybe she'd be climbing trees or jumping off a cliff. Certain outfits are going to let her have that athleticism. But if she's wearing a narrow skirt, she's not going to be able to do very much."

Voice: *Auli'i Cravalho*

Personality traits: *Trailblazer, Independent, Community-Oriented*

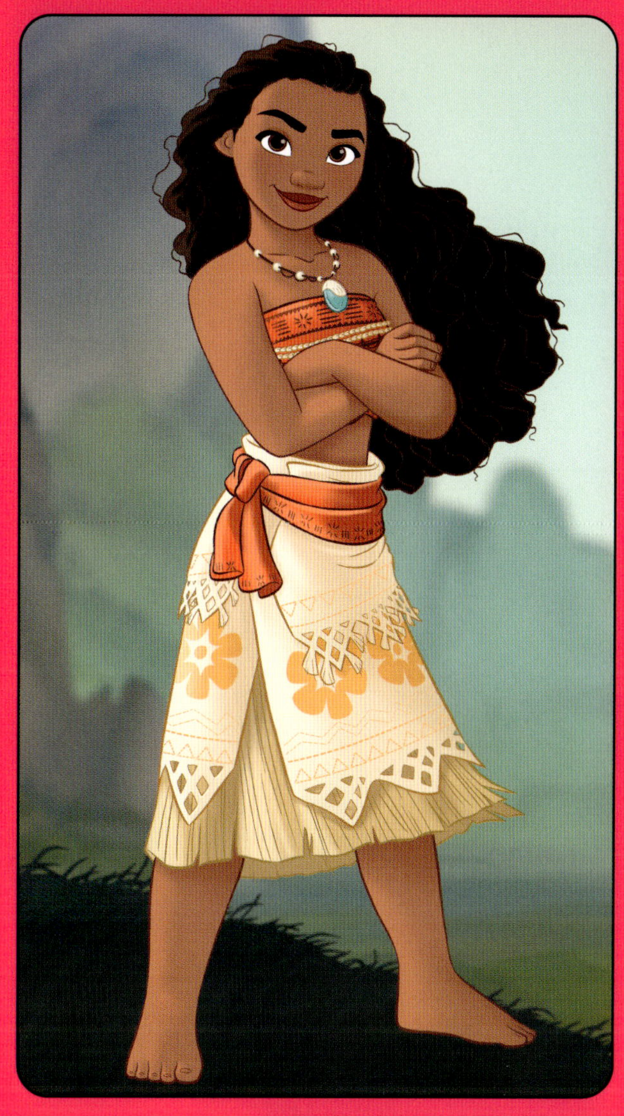

From left: Auli'i Cravalho; Pacific Island-inspired art sketches.

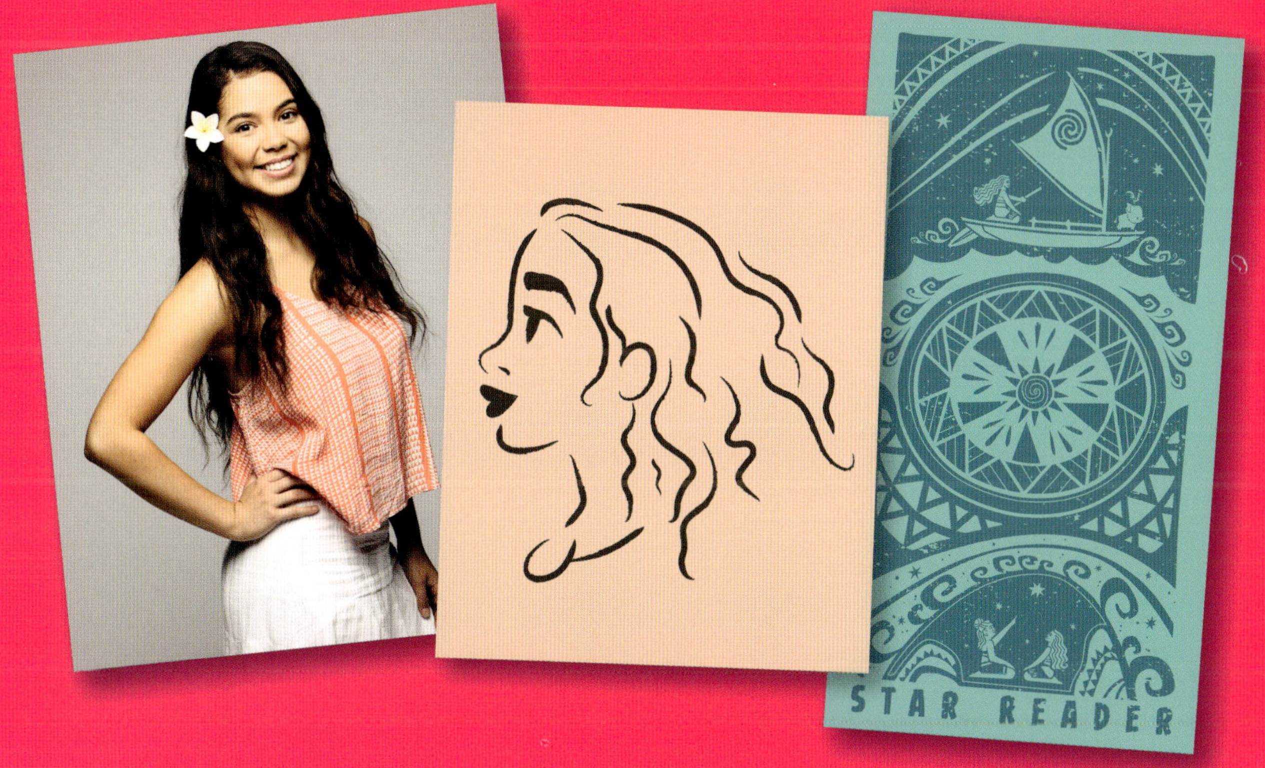

Like all of the Disney Animation filmmakers, the creators of *Moana* wanted to make their hero reflective of her moment, but also as timeless as possible. "We're of our time," Shurer says. "What we look to do in any Disney animated film is to hone the story and hold ourselves to a really high standard—there's almost one hundred years of this studio's history to be intimidated by if you so choose or to be responsible to. You try to tell the best story you know. You try to make the characters as strong as you know."

THE DISNEY QUEENS

Disney Animation's legacy of portraying strong, adventurous heroes is vast, Disney Princess or not. In 2013, *Frozen*, written by Jennifer Lee and directed by Lee and Chris Buck, became a pop culture phenomenon. The film, loosely inspired by Hans Christian Andersen's fairy tale *The Snow Queen*, felt like a revelation for audiences, thanks to its determined, courageous female characters and its memorable songs. The story of its heroes, Anna and Elsa, reflects a thematic idea Lee was thinking about while making the film.

"Suddenly I was watching a world where the power of fear was really taking over," Lee explains, pointing to the news. "Everything we're supposed to fear, everyone we're supposed to fear. I thought about that wrestle between the power of love and the power of fear. And many times I was concerned or afraid that fear would win. So we started looking at that wrestle and in the film there are times where fear wins. But, in the end, love shows that it's stronger than fear."

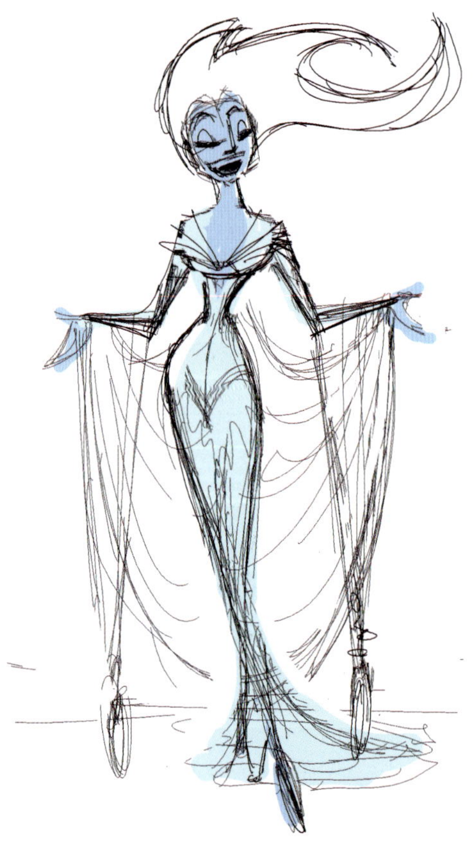

Early concept art for Elsa and Anna by Claire Keane *(top left)*, Bill Schwab *(left)*, and Jean Gilmore *(above)*.

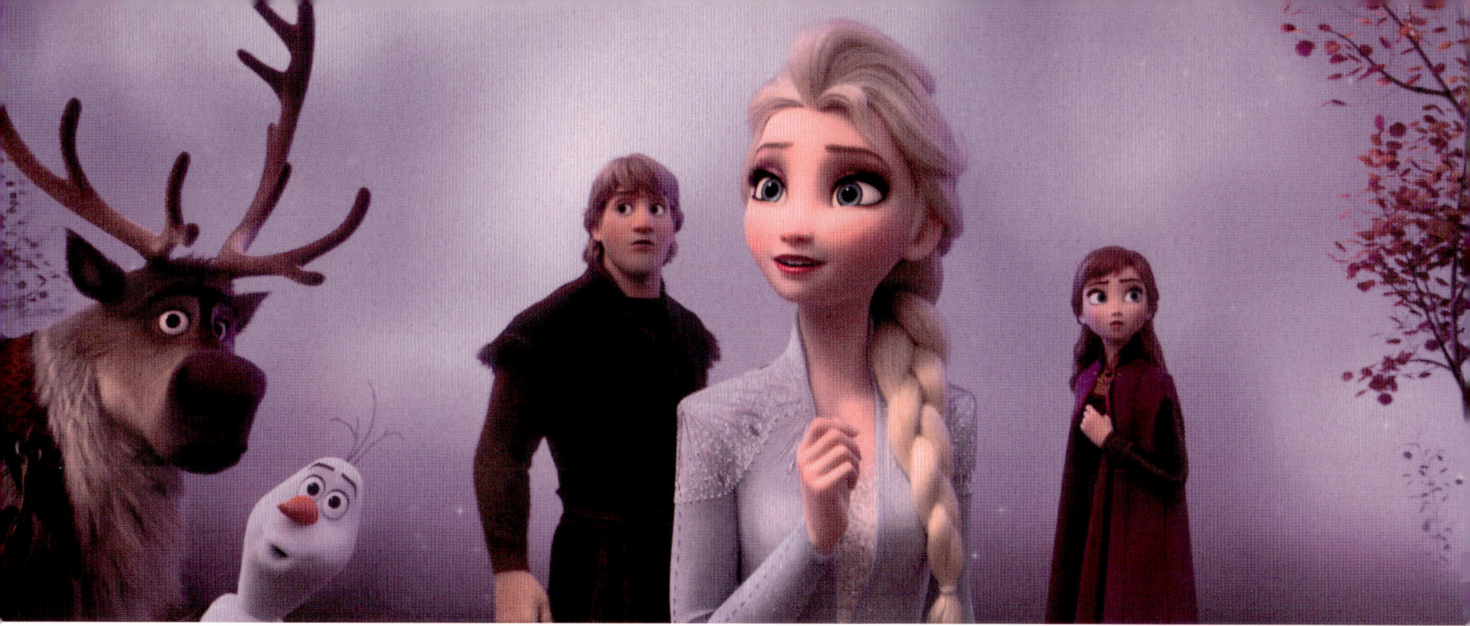

Elsa leads Anna and Kristoff, along with Sven the reindeer and Olaf the snowman, on a journey in *Frozen 2*.

Inspired after a research trip to Norway, the filmmakers looked at Norwegian folk designs and patterns as early reference for costume design. Visual development artist Brittney Lee began with folk art from the 1840s and 1850s, but expanded to other inspirations, bringing in both historical and modern elements. "In the case of every Disney film, we always strive to make nods to the current time period, whether it's intentional or not," she explains. "There's always this idea of 'We've got to look at what's happening around us to try to influence these characters.'"

That played into Elsa and Anna's hair styles, and also as Elsa's dramatic, magical blue cape dress, which has a straight silhouette and contemporary look, in contrast to her heavy coronation gown. "Sometimes we just have to make those leaps," Brittney Lee adds. "That's the fun dance that we try to do. We want it to feel like it's motivated and it's of the world, but also have a little bit of fantasy element included."

Elsa's transformation during the song "Let It Go" is a direct callback to *Cinderella*, Jennifer Lee's favorite Disney Princess film. Here, though, Elsa acts as her own Fairy Godmother. The protagonist's fluid movement as she embraces her power was drawn from Martha Graham's choreography, as well as from a moment animator Becky Bresee noticed on the television series *Glee* (2009-2015)—again, a combination of past and present. "For years, I had watched the *Cinderella* transformation over and over again and knew how beautiful that was," Bresee notes. "I feel very lucky to have gotten a chance to collaborate with visual effects animator Dan Lund on that scene. He did an amazing job with the dress and the sparkles. It was a really fun collaboration."

The filmmakers revisited the characters in *Frozen 2* (2019), unveiling a story where both Anna and Elsa fully embrace their talents. Elsa gained a deeper understanding of her magical powers and entrusted Anna to lead the kingdom of Arendelle. Like the Disney Princesses, Anna and Elsa lead the way toward stronger, more complex female characters in the years to come. And like their fellow heroes, the *Frozen* queens have had a distinct impact beyond their films.

"When we're making the films, we all obviously have very deep connections to these characters because we live with them for five or more years," says Jessica Julius, Vice President, Creative Development at Walt Disney Animation Studios. "We feel like we know them super well. And then we release them out into the world and audiences make them their own and react to them in a way we never could have foreseen. It's really incredible. They become living and breathing people."

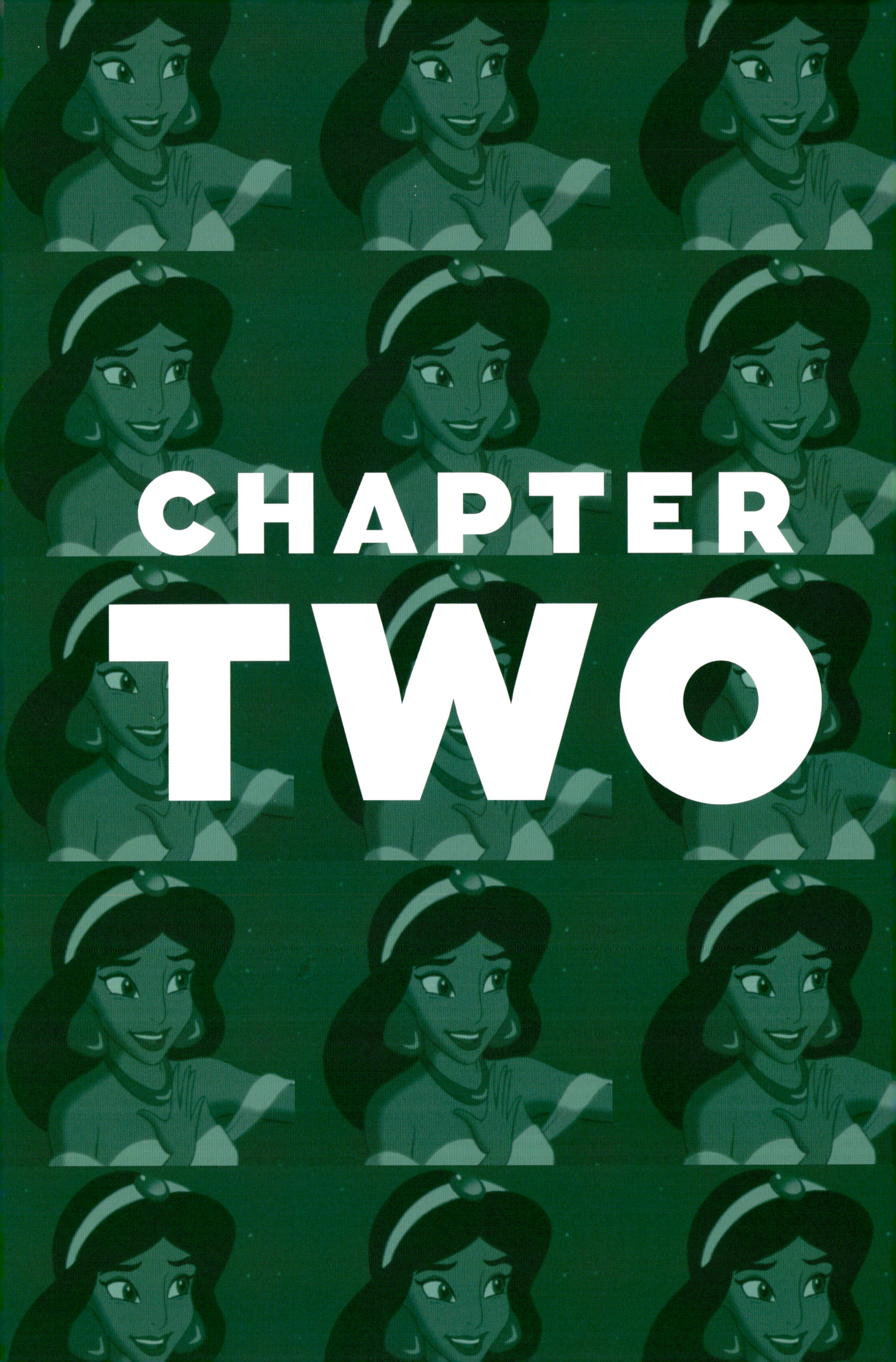

CHAPTER TWO

A WHOLE NEW WORLD

REIMAGININGS

While the definitive rendering of each Disney Princess was established by Walt Disney Animation Studios' classic films, the characters have always been given opportunities to venture out beyond the borders of their original stories. Snow White appeared in serialized comic strips and children's books in the 1930s, as did Cinderella and Aurora in the 1950s. In more recent decades, Disney has expanded the Disney Princess universe to include sequels, live-action reimaginings, television series, animated shorts, and, of course, books. These spin-offs provide new ways of looking at the characters and offer insight into their backstories, as well as where they might end up later, after their happily-ever-afters.

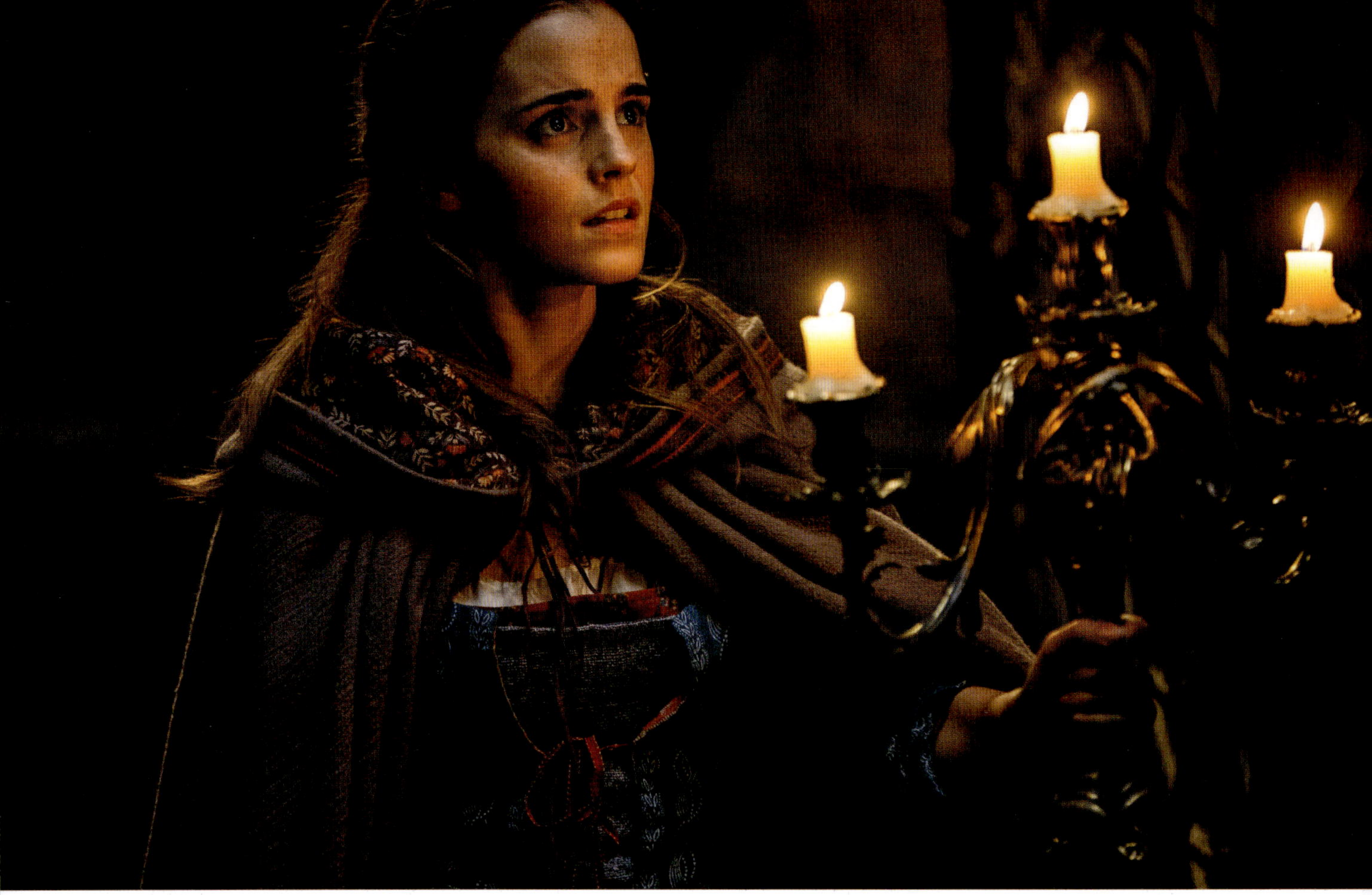

Above: Emma Watson as Belle in the live action version of *Beauty and the Beast*. ***Below:*** Sean Bailey on the set of *Mulan*.

Walt Disney cut his teeth on animation, he soon branched out and began leading his studio into the production of original live-action films, including *The Reluctant Dragon* (1941), *Treasure Island* (1950), and *20,000 Leagues Under the Sea* (1954). The studio continued creating live-action films in the years that followed, and it was an easy leap when, a few decades later, The Walt Disney Studios began producing movies like *Pirates of the Caribbean: The Curse of the Black Pearl* (2003) and *Alice in Wonderland* (2010), which thrilled audiences by transforming familiar animated films and Disney Parks attractions into blockbuster films. These live-action films had the added advantage of appealing to viewers of all ages with their more mature stories and exciting action sequences. It was clear there was real potential in reviving past stories and characters for a modern generation with new adaptations.

"After *Alice* worked the way it did in 2010, we asked ourselves, what does it mean?" The Walt Disney Studios President of Production Sean Bailey told *Deadline* in 2017. "There was opportunity with the female audience, and we had a lot of big characters here that we consider to be ours. Marvel has Iron Man, Captain America, and Thor; we have Cinderella, Snow

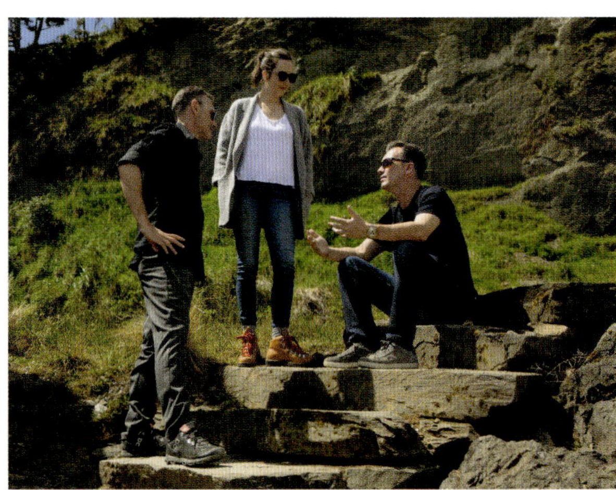

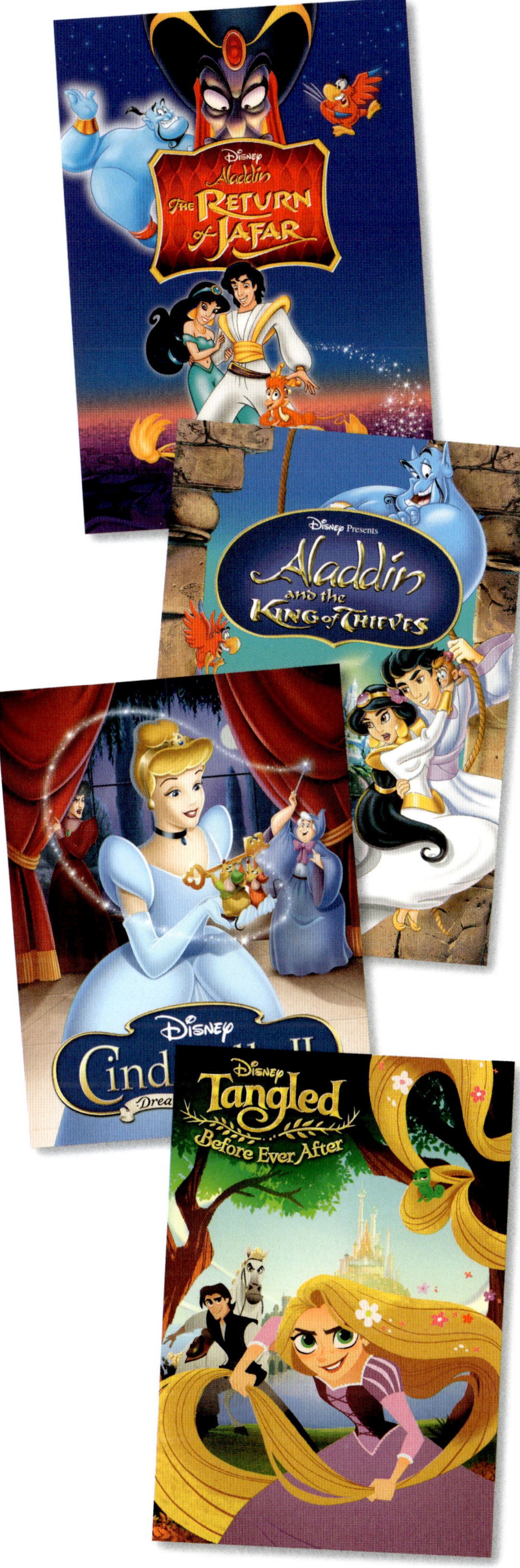

The Walt Disney Studios began releasing sequels to its popular films in the 1990s.

White, and Belle. Pairing those characters with great live-action talent and technology, something that Walt always aspired to, with technology that has moved so far forward, just seemed a smart way to go."

Several of the Disney Princesses, including Cinderella, Jasmine, and Belle, have been at the center of these live-action reimaginings. Kenneth Branagh's *Cinderella*, released in 2015, ushered in a new era for The Walt Disney Studios (Branagh described it to D23.com in 2015 as "the start of a reinvention"), which has continued with live-action reinterpretations of films like *Aladdin* and *Mulan*. At the same time, the Disney Princesses have reemerged in everything from ABC television series *Once Upon a Time* (2011-2018) to Disney Channel Original Movie *Descendants* (2015).

"These stories have proven to be timeless," Bailey says. "And we've said, 'How do we honor what's timeless in these stories, but look at how we enhance, expand in a way that feels relevant and timely for our time?'"

MORE TO THE STORY

While there have always been spin-off books and comic strips created to accompany the Disney Princess films, the studio hasn't always pursued sequels or spin-offs onscreen. In the mid-1990s, as the "Disney Renaissance" saw great success with audiences, The Walt Disney Studios ventured into animated sequels. In 1994, the studio released its first straight-to-video sequel: *The Return of Jafar*. The film, a follow-up to *Aladdin*, featured several of the original voice actors, including Linda Larkin as Jasmine. The sequel offered a slight revision of *Aladdin*'s original ending, with Aladdin and Jasmine deciding to see the world instead of ruling Agrabah. The story was initially intended as a TV series, but director Tad Stones suggested it would do better as a home video release. It did: *The Return of Jafar* sold 1.5 million VHS copies in the first two days

Filling Our Bookshelves

Starting with *Snow White and the Seven Dwarfs*, illustrated picture books and novelizations have been released for every Walt Disney Animation Studios feature film. Simon & Schuster added *Snow White and the Seven Dwarfs* to their Little Golden Books series in 1937, selling the books for 25 cents each. In the years that have followed, thousands of books featuring the Disney Princesses have found their way to shelves. Some replicate the films' stories, while others allow the reader to imagine how new events might transpire. There have been graphic novels, comic books, how-to-draw books, and even a series set in the "Enchanted Stables," where the princesses' love for horses takes them on whimsical adventures.

While many books expand the worlds of the animated films directly, others take more creative approaches. *The Twisted Tale* series imagines "what if?" scenarios for the characters, like "What if Cinderella never tried on the glass slipper?" Younger versions of the Disney Princesses and the *Frozen* queens appear in the *Disney Before the Story* series, while the young adult series *The Queen's Council* envisions the princesses as young rulers of their lands. To honor the Ultimate Princess Celebration, Disney Publishing released *Tales of Courage and Kindness*, a collection of fourteen illustrated stories. Over the years, each book observes the heroes through a new lens while also staying true to what makes each character so unique and inspirational.

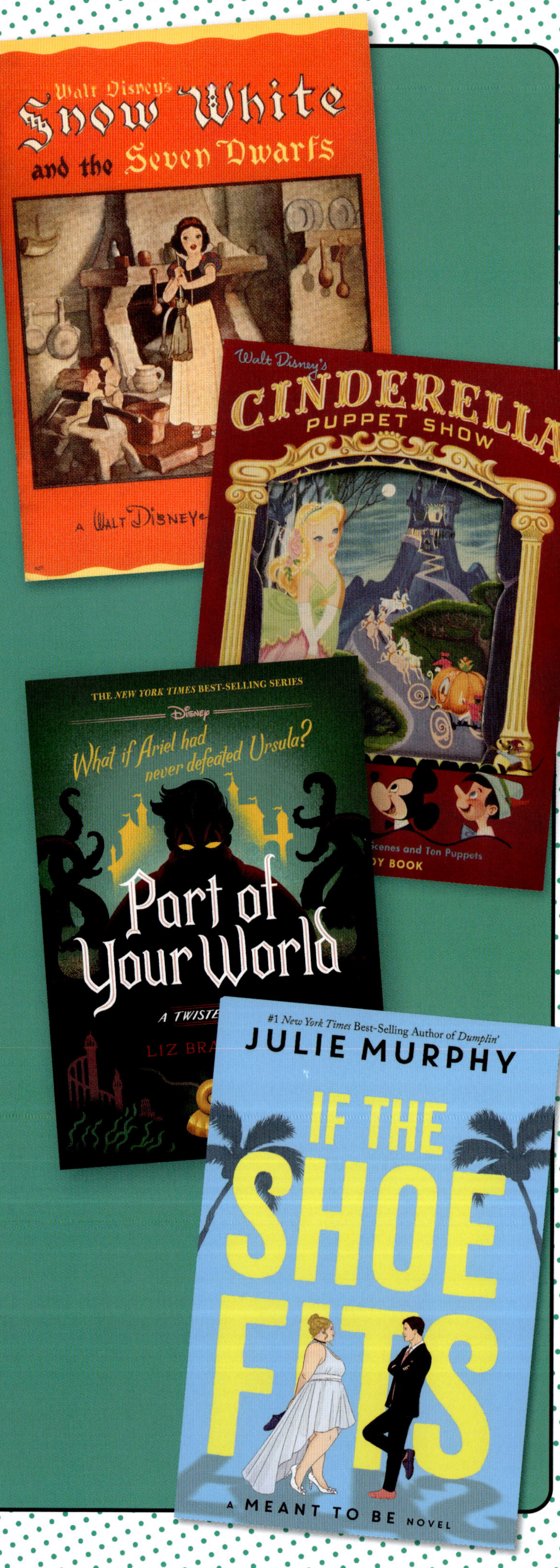

Right: Many of the Disney Princesses have had their stories continued and expanded in written form, both in picture books and novels.

of its release, setting the stage for Disney's extensive home video market, which burgeoned in the mid-'90s. *Aladdin and the King of Thieves* followed in 1996.

Clearly, there was a demand for new tales with familiar characters. The home video sequel—and prequel—became part of Disney's marketing strategy in the years that followed, modeled after the success of the *Aladdin* sequels. The goal was to create sequels that were as appealing as the originals, in order to captivate the Disney audience from home. Walt Disney Television Animation brought Ariel back for an animated TV series, titled *Disney's The Little Mermaid,* in 1992, for three seasons on Saturday mornings on CBS, and the character later found a renewed focus with the home video sequel, *The Little Mermaid II: Return to the Sea,* in 2000, and again in 2008 with *The Little Mermaid III: Ariel's Beginning.* In 2002, Disney released *Cinderella II: Dreams Come True,* a collection of three shorter narratives that take place after *Cinderella,* and followed with *Cinderella III: A Twist in Time* in 2007.

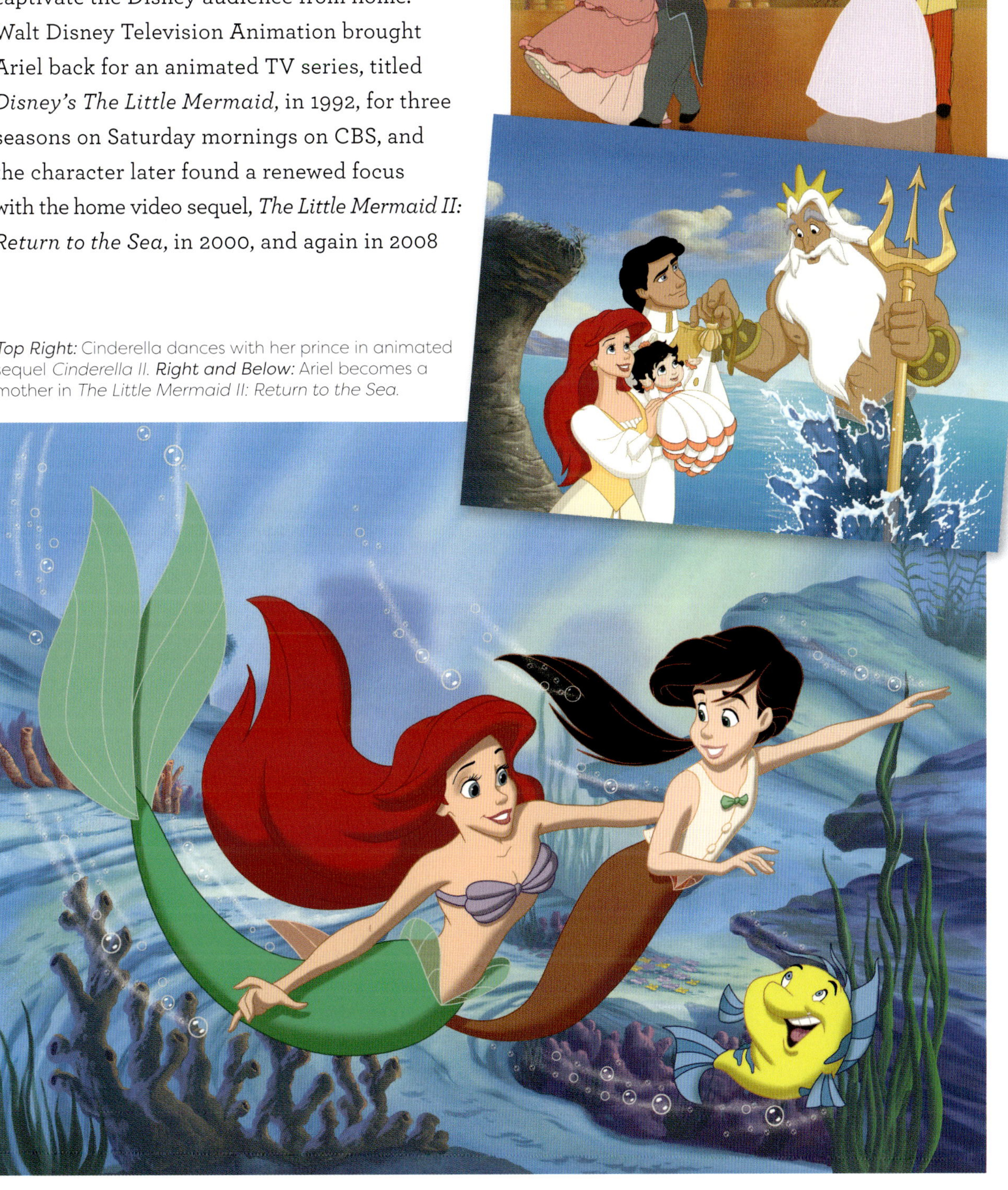

Top Right: Cinderella dances with her prince in animated sequel *Cinderella II.* ***Right and Below:*** Ariel becomes a mother in *The Little Mermaid II: Return to the Sea.*

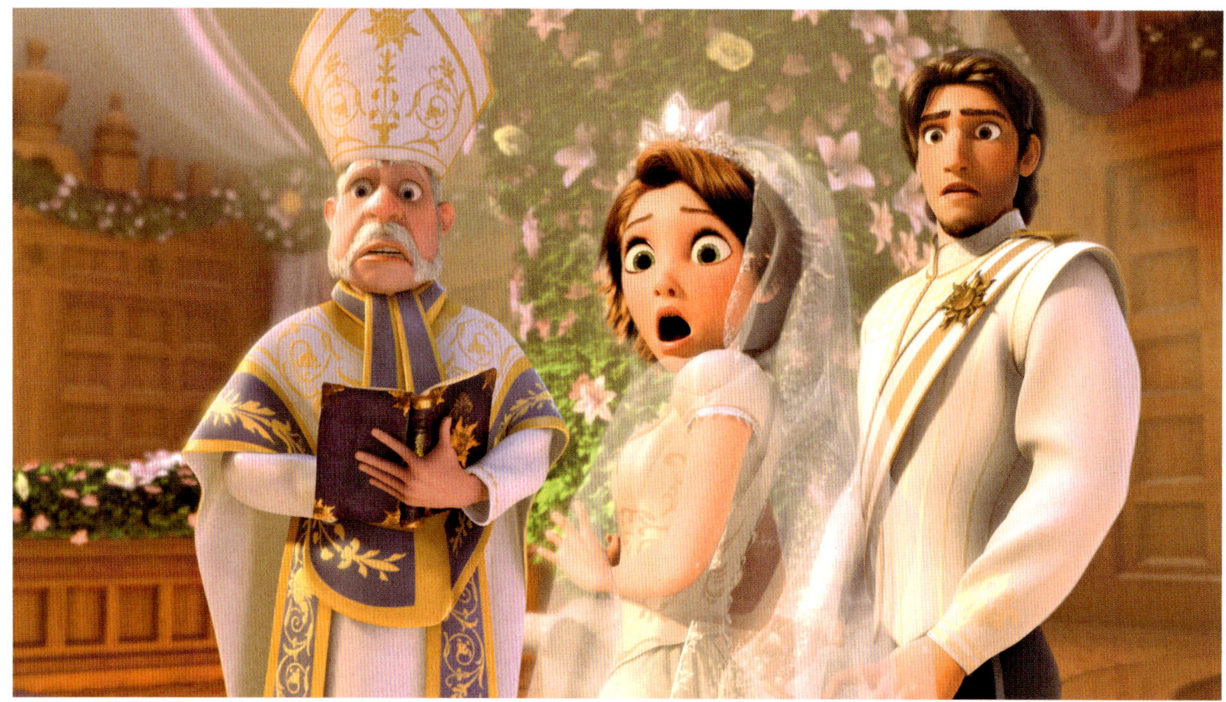

Rapunzel has a moment of surprise during her wedding to Flynn Rider in sequel *Tangled Ever After.*

"We were trying to match the originals as closely as possible," explains animator Amy Mebberson, who worked at Walt Disney Animation Australia on many of the sequels. "With Ariel, we got all of Glen Keane's notes. We had several weeks of training and we analyzed those to death. With Cinderella, as well, we had the original notes. We set out to honor the animation legacy that these original characters set up."

More recently, Disney Television Animation released a spin-off of *Tangled, Rapunzel's Tangled Adventure*, which aired on Disney Channel from 2017 through 2020 and again featured Mandy Moore as Rapunzel. Several of Disney's upcoming series, like *Tiana*, a continuation of *The Princess and the Frog* (2009) and *Moana*, a sequel to the 2016 film, are similar opportunities to see what else is possible for the characters. Spin-offs, like Kristen Wiig and Annie Mumolo's upcoming evil stepsisters film, a spin-off of *Cinderella* (1950), retell the classic stories from new perspectives. Even animated shorts, like *Tangled Ever After* (2012) and *Frozen Fever* (2015), expand how fans see their favorite heroes.

"We fall in love with these characters and we fall in love with these worlds and we tell a complete story—but then, there's more we could tell," explains *Moana* producer Osnat Shurer. "It's less someone saying 'We should make a sequel' and more asking ourselves 'what if?'"

FAIRY TALE REMIXES

Fairy tales have been told and retold for centuries, but most modern audiences now recognize a Disney version of a fairy tale as the most familiar interpretation. The animated classic films are so ingrained in our collective consciousness that *Once Upon a Time* creators Adam Horowitz and Edward Kitsis didn't even realize they were pitching Disney characters when they came up with an idea for a TV series that brought many fairy tales together into one universe. The duo first tried to sell the series in 2002, but it wasn't until the success of *Lost* (2004-2010), on which both were writers, that television executives were willing to consider their wild idea.

"Because Disney is so iconic we didn't understand that Jiminy Cricket is their thing and that Grumpy and Sneezy were their thing," Kitsis remembers. "It wasn't until we sold it to Disney that we understood had we sold it anywhere else it would have been a different show."

"What people know and remember are the Disney versions," Horowitz adds. "You think about these princesses in certain colors and in certain configurations. For us, it was taking that collective memory and playing with it a little bit."

The series, which premiered in 2011, was centered on "what if?" The story started with the premise that the evil Queen from *Snow White and the Seven Dwarfs* had cursed the inhabitants of the Enchanted Forest, including Snow White and Prince Charming, and relocated them to the non-magical town of Storybrooke, Maine, erasing their memories in the process. It's only after the arrival of Emma Swan, the long-lost daughter of Snow White and Prince Charming, that things begin to be set right. Using narrative time jumps, the writers offered backstories on all the characters, including Snow White, Cinderella, and Merida, allowing the old familiar tales to overlap and intersect in new ways.

"I loved things like making Ariel and Snow White friends, or Red Riding Hood and Snow friends," Horowitz says. "It's fun to ask 'What if Snow and Red Riding Hood were best friends? What would they talk about? How would they help each other out?'"

Once Upon a Time captivated audiences from the outset. While characters like Snow White, Rumpelstiltskin, Captain Hook, and

Jennifer Morrison's Emma Swan joins forces with Ginnifer Goodwin's Snow White, Sarah Bolger's Aurora, and Jamie Chung's Mulan in ABC's *Once Upon a Time*.

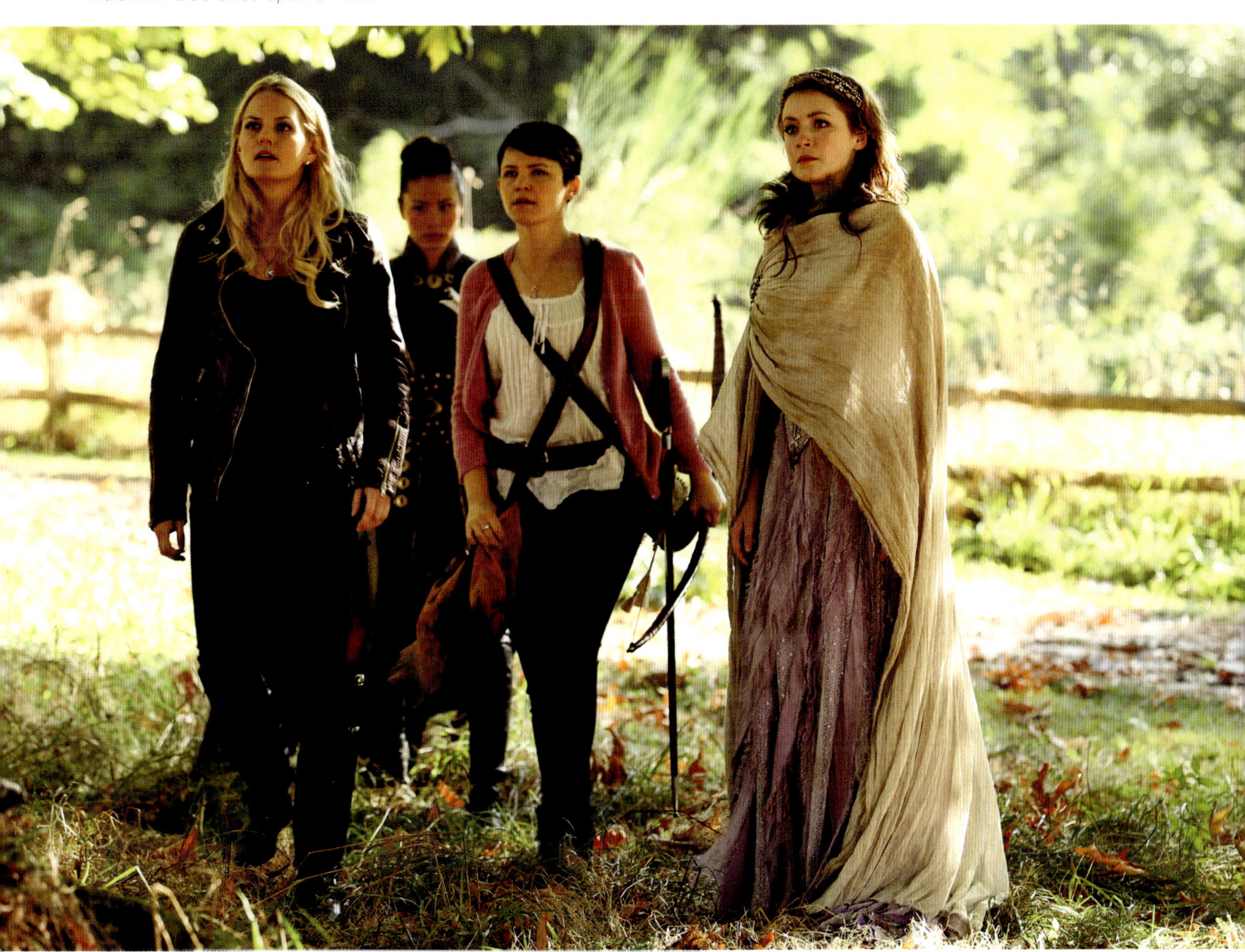

Prince Charming comprised the core of the story, the writers introduced other well-known characters along the way. Belle, played by Emilie de Ravin, appears midway through season one and falls in love with Rumpelstiltskin, a beastly man with more to him than meets the eye. In the second season, Mulan and Aurora join forces with Snow White and Emma to escape the Enchanted Forest, and later Mulan trains Merida in new fighting techniques. During the show's seven seasons, ten of the Disney Princesses found their way into the episodes.

"With each season, we would talk about what we wanted to accomplish with our regular characters and what we thought the best way was to do that," explains Horowitz. "That conversation would often lead to who they would encounter and what parts of their past would come to light. What part of the Disney canon could we dip into? It often would naturally reveal itself."

The writers also wanted to ensure that their interpretations of the Disney Princesses shed new light on the characters. "You bring on Ariel and you know she's beloved, so the pressure is that you have to add something," Kitsis says. "You don't want to take the favorite toy off the shelf only to get viewers."

Shortly after the release of *Frozen*, Kitsis and Horowitz wrote a half-season storyline introducing Anna and Elsa into Storybrooke. The episodes created an extensive backstory for the characters, including new family members and a past connection between Belle and Anna. It gave the viewer a different perspective on the sisters, including how their bond had grown stronger since the events of the original animated film. There was a real awareness on all sides that the characters in *Once Upon a Time* didn't have to be the same as those in the movies. Elsa was one possible take on an iconic hero; not the definitive version.

"We didn't have to be canon because people understood that *Once* could exist here, but you could still do a big Cinderella movie and

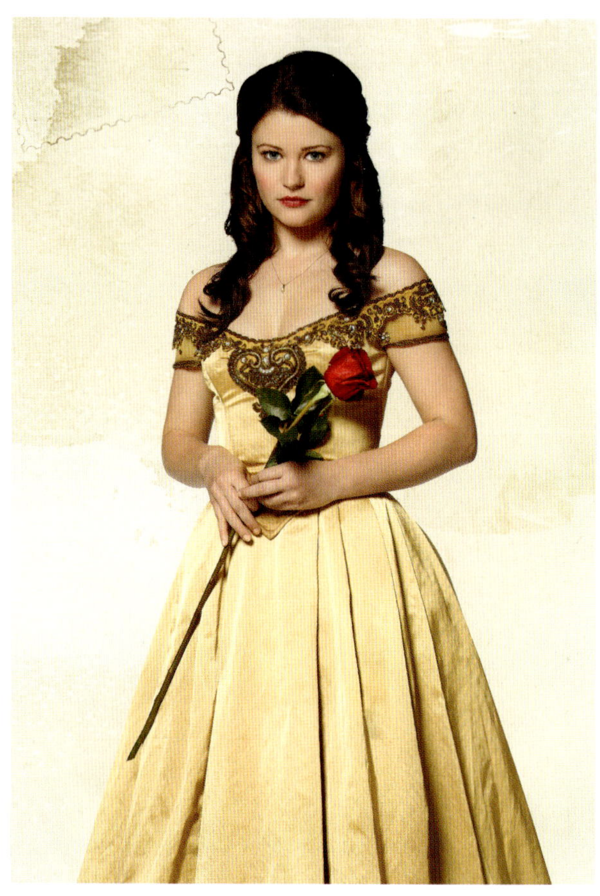

Emilie de Ravin as Belle in ABC's *Once Upon a Time*.

no one was expecting the two to talk," notes Kitsis. Horowitz adds, "We were allowed, very graciously, to do our own thing. Everything could have its own clear identity."

While *Once Upon a Time* was riffing on fairy tales on primetime, Disney Channel's *Sofia the First* embraced younger viewers in an animated daytime series. The show premiered in 2012 with a special episode called "Once Upon a Princess," and aired on both Disney Channel and Disney Junior networks. The show, aimed at a preschool audience, followed a young princess named Sofia, who becomes princess of Enchancia. As she explores the kingdom, Sofia, voiced by actress Ariel Winter, gains the magic Amulet of Avalor, which has the ability to summon the Disney Princesses in times of need. The series ran for four seasons, with 107 total episodes, during which several of the Disney Princess voice actresses reprised their original roles, including Jodi Benson as Ariel and Mandy Moore as Rapunzel.

Reimagining Disney Princess Costumes

While we recognize the Disney Princesses in specific outfits, the live-action reimaginings and spin-offs have been an opportunity for costume designers to get creative. For example, recreating Cinderella's ball gown gave costume designer Sandy Powell the chance to update a classic. "In a way, I had to stick to certain rules, like it had to be the prettiest dress at the ball, and it had to fulfill every little girl's dream," Powell explained. "But still, I wanted it to be different and slightly more contemporary."

Emma Watson was involved with designing of Belle's costumes for *Beauty and the Beast*, working with costume designer Jacqueline Durran to make Belle's everyday look more functional. That included adding pockets and swapping out ballet flats for sturdy riding boots. Belle's vibrant yellow ball gown got a fresh approach that left out the corset to show she is an emancipated princess. The team also wanted to pay homage to the iconic yellow gown from the original film in the design. "The animation was very important to me," Durran said. "It was about bringing a combination of history and the animation."

The same held true for *Once Upon a Time*, for which costume designer Eduardo Castro made the classic looks more modern and more functional for action scenes. "I knew all of these characters well," he said. "I knew what Belle looked like, I knew what Sleeping Beauty looked like—we just made it classic, but with a modern twist."

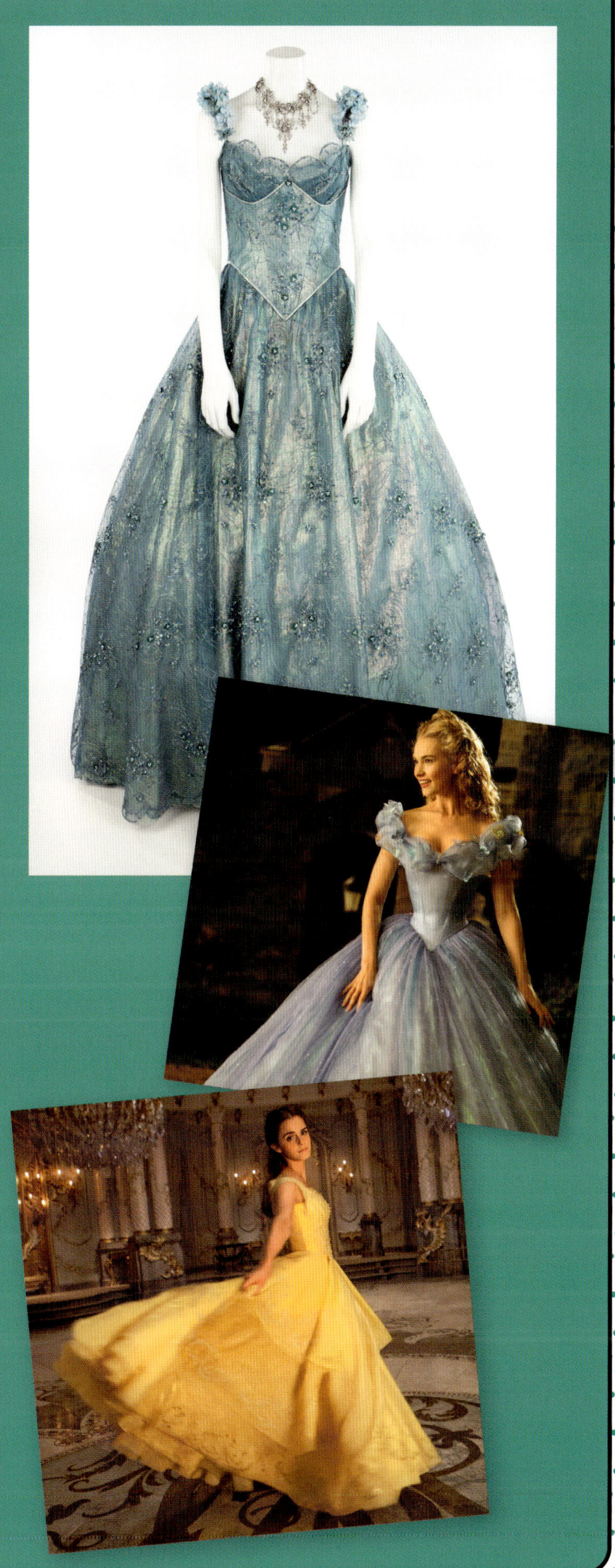

Right: (top): Cinderella's gown from ABC's *Once Upon a Time*; *(middle)* Sandy Powell designed Lily James's gown for the live-action film of *Cinderella; (bottom)* Emma Watson in Belle's sweeping yellow dress.

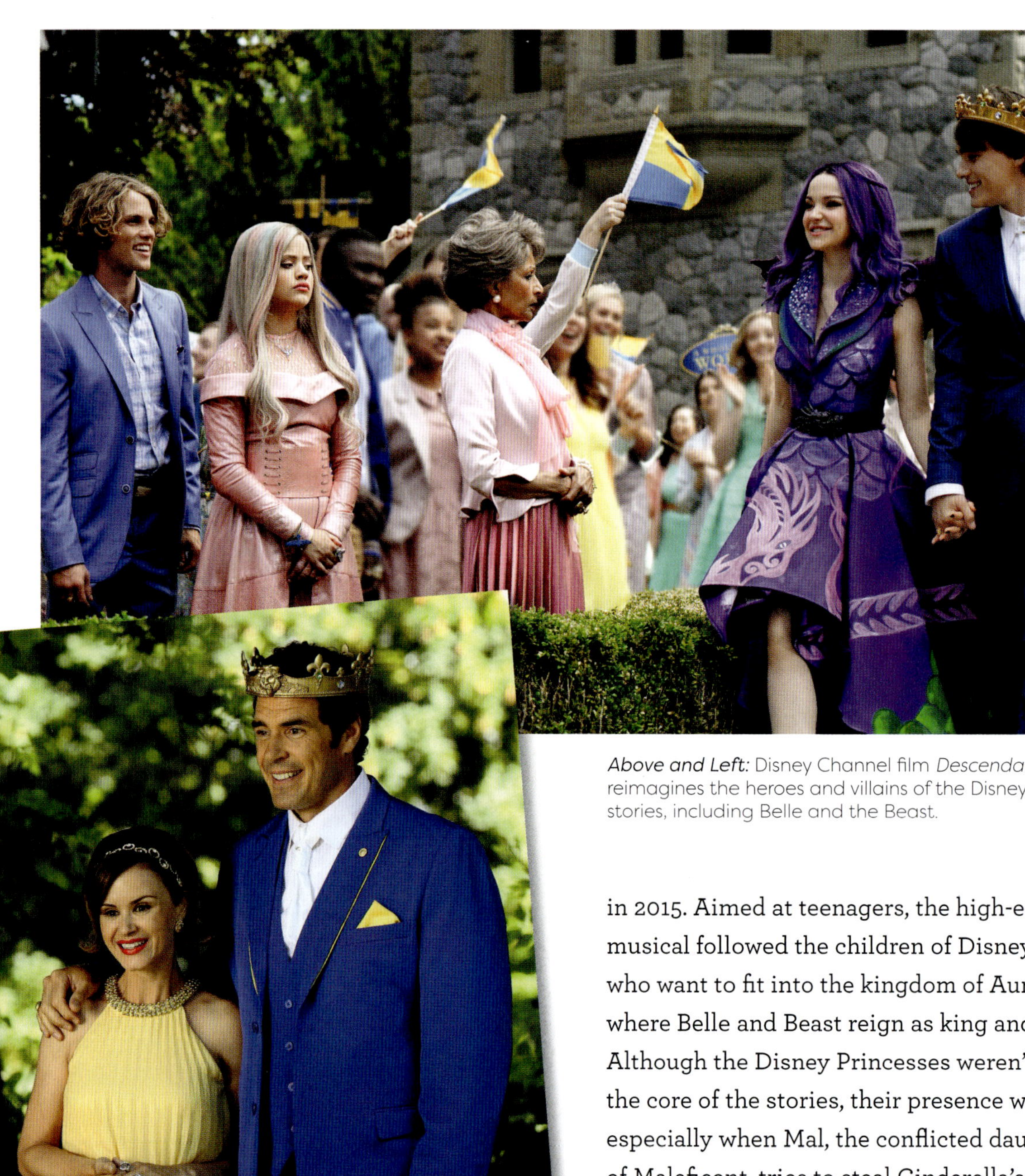

Above and Left: Disney Channel film *Descendants* reimagines the heroes and villains of the Disney Princess stories, including Belle and the Beast.

The series aimed to redefine who a princess could be, as well as appeal to a broad audience—not just those who might already be obsessed with princesses.

Likewise, the Disney Channel film *Descendants*—and its two sequels—veered away from the original films and showcased the characters through a new lens upon its release in 2015. Aimed at teenagers, the high-energy musical followed the children of Disney villains, who want to fit into the kingdom of Auradon, where Belle and Beast reign as king and queen. Although the Disney Princesses weren't at the core of the stories, their presence was felt, especially when Mal, the conflicted daughter of Maleficent, tries to steal Cinderella's Fairy Godmother's wand.

"I've always been a big fan of the Disney animated films and their heritage," director and Disney Legend Kenny Ortega said, speaking to D23.com in 2015. "What was thrilling for me was suddenly to find myself in a position to be able to be a part of the development and creation of brand-new Disney characters and—at the same time—get to play with refreshing classic characters, both the good and the evil characters of the Disney stories. There was also a lot of responsibility, being a part of the creation and development of a brand-new generation of Disney characters."

SHIFTING TO LIVE-ACTION FILMS

In 2010, a year before the premiere of *Once Upon a Time,* Disney announced plans to develop and release *Maleficent* (2014), the untold story of Disney's most iconic villain from the classic *Sleeping Beauty* tale, with Angelina Jolie attached as star and executive producer, and longtime Disney screenwriter Linda Woolverton penning the script. For the script, Woolverton drew her inspiration from the 1959 animated film, in which animator Marc Davis brought both Aurora and Maleficent to life. Woolverton also wanted to create a mother-daughter relationship between Maleficent and Aurora, who was given more agency.

"Aurora got to be brave," Woolverton notes of this new version of the Disney Princess from *Sleeping Beauty*. "She was raised as the princess that she is, in the forest, and she got to bond with the fairies. We got to see what an absolutely wonderful person Aurora is and her total love of nature."

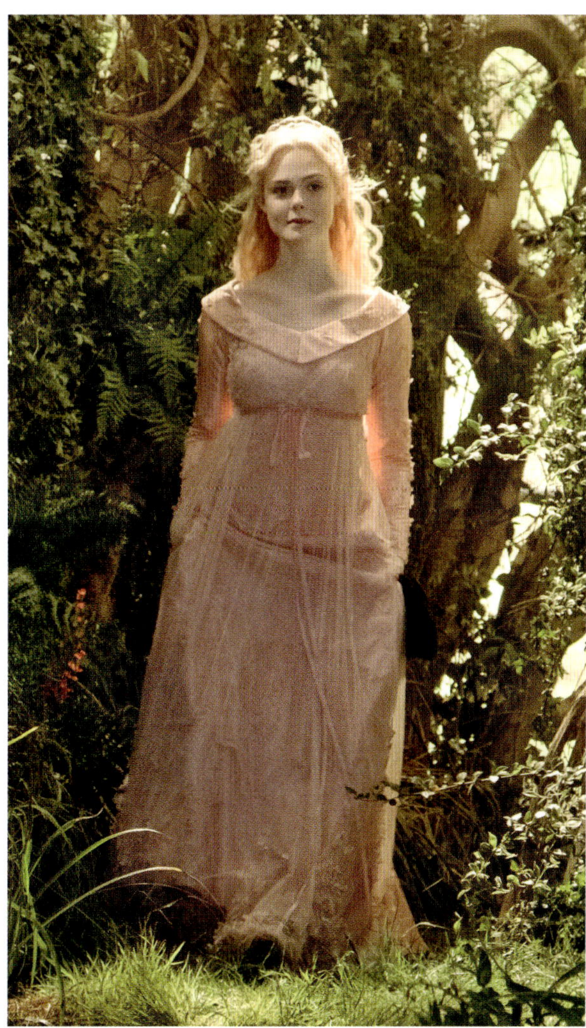

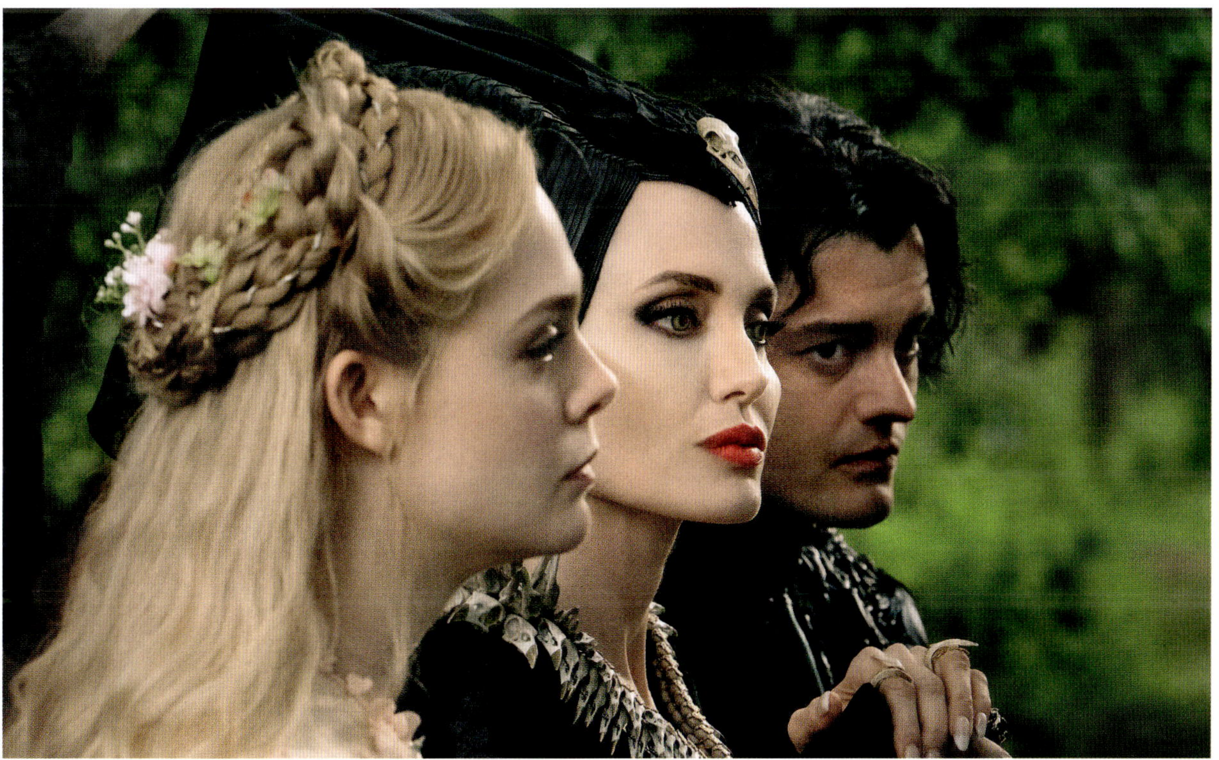

Above (top and bottom): Elle Fanning embodies Aurora in *Maleficent* and its sequel, with Angelina Jolie portraying the iconic villain.

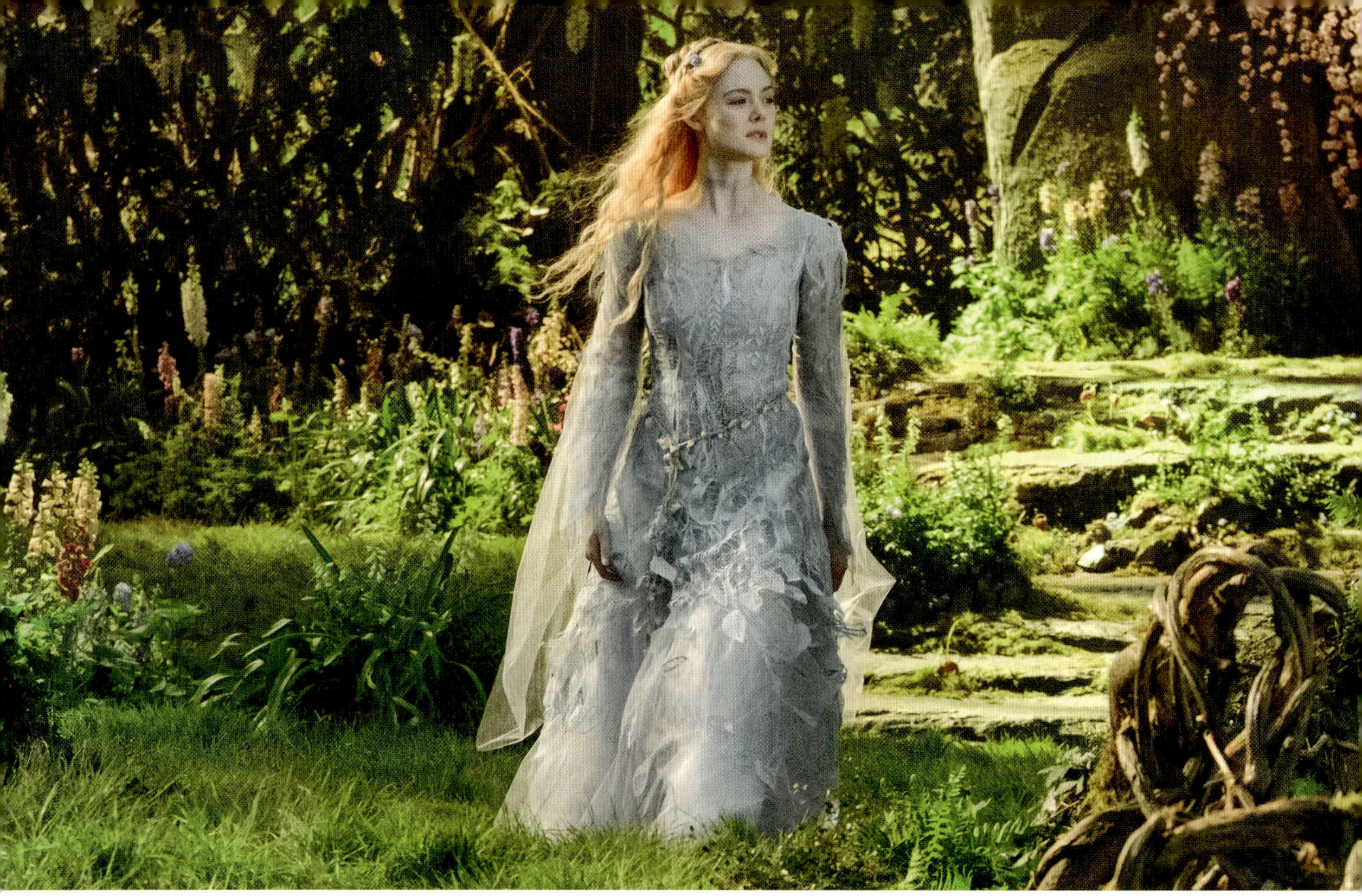

Elle Fanning as Aurora in *Maleficent: Mistress of Evil.*

The filmmakers cast Elle Fanning, then fourteen years old, as Aurora. Fanning's Aurora evoked her animated counterpart, with long, flowing blonde hair and a kind-hearted demeanor, but director Robert Stromberg set out to re-envision the character. Costume designer Anna B. Sheppard dressed Aurora in organic, flowing dresses inspired by the Renaissance and the late-Medieval period, emphasizing her connection with nature. "Elle has a personality full of light," Sheppard told *Vanity Fair*. "She is incredibly innocent, she has got this very fair complexion, beautiful hair, and never really needs makeup. I wanted to give her the same light, like she has got in the real life."

It's that light that defines Aurora as we know her in *Maleficent* and its sequel, *Maleficent: Mistress of Evil* (2019). But she's also characterized by an emotional gravity and fortitude, and is able to experience the full scope of her humanity. Like her animated inspiration, Fanning's Aurora is kind and curious. But the films also allow her to be thoughtful and empathetic, traits that feel appropriate for a contemporary hero.

"What I like about our film is that you get to know her more," Fanning explained when the first film came out. "Because in the animated movie, she's this pretty girl who is asleep most of the time. And in our film, you get to see her have different emotions and really get the essence of her. I love how she's very free-spirited, and since she has been kept away from normal life, she's very open to things and innocent. But that's what makes her very likeable and charming."

Cinderella (2015), a more traditional live-action reimagining of a Disney Princess animated film, also centered on showcasing a modern version of its lead character. The film went into production in 2010, with several directors and screenwriters involved in the early stages. Eventually, The Walt Disney Studios hired Chris Weitz to pen the script and Kenneth Branagh to direct. Their vision was to retell a familiar tale without emphasizing Cinderella needing to be rescued by a man. They wanted to make it feel current, even while it's set in the nineteenth century.

"Figuring out a way to build on the legacy of fairy tales at The Walt Disney Company was a high priority," producer Alli Shearmur explained. "They had a real desire to modernize the character of Cinderella without turning their back on the animated classic." Branagh added, "My dream was to not only a find a way of combining the best inspirations from [Charles] Perrault and from the Disney animated film, but also to make our own new and original contributions to the 'Cinderella' myth."

Played by Lily James, Cinderella is inherently kind and a friend to all, like the 1950 version. But she also takes more control over her life. She's proactive, with an ability to ask for help when needed—which makes her transformation before the ball even more poignant. While James wanted to evoke the 1950 film, she also wanted this Cinderella to present a fresh point of view, offering a new twist on the character.

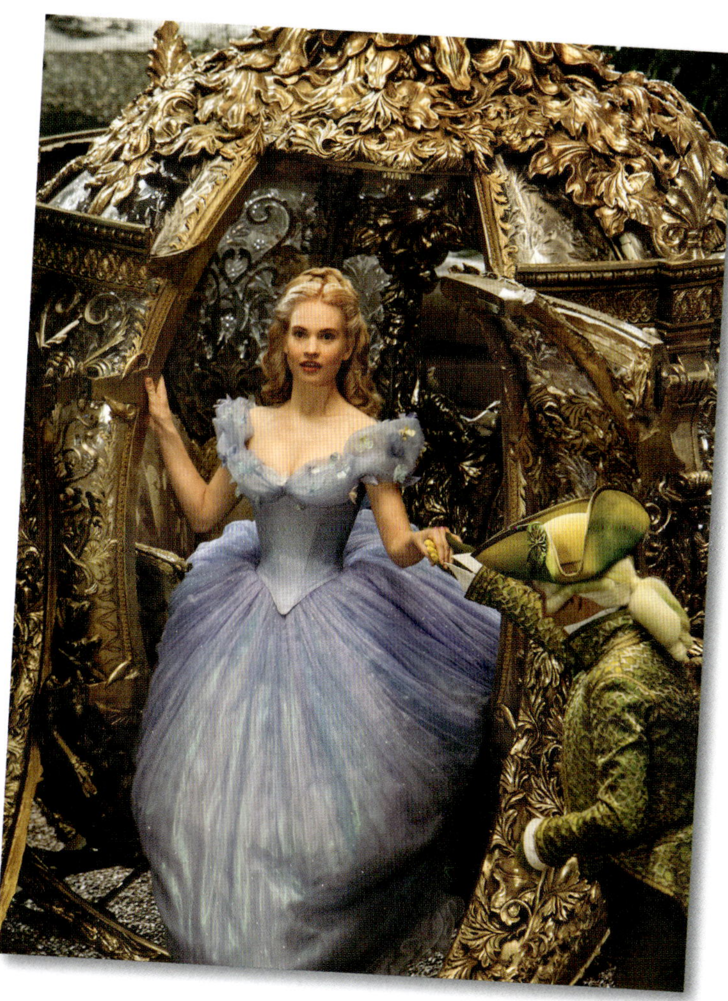

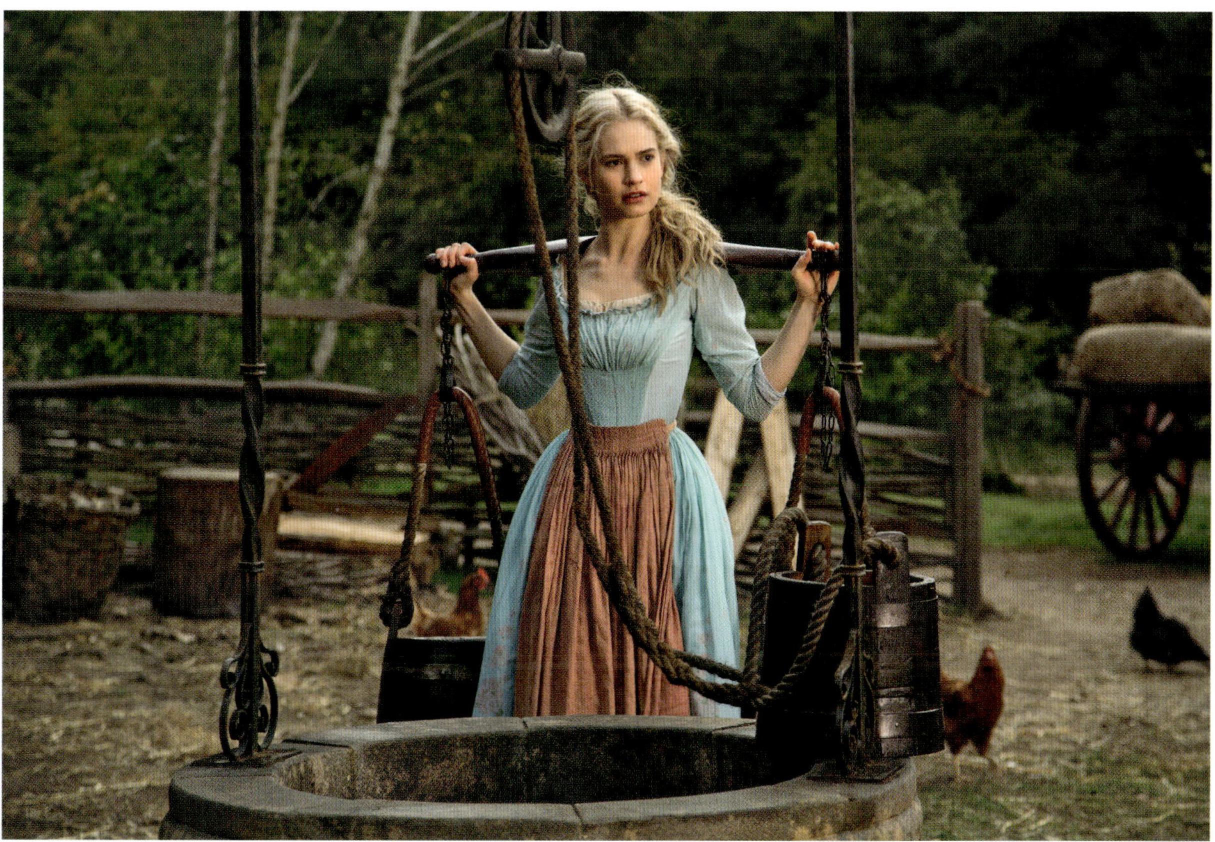

Above (top): Lily James arrives at the ball as Cinderella. ***(bottom):*** Cinderella embraces hard work and kindness in the live-action reimagining

FEMINIST PRINCESSES AND AUTHENTIC HEROES

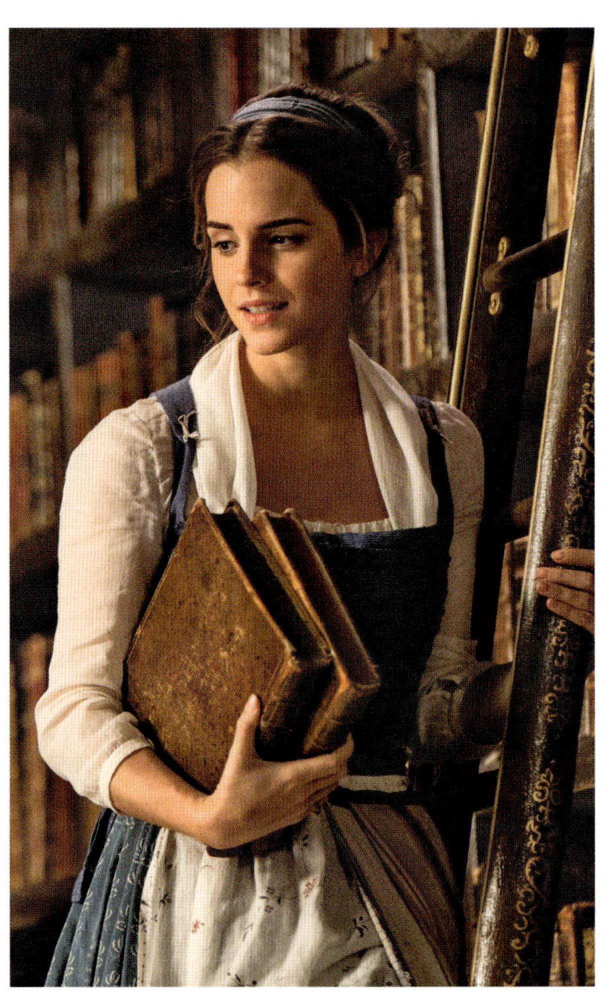

In the original 1991 film *Beauty and the Beast,* Belle was an intelligent, independent thinker, fearlessly walking her own path. To reimagine the film, director Bill Condon wanted to amp up those liberated undertones. Belle became an educated woman who recognizes the power of the written word, something that almost politicizes her.

"What I'm proud of in our movie is that [Belle's] also become an activist 25 years later," Condon told *Los Angeles Times.* "That she not only has a private interest in [reading], but she wants to share it and figure out how to help other little girls discover books too."

Actress Emma Watson was the perfect fit for an updated approach to Belle. Watson, who grew up loving the animated film, famously champions books and encourages her followers on social media to read as well. She's also an outspoken feminist. The actress famously brought feminist

Above: Emma Watson brings the spirit of feminism to Belle in *Beauty and the Beast.* ***Below:*** Belle investigates the Beast's rose in *Beauty and the Beast.*

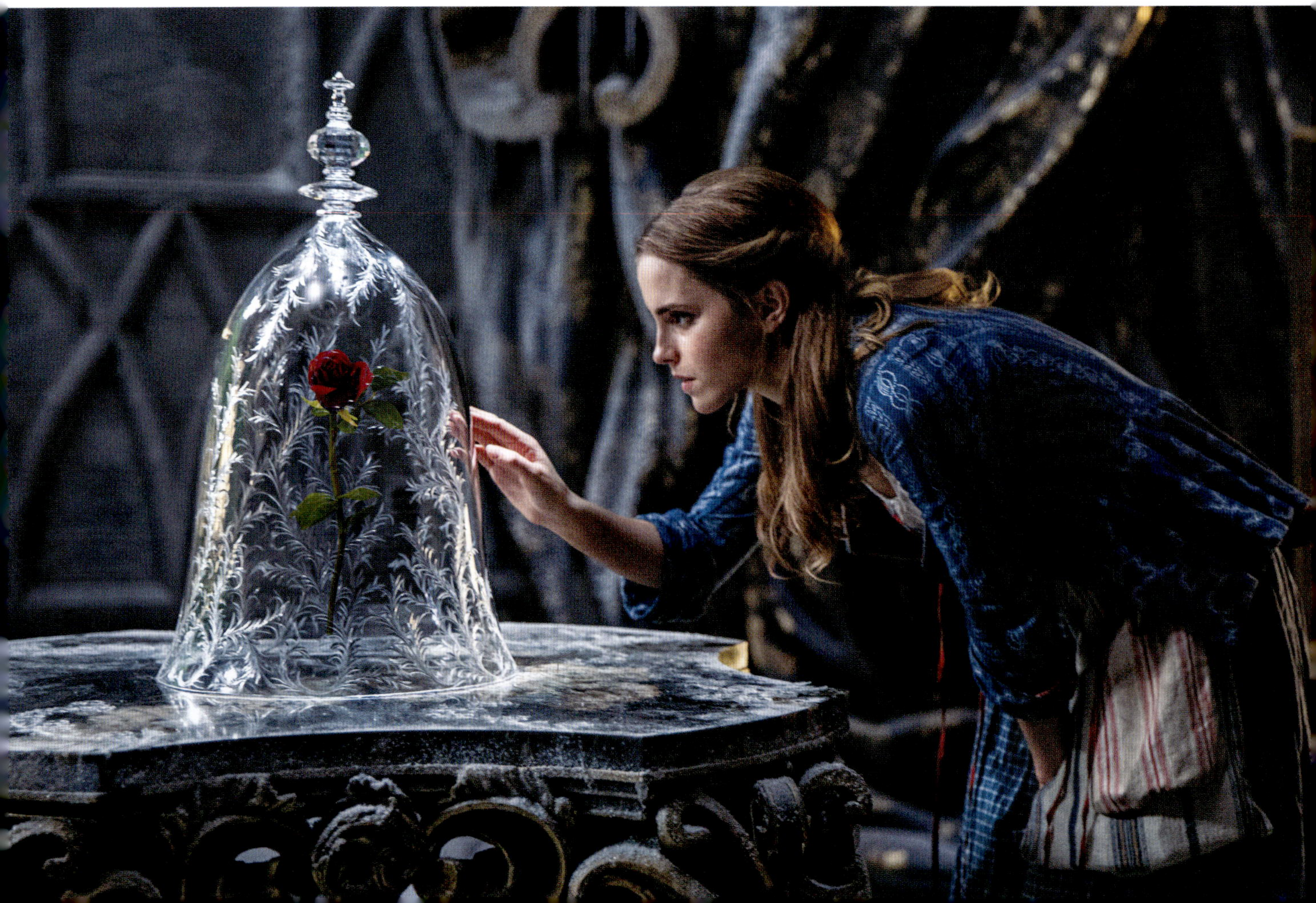

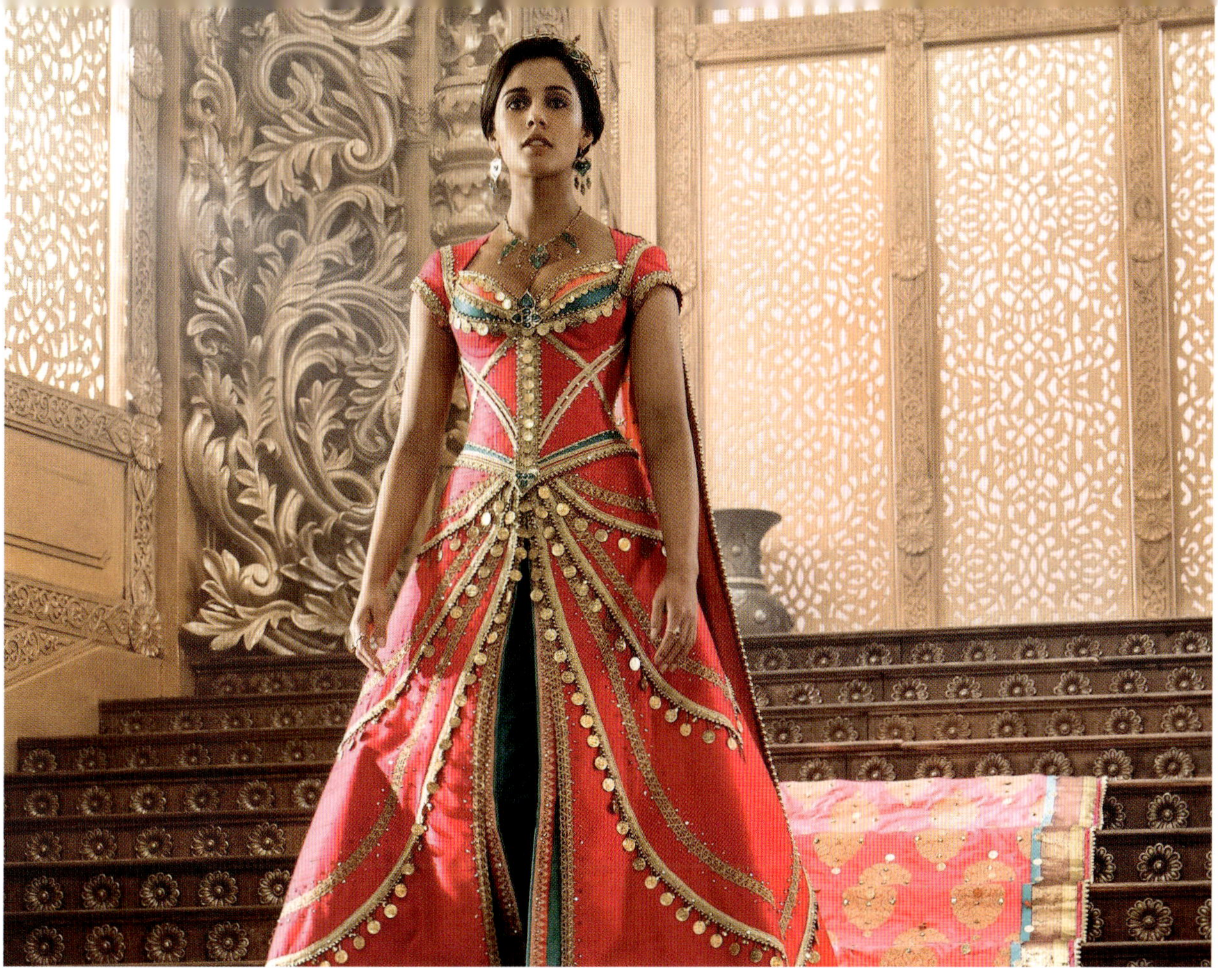

Gloria Steinem with her to a screening of *Beauty and the Beast* (2017) in London, seeking her approval on this new representation of Belle, which Steinem gave. "It was fascinating that [Emma's] activism could be so well mirrored by the film," Steinem noted in *Vanity Fair*. "It's this love of literature that first bonds the Beauty to the Beast, and also what develops the entire story."

In Guy Ritchie's 2019 reimagining of 1992's animated classic *Aladdin*, Jasmine was given a similar feminist update. While the original animated character is outspoken and adventurous, the filmmakers felt she needed a next-level evolution. In the reimagining, Jasmine aspires to succeed her father as leader of Agrabah, rather than simply marry into the position. She has aspirations, as evidenced by the books and maps that fill her bedroom, but she's also vulnerable enough to fall in love. The filmmakers, who cast Naomi Scott in the role, even added a solo musical number for Jasmine, titled "Speechless."

"In the original movie, I always remember Jasmine as strong and someone who knows her own mind," Scott said, describing her view of

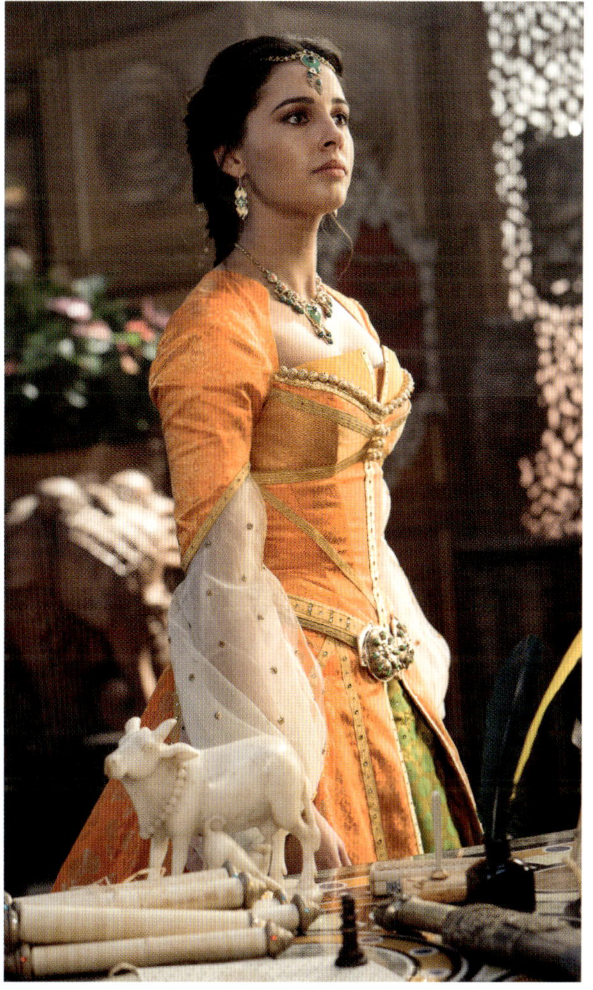

Naomi Scott embodies Jasmine in the live-action reimagining of *Aladdin*.

Like a Princess

After the success of animated film *Wreck-It Ralph* (2012), it occurred to screenwriter Pamela Ribon that its hero, Vanellope, shared numerous attributes with the Disney Princesses.

In the film's 2018 sequel, *Ralph Breaks the Internet*, Vanellope, voiced by Sarah Silverman, fully comes into her own as a royal, acknowledging that she too lacks a mom and has big dreams.

"I thought, 'Gosh, Vanellope is a princess. How come they never talk about that?'" Ribon said in an interview. "For her to move into this new land and learn about a new world, I wondered about what Vanellope could take away from that. In the first movie, we learn about her past, and this is another way to learn a little bit more about her."

Vanellope even got her own "I want" song written by longtime Disney composer Alan Menken, along with Phil Johnston and Tom MacDougall. With the poignant tune, "A Place Called Slaughter Race," Vanellope breaks into song, just like the Disney Princesses before her. She may not be an official Disney Princess, but Vanellope certainly embodies the spirit and qualities of a kind-hearted, courageous princess.

Vanellope channels her dreams into her own "I want" song in *Ralph Breaks the Internet*.

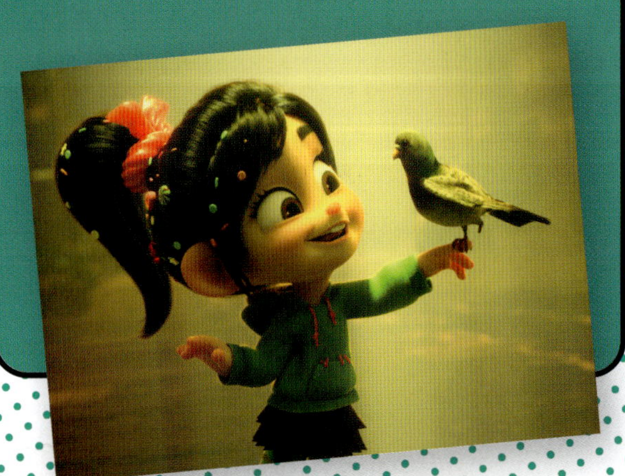

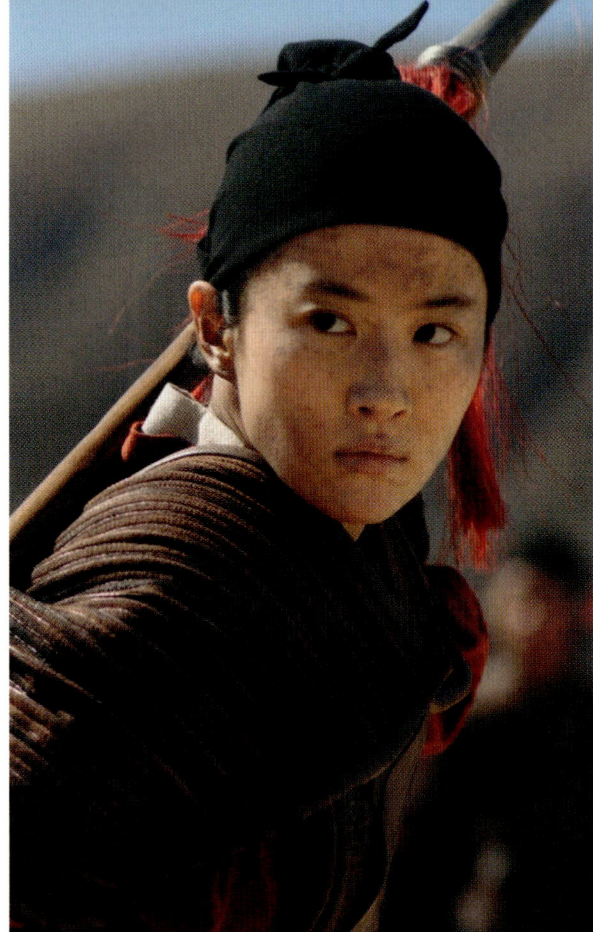

Liu Yifei as the warrior Mulan.

the princess. "Those are fantastic qualities that I obviously wanted to replicate. In this adaptation, Jasmine wants the best for her people. She wants the best for Agrabah and she feels like what's best for them is that she leads. That's really where Aladdin comes in and that's what Aladdin shows her. He really opens her eyes to the kingdom that she loves so much. She really wants to lead, and the story is a progression of how she finally speaks out and steps out and no longer goes silent."

Like *Aladdin*, the original *Mulan* (1998) captivated audience thanks to its adventurous story and strong hero. In fact, there wasn't much about the character of Mulan that needed to be updated for 2020. She was, after all, the Disney Princess who earned her royal status not through birth or marriage but because she saved China. Instead, the filmmakers focused on authenticity. Every detail of the film was based on extensive research by all of the department heads, as well as director Niki Caro. The screenplay took its cues both from the animated classic and from the original poem, *The Ballad of Mulan*, which dates back over 1,300 years. "The audience that loved Mulan as a character is taken on another journey with her—a slightly different journey," Caro noted to *Forbes*.

Mulan (2020) marked the first time a female director stepped behind the camera for a Disney live-action film, and Caro made sure that her crew was also comprised of a lot of women, including cinematographer Mandy Walker. "I think it's the only movie of this scale and genre where all the voices—all the people running it were women," Caro said. "[It was] very female-led, this production."

Star Liu Yifei, who was cast as Mulan, trained for six or seven hours every day to hone her strength and learn how to fight to best showcase Mulan's determination. The actress also wanted to convey the strength that comes from embracing who you are. "We can do everything we decide to," Yifei said. "Take every path we want to take. But we have to be responsible for ourselves."

For Sean Bailey, the aim is to bring more gender equality into these narratives while also maintaining the love stories to which fans connect. "Audiences want to see, in my opinion, empowered characters who still feel that depth of emotion that is the timeless part of the story," Bailey notes. "So striking that balance is what we really work hard to achieve."

Several more Disney Princesses will be coming to the screen in the next few years, offering reinterpretations of the characters with more inclusive casting. *The Little Mermaid* live-action adaptation, in theaters May 2023, stars singer Halle Bailey as Ariel, and a live-action adaptation of *Snow White and the Seven Dwarfs*, directed by Marc Webb, will follow. The updated take, with a script from Greta Gerwig, will embrace a new perspective, starring Rachel Zegler as Snow White.

"We are making it a priority to, in these fairy tales, reflect the world as it looks," Bailey says. "We really feel it's an incredible opportunity to open up and show and reflect for people everywhere what these characters can be. Hopefully, it makes these stories all the more powerful when everyone can see themselves as a part of them."

Liu Yifei's Mulan is loyal, brave, and true.

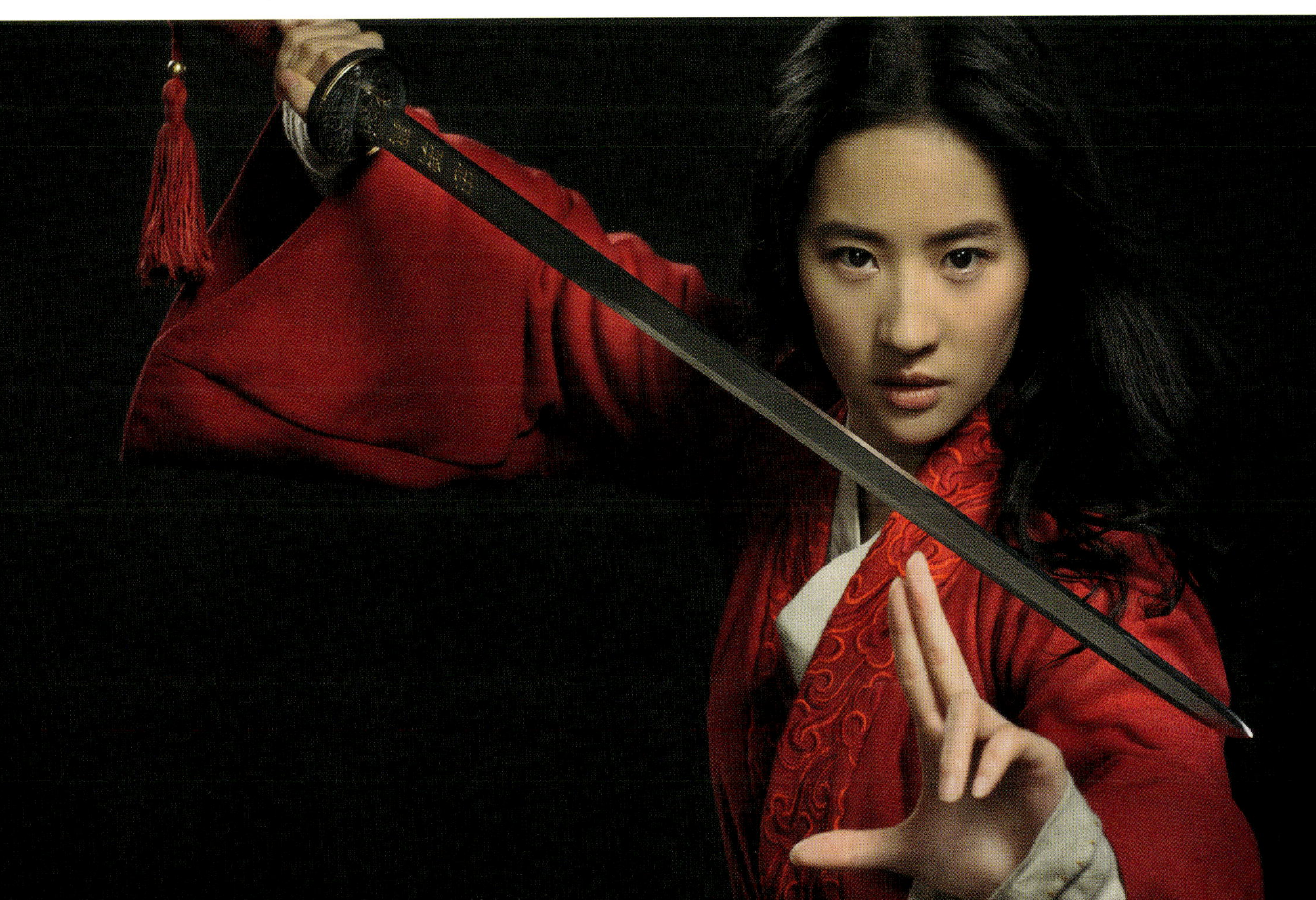

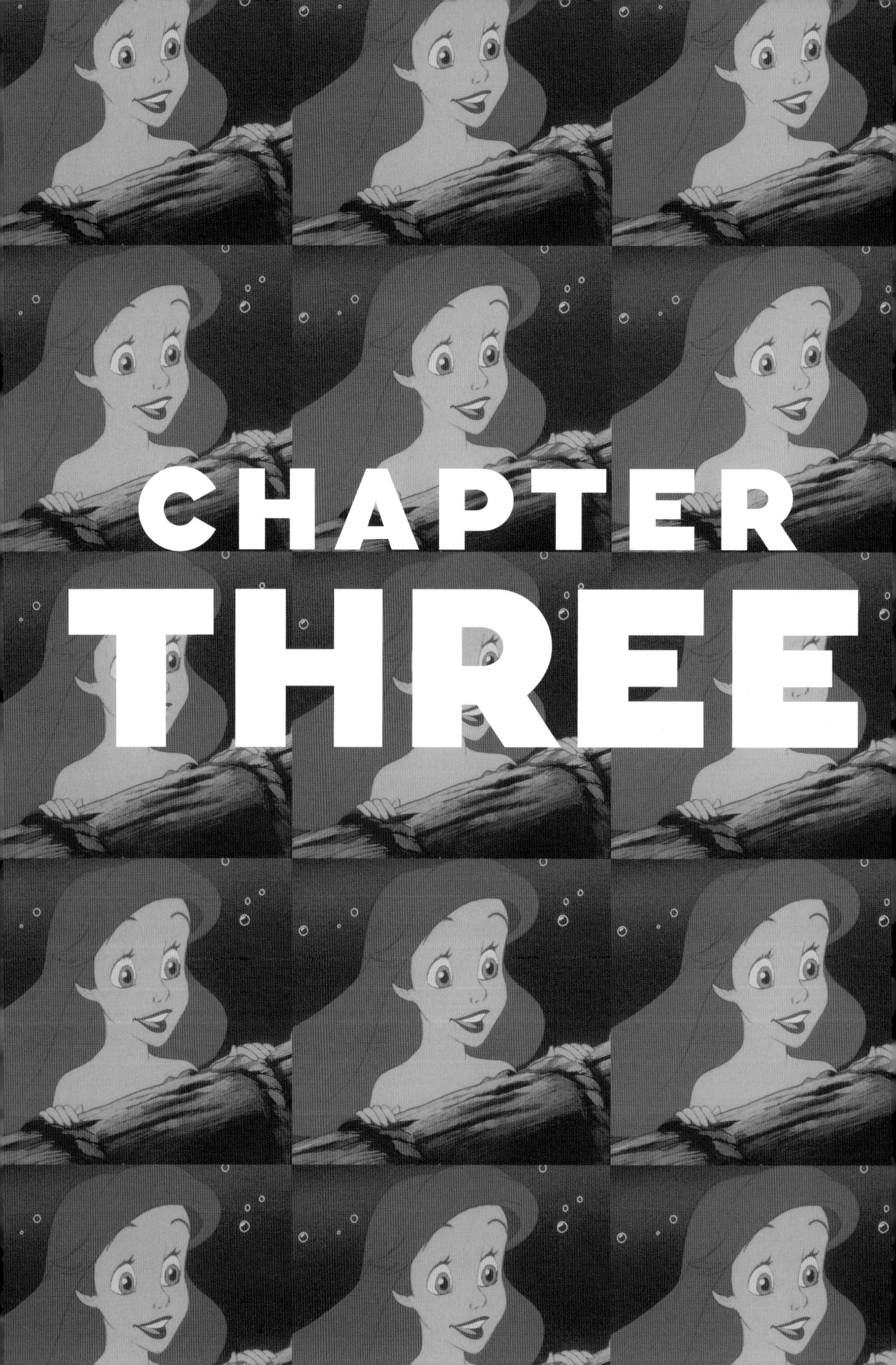

CHAPTER THREE

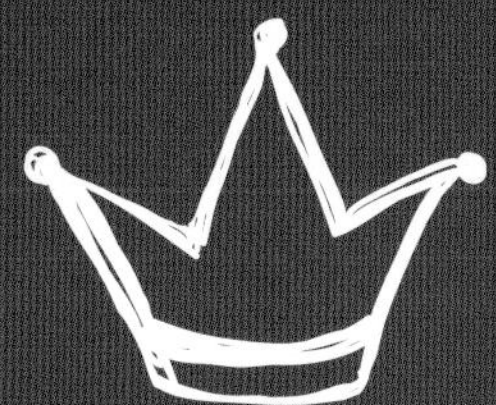

PART OF YOUR WORLD

TOYS, COLLECTIBLES, AND GAMES

From the beginning, Walt Disney knew that moviegoing audiences would want to see animated characters brought out into the world in different ways, both before and after a film's release. Products that celebrate a film's characters being unveiled ahead of a movie can create excitement and demand, while a burst of merchandise after it hits theaters allows the story to continue and to be retold in new ways with toys, games, dolls, and other themed products.

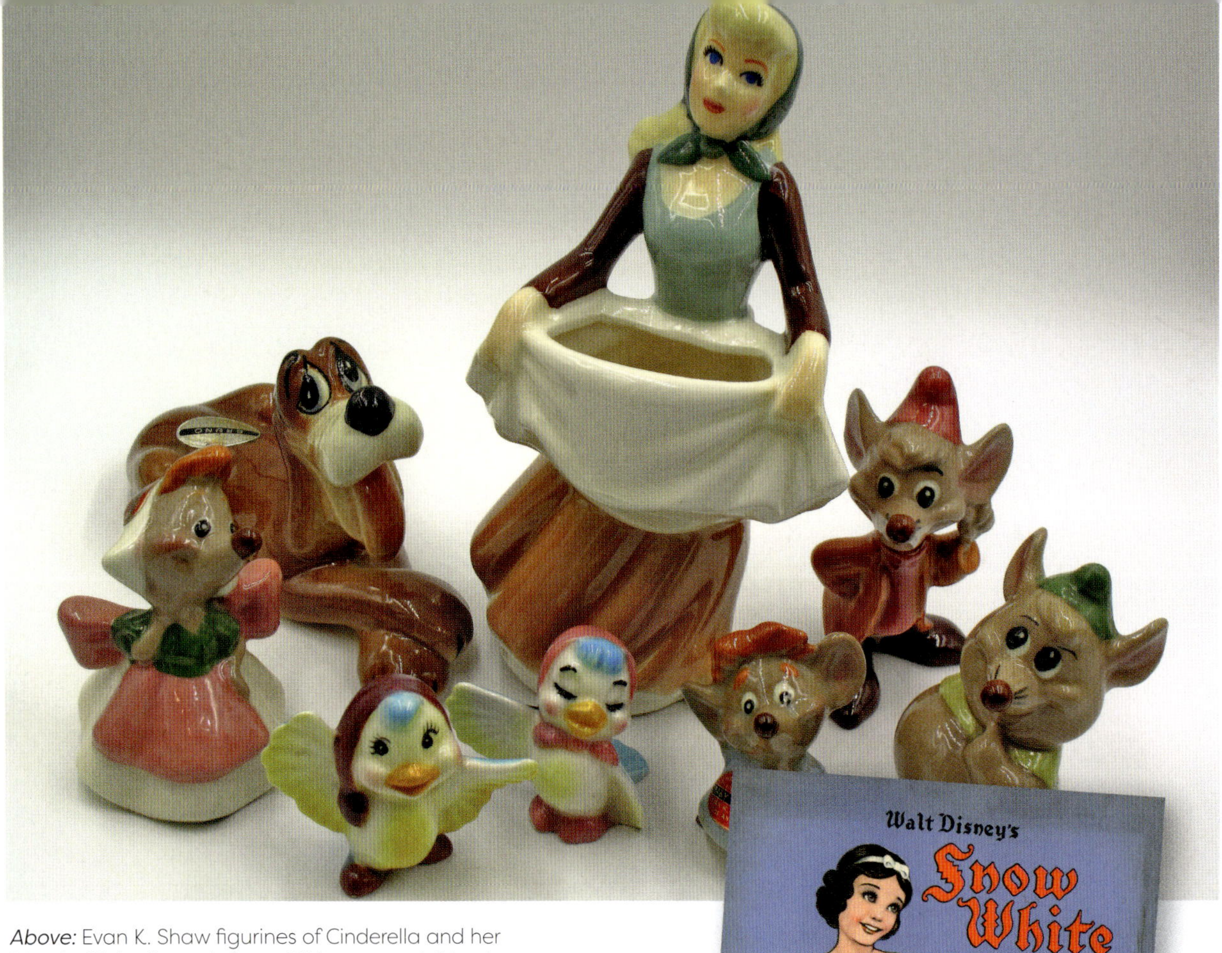

Above: Evan K. Shaw figurines of Cinderella and her friends. *Right:* An early Snow White paper doll book.

Today, Disney is known for its vast array of merchandise, which engages fans of all ages and comes at a variety of prices. This is notably evident with the Disney Princesses. Disney Consumer Products now releases around 15,000 different Disney Princess-themed toys and dolls in total each year. And it's no accident that all of these items accompany Disney's beloved stories—Disney products have been a staple since the early days of Mickey Mouse, back in 1930. We can now fill our homes with everything Disney Princess thanks to a legacy of creative merchandising at Disney, which dates back even before *Snow White and the Seven Dwarfs*.

Disney products embrace new films alongside classic releases, and the company continues to revitalize the characters, especially the Disney Princesses, to keep them modern and reflective of contemporary values. "At Disney, one of the great things we have is almost one hundred years of nostalgia," says historian Stacia Martin. "But our history is not dormant. If you show a five-year-old *Snow White and the Seven Dwarfs*, it's a good movie. They have no idea where it came from chronologically; it's just a good movie. Our characters and stories are kept alive and simultaneously they're kept current. What a tremendous feat it is to look back to the '30s and yet be able to meet Snow White at the parks or take home a doll of her still today."

Over the years, Disney's toys and games have evolved, but they've always captured the essence of the characters—such as Snow White's kindness or Moana's spirit of adventure. It's no wonder a vast contingent of Disney collectors has emerged and that so many fans are attracted to both vintage and new products. The love of Disneyana—any Disney-related item—is endless.

There's an ageless feeling to many of these items, which connect us to the meaningful, timeless films and stories that have stayed with us for generations. The Disney Princesses live in our collective memories and imaginations, but also in our bedrooms, living rooms, and display cases.

A DISNEY CHARACTER IN EVERY HOME

In 1932, Walt and Roy O. Disney hired Herman S. Kamen, an advertising executive known as Kay Kamen, as the merchandising man for Mickey Mouse. Over the next three years, Kamen oversaw the creation of thousands of pieces of Mickey Mouse merchandise, from wristwatches to breakfast cereal to figurines. He worked with manufacturers as well as department stores to ensure that Disney characters were familiar in the lives of the American public, generating a demand for branded items and creating an expectation that those products would be constantly available, as well. It was a strategy that become common throughout Hollywood. "Kay Kamen invented the whole licensing industry," noted Tom Tumbusch, publisher of *Tomart's Disneyana Update*. "Not just for Disney, alone; others followed suit."

A year before the release of *Snow White and the Seven Dwarfs*, Kamen began to prepare an extensive marketing campaign intended to bring the film's story and characters into the homes of their audience. Traditionally, film merchandise was unveiled after a film's release, and only if the story was popular and resonated with the public; *Snow White* marked the first time movie merch was available before anyone had even seen the film. By October of 1937, months ahead of the premiere of *Snow White*, toys and themed items appeared on store shelves. Seiberling Latex Products Co., which had previously created Mickey Mouse and Donald Duck figurines, made hand-painted rubber figurines of Snow White and the Seven Dwarfs, which became so popular that they sold out several times even before the film's release. Seiberling quickly realized it had to ramp up production to prepare for the release of

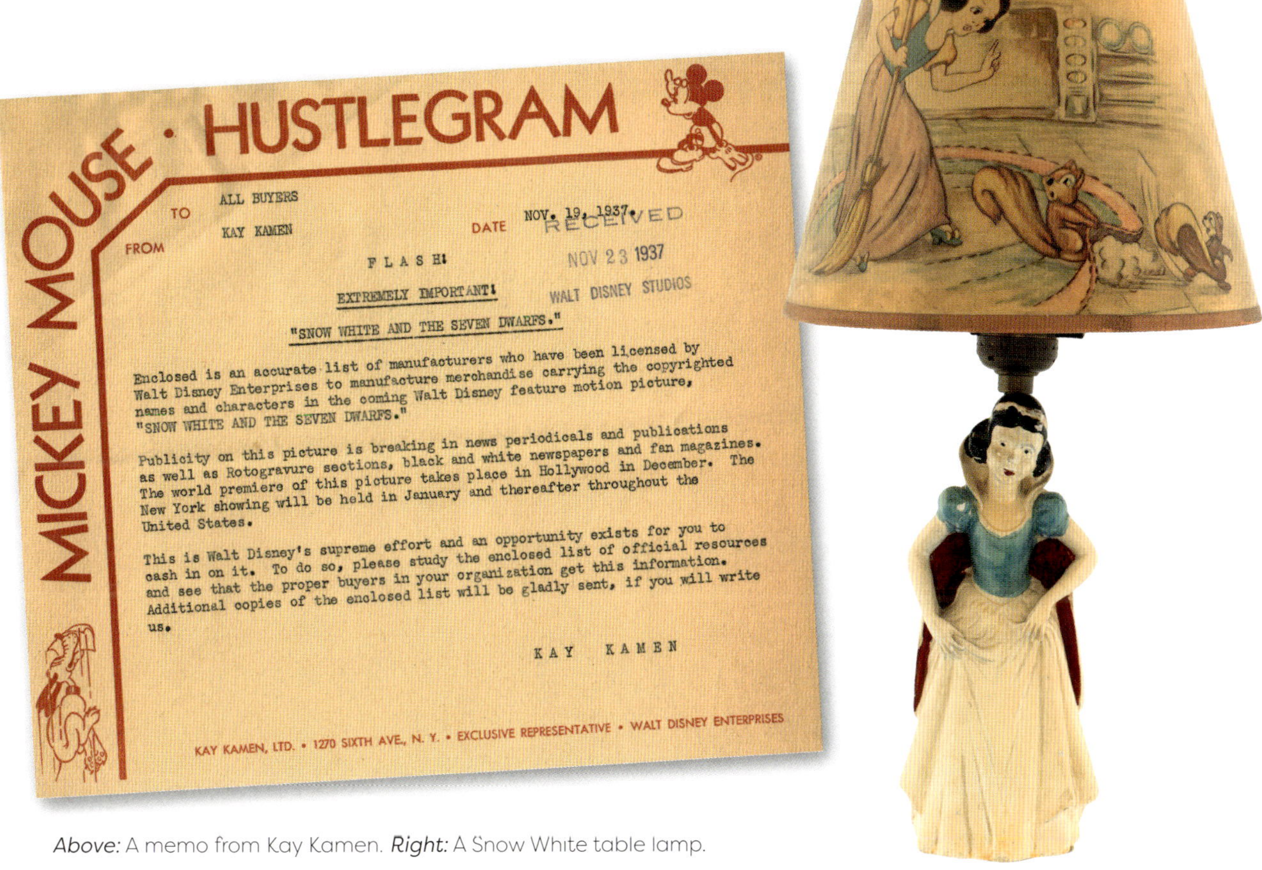

MICKEY MOUSE · HUSTLEGRAM

TO ALL BUYERS

FROM KAY KAMEN

DATE NOV. 19, 1937.

RECEIVED NOV 23 1937 WALT DISNEY STUDIOS

F L A S H!

EXTREMELY IMPORTANT!

"SNOW WHITE AND THE SEVEN DWARFS."

Enclosed is an accurate list of manufacturers who have been licensed by Walt Disney Enterprises to manufacture merchandise carrying the copyrighted names and characters in the coming Walt Disney feature motion picture, "SNOW WHITE AND THE SEVEN DWARFS."

Publicity on this picture is breaking in news periodicals and publications as well as Rotogravure sections, black and white newspapers and fan magazines. The world premiere of this picture takes place in Hollywood in December. The New York showing will be held in January and thereafter throughout the United States.

This is Walt Disney's supreme effort and an opportunity exists for you to cash in on it. To do so, please study the enclosed list of official resources and see that the proper buyers in your organization get this information. Additional copies of the enclosed list will be gladly sent, if you will write us.

K A Y K A M E N

KAY KAMEN, LTD. • 1270 SIXTH AVE., N. Y. • EXCLUSIVE REPRESENTATIVE • WALT DISNEY ENTERPRISES

Above: A memo from Kay Kamen. *Right:* A Snow White table lamp.

the film. In total, more than 2,000 products were created for *Snow White and the Seven Dwarfs*.

"Walt saw an opportunity to have merchandise be made available before a film was in theaters to get his version of the characters in front of people so they were ready for that film," explains Libby Spatz, Disney Consumer Products Senior Librarian and Archivist. "This changed the entertainment merchandising business structure. Suddenly, there was more conversation going on about films, about what was coming, about the characters. People became accustomed to having the merchandise available as soon as they realized the film was something they were interested in."

The amount of Snow White-themed merchandise was staggering, even by today's standards. Consumers could buy everything from Snow White watering cans to carpet sweepers to household bleach and ammonia to Armour's specially branded Star Jubilee Ham and Star Bacon. Kroger's grocery stores sold an exclusive set of collectible glasses, while Swift's Allsweet Margarine ran a campaign where fans could mail in package clippings along with ten cents to receive Snow White seed packets. There were wristwatches, cut-out books, coloring sets, children's blocks, doll-shaped soap, board games, paper dolls, and even a lamp that showcased the princess standing over her wishing well. It was evidence that consumers, when faced with the choice between an ordinary product and an experiential one, would always opt for magic.

Previously, several companies, including the Knickerbocker Toy Company and Richard G. Krueger, had sold Disney character dolls, from Mickey Mouse to Red Riding Hood. The arrival of Snow White, a charming, beautiful princess, meant many Snow White dolls, most of which were released in 1938. Ideal Toy Company manufactured three different editions of Snow White in doll form, one of which was made using the brand's Shirley Temple head mold, and

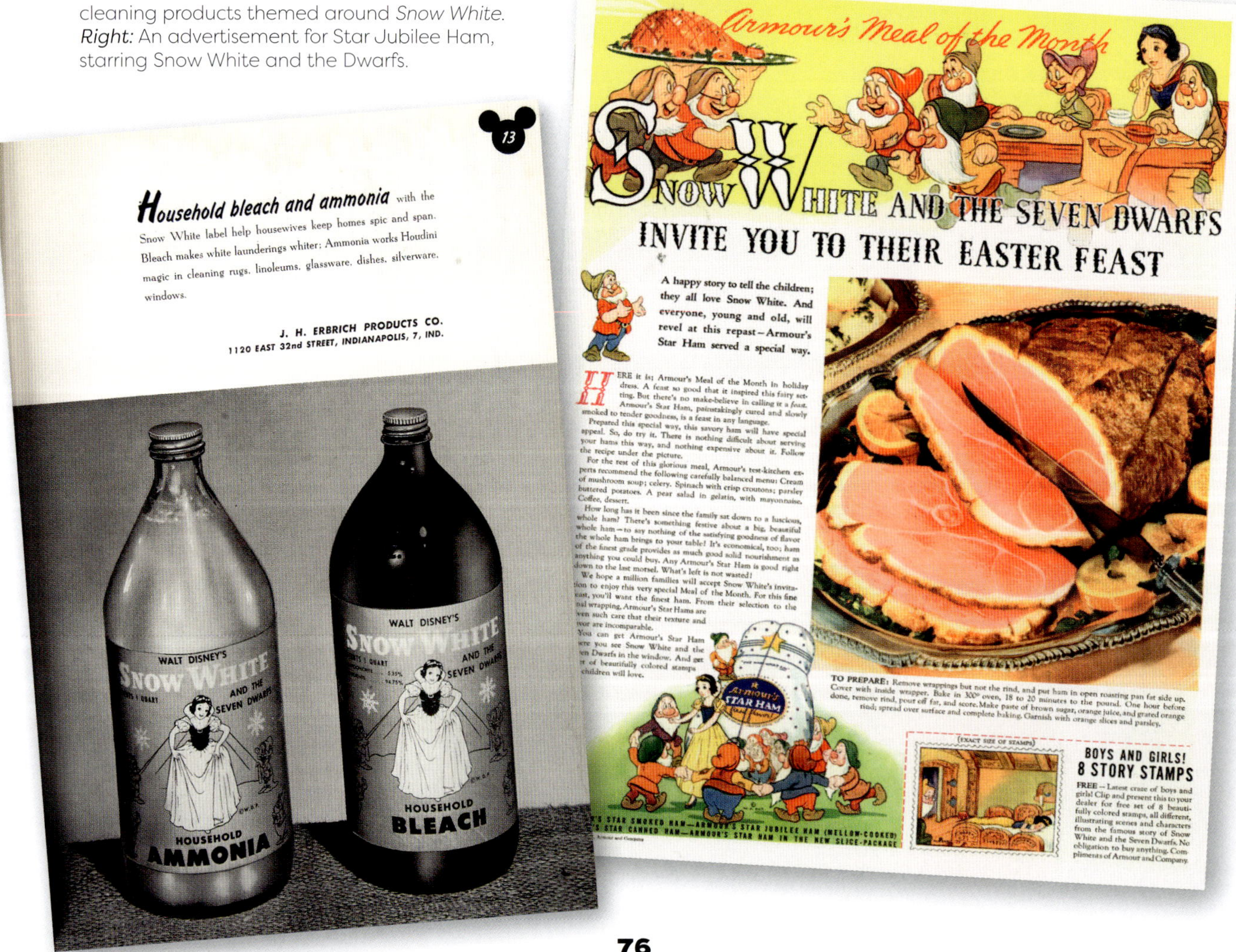

Below: An advertisement for household cleaning products themed around *Snow White*. *Right:* An advertisement for Star Jubilee Ham, starring Snow White and the Dwarfs.

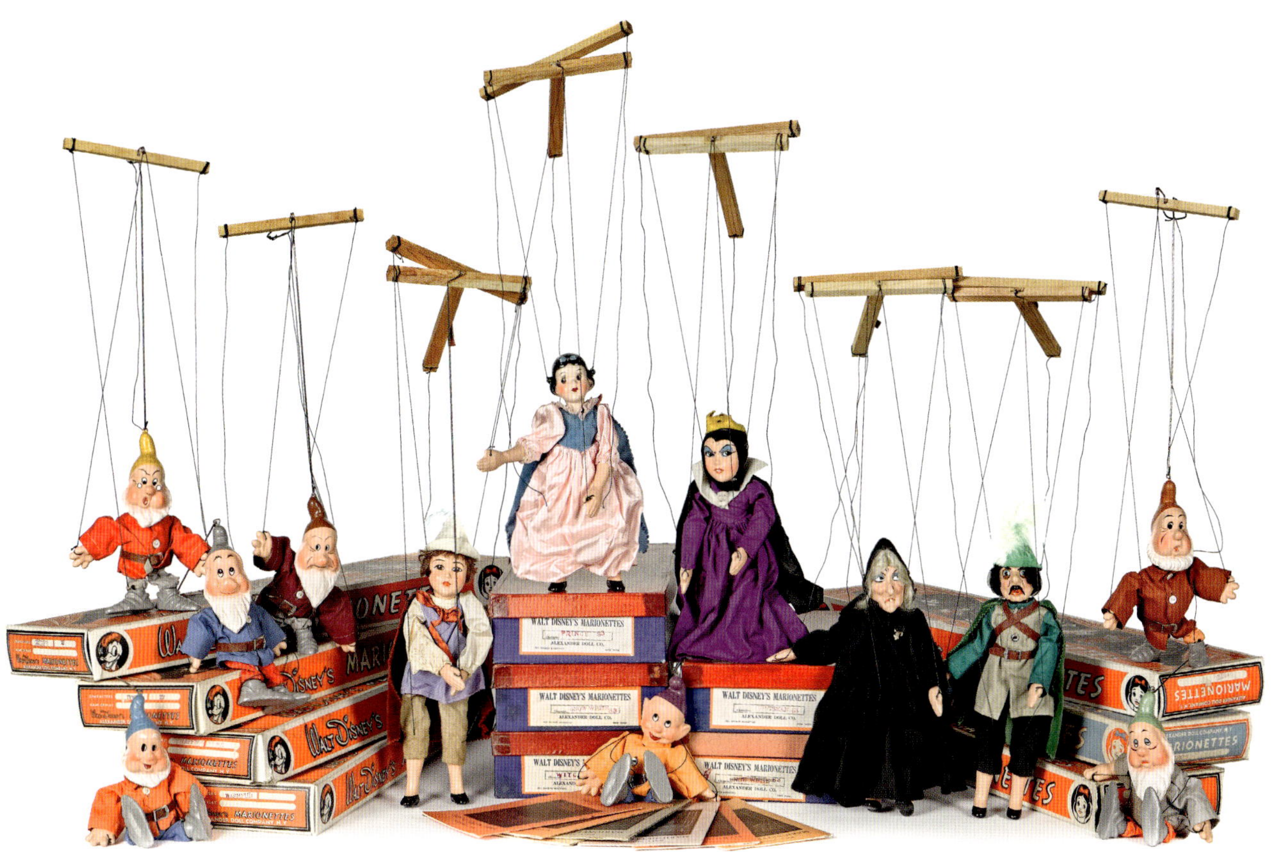

Above: Madame Alexander marionette dolls released in 1938.
Right: An example of an early Snow White doll.

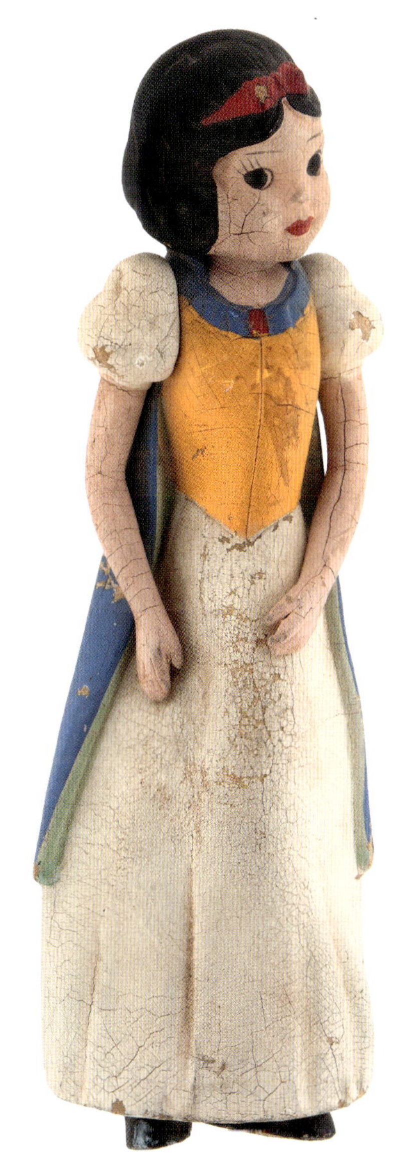

Richard G. Krueger Company sold cloth dolls with velvet and organdy dresses. Madame Alexander, a doll maker known for its high-end fashion dolls, released a series of *Snow White and the Seven Dwarfs* marionettes in 1938, featuring Snow White and all of the Seven Dwarfs, as well as the evil Queen, the Witch, Prince Charming, and the Huntsman. In 1939, the Snow White marionette, whose head was designed by illustrator Tony Sarg, was advertised as being sold for $3.65. Several types of paper dolls, with cut-out dresses, were also notably popular with consumers in those days.

Games, too, were a must-have item for fans of the film. Several *Snow White* board games were produced, including Parker Brothers' *Walt Disney's Own Game – Snow White and the 7 Dwarfs*, a *Candyland*-style boardgame where players rushed to wake up Snow White. There were also playing cards, puzzles, and card games. The film products provided lots of opportunities for lovers of *Snow White and the Seven Dwarfs* to enjoy their favorite movie characters at home, putting Disney on a path to present merchandise for each new film release with more and more fervor.

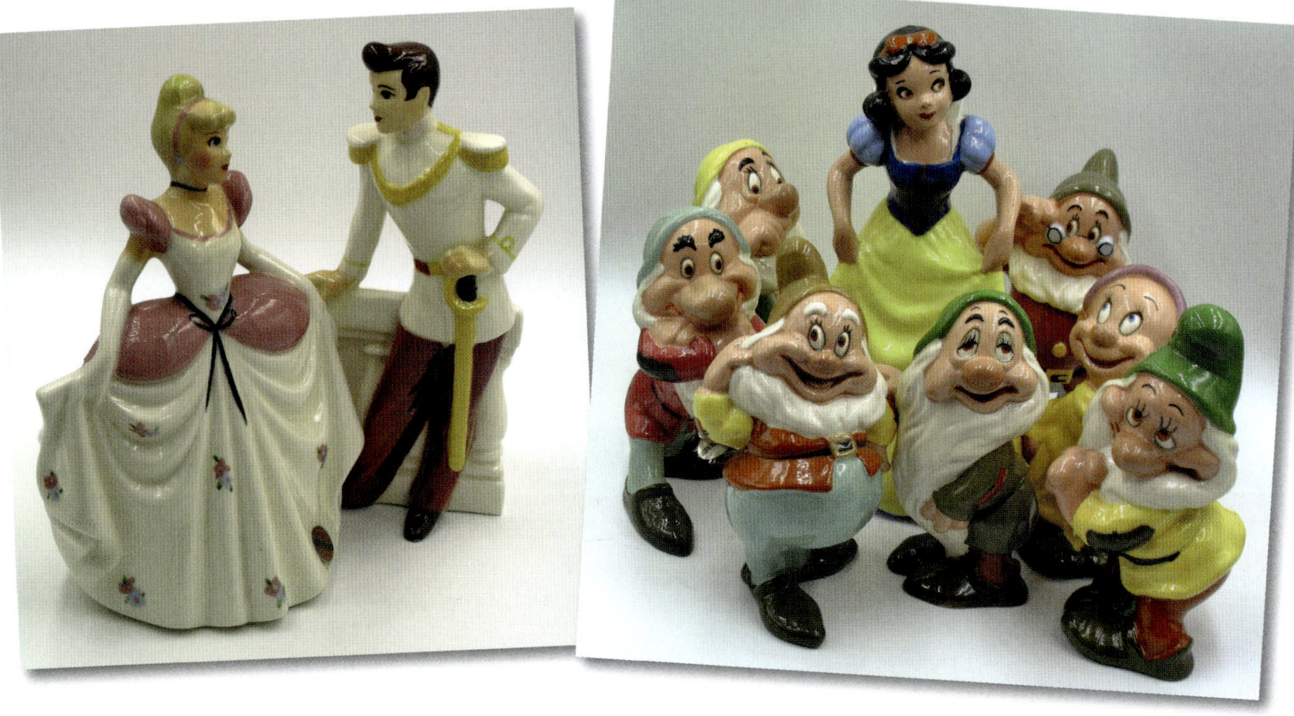

Evan K. Shaw ceramic figurines created for *Cinderella* and *Snow White and the Seven Dwarfs*.

Kamen remained with The Walt Disney Company until his untimely death in 1949, when he was killed in a plane crash in the Azores. His death meant that the plan for *Cinderella*'s merchandising was halted, with the merchandising strategy on pause until someone new was placed in charge in December later that year. Still, by 1950, when *Cinderella* arrived in theaters, Disney had established itself as having a strong marketing arm, with each new production celebrated with hundreds of products ahead of its release.

Postwar also meant new toy technologies, resulting in more detailed figurines, more advanced products, and more ornate dolls. While early Snow White figurines were made from rubber or unfired porcelain, Cinderella figurines were made of glazed ceramic. Ceramics company Evan K. Shaw's figurines, which remain collectible today, were one of the best representations of Cinderella outside of the film. "The Shaw figures have that same sort of slightly distant beauty and veneer that the film has," Martin explains. "I think they're the most effective at capturing the visual aesthetic of the film. They look as glamorous as the film itself."

Cinderella was marketed as a date movie, with the tagline "Midnight never strikes when you're in love," and Walt intended the film for audiences of all ages, not just children. This translated into the merchandise released around the film, which was targeted as much to adults as it was to kids. "Walt made what he felt were good stories for everybody," Martin notes. "He made what suited his taste, and his taste was very much in tune with the general American psyche of the times he inhabited. The market for these objects was everyone."

Like with *Snow White, Cinderella* was an opportunity to spread the beloved characters from the film far and wide. There was a Cinderella wristwatch, housed in a plastic glass slipper. There was a Cinderella doll that danced with her prince, and a Cinderella topsy-turvy doll, a rag doll that one could flip between costumes by turning it upside down. Cinderella dolls continued to be released for the next decade, with notable new editions in 1964, and the film's story was retold several times in Little Golden Books and Tell-A-Tale Books.

By the time *Sleeping Beauty* was released in 1959, it had been nearly a decade since the previous Disney fairy-tale princess film. Disney launched a massive marketing campaign around the movie, which was, like *Cinderella*, presented as an extremely glamorous film.

Because many of the products were designed and manufactured before the final cut of the film was finished, some of the items released in 1959 showcase scenes that never actually made it into *Sleeping Beauty*. Toy company Gong Bell manufactured a toy doll cradle made from particle board and paper appliques, which featured artwork of an adorable, wide-eyed child version of Aurora surrounded by forest animals, as did a Gong Bell puzzle. That young Aurora, who was originally meant to appear in the film, also showed up in a comic book series published by Gold Key, which debuted in 1970. Madame Alexander created a Sleeping Beauty doll with a shimmering turquoise gown and golden tiara, and figurines continued to be popular display items for fans of the characters. The early Disney Princesses took many forms, as dolls, toys, and more, and some these have become highly collectible all these decades later.

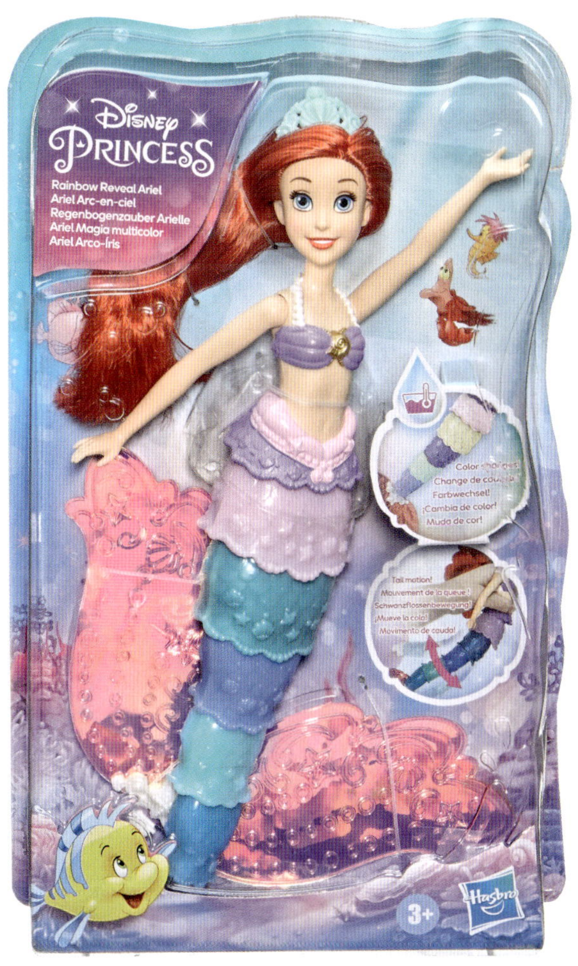

A MERCHANDISING BOOM

The late 1980s and 1990s, heralded by *The Little Mermaid*, weren't just a renewal for Walt Disney Animation Studios. After decades without a new Disney Princess, there were suddenly popular new stories and characters to bring to the shelves. From the late 1980s, the era marked a revolution in marketing and merchandising, as first evidenced by the public clamor for Ariel-themed products when *The Little Mermaid* was released in 1989.

"*The Little Mermaid* was a tremendous success in its first release," says Dave Pacheco, Disney Master Artist and Creative Director. "There was such a demand for product. That demand continued for years and years—it was just amazing. Today, the demand for *The Little Mermaid* merchandise is still there, all these years later."

Spatz explains that *The Little Mermaid* was an opportunity for Disney to create an arc of merchandising that allowed fans of the film to engage in role-play as the characters. The deep blues and greens of the film were used to great effect on merchandise, recalling the colors of the ocean. The colors worked well on all kinds of products, including musical microphones and fishtails. Many children already dreamed of becoming mermaids, so there was a fan base in place, and today Ariel continues to be one of the most popular princesses when it comes to toys, dolls, and dress-up costumes. "There were many opportunities for guests to relate to Ariel," Spatz says. "The merchandise was fairly robust in support of all of that."

Originally, there was a concern from the merchandising standpoint that red-haired dolls wouldn't sell. That, of course, was not an issue thanks to Ariel's immediate popularity. "The first time the toy company saw that Ariel had red hair, they were horrified because their

Left: Ariel dolls have been consistently among the top-selling Disney Princess toys.

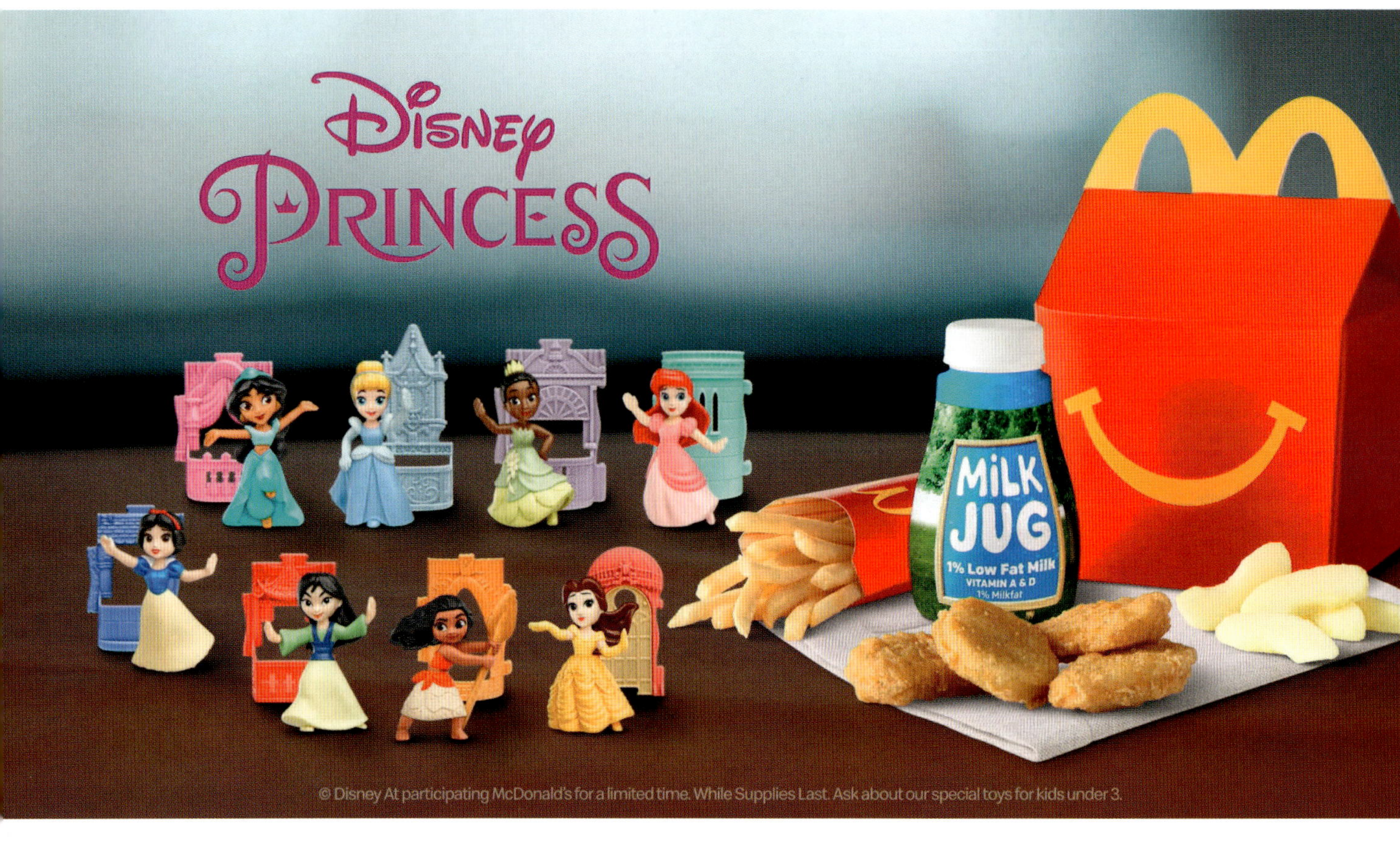

McDonald's Happy Meal toys featuring the Disney Princess characters.

research had shown that redheaded dolls do not sell," Ron Clements recalled in an interview. "To everyone's relief, sales of Ariel dolls proved their research wrong."

The era was a heyday for Disney Animation, reigniting the public's love for animated stories and characters through films like *Aladdin* and *Beauty and the Beast*. With each film's release, themed toys and products became plentiful. Fans could collect plastic figurines and toys of their favorite characters just by buying McDonald's Happy Meals and Burger King Kids' Meals around the release of every new film—the figurines came free with every purchase. *Pocahontas*, in particular, had a huge amount of promotional tie-ins, from Burger King toys to Payless Shoes moccasins to Barbie-style fashion dolls. These made it possible for audiences to bring the characters to life beyond their existing stories with play and imagination.

It was also around this time, in 1994, that the Walt Disney Masterpiece Collection brought VHS versions of the films to store shelves. While the Walt Disney Classics series had been available from 1984 to 1994, offering VHS releases of movies like *Cinderella* and *The Little Mermaid*, the mid-to-late '90s saw even more public demand for home entertainment. This was also notably the first time *Snow White and the Seven Dwarfs* was available for home release.

The creation of the Disney Princess franchise by Disney Consumer Products in 2000 expanded the possibilities for merchandise exponentially. It was an opportunity to bring the characters together on various products, and for young fans to pick a favorite Disney Princess from a large array of options. Disney Consumer Products added items like Disney Princess rolling suitcases, Disney Princess karaoke machines, Disney Princess fishing sets, and Disney Princess bicycles made by Huffy, to the product lineup. Action toys, like a Merida or Rapunzel bow and arrow set, or a light-up Moana

Evolution of the Dolls

Dolls have been an important representation of the Disney Princesses ever since the release of *Snow White and the Seven Dwarfs*. Numerous types of dolls have been released over the years, from composition dolls to plush dolls to fashion dolls, and all of them have been a way for children and adults alike to celebrate their favorite animated characters. Dolls have always been a reflection of culture, allowing children to express themselves and grow through a particular princess—and today, the values of the Disney Princesses are reflected through all the available dolls. "The doll becomes almost like an avatar," notes Elaine Carovilla, Director Commercialization at Disney Parks, Experiences, and Products. "I want children, when they're playing with a princess doll, to call to mind those subliminal messages and all the character qualities they witnessed in the film."

In the past decade, the number of Disney Princess dolls has increased substantially. Carovilla estimates that there are four times more dolls now than a decade ago, and in 2020 Disney Consumer Products released 1,200 different Disney Princess dolls. Today, the Shimmer Doll line—which has also been known as Sparkle Dolls or Classic Dolls—is the best-selling, with over five million being sold per year.

The evolution of the Disney Princess dolls is visually striking when compared from decade to decade, particularly in the subtle changes to their faces, fashions, and even heights. When the Disney Princess franchise was first created, Disney worked with Mattel, a company Disney had partnered with since 1955, back when Mattel was the first sponsor of the Mickey Mouse Club. Later, in 2016, Hasbro took over production of the dolls (Mattel will take over the production again in 2023). Looking back at Snow White, the dolls reveal how our perceptions and technologies have shifted, as well as how Disney wants to present their characters in doll form.

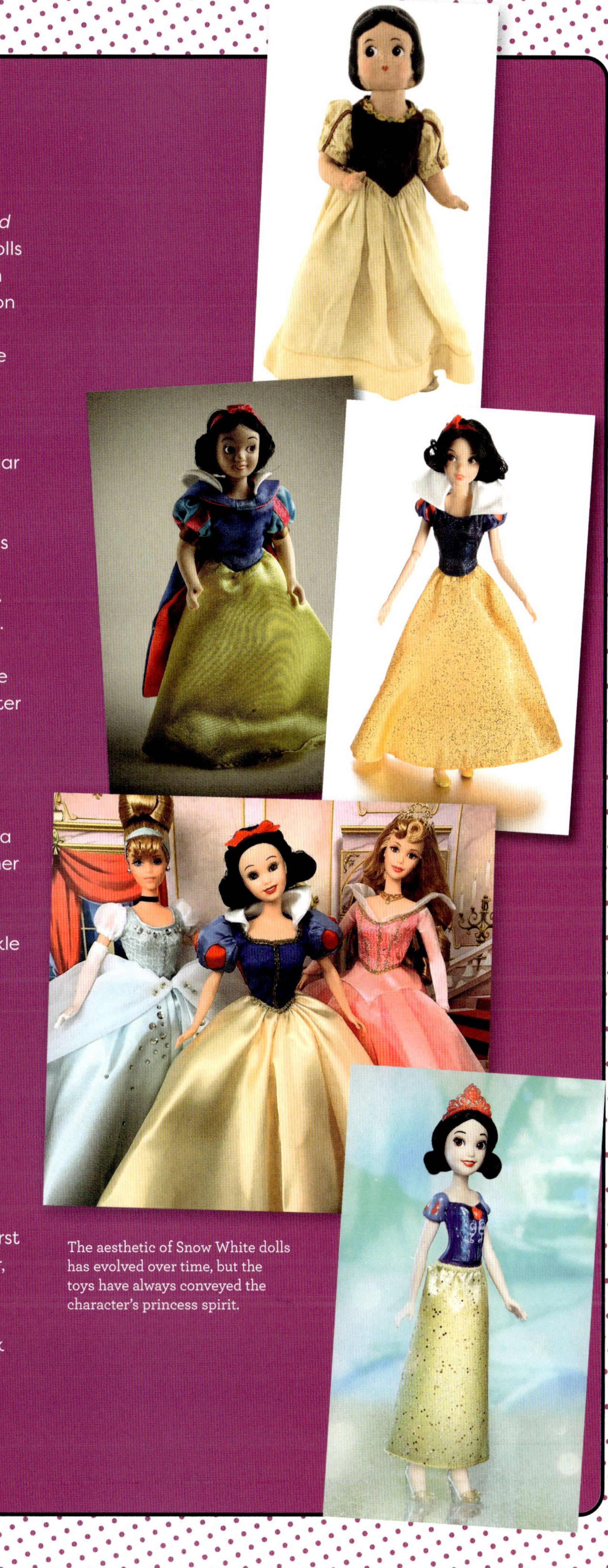

The aesthetic of Snow White dolls has evolved over time, but the toys have always conveyed the character's princess spirit.

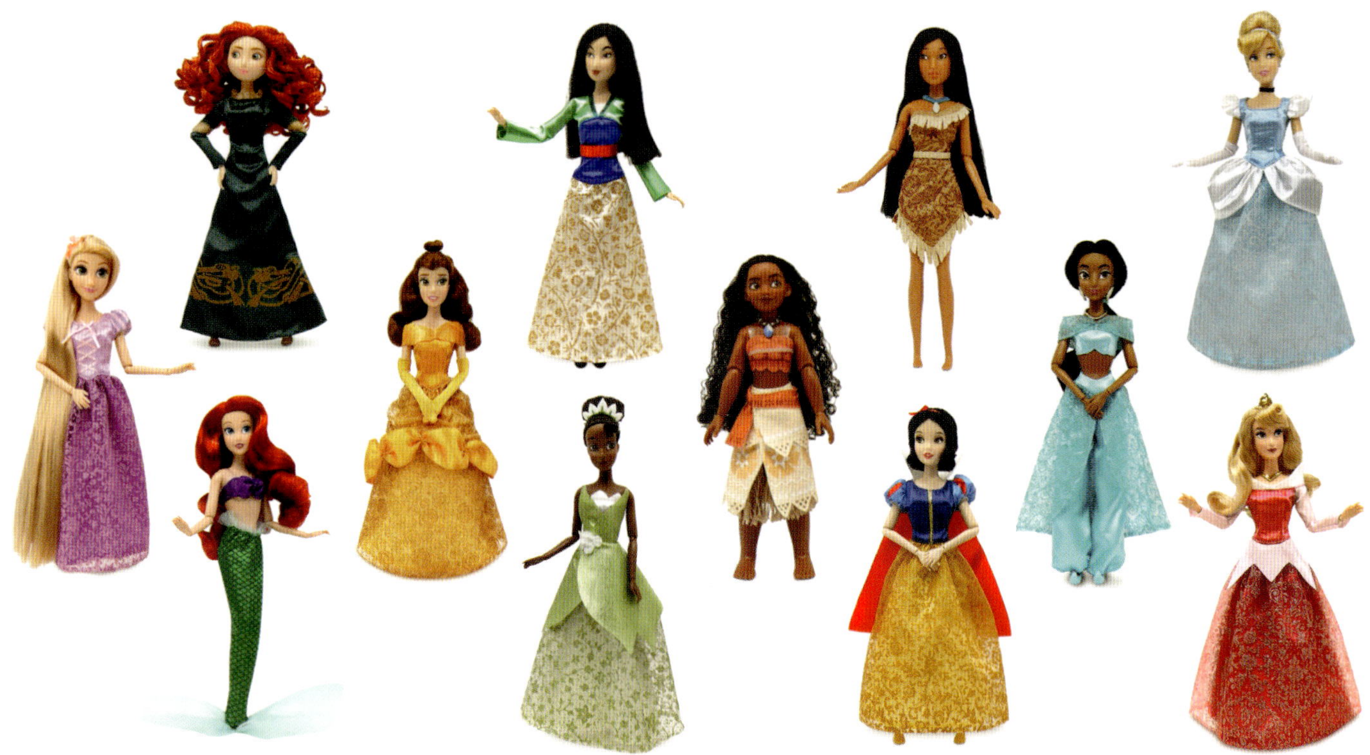

Above: A set of Hasbro's Disney Princess dolls. *Below:* A bow and arrow toy set, released as part of the *Tangled* franchise.

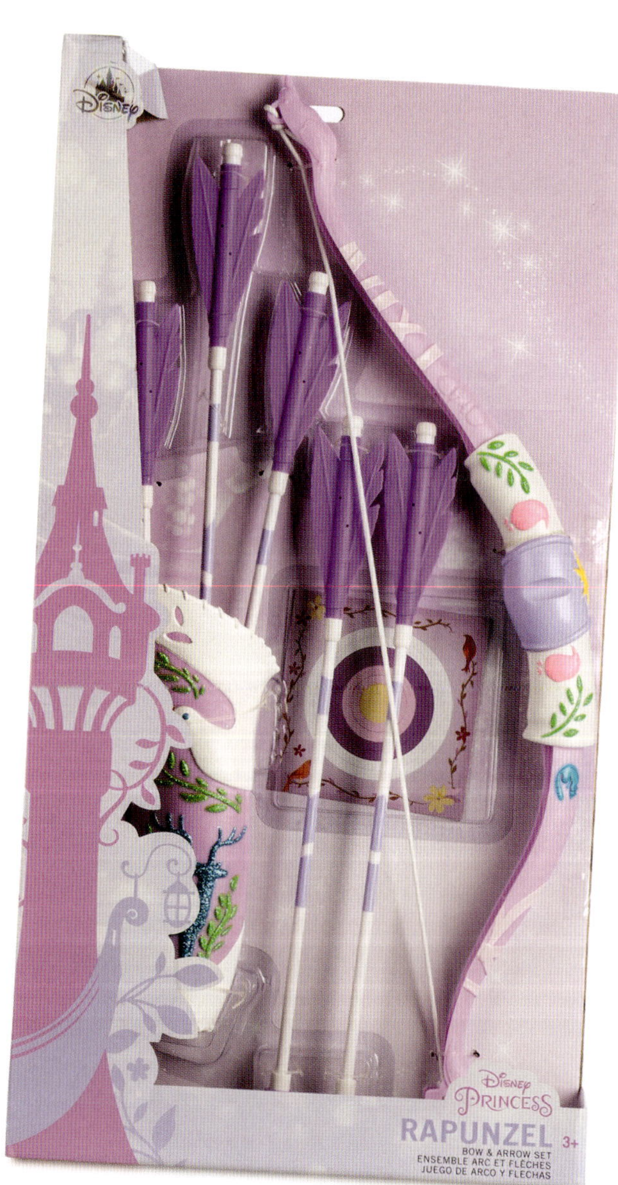

oar, can empower kids, offering inspiration and positivity along with fun.

"That's when the interest in Disney Princesses really took off," Pacheco explains of the Disney Princess franchise. "It allowed us to focus on the idea that 'You too can be a princess. And you can be whatever princess you want.' Everyone has their favorite. You can role-play or dress up as your favorite princess, you can have a princess party, you can have jewelry or makeup or dolls or storybooks. The demand for everything Disney Princess just overwhelmed us."

Elaine Carovilla, Director Commercialization at Disney Parks, Experiences, and Products, has seen that demand continue to grow. "One of the things that's been exciting in the past few years is how The Walt Disney Company has changed what princess means," Carovilla says. "We have morphed and changed and evolved with the culture, and the character qualities reflect today's women. They're evocative of really strong, determined women who are also kind, caring, and doing good in the world. We want each item to be innovative and right for the toy industry. Our toys are competing with all the very best toys out there, but we have something better than that because we are reflecting a film that is the leading voice in pop culture at any given point in time for consumers, and especially for kids."

Many products are designed and made by Disney licensees, although Disney continues to innovate toys from within the company as well. A prime example is the Disney Animator's Collection Dolls, which were inspired by the success of a Tiana toddler doll released in 2009. The Disney Store tapped animators Glen Keane and Mark Henn to bring wide-eyed toddler versions of the Disney Princesses to life using art from the Walt Disney Animation Research Library, as well as their own work on films like *The Little Mermaid* and *The Princess and the Frog*.

"I had them pull a lot of the original concept art that the Disney artists had originally created for this film back in the mid-1930s," Keane told website Jim Hill Media. "And there—on a yellowing piece of paper—I found some drawings for a sequence that they'd discarded for this animated feature which showed Snow White as a toddler right after her father, the king, had died. So I used those concept drawings as my jumping-off point when I was designing the Snow-White-as-a-toddler doll."

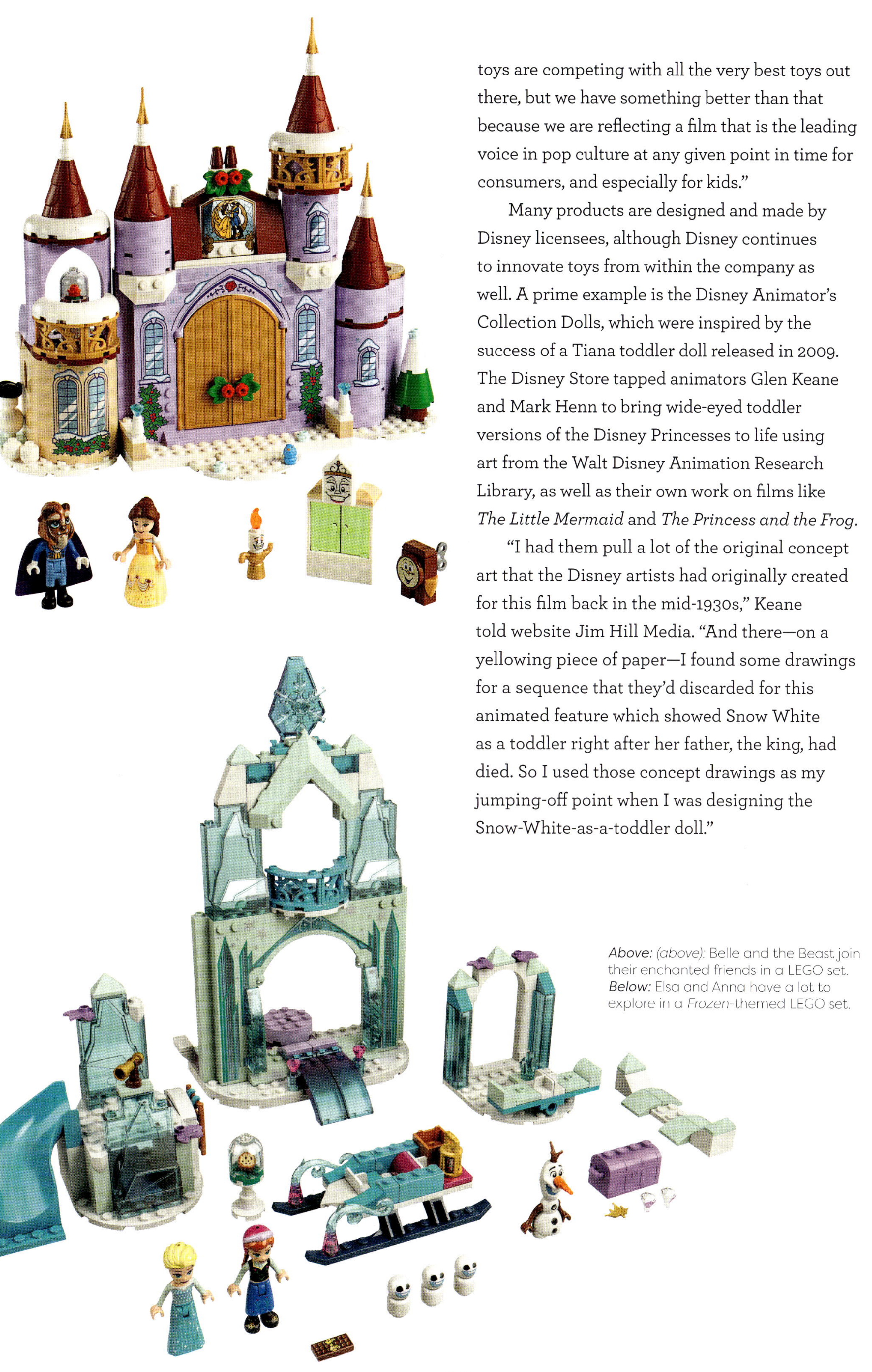

Above: (above): Belle and the Beast join their enchanted friends in a LEGO set. *Below:* Elsa and Anna have a lot to explore in a *Frozen*-themed LEGO set.

While everyone has their favorite Disney Princess toy or game, Carovilla points to the LEGO Disney Princess sets as an important product line because they encourage young girls to engage in toy building. LEGO Disney Princess first arrived in 2014, with six sets initially offered to consumers, including the 646-piece Cinderella's Romantic Castle. Since then, the Disney Princesses, as well as the *Frozen* queens, have been featured in various sets, from Ariel's Undersea Palace to Elsa's Winter Throne to Belle's Castle Winter Celebration. LEGO creates marketing pieces that bring the characters to life—another reason Carovilla finds them so engaging. LEGO's YouTube "Minisode" retelling of films like *Beauty and the Beast* with LEGO bricks give agency to the children, allowing them to create narratives in which the princesses help each other and save the day.

GAMES, GAMES, GAMES

The advent of video games and mobile games has brought the Disney Princess characters to life in many new, dynamic ways. In the 1990s, video games like *Beauty and The Beast: Belle's Quest*, released in 1993 for Sega Mega Drive and Sega Genesis, and 2003's *Disney Princess* for Game Boy Advance, offered actionable retellings of the animated films. More recently, video games have been an opportunity to create brand-new situations and adventures for the Disney Princess characters, rather than simply retelling their original stories.

"As video games continue to grow and evolve as a medium, we've been able to expand the characters' stories, including the Disney Princesses, and give fans all new ways to connect with these very iconic characters," explains

Below and Opposite (top): Rapunzel goes into battle in a *Kingdom Hearts* game.

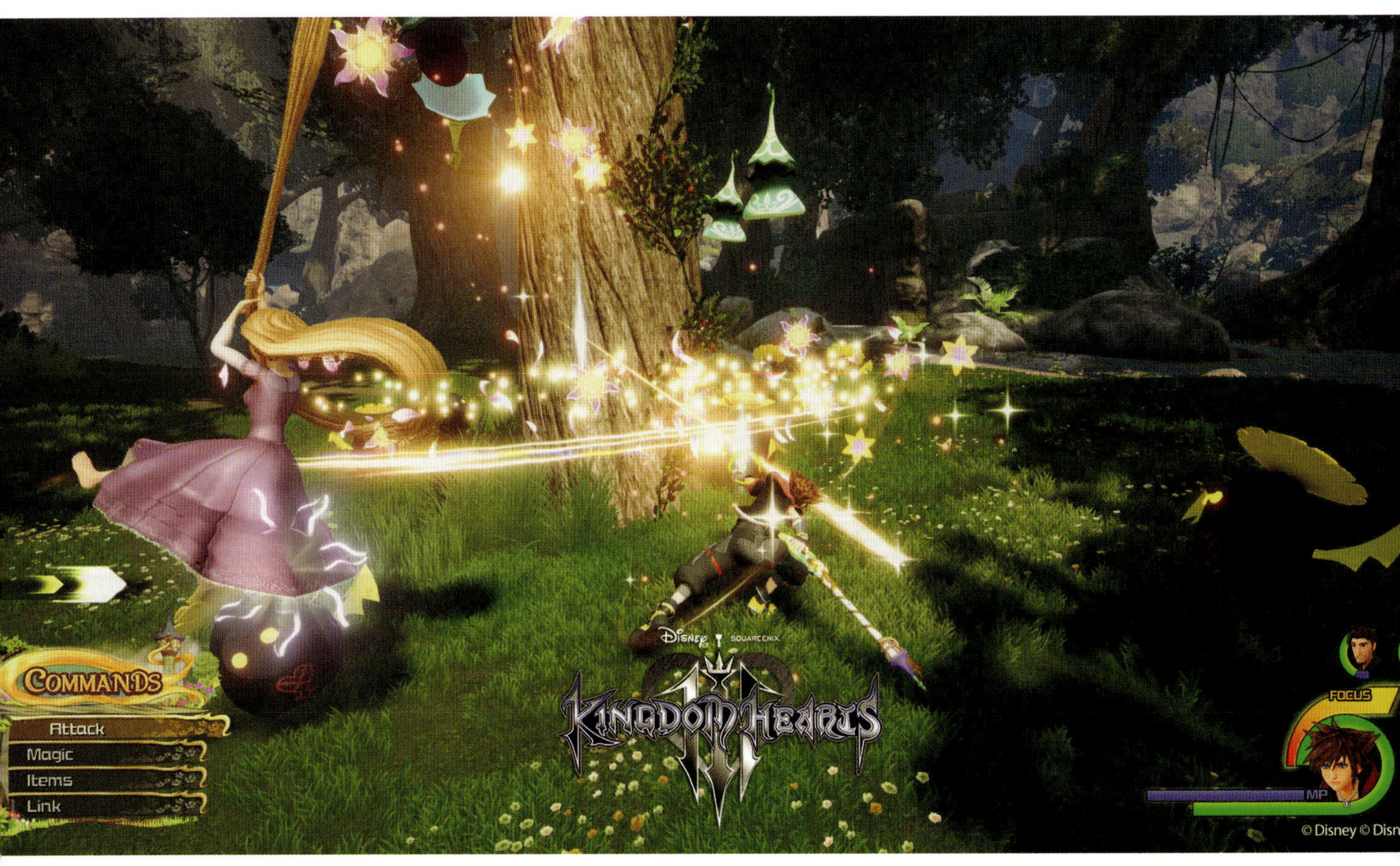

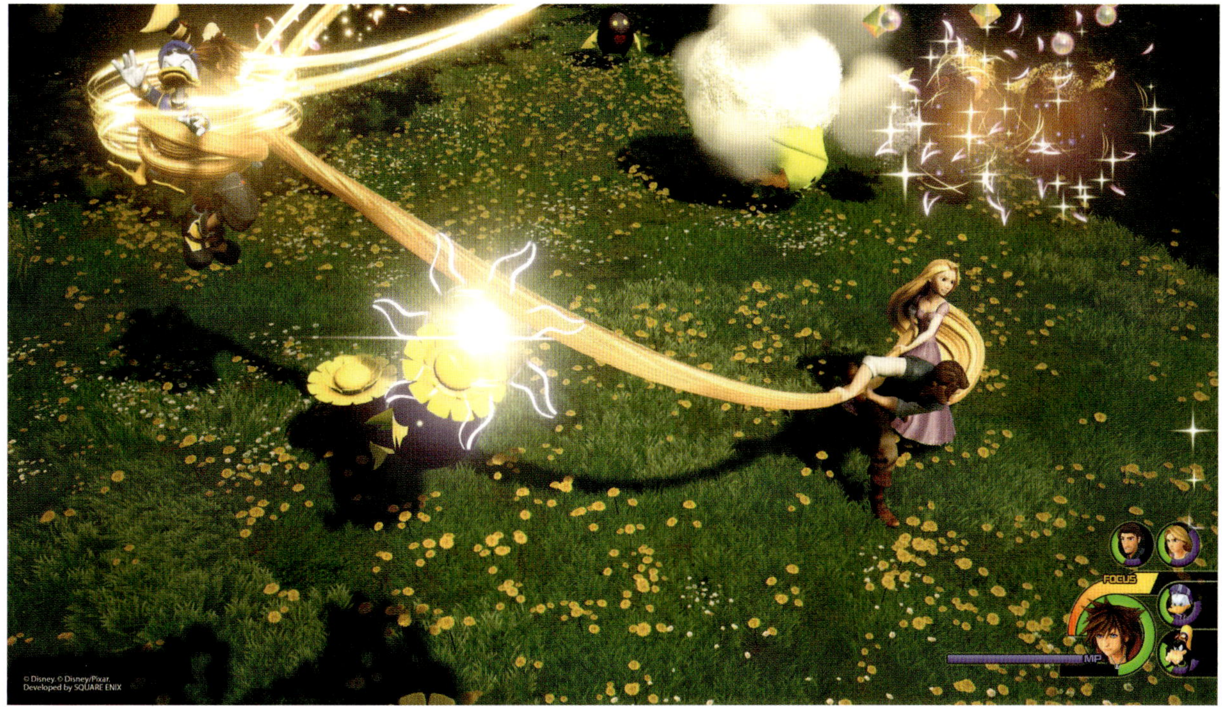

Lauren Preston, Manager of Game Design and Narrative at Disney. "The game worlds the Disney Princesses inhabit create new circumstances to show off their strengths and skills, and also bring the empowered, independent qualities of these fantastic female leads into clear focus."

In 2002, Square Enix debuted *Kingdom Hearts* for PlayStation 2, a crossover video game in a fictional universe featuring several Disney and *Final Fantasy* characters. The protagonist, named Sora, encounters everyone from Goofy to Dumbo in his adventures, and ultimately he's tasked with rescuing the Princesses of Heart—which includes Snow White and Jasmine—from Maleficent. Several sequels have followed, including *Kingdom Hearts III* in 2019 for PlayStation 4, Xbox One, and Microsoft Windows. *Kingdom Hearts III* revised the Princesses of Heart lineup to include Rapunzel, Anna, and Elsa.

While the Disney Princess characters are not the protagonists of the *Kingdom Hearts* series, they have featured more significantly in other video games, including 2008's *Disney*

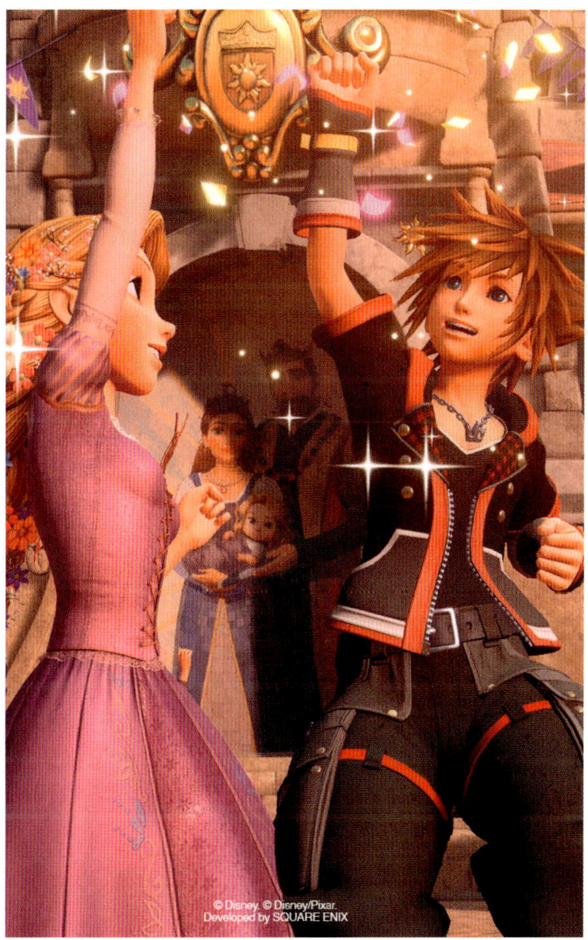

Rapunzel celebrates a victory in *Kingdom Hearts*.

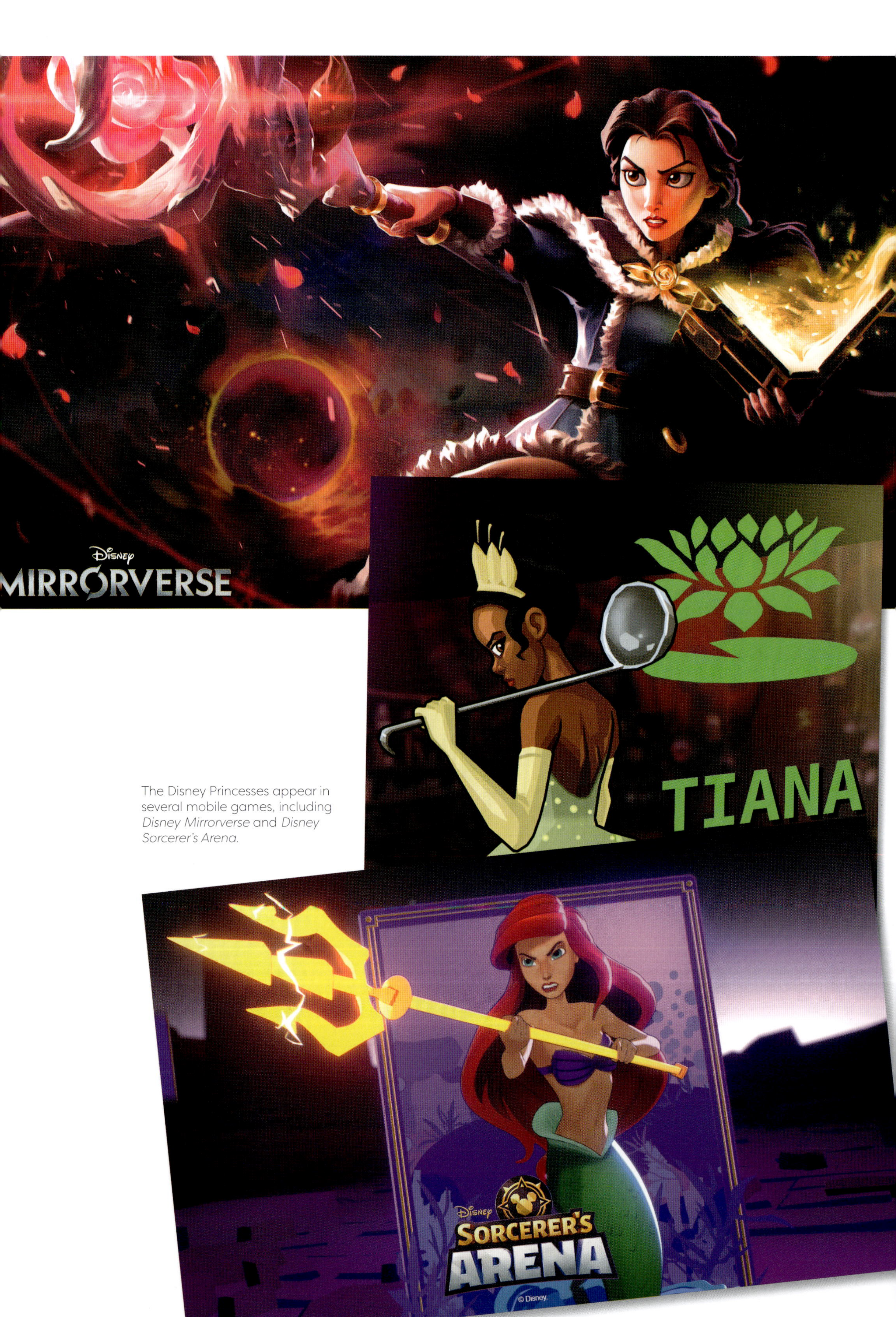

The Disney Princesses appear in several mobile games, including *Disney Mirrorverse* and *Disney Sorcerer's Arena.*

Princess: Enchanted Journey for PC and 2012's *Disney Princess: My Fairytale Adventure* on Wii, Nintendo 3DS, and PC. *Disney Princess Majestic Quest*, released in 2019, encourages players to restore four kingdoms belonging to Jasmine, Belle, Ariel, and Mulan by embarking on mini games and tasks. Elsa and Anna feature in *Disney Frozen Adventures*, a mobile puzzle game released as a tie-in to the storyline of *Frozen II*. By interpreting the princesses into highly expressive emojis, the 2016 mobile game *Disney Emoji Blitz* weaves the princess emojis into players' daily lives of gaming and messaging in a very modern way.

In 2019, Disney unveiled *Disney Sorcerer's Arena*, a crossover mobile role-playing game that allows players to compete as legendary Disney and Pixar characters. One of the most exciting inclusions was Ariel, who fiercely wields her father's trident in battle. The Disney game designers have further expanded on bringing more action to the Disney Princess characters in the mobile role-playing game *Disney Mirrorverse* in 2022. The game evolves several of the princesses, including Belle, Mulan, and Raya, into battle-ready defenders against an unrelenting enemy known as the Fractured.

"We're always trying to take characters and think about them in new ways for adult audiences of today," Preston explains. "We created this deep, expansive alternate universe filled with Disney characters, and the *Disney Mirrorverse* evolutions of our Disney Princesses are especially exciting. They are amplifying their core, authentic characteristics in unexpected and surprising ways."

Video games are an especially immersive medium, which means players may spend hours upon hours with the stories and the characters—not just as an audience member but as an actual participant. "Games are super special in that you get to control what's happening," Preston notes. "When Disney fans play Disney games, they are part of the story. As the princesses outwit and defeat challenges with their skills and powerful abilities, that's a very relatable moment for contemporary fans. They are at the heart of the action, and it gets people closer to those characters that they love. The Disney princesses have so much to offer in games storytelling, and also as actively connective heroes in the player experience."

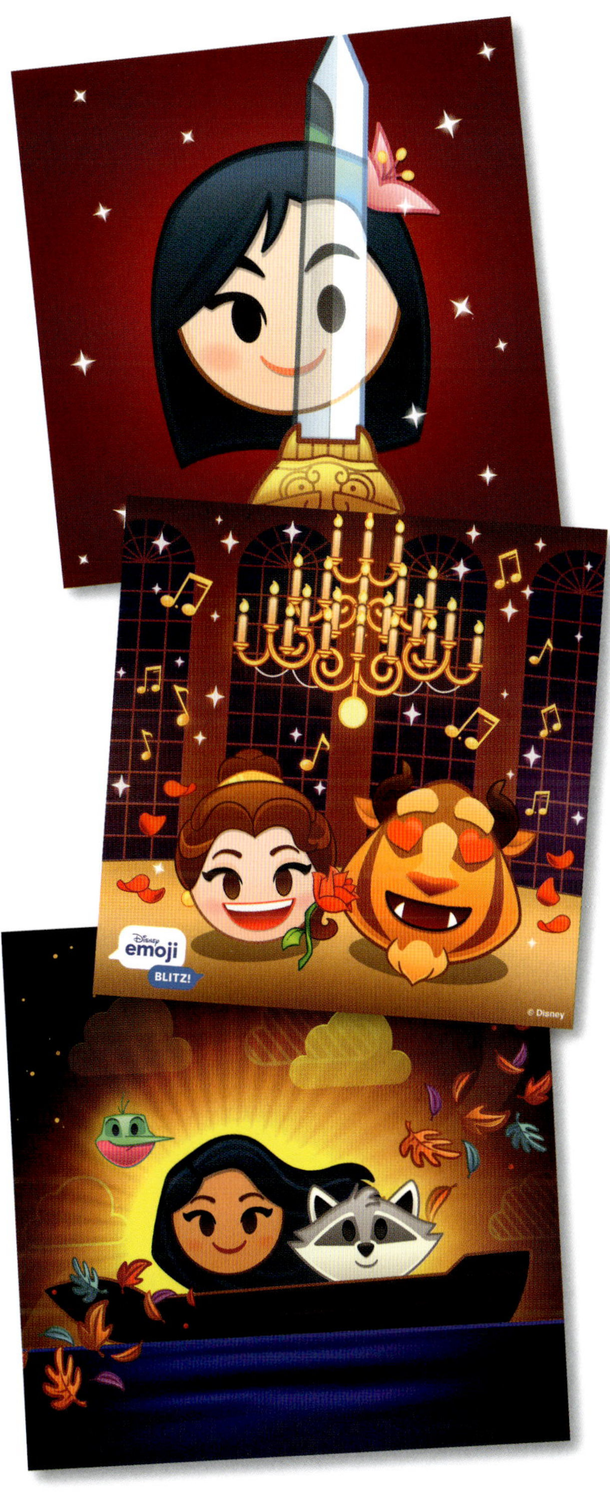

The Disney princess characters in *Disney Emoji Blitz*.

Limited Edition Stamps

Not all collectibles have to come at a high price or be vintage to be valuable. Disney has had a relationship with the U.S. Postal Service since 1918 when Walt sorted and delivered mail for the Chicago Post Office (Mickey Mouse later also worked for the Post Office in a 1933 animated short titled *The Mail Pilot*). The first official Disney stamp was released in 1968, showcasing Walt with a group of children of the world in front of a castle, and Snow White appeared on a 32-cent stamp in 1998 as part of the "Celebrate the Century" stamp series. Dave Pacheco understood this appeal when he launched the "The Art of Disney" stamp series with USPS in 2003, working with artist Peter Emmerich. To date, it's the most collected stamp series in history, with 211.5 million sets purchased by Disney lovers.

Five different "The Art of Disney" collections were released between 2004 and 2008 under themes like "Romance" and "Imagination." These were so popular that USPS rejoined with Disney in 2012 for a Pixar stamp set, which saw 125 million stamps printed, and again in 2017 for a Villains series, which paid tribute to traditional ink and paint as applied on animation cels. Pacheco and Emmerich designed a similar Disney Princess series, also done as a tribute to ink and paint animation, for release in 2019, but USPS canceled the series before the stamps were made public. The original artwork for those unreleased Disney Princess stamps is now preserved in the Walt Disney Archives, and shown here publicly for the first time.

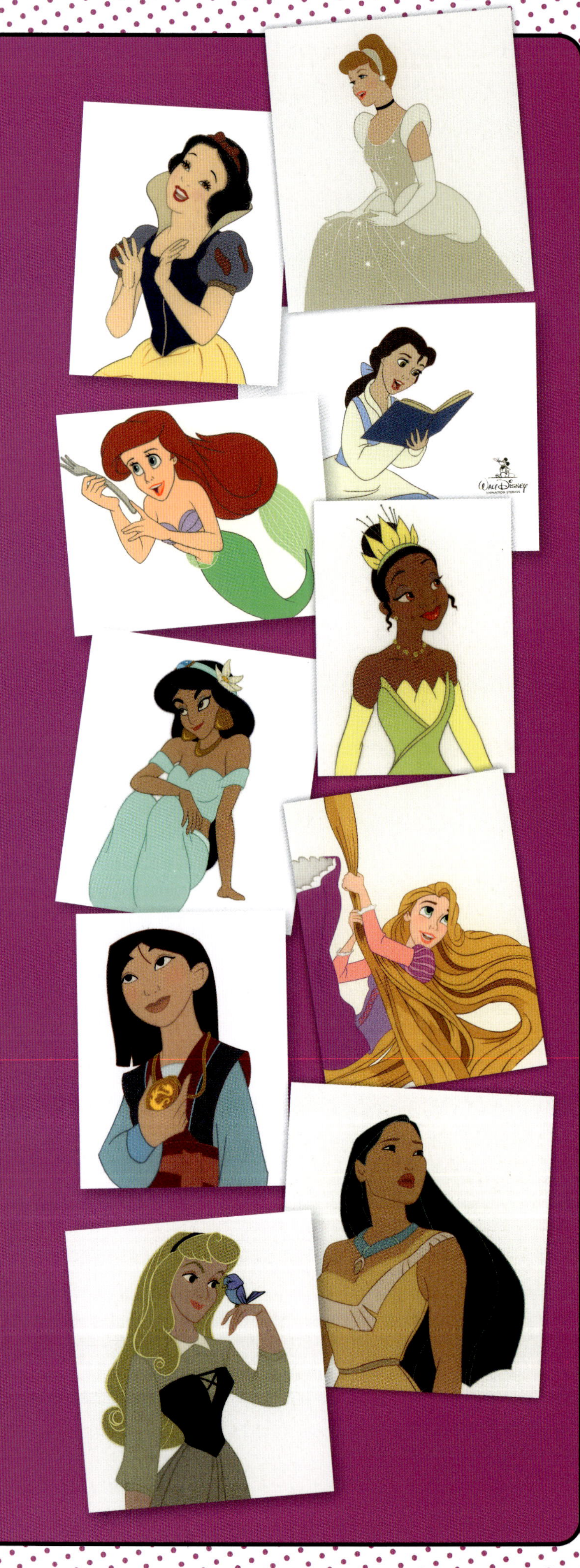

The previously-unseen concept art for Disney Princess postage stamps, which were never released.

DISNEYANA AND COLLECTIBLES

While many early Disney products were crafted as collectible items, collecting Disneyana, the term for any items associated with The Walt Disney Company, has grown exponentially in the past few decades. Shortly after Disneyland Park opened in 1955, it featured a shop in Tomorrowland called The Art Corner, which remained open until 1966 when the area was renovated. The store sold souvenirs and Disneyana items, but it was most notable as an outlet for Disney animation artwork, including cels and background paintings. Similar animation cels had first become available in 1937 on the sales market through San Francisco art gallery Courvoisier, which sold animation art for *Snow White*, but The Art Corner provided a more accessible venue for collectors.

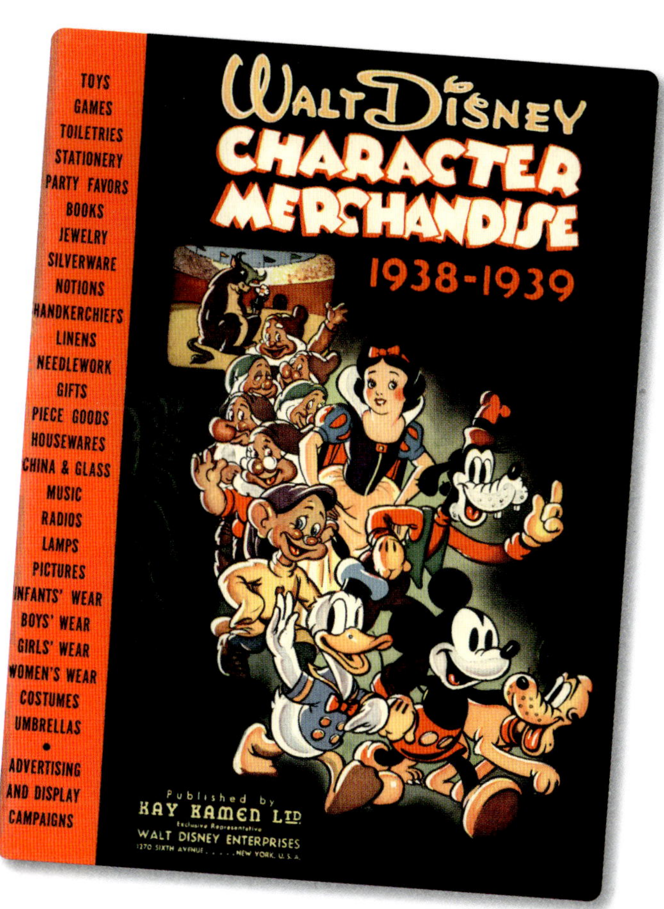

Above: A Walt Disney Character Merchandise catalogue created by Kay Kamen. *Below:* The Disneyana shop on Main Street, U.S.A. at Disneyland.

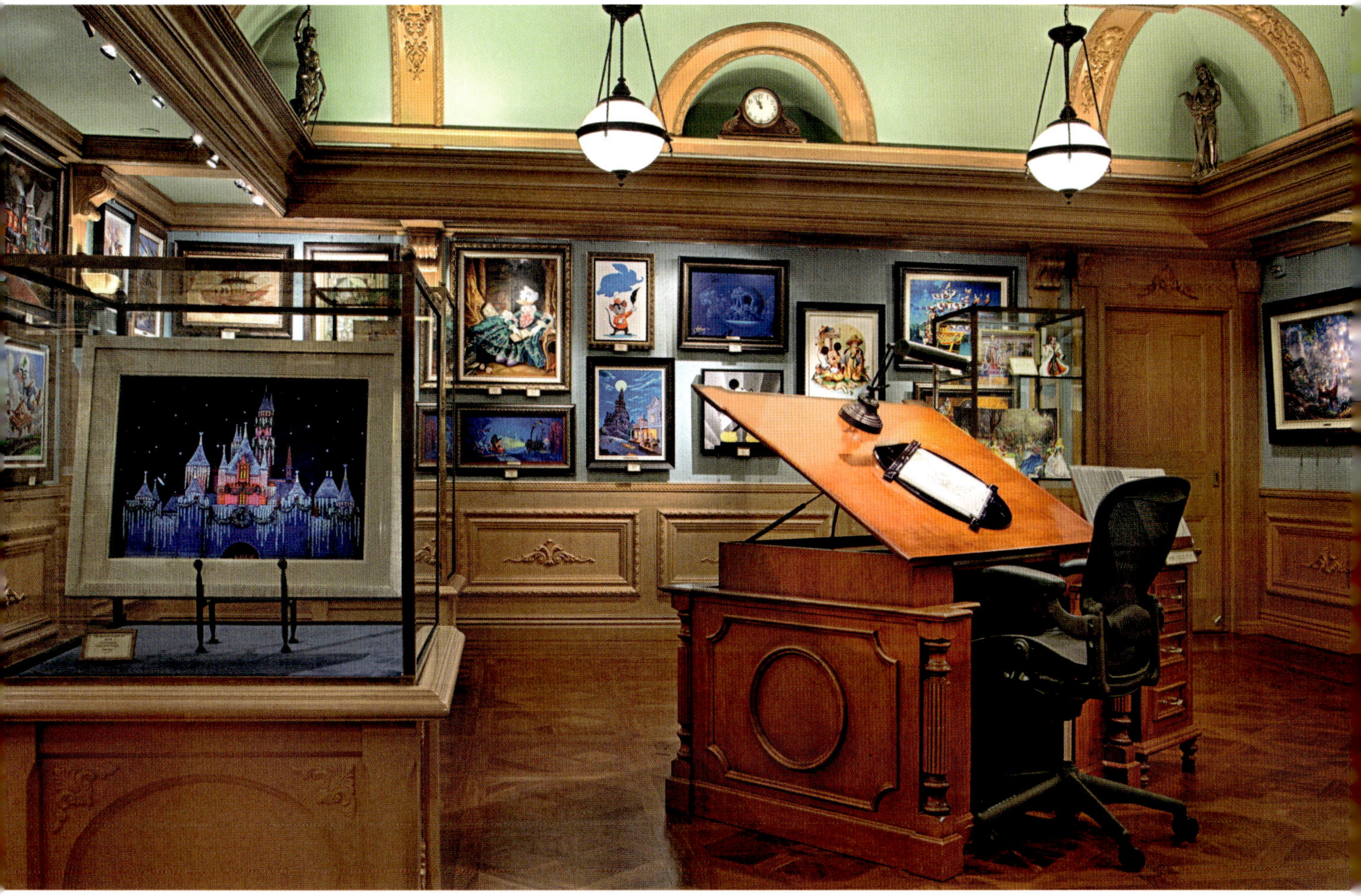

Eras of Film Posters

There are a lot of ways to market a film, but movie posters are one of the most iconic. *Snow White and the Seven Dwarfs* had one of the biggest promotional campaigns in the history of cinema, with a variety of posters, lobby cards, standees, and banners created for movie theaters. The original release poster, which announced Walt Disney's "first full length feature production," was designed by illustrator Gustaf Tenggren. *Cinderella's* poster declared the film to be the "Greatest since *Snow White*," while *Sleeping Beauty* was advertised as "Wondrous to see... Glorious to hear..."

Today, these vintage posters sell for thousands of dollars, while early posters for *The Little Mermaid* go for hundreds. For many people, the posters create a nostalgic feeling, reconnecting them to that first moment when they experienced a magical Disney film in a darkened movie theater.

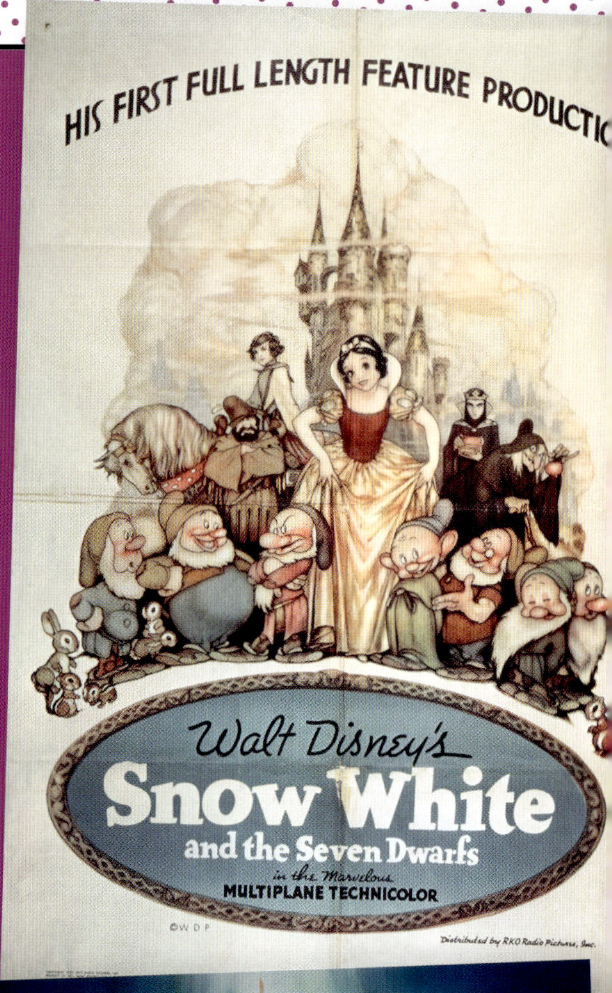

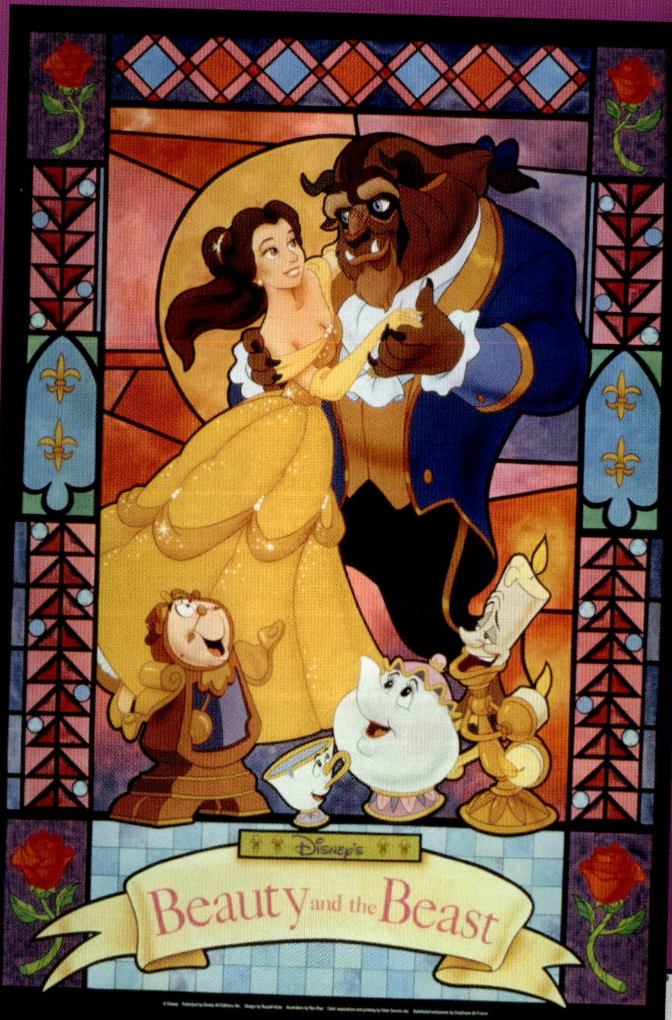

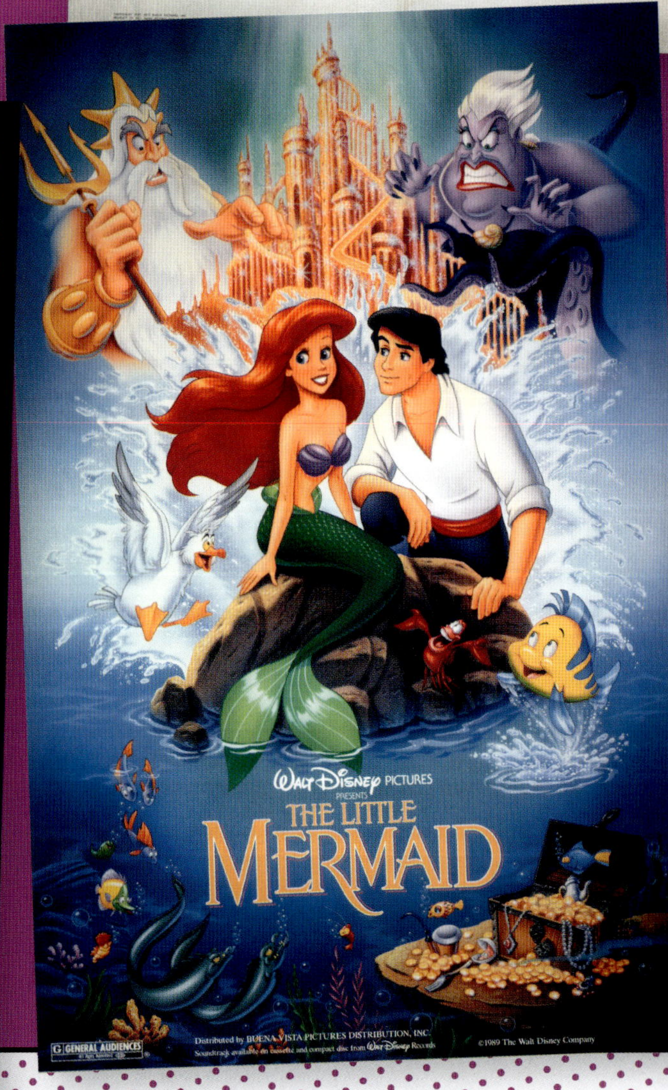

Original theatrical movie posters released for Disney Princess films.

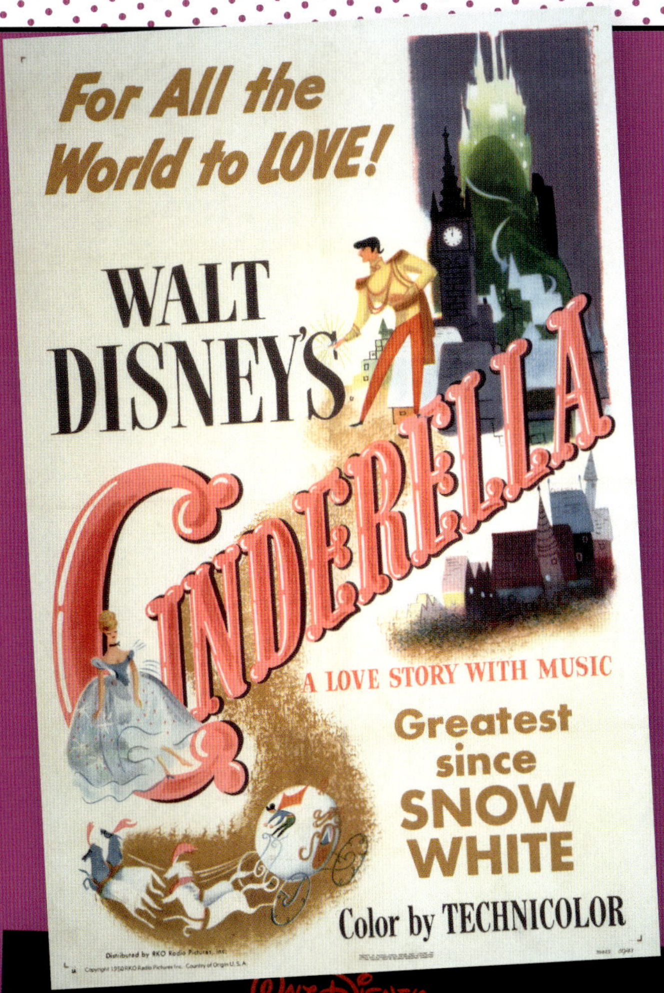

For All the World to LOVE!

WALT DISNEY'S

CINDERELLA

A LOVE STORY WITH MUSIC

Greatest since SNOW WHITE

Color by TECHNICOLOR

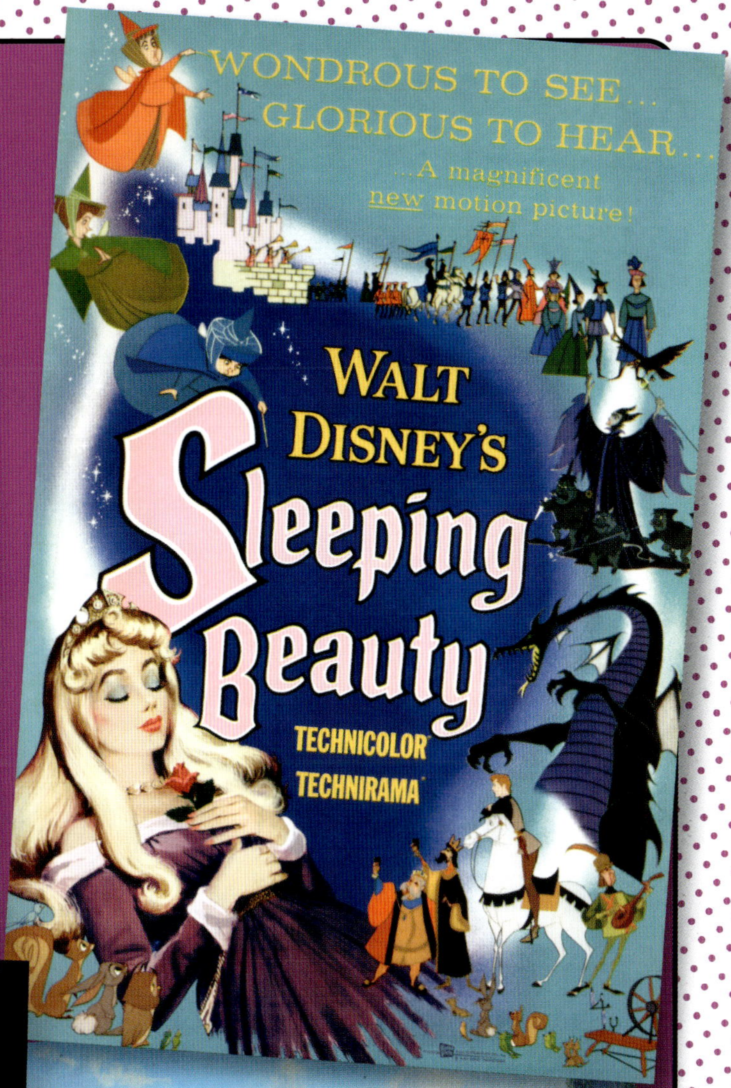

WONDROUS TO SEE...
GLORIOUS TO HEAR...
...A magnificent new motion picture!

WALT DISNEY'S

Sleeping Beauty

TECHNICOLOR

TECHNIRAMA

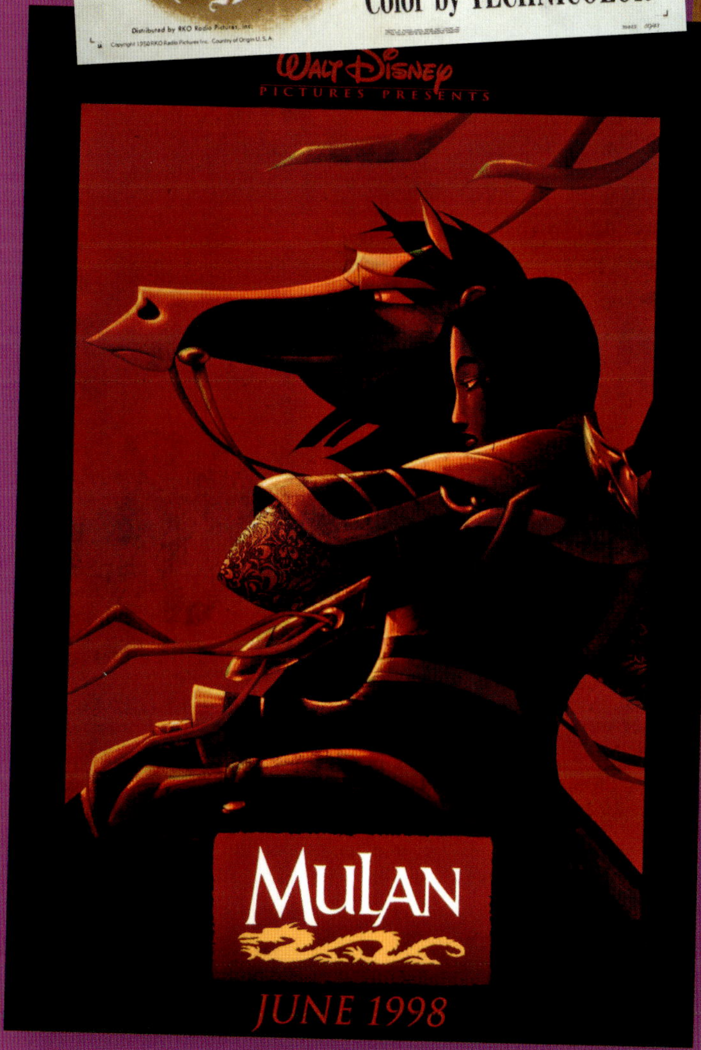

WALT DISNEY PICTURES PRESENTS

MULAN

JUNE 1998

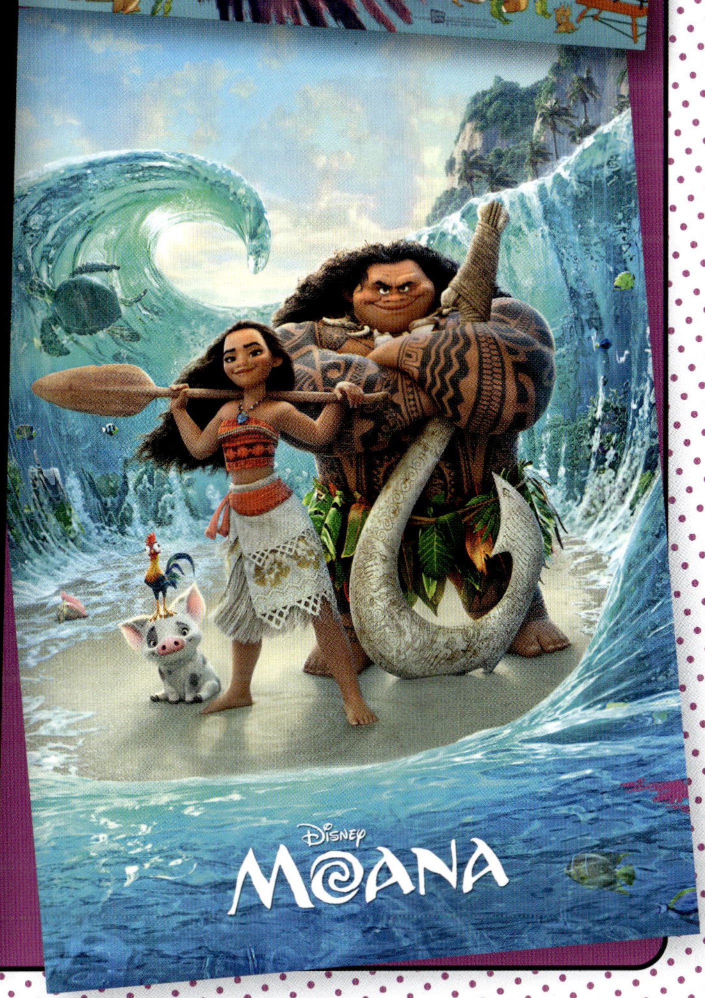

DISNEY

MOANA

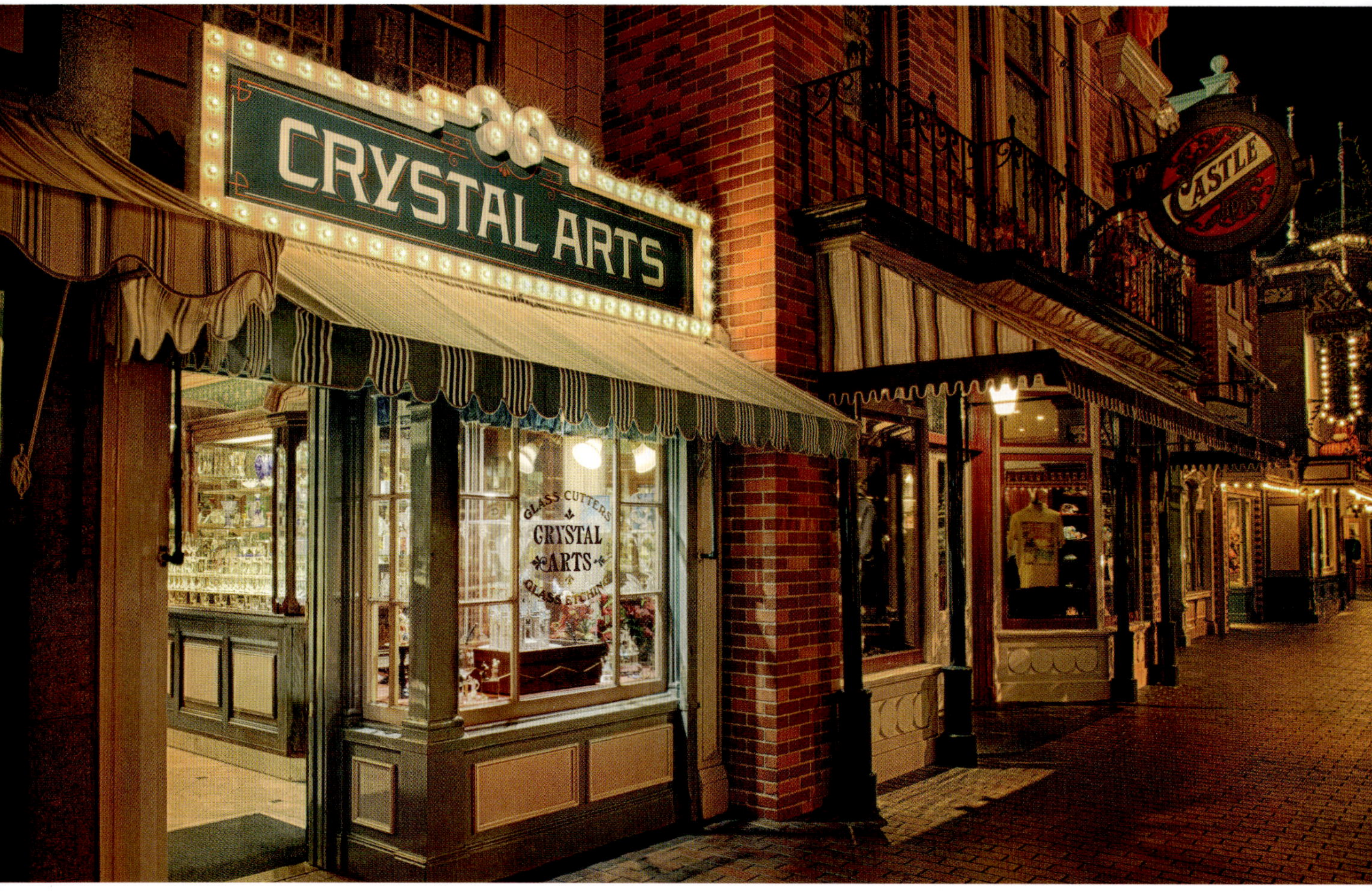

The Crystal Arts shop at Disneyland, on Main Street, U.S.A.

The shop hosted an exhibition called "The Art of Animation" in 1960 to promote *Sleeping Beauty*, and a significant amount of animation art from the film was available to buy.

The term "Disneyana" was used informally by collectors before Cecil Munsey published *Disneyana: Walt Disney Collectibles* in 1974. The book, a history of Disney merchandising, lit the fuse for collectible items, with fans beginning to recognize that Disney products had the potential to be viewed as an art form rather than something gathering dust in the attic. In 1976, Disneyland opened its Disneyana Shop on Main Street, U.S.A., selling limited edition and collectible merchandise (a Disneyana Shop also opened in the Magic Kingdom at Walt Disney World in 1983 in Fantasyland, and in Disneyland Paris in 1992). The Walt Disney Classics Collection, launched in 1992, includes figurines designed in conjunction with the animators, using the original colors from the studio's ink and paint department, and Disney formed the Walt Disney Collectors Society in 1993 to celebrate their love of the pieces.

Unofficially, the Disneyana Fan Club has existed since 1984 and now has twenty-four chapters around the world. It hosts the annual Disneyana Collectibles Show and Sale, where members buy and sell rare items. Today, there are dedicated Facebook groups for Disney collectors and eBay is filled with vintage dolls, figurines, and old games. At a given time, there is always someone looking for a specific item created around a Disney film or character. And when it comes to Disney collectibles, their value isn't always defined by rarity or cost.

"In Disneyana collecting, the strongest demand is often generated by people wishing to obtain items of special interest," Tom Tumbusch wrote in *Tomart's Illustrated Disneyana*. He added, "Character popularity, crossovers to other collecting fields (such as pocket knives, plates, dolls, books, etc.), and the type of item (anything showing a camera, Santa Claus, or telephone, for example) may become stronger factors."

Devoted Disney collectors don't usually focus exclusively on Disney Princess items, but there are groups who seek out items from specific films, particularly *Snow White and the Seven Dwarfs*, or who focus on Disney character dolls. Two such collectors, Mario Menendez and Lazaro Roque, were featured in the press in 2017 for their collection of hundreds of Disney dolls, worth over $65,000. Another collector, Nick Theodoulou, has dozens of limited edition dolls, mostly Belle, and noted in an interview that he loves "the way the dolls capture their characters and bring them to life." Disney Princess Funko dolls and the adorable Disney Princess Comics Minis (based on Amy Mebberson's Disney Princess comics) have a similarly impassioned following.

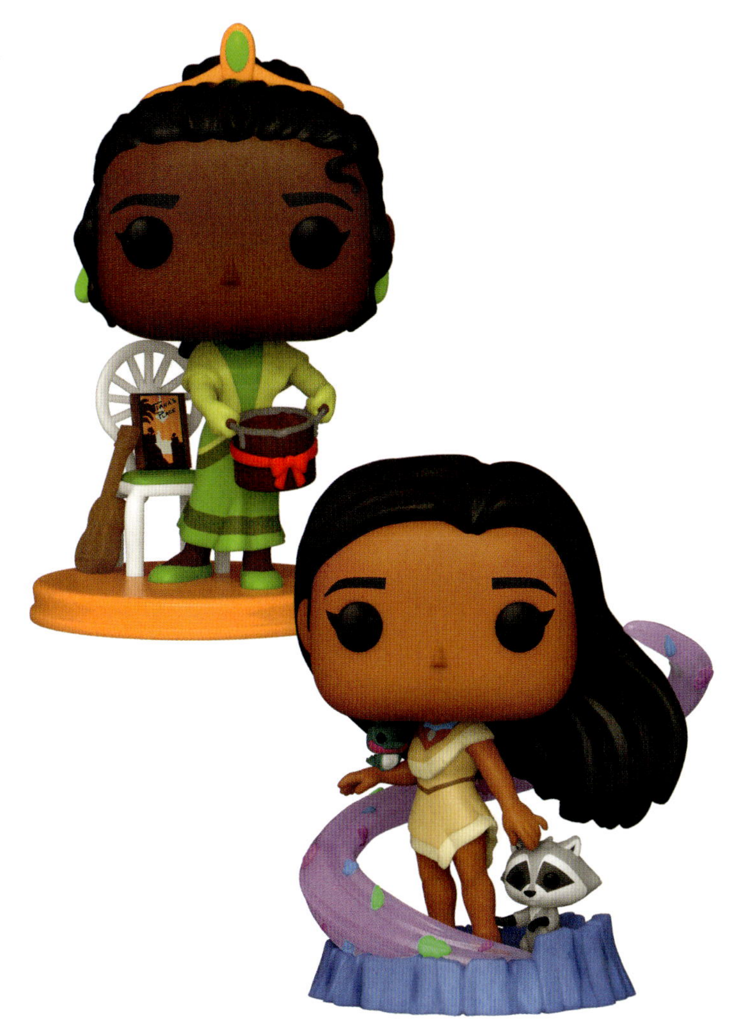

Above: Disney Princess Funko dolls are popular collectibles. *Below:* Mario Menendez and Lazaro Roque have collected hundreds of official Disney dolls.

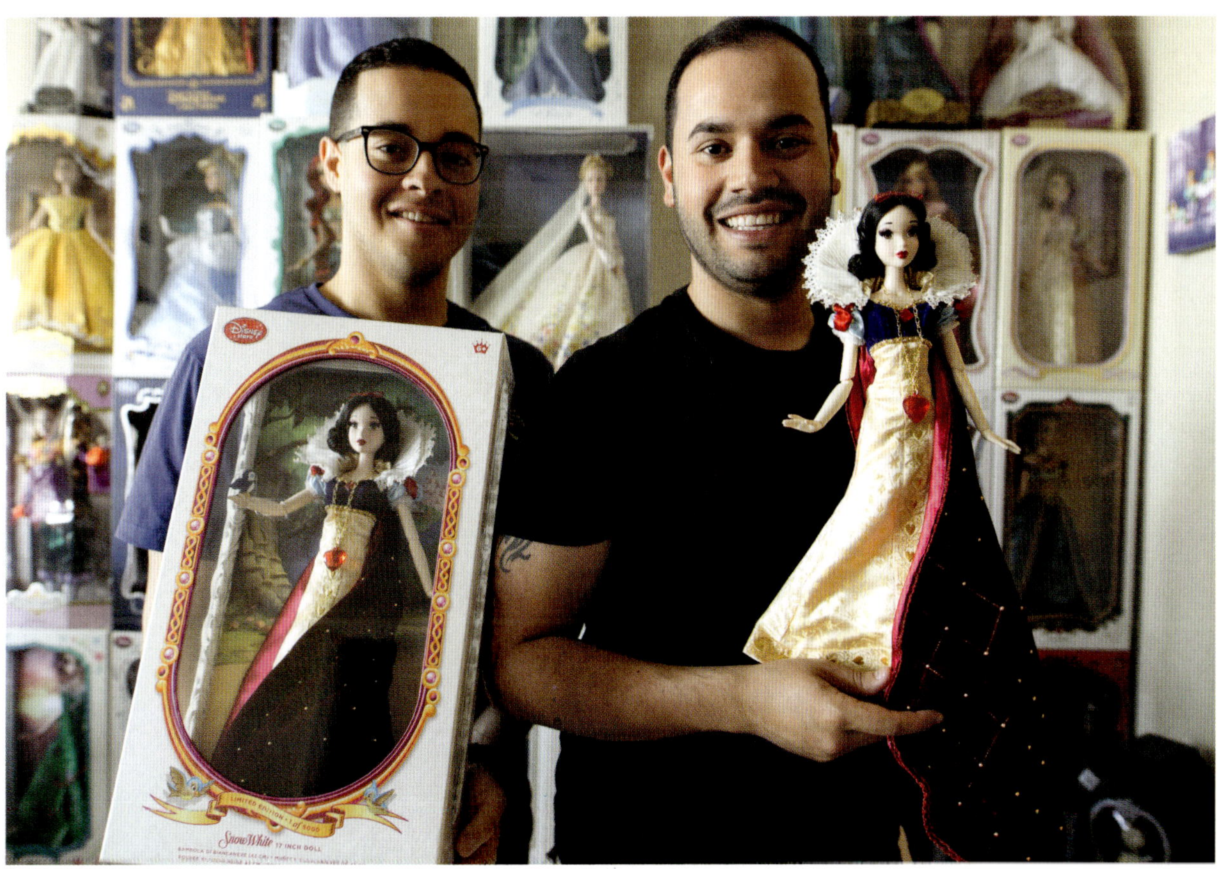

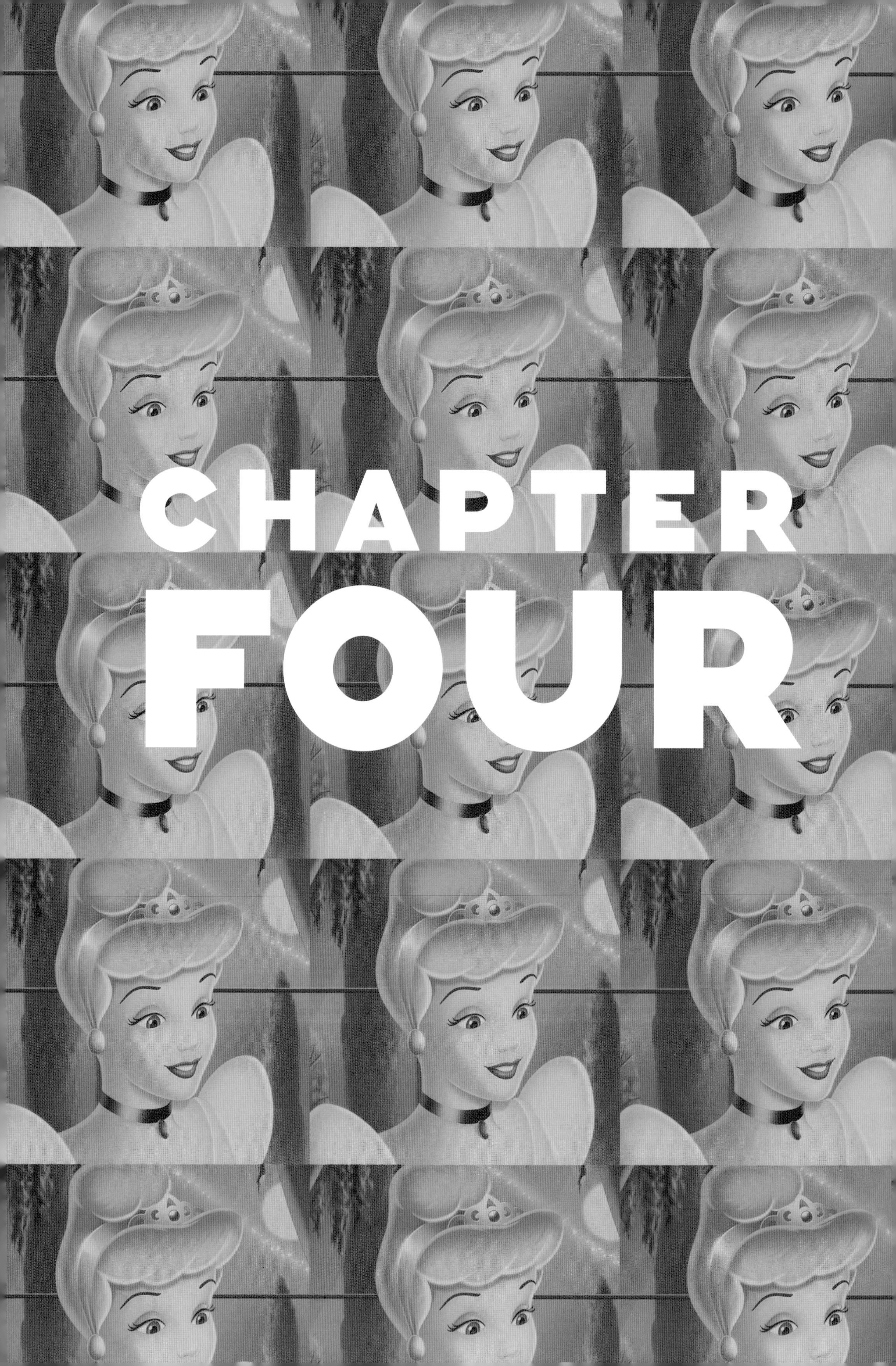

CHAPTER FOUR

BIBBIDI-BOBBIDI-BOO

FASHION

Each Disney Princess has a unique style. Cinderella wears an icy-blue ballgown, Ariel a chic purple shell bikini top, and Tiana a bayou-inspired green dress. Each ensemble is memorable in its own way and has become part of the iconography of fashion. The animated looks come from a variety of sources—historical, contemporary, and fantasy—and Disney Princess fashion is now almost a genre of style unto itself.

"The power of Walt Disney's imagination was global and hugely influential," explains fashion designer Zac Posen, who has created several Cinderella-inspired pieces. "When Walt Disney and the animators were building the characters, there was so much of the fashion plate of the time. You can see the references to the fashion of the time mixed with the historical time period of the story. And these characters were hugely impactful. I think nonliving creations can sometimes become even more powerful than living imagery."

Over the decades, Disney Princess fashion has played out in several different ways, both in official collaborations with designers and brands, and through imaginative, unofficial homages. Each year, Disney Consumer Products partners with licensees to create innovative apparel, accessories, jewelry, and home goods based on the Disney Princesses and their stories. These can be more obvious pieces, like a Belle-inspired Disney's Fairy Tale Weddings & Honeymoons gown, or more subtle, like adidas' *The Little Mermaid* sneaker collection or TOMS Disney Collection shoes.

"There's a princess for everyone and there are women from all walks of life, with all kinds of styles and design aesthetics," Karen Torpey, Director Licensing, Princess and Fairies at Disney Consumer Products, notes. "What I love about the princesses is that you can be inspired by many things. Yes, there are ballgowns, but there are also characters and their personalities and stories, or key movie moments or scenes to be inspired by."

Because the Disney Princesses' animated costumes always convey a sense of magic and color, that plays into how designers and brands interpret the clothing, whether it's a red-carpet

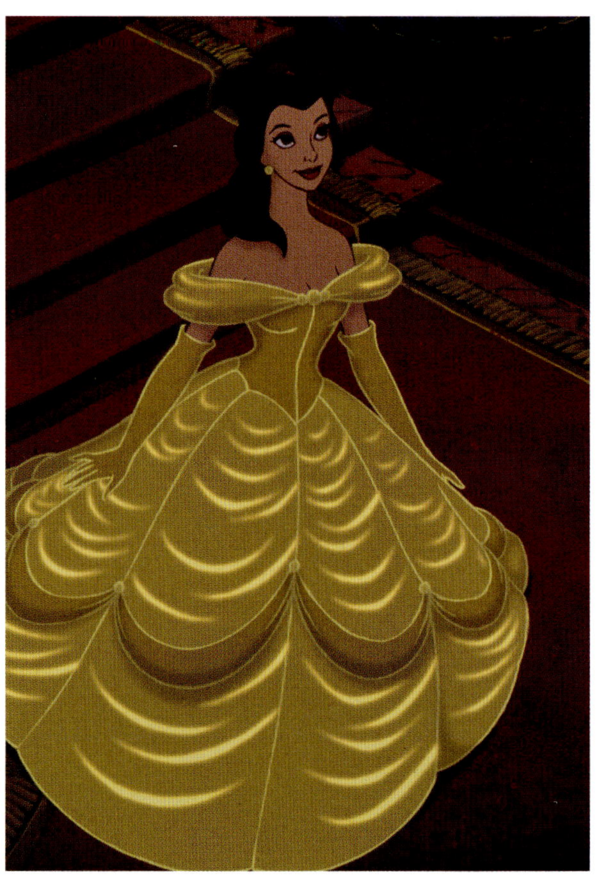

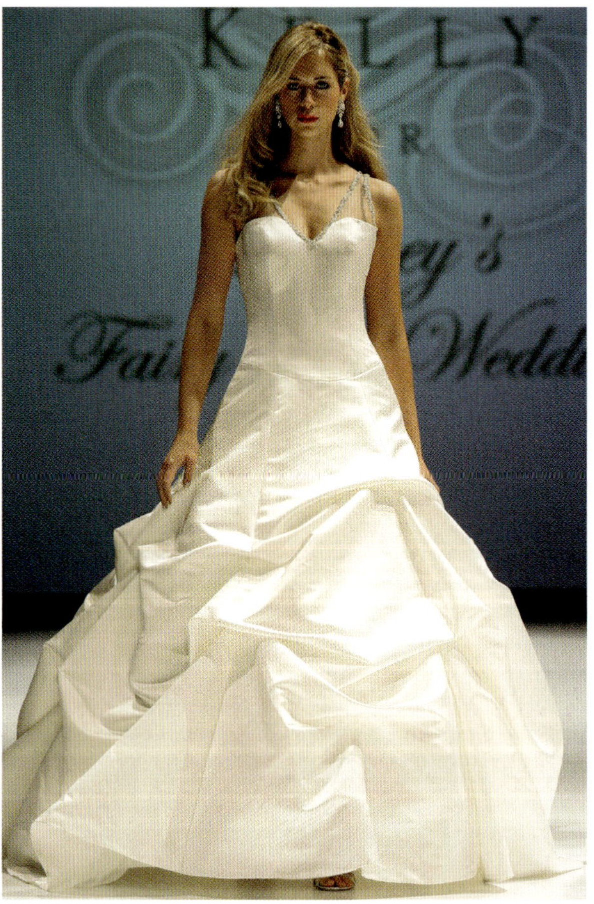

Right (top): Belle's gold ballgown has become an icon for fashion designers. *Right (bottom):* A Belle-inspired wedding gown by Kirstie Kelly. *Opposite:* Elsa's beloved blue cape in *Frozen 2* has inspired fashion lovers.

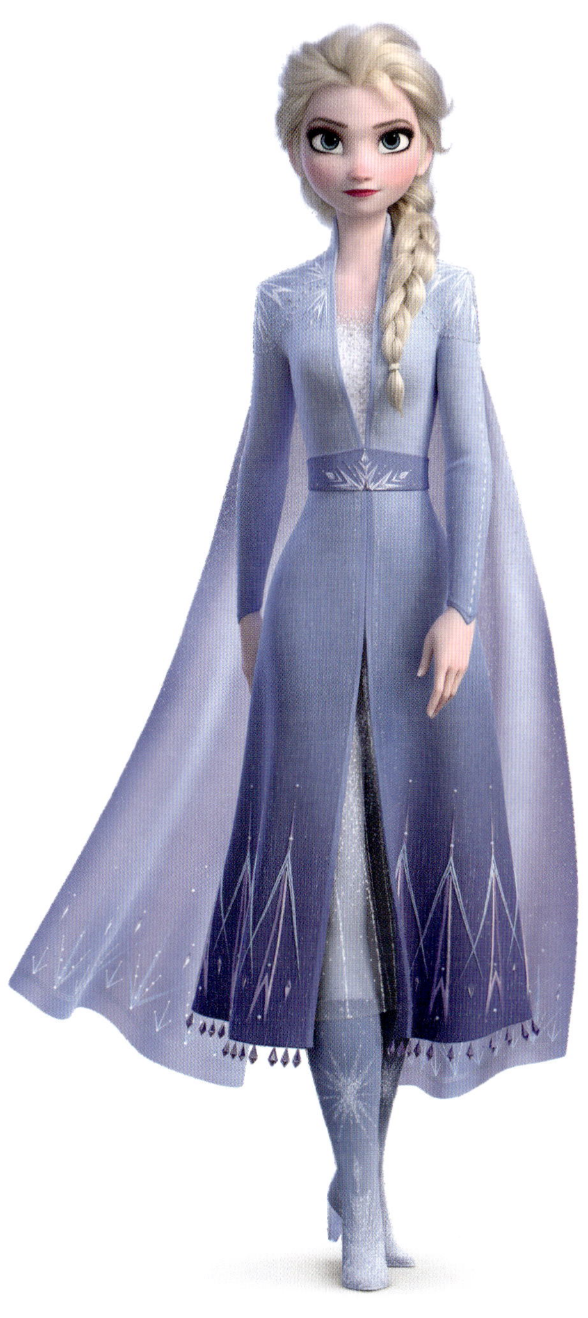

gown or a t-shirt. By wearing ensembles similar to those of a Disney Princess, one can evoke the vibrant world of a Disney film and the aura of that princess.

"The crossover with fashion and a Disney Princess is this idea of a fairy tale and a dream," explains Bethan Holt, Fashion News and Features Director at the *Daily Telegraph*. "When you watch a Disney film, you're entering into this dream world. And that's what fashion does as well, whether that's a catwalk show, or whether it's walking into a shop and putting on a dress that makes you feel like a different person."

Designer Christopher Kane, who created a line of *Beauty and the Beast*-inspired looks, also made this correlation. "Where would we be, as fashion people, without fantasy?" the designer said in an interview with *ELLE*. "We fuel our whole industry on it. And for most of us—definitely for me—Disney was one of the first places to give us images of fantasy. They run on dreams, and daydreams, don't they? So do we."

More recent heroes, like Merida and Moana, wear costumes based largely on historical and cultural research, although the animators and visual development artists always use a variety of sources to ensure a character's look feels genuine. Thinking back, however, it's easy to see how the fashions of a particular era inspired the costumes and beauty looks of Disney Princesses like Snow White, Aurora, and Ariel. "It was about what was happening culturally and in terms of fashion and women's looks at the time," notes Dave Pacheco. "That was very influential as to how the princesses were going to look."

Thanks to the careful efforts of the filmmakers, it's fair to say the Disney Princesses are style icons in their own right. Holt even uses the princesses as a reference point when writing about red-carpet style or a new designer collection. This is true for the *Frozen* queens, as well, particularly Elsa, who is now synonymous with blue sparkles. It's no accident that after the release of *Frozen*, capes appeared on the runways.

"As a fashion journalist, when you're watching a fashion show, you're always looking for 'Where has this come from?'" Holt notes. "Whether it's on a conscious level or a subconscious level. When a huge film like *Frozen* comes out, of course if you see a cape or blue sparkles, you think about it, even if the designer themselves didn't necessarily think they were making that reference. It's all part of the cultural zeitgeist."

ART IMITATING STYLE

The stories may have been set centuries in the past, but the style in films like *Snow White and the Seven Dwarfs, Cinderella,* and even *The Little Mermaid* reflected what was fashionable at the time they were made. Snow White's work dress evoked the Peter Pan collars and puffed sleeves of the 1930s. Her pencil-thin eyebrows mirrored those of popular film stars Claudette Colbert and Jean Harlow, as did her rosy cheeks and ruby-red lips. Her wavy bob, tied up with a bow, was seen on actresses like Loretta Young and child stars like Shirley Temple. The character's primary costume, in blue, red, and yellow, suggested a sixteenth century influence. But it was the smaller details that reminded the viewer of what was elegant in 1937.

Similarly, the visual design of Cinderella and her clothes reflected the postwar era. Disney began work in earnest on *Cinderella* in the late 1940s, a few years after the culmination of World War II. Around that same time, in 1947, fashion designer Christian Dior debuted a collection he dubbed the "New Look," a style that emphasized femininity and opulence. "New Look" ensembles were defined by cinched waists, rounded shoulders, and voluminous skirts, all of which stood in direct contrast to the stark fashion of the war era. After years of rationing, including that of clothing and fabric, the public was starved for these embellished pieces. Dior described his ideal customer as "flowerlike women, with rounded shoulders, full feminine busts, and hand-span waists above enormous spreading skirts." That description feels akin to the shimmering ballgown created by Cinderella's Fairy Godmother.

Cinderella's ballgown was conceived and animated as silver, although we now assume it is pale blue because that's how the dress looks as Cinderella dances in the moonlight. There are glimmers of historical court dress in the design, but ultimately Cinderella evokes contemporary couture as she appears at the ball. "Cinderella

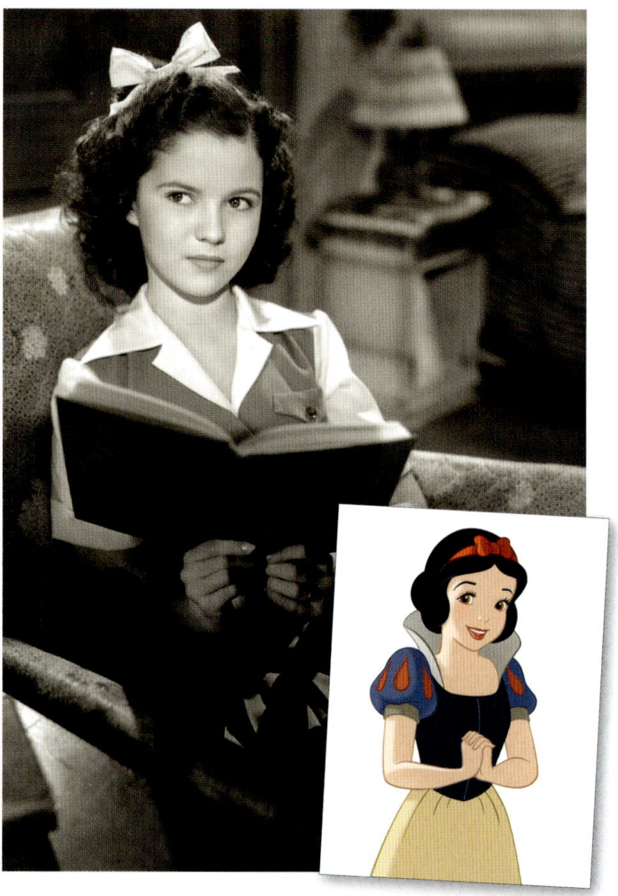

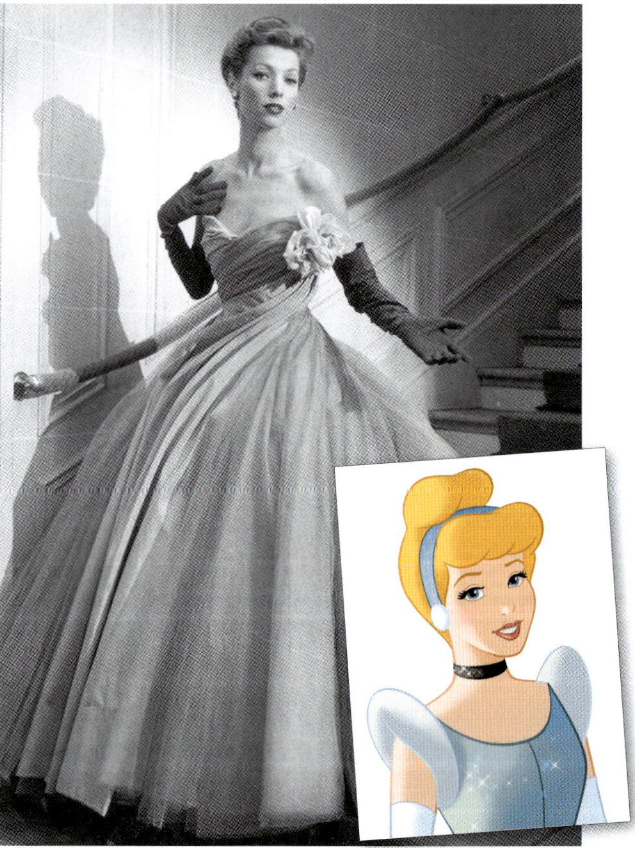

Above (top): Shirley Temple wears a hair bow similar to Snow White's. *Above (bottom):* A Christian Dior "New Look" gown from 1953.

may be living in a nineteenth century French chateau, but her ballgown is pure 1950s Dior," notes Jill Breznican, Senior Archivist at the Walt Disney Animation Research Library.

Sleeping Beauty, created a few years later, appears rooted in medieval Europe, but there are several details that suggest the animators were also taking cues from the 1950s. Aurora's everyday dress has a pointed white collar, a detail straight out of mid-century patterns, and its mid-length brown skirt reflected current silhouettes. "Aurora's dress, with the pointed collar, is a stylization of a 1950's portrait collar, similar to one Audrey Hepburn wore in *Roman Holiday*, her first film," Pacheco explains. Aurora's iconic gown, which transforms from

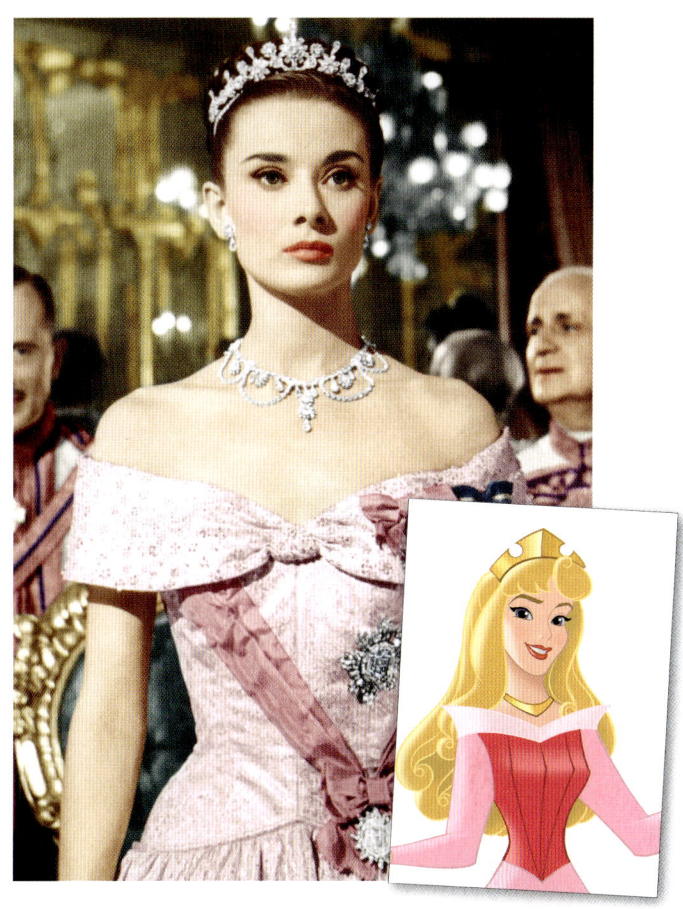

Right: Audrey Hepburn in a colorized still from the film *Roman Holiday*. *Right inset:* Aurora's iconic dress with its deep V collar. *Below:* Princess Diana at her wedding to Prince Charles. *Below inset:* A concept sketch for Ariel's wedding dress in *The Little Mermaid*.

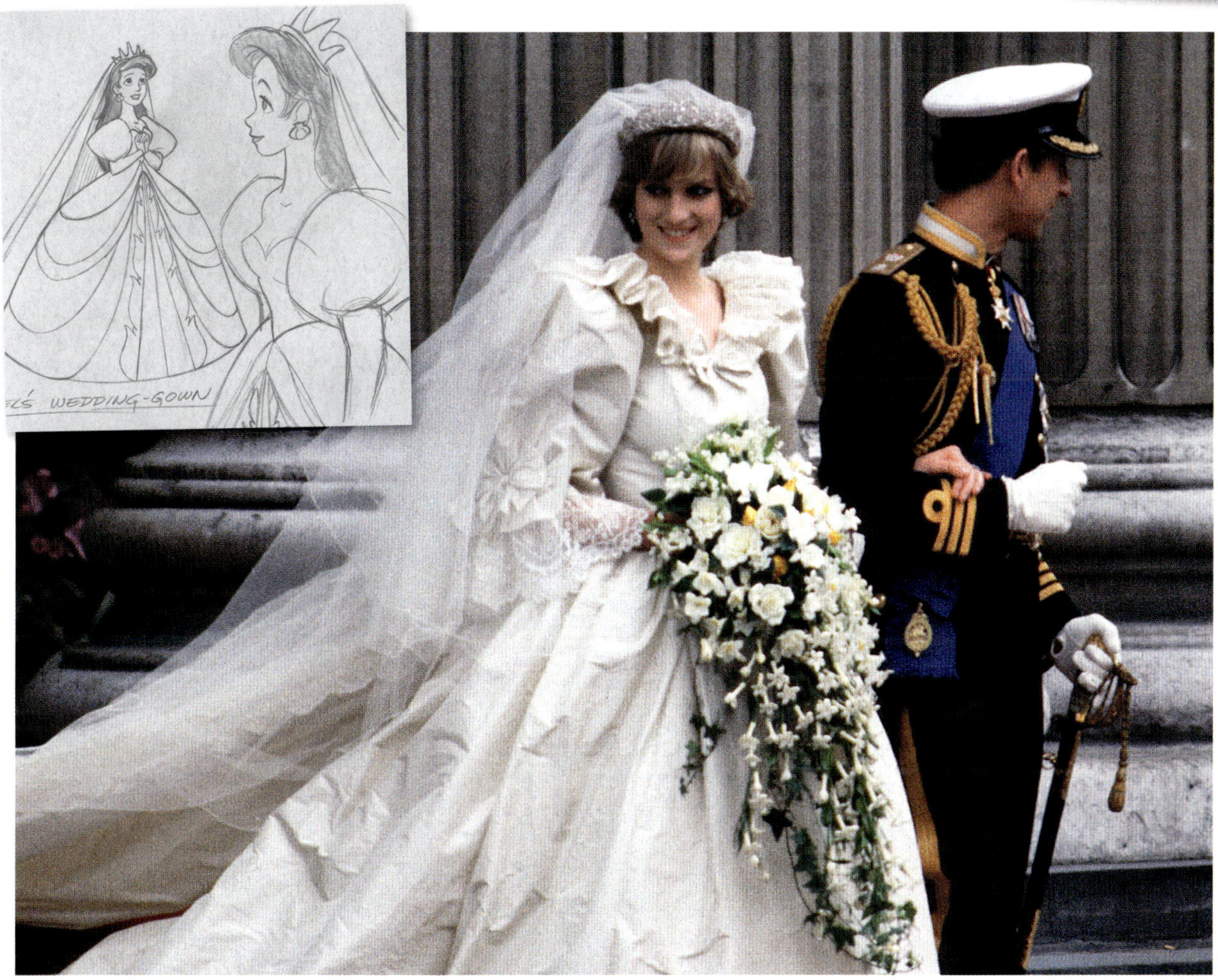

blue to pink and back again, is more evocative of silhouettes from the 1950s than the 1300s, says Breznican, who notes that both time periods had an appreciation for tight-fitting designs.

"Outfitted in a gown that featured an exaggerated collar, cinched waist, and peplum detail, Aurora could have easily stepped out of a classic *Vogue* magazine spread instead of a medieval castle," Breznican says. "African American designer Ann Lowe, haute couture French fashion designer Hubert de Givenchy, and *Roman Holiday* costume designer Edith Head are some of the few influential artists who incorporated the deep V collar into their designs."

By the time of the "Disney Renaissance," fashion trends had shifted dramatically. It's hard to point to a specific influence for Ariel's purple shell bikini top, but her puffy wedding dress evokes the iconic silk taffeta wedding dress worn by Princess Diana at her wedding to Prince Charles in 1981. Meanwhile, Ariel's dual-toned blue dress with a navy-blue corset, which she wears on her tour of the kingdom with Prince Eric, harkens back to earlier Disney Princesses. The dress brings to mind similar outfits from previous films, including Cinderella's scullery maid dress and Aurora's Briar Rose gray dress, which also has a black corset.

Tiana's green gown is a direct callback to *Cinderella,* although it also has some historical connections to the 1920s. A gown worn by Mary Eaton at the Ziegfeld Follies in 1923 featured layers of "petals," just like Tiana's. That gown has been cited as a possible inspiration for Dior, who also designed layered ball skirts. For animator Mark Henn, the vision was to mirror Tiana's connection with the bayou in her gown. "The goal of her gown at the end was to reflect the environment," Henn notes. "It was created there in the swamp by Mama Odie, kind of like Cinderella's Fairy Godmother when she gives her a beautiful dress. We wanted the dress in Tiana's case to have more organic qualities since it came out of nature."

Because many of the characters come from historical moments and time periods, the filmmakers have always embraced a combination of authentic reference and fantastical imagination in the princesses' clothes. And even if the characters exist in what's sometimes referred to as "fairy-tale time"—a fantastical amalgam of time periods as seen in movies like *Tangled*—it's essential that each hero is designed in a way that allows her to seem genuine.

"We want the designs to fit the story," explains animator Kira Lehtomaki, who worked on *Tangled* and *Moana*. "Whatever the story and the needs are, we want the designs to make sense for their circumstance and the situations they're in. We're never trying to go for realism. We're always trying to go for believability. As much as you can try to make the character believable and you believe there's that real soul inside this girl and that she would really be like this—that's the driving force behind how she looks and how she moves and what she dreams about."

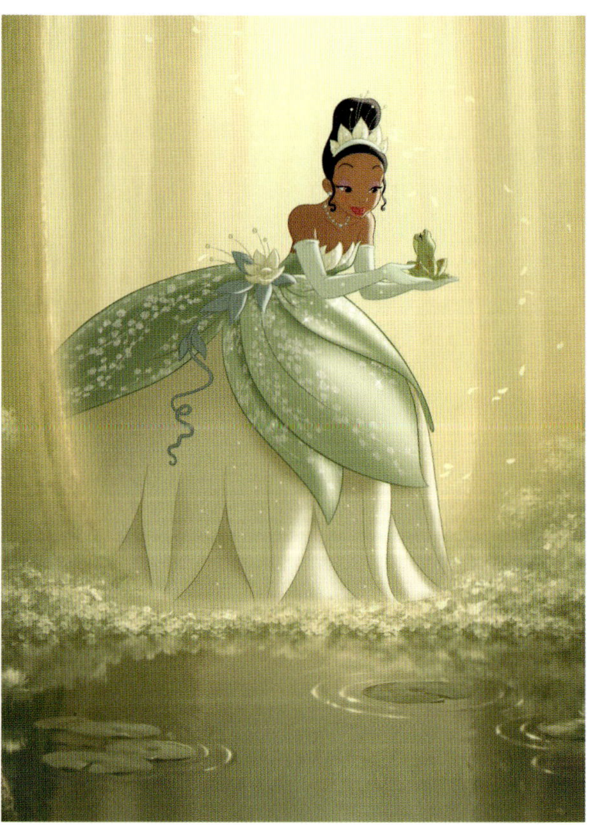

Tiana's green dress was partially inspired by Cinderella's ballgown.

FASHION COLLABORATIONS

Disney has been partnering with fashion brands to bring Disney Princess looks to life since *Snow White and the Seven Dwarfs*. Before the film was even in theaters, French silk company Colcombet created fabrics from design patterns sent to Paris by Disney merchandising man Kay Kamen. Several French fashion houses, including Lelong, Paquin, and Patou, also produced pieces based on the designs. Back in the U.S., the company Marshall Field manufactured six cotton print fabrics with Snow White motifs to be used for dresses, pajamas, house coats, and beachwear. An article in the *Decatur Daily Review*, titled "Snow White Film to Influence All Styles, Accessories," in January 1938 heralded the importance of the film's impact on the fashion world, noting that "the spring openings in the French capital will demonstrate a strong 'Snow White' influence."

Snow White's style impacted accessories, too. A series of hats based on the film's characters debuted in 1938, featuring looks inspired by some of the Seven Dwarfs, as well as a pastel blue headpiece with a forehead bow much like Snow White's own hairpiece. An advertisement for the hats appeared in several newspapers, including the *Millinery Monitor*, and showcased the hats on up-and-coming RKO studios' actresses like Lucille Ball and Ann Miller. Lapin-Kurley Kew Inc. sold themed hair bows and barrettes, and there were even Snow White brush-and-comb sets available by 1938.

On the pricier side, Cartier designed a charm bracelet made of gold and enamel, which sold in 1937 and has since become a highly sought-after collectible. One bracelet sold at Christie's for $118,750 in 2019 and another for $43,750 in 2020. Lillian Disney wore one of the bracelets to the premiere of *Snow White and the Seven Dwarfs* and it is now on display in The Walt Disney Family Museum in San Francisco, California.

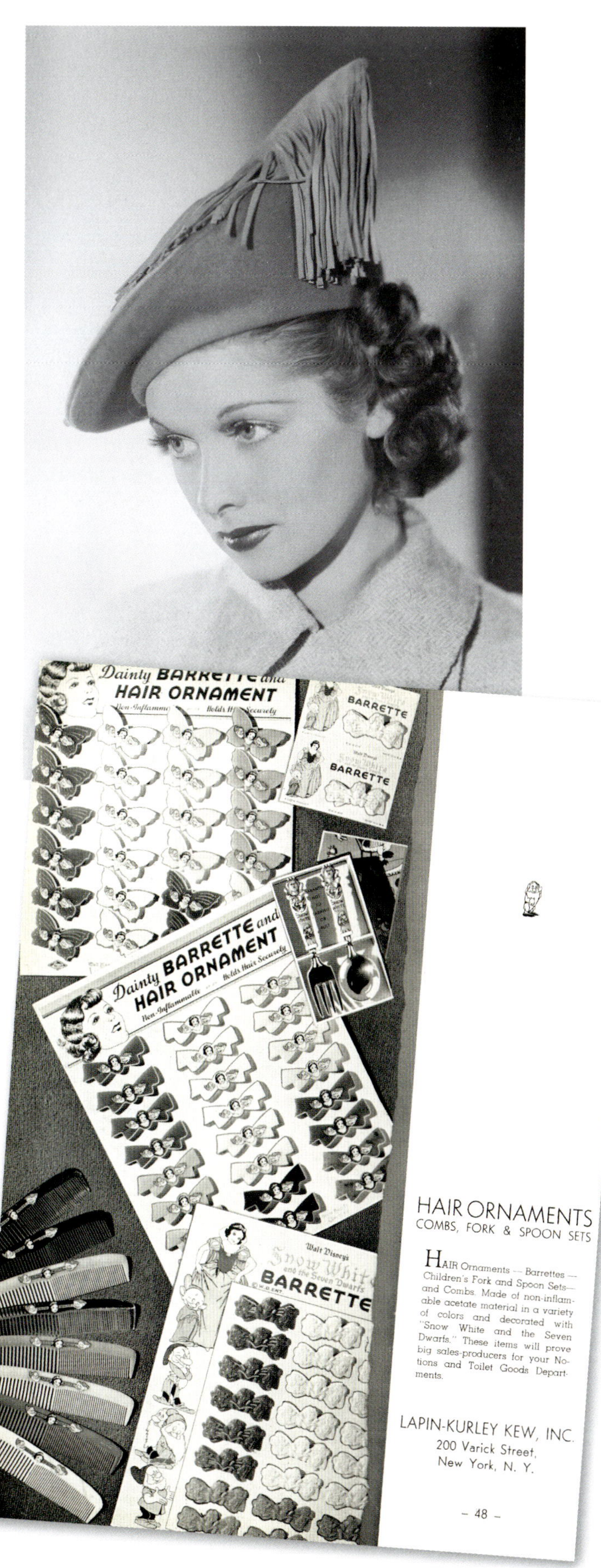

Above (top): A Huntsman-inspired hat designed to promote *Snow White and the Seven Dwarfs*. *Above (bottom):* An advertisement for hair ornaments inspired by Snow White.

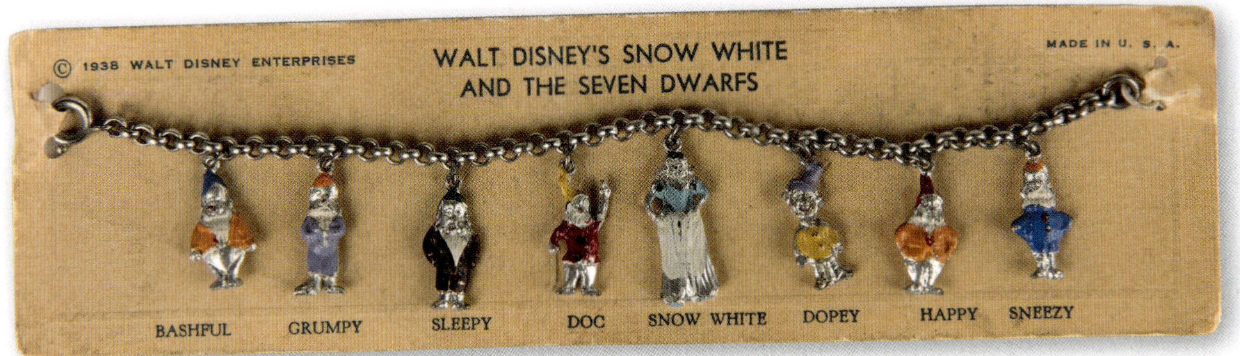

Above: A charm bracelet featuring *Snow White and the Dwarfs*. *Below:* JCPenney sold apron patterns inspired by Cinderella's style.

Audiences of the 1930s already gravitated to the style of beloved screen stars, but this was the first time an animated character had such a strong sartorial reach. That influence continued with *Cinderella*, although not quite to such an expansive degree. Retailer JCPenney unveiled a Cinderella apron pattern in 1950, allowing audiences to sew their own version of the character's ensemble for everyday wear. *Cinderella* wristwatches became something of a status symbol for fans after the film's release, and U.S. Time released a pink chrome-plated bezel stainless watch in 1951 that was sold nestled in a transparent plastic slipper. Even dry cleaners, like Sanitone, encouraged Disney Princess style. In 1958, Sanitone wrapped clean clothes in cut-out paper costume bags with Snow White and Cinderella's gowns, which customers could wear at home.

There were fewer designer collaborations coordinated with Disney during the 1980s and 1990s. Many more of these brand collaborations developed after the official founding of the Disney Princesses franchise in 2000, particularly in the last decade. These days, Disney Consumer Products works with many different fashion and beauty brands, focusing on licensed clothing lines that are either inspired by the Disney Princesses in general, or by a specific film and character. Many brand collaborations arrive alongside a film's anniversary, and Disney Consumer Products aims to be as diverse and creative as possible in their offerings. "We want to make sure we've got product where our fans shop," Torpey says. "And they shop all over the place. Inclusivity is important to us and we look for brands that have that bent to them."

On the upscale side, fashion designers have interpreted the characters' costumes in various ways in recent years. In 2012, London department store Harrods celebrated the holiday season with a series of window displays that featured designer takes on Disney Princess fashion. The dresses, by designers like Valentino and Jenny Packham, were later auctioned by Christie's to benefit Great Ormond Street Hospital Children's Charity in London. A few years later, in 2017, New York's Saks Fifth Avenue heralded the 80th anniversary of *Snow White and the Seven Dwarfs* by transforming fourteen display windows into scenes from the fairy tale. Four designers—Alberta Ferretti, Naeem Khan, Monique Lhuillier, and Marchesa—created original gowns for the displays.

A Real Glass Slipper

There is perhaps no shoe more famous than Cinderella's glass slipper. A modern day Cinderella, of course, would find her iconic footwear with Christian Louboutin's red sole, so it makes sense that the designer partnered with Disney in 2012 for an interpretation of the glass slipper. Tied to the *Cinderella* Diamond Edition Blu-ray disc release, as well as Louboutin's 20th Anniversary Retrospective Exhibition at the London Design Museum, the shoe was a limited edition.

Featuring the red sole and a five-inch heel, Louboutin's version of the glass slipper was technically not glass, although the design incorporated white lace and Swarovski crystals to give it the effect of a shimmering clear shoe. Unlike Cinderella's slipper, Louboutin's included crystal butterfly details. In a making-of clip, Louboutin explained that the reason the back of the slipper was coated in crystals was because the butterflies had landed on it and left behind the illumination. Costume designer Sandy Powell also introduced butterflies into Cinderella's look for the 2015 live-action reimagining, this time on Cinderella's gown.

Louboutin's 2012 design was unveiled at Paris Couture Fashion Week during an event at the Palais Brongniart, where the shoe was showcased alongside images from the making of the animated classic. "Her character and her story dictated the design to me, it was all there in the pages and the words of this tale," the designer said when the shoe was revealed. "Cinderella is not only an iconic character when it comes to grace and fairy-tale love, but also shoes. The dream is a major factor in my language of design. There are no limits in the world of fantasy and there is always a happily ever after."

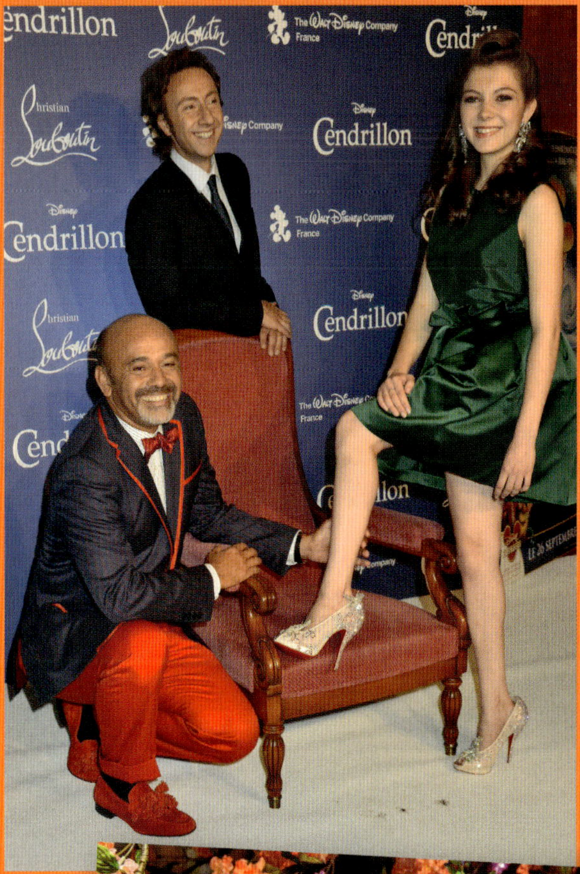

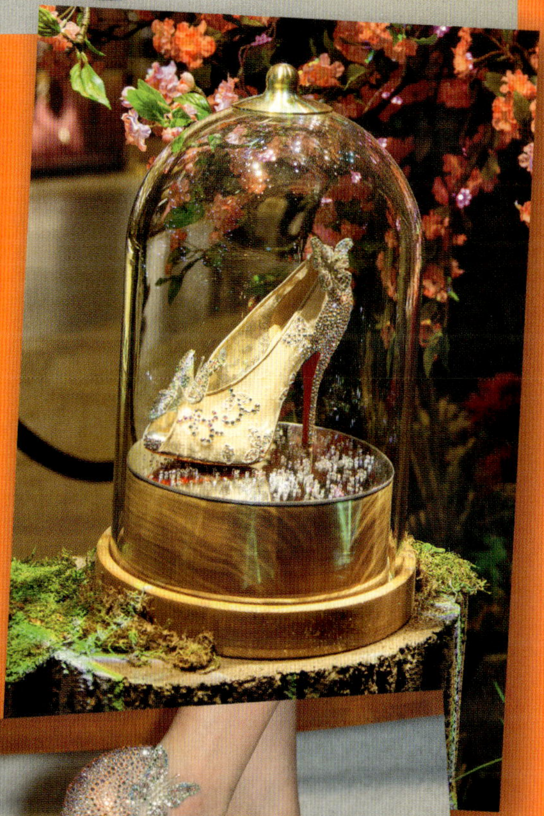

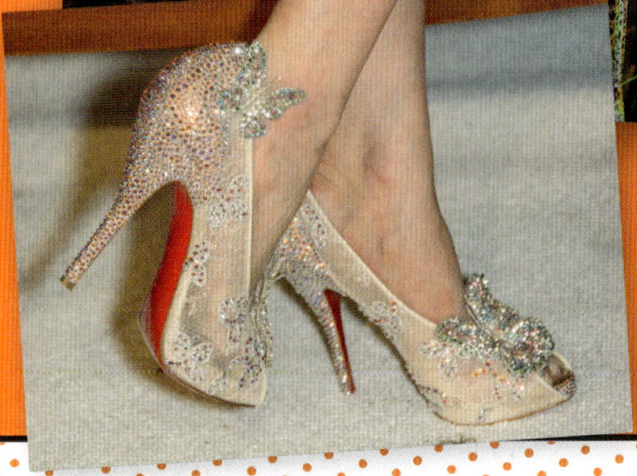

Christian Louboutin, kneeling, reveals a limited edition glass slipper.

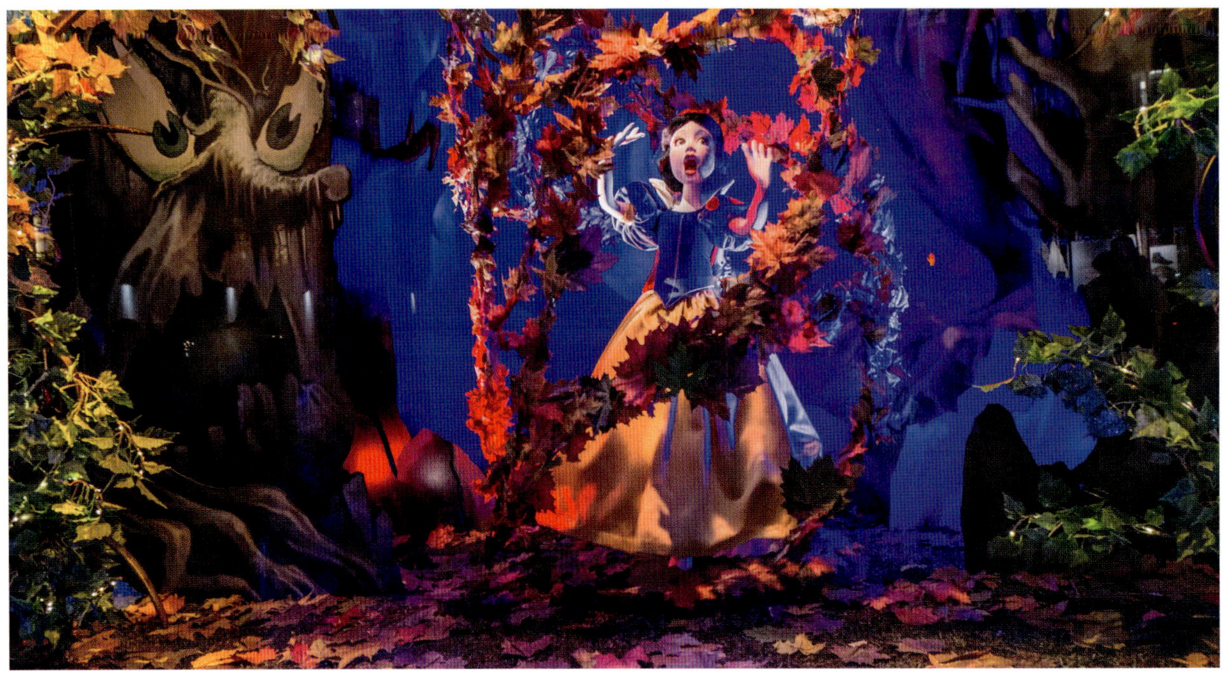

Saks Fifth Avenue celebrates the 80th anniversary of *Snow White and the Seven Dwarfs* with vibrant window displays.

That same year, Christopher Kane's *Beauty and the Beast* thirty-three-piece capsule collection arrived hand in hand with the live-action film adaptation. While the looks embraced the whimsical fantasy of the original fairy tale, each piece had its own real-world appeal, with Kane opting for biker jackets over gowns for the collection. "I didn't want to do the yellow dress," Kane explained to *Vogue*. "I think people were expecting that, and to me it just seems too obvious. I don't think it's necessarily something that should be taken out of the world of the film."

The Disney Princesses also lend themselves well to whimsical couture. Paolo Sebastian's 2018 Spring/Summer Couture collection, titled "Once Upon a Time," paid homage to iconic fairy tales without directly copying from the films. Several of the collection's flowing gowns featured lyrics to memorable Disney Princess songs, including "I Wonder" from *Sleeping Beauty*. Sebastian wrote that he was "following the timeless narrative of a heroine, who in the quest for happiness is challenged by a wicked evil." He added, "Through her strength and bravery, light prevails and she lives happily ever after."

Not all collaborations have been so obviously linked to the animated characters. For capsule

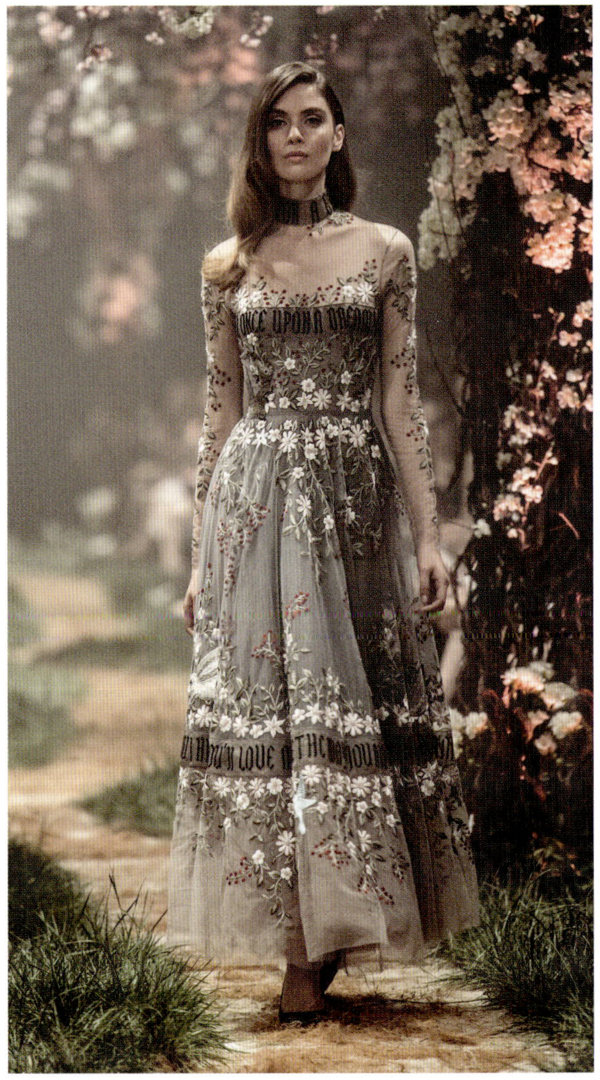

A gown from Paolo Sebastian's 2018 Spring/Summer Couture collection.

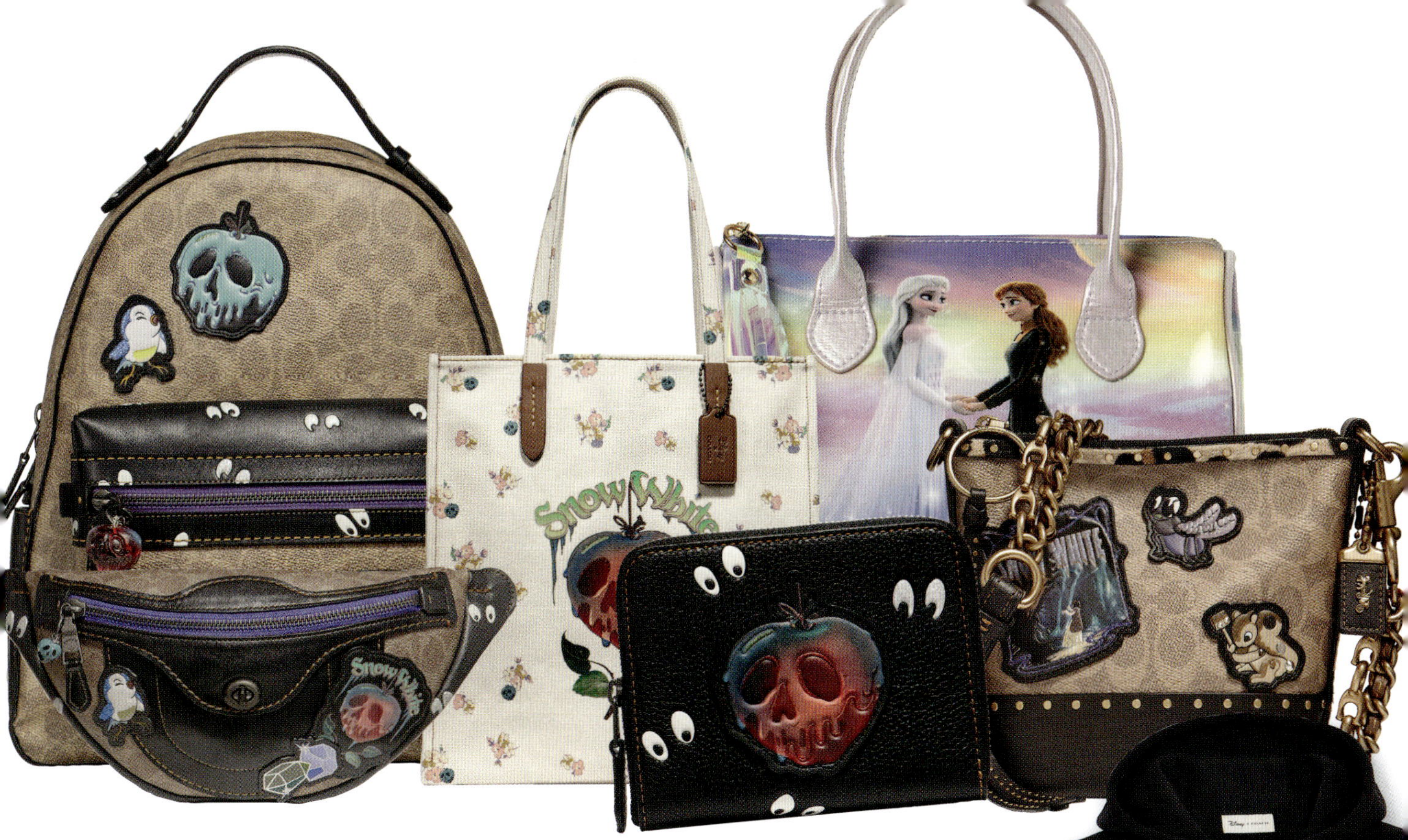

Above and right: Apparel and accessories, including a skateboard deck, from the "Disney X Coach: A Dark Fairy Tale" capsule collection, and a *Frozen*-inspired purse from H&M.

collection "Disney X Coach: A Dark Fairy Tale," in 2018, designer Stuart Vevers subverted the traditional fairy-tale aesthetic, giving a youthful streetwear twist to princess fashion with ready-to-wear garments, accessories, and even skate decks. While iconography from the Disney Princesses' stories appeared on the pieces, including Snow White's apple and *Sleeping Beauty*'s castle, the collection was edgy and unexpected.

"We were looking at an American gothic fairy tale," Vevers told *ELLE*. "A lot of our references have that feeling—it was a dark take on a romantic feel. We started to look at the scary moments in *Snow White and the Seven Dwarfs* and *Sleeping Beauty*, and it felt very natural with the collection."

Over the past decade, Disney Consumer Products has collaborated with everyone from adidas to Torrid, which has made several inclusive lines of fashion inspired by several princesses. Cath Kidston created a Snow White collection, while Coach Outlet released a themed line of Disney Princess handbags. There have also been collections of Disney

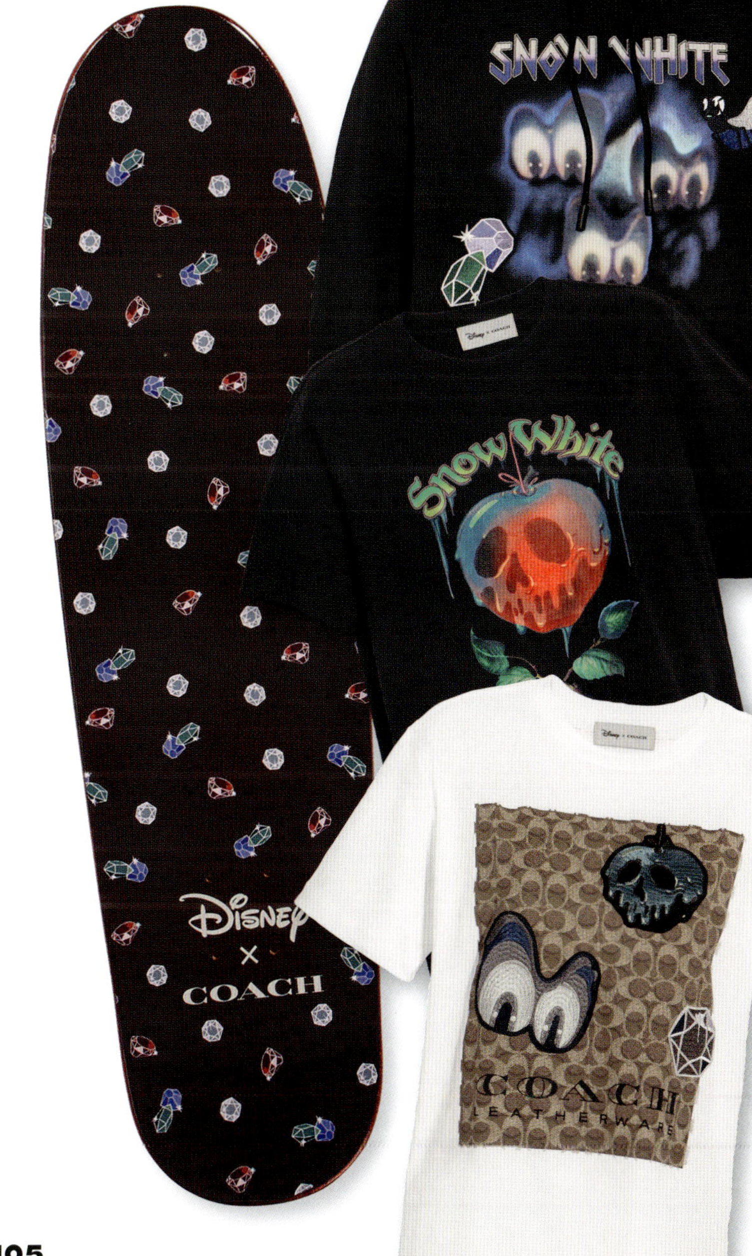

Princess-inspired engagement rings and jewelry, from brands like Roberto Coin, as well as Disney's own Enchanted Fine Jewelry. *Frozen*'s Anna and Elsa have also popped up in brand collaborations, including in the "COMME des GARÇONS x *Frozen*" collection, a line of Columbia winter jackets, and Ruthie Davis's *Frozen 2* shoe line in 2019.

The shoe designer also debuted a "Disney Princess x Ruthie Davis" collection, which featured avant-garde footwear inspired by characters like Mulan and Jasmine. "What my brand stands for and what Disney Princess stands for are totally in sync," Davis said. "My design aesthetic is to create shoes that make the woman wearing them feel special, powerful, confident, and beautiful. These characteristics also describe the Disney Princesses."

Beauty products, too, have been popular for collaborations involving the Disney characters. Sephora and Disney Consumer Products have teamed up for several collections, including a line of compact mirrors in 2015. Bésame Cosmetics has made some particularly elaborate makeup collections inspired by *Snow White and the Seven Dwarfs* and *Sleeping Beauty*, as well as a limited edition compact and lipstick collection for the Ultimate Princess Celebration. Dave Pacheco helped Bésame design the Snow White collaboration in 2017. The makeup came in the exact colors found in *Snow White and the Seven Dwarfs*, matching the precise shades of Disney's ink and paint department. The cosmetics set was extremely detailed, including an animation cel from the film drawn by Pacheco. The favorite product, though, came from the Aurora-themed set, the 1959 *Sleeping Beauty* Collection. Bésame's "Make It Blue, Make It Pink" lipstick transformed from blue to pink, just like Aurora's gown in the final scene of the movie.

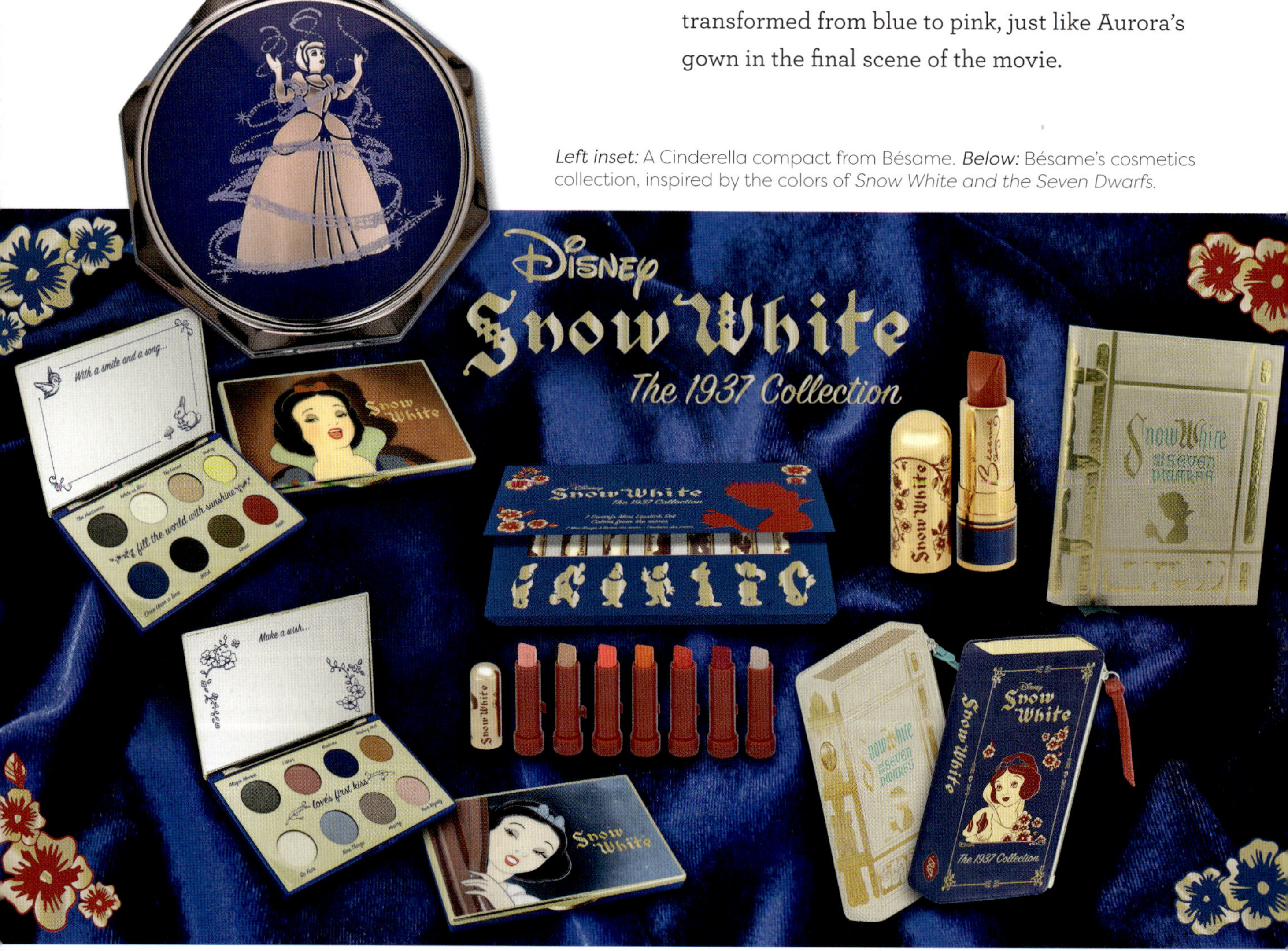

Left inset: A Cinderella compact from Bésame. *Below:* Bésame's cosmetics collection, inspired by the colors of *Snow White and the Seven Dwarfs*.

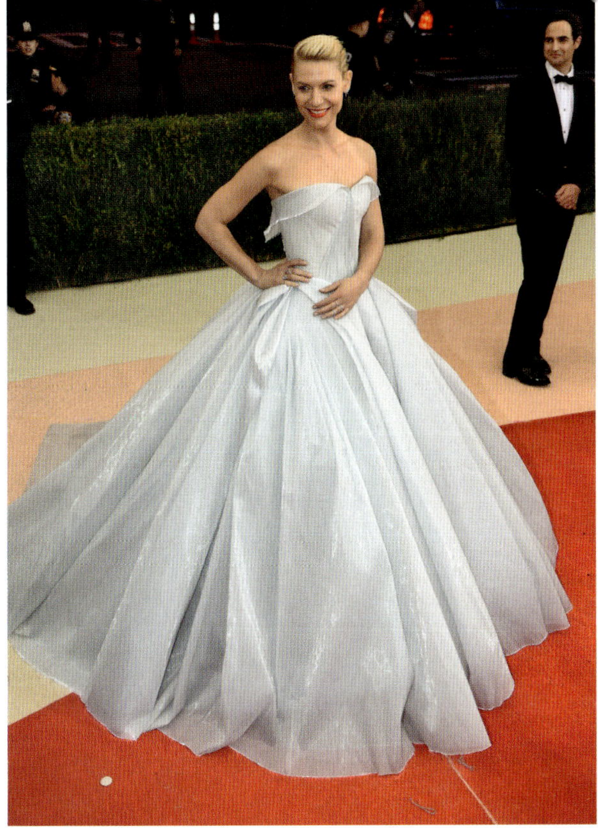

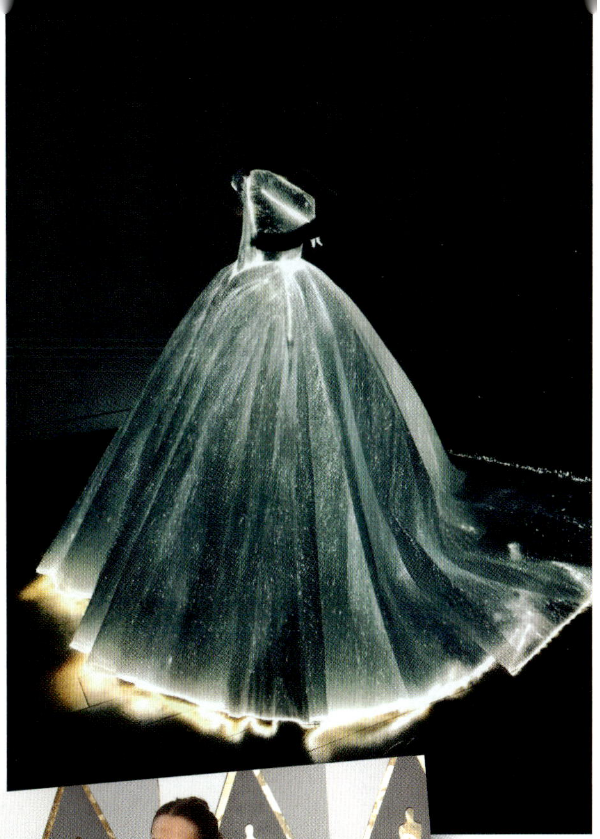

Above: Zac Posen's Cinderella-inspired gown, as worn by Claire Danes, illuminates with hidden fiber optics. *Right:* Alicia Vikander and Lupita Nyong'o embrace Disney Princess style on the red carpet with looks inspired by Belle and Cinderella.

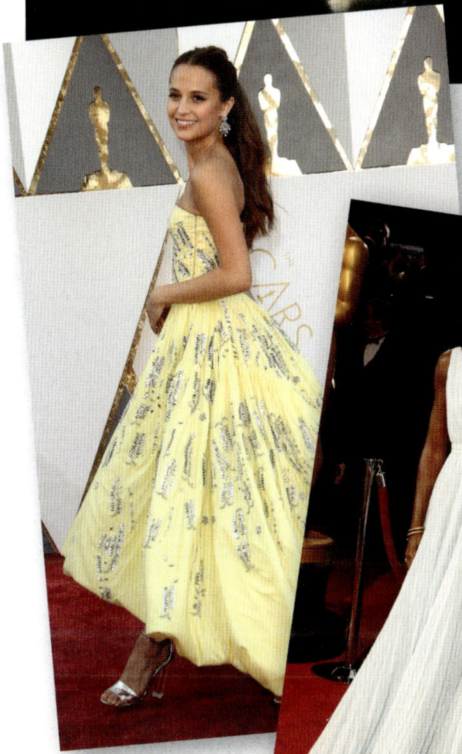

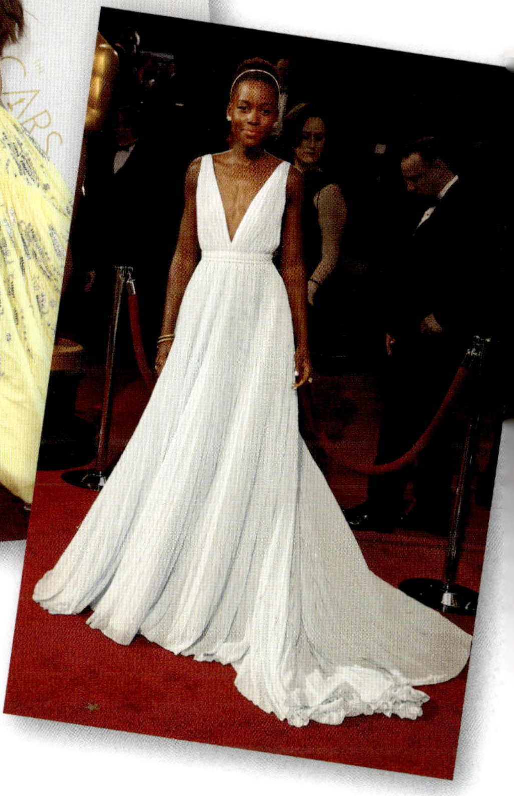

STYLE IMITATING ART

Just as our entertainment reflects the world in which it was made, the world also takes its inspiration from art. Of the Disney Princesses, Cinderella has been the most influential on designer fashion. For the 2016 Met Gala, Zac Posen recreated Cinderella's famous blue ballgown for Claire Danes. Taking the theme of "Fashion in an Age of Technology" to heart, Posen designed the dress with fiber optic woven organza, which allowed the fabric to illuminate with the help of thirty tiny battery packs sewn into the skirt. The designer, who spent over five hundred hours making the dress, says he was inspired by the classic Cinderella film, as well as the luminosity of her animated glass slipper. The voluminous gown appeared traditional on the red carpet, but its fiber optics began to glow as Danes entered the ball.

"The second that she walked through the doorway into the museum, the glow became apparent to the viewer," Posen recalls. "There was a transformational quality to the experience of seeing this dress, which in itself is a Cinderella moment. So it wasn't just the shape of it, it was the experience of it as well. That's the magic of Disney. And if you can capture that in high fashion to a crafted level, that's the dream."

Cinderella has been a favorite inspiration for red-carpet dresses. From Cardi B's Christian Siriano at the Diamond Ball in 2017 to Blake Lively's Vivienne Westwood Couture at Cannes

Fairy Tale Weddings

Romance is often entwined with fairy tales, particularly in Disney's classic animated versions. Several of the films, including *Cinderella*, end with a wedding—or, at least, the promise of one. So it was only natural for Disney to get into the wedding business, including the wedding gown business. Disney Bridal partnered with designer Kirstie Kelly in the spring of 2007 for its debut "Kirstie Kelly for Disney's Fairy Tale Weddings" line. The line featured bridal looks based on each Disney Princess, as well as jewelry and veils. Today, the wedding gowns are by Allure Bridals, who relaunched the "Disney's Fairy Tale Weddings" collection in 2020. The gowns are available in a wide range of sizes, making them perfect for any bride. They also take their design inspirations directly from the Disney Princesses.

"We know that every bride wants to feel like a princess on her wedding day," explains Karen Torpey, Director Licensing, Princess and Fairies, at Disney Consumer Products. "Each character's personality is incorporated in with styling cues. For example, Ariel's debut gown was a mermaid-style silhouette encrusted with sea pearls. Some of Belle's gowns feature gentle pick-ups reminiscent of her yellow ballgown, and others have a rose motif in the lacing."

Each year, Disney's Fairy Tale Weddings & Honeymoons spotlights a different Disney Princess. In 2020, for the 70th anniversary of *Cinderella*, they created a Cinderella wedding gown made with 4,600 crystals and 44,000 sequins and beads to evoke the sparkle of the character's glass slipper. It even came in a shade of blue.

Other designers have created their own Disney Princess-inspired wedding gowns, as well. Nephi Garcia, known as Designer Daddy, has built a business designing princess-themed gowns, cosplay ensembles, and wedding dresses for Disney fans. Garcia got his start making "transformation dresses"—dresses that twirl from one look to another—for his daughters, and once those gained traction on social media, the requests began to pour in. The designer had made his wife's wedding dress, which was inspired both by Grace Kelly's bridal look and Aurora, and he quickly built a client roster of women hoping to feel like royalty on their special day. Garcia explains he wants to give people the magical feeling that he felt while watching the Disney films as a child.

"It's about the happily ever after of it," Garcia says. "People are too realistic these days, like 'Yeah, it's hard. Life is tough.' But why not believe in happily ever after? It still happens, just in different ways than we expect from what the story tells you. It's still out there and I love giving a glimpse of that through the dresses that I make."

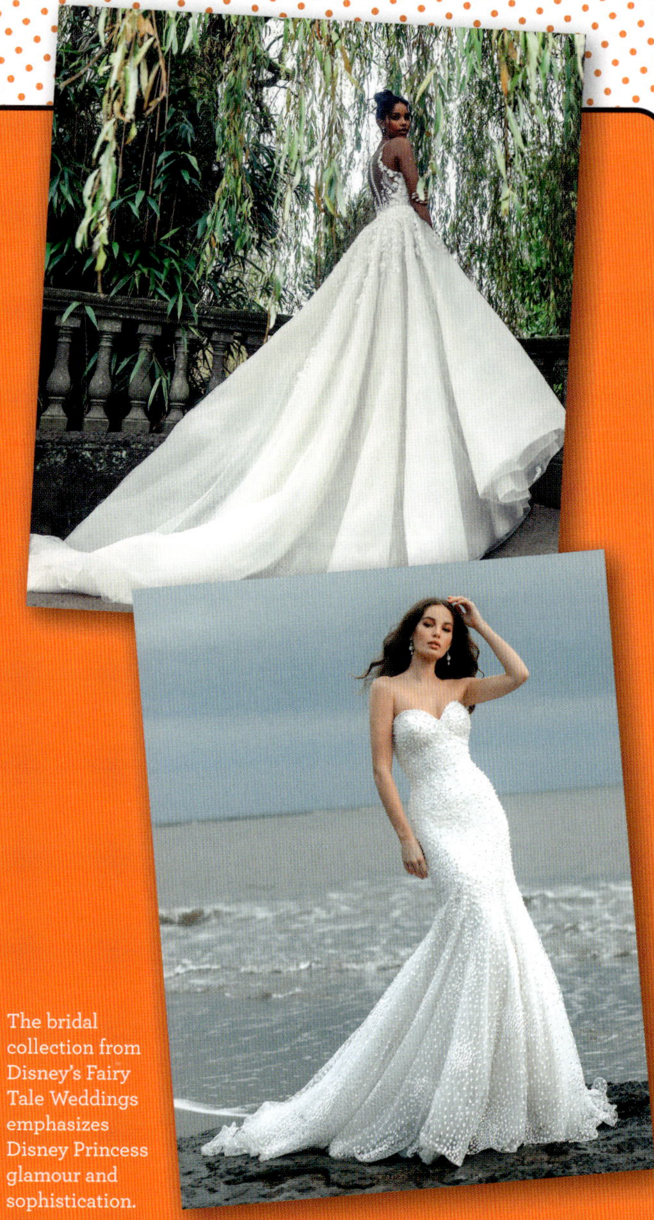

The bridal collection from Disney's Fairy Tale Weddings emphasizes Disney Princess glamour and sophistication.

in 2016 to Lupita Nyong'o's flowing Prada at the Oscars in 2014, a glamorous blue gown always evokes a fairy-tale moment. Posen was responsible for a sumptuous ballgown designed for Ariana Grande to wear to the Grammys in 2019, an idea that came from Grande herself. The designer was enlisted by the singer's stylist, Law Roach, after Grande said she wanted "to feel like a princess."

"If you say you want to feel like a princess, then that means you want to look like a princess," Roach explains. "That's when I go into the repertoire of all the Disney Princesses and figure it out. Their looks are part of Americana. At some point in every little girl's life—and some little boys as well—they want to be a Disney Princess. Our idea of that, in America, isn't necessarily about actual royalty. The Disney Princesses are our royalty."

Dressing in the image of a Disney Princess is as much about a collective appreciation for an iconic gown as it is about the style itself. "If you held up a picture of Cinderella's gown, we all know that gown," Roach notes. "I know that gown. My mother knew that gown. Her mother knew that gown. When it comes to impact and influence, all of the Disney Princesses are fashion icons."

There's also a performative aspect to a Disney Princess-inspired look. In 2019, Roach accompanied Zendaya to the Met Gala and acted out the part of the Fairy Godmother—dubbing himself the Fairy Godbrother. Roach commissioned a custom Tommy Hilfiger gown for the former Disney Channel actress, inspired by the yearly theme of "camp." On the red carpet, Roach waved his magic wand and Zendaya's blue gown slowly illuminated.

"The inspiration was a bit of Disney Princess and Cinderella, of course, but also Zendaya was, in my opinion, the reigning Disney Princess for

Stylist Law Roach accompanies Zendaya to the Met Ball in 2019.

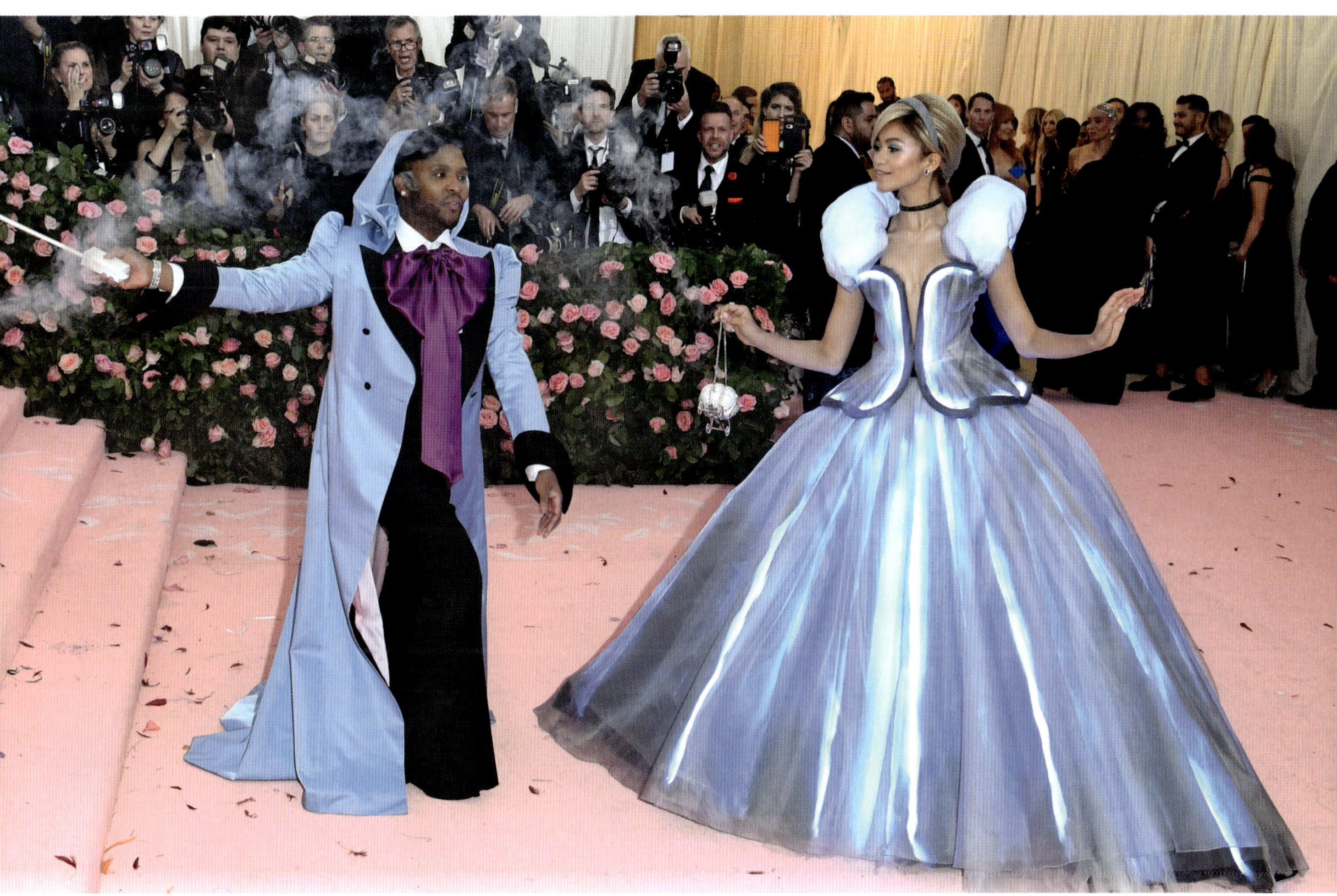

the Disney Channel network for years," Roach says. "She was coming to the end of that Disney career. I thought it would be a beautiful story to leave it all on the stairs of the Met."

Zendaya did, in fact, leave her glass slipper behind on the Met stairs, just like Cinderella. But for Roach, it was far more than just a great photo opportunity. "A big red-carpet moment is about being able to evoke the kind of confidence the Disney Princesses have," the stylist explains. "They may not have started out that way at the beginning of the story, but by the end they were comfortable and confident with who they are. It's that climactic moment when the gown is on and they walk into the ball and all eyes are on them. It takes a lot of confidence to go into a room and know all eyes will be on you. That's what I give to my girls and they take along with them, and it all comes from the Disney Princesses."

It's not always about Cinderella either, whether it's Katie Holmes's yellow Marchesa in 2014 or Lily-Rose Depp's off-shoulder pink Chanel in 2017. In 2016, Alicia Vikander accepted the Best Actress Oscar for *The Danish Girl* (2015, Focus Features) while wearing a custom yellow Louis Vuitton gown, and Twitter was

Below (left): Katie Holmes at the Met Gala in 2014 in a Belle-inspired gown. ***Below (right):*** Lily-Rose Depp in Chanel at the 2017 Met Gala evoking Aurora.

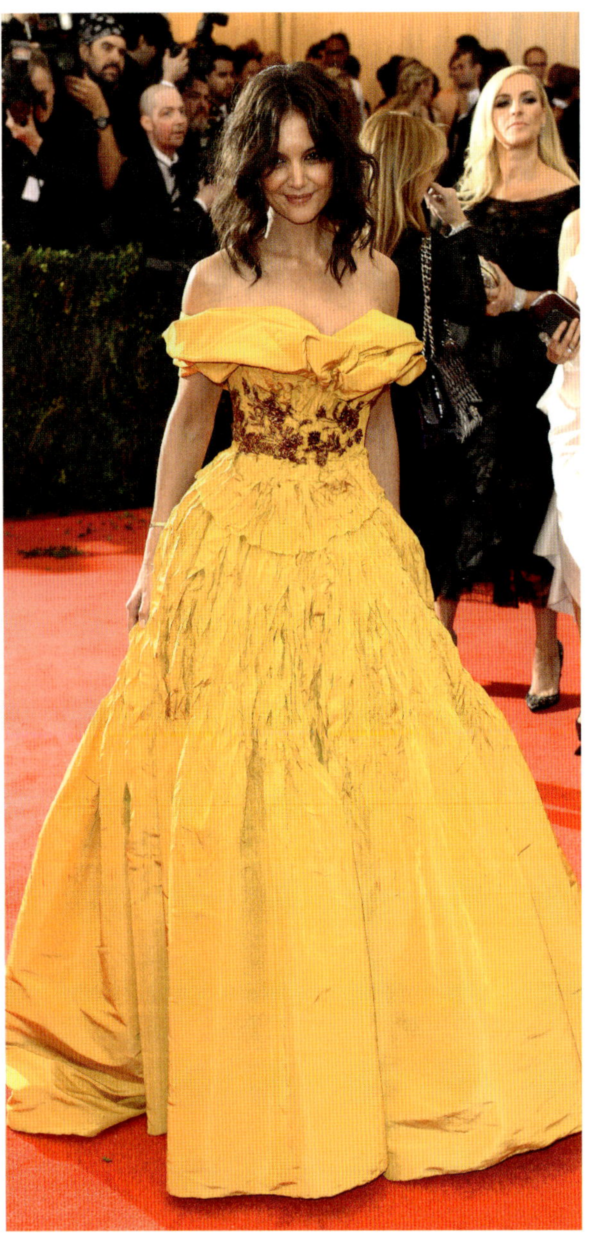

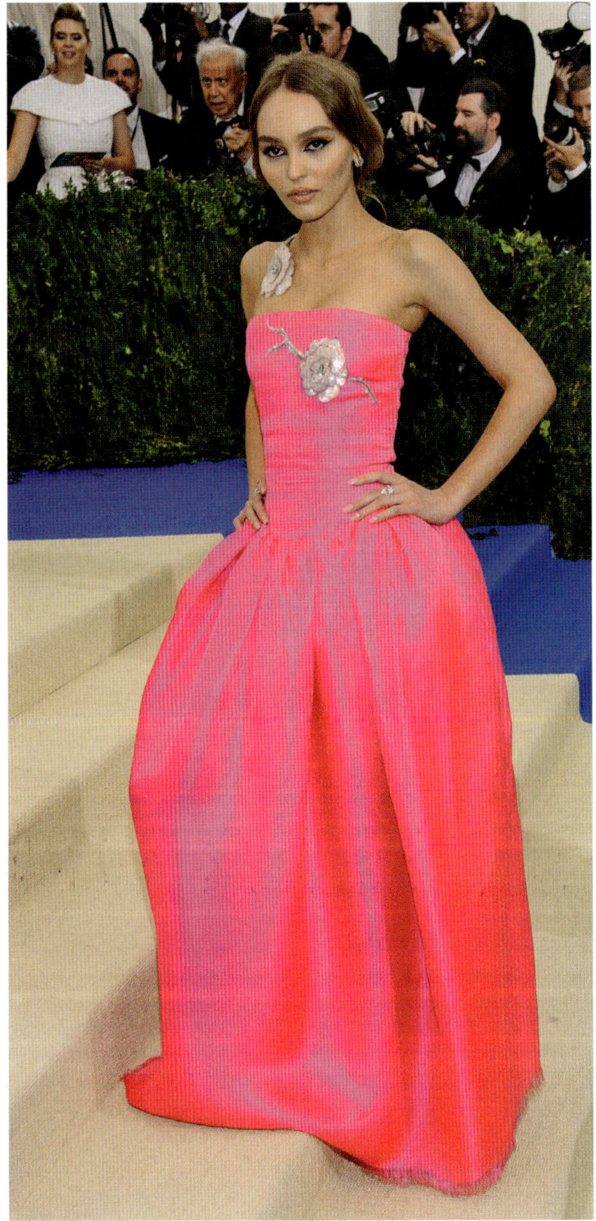

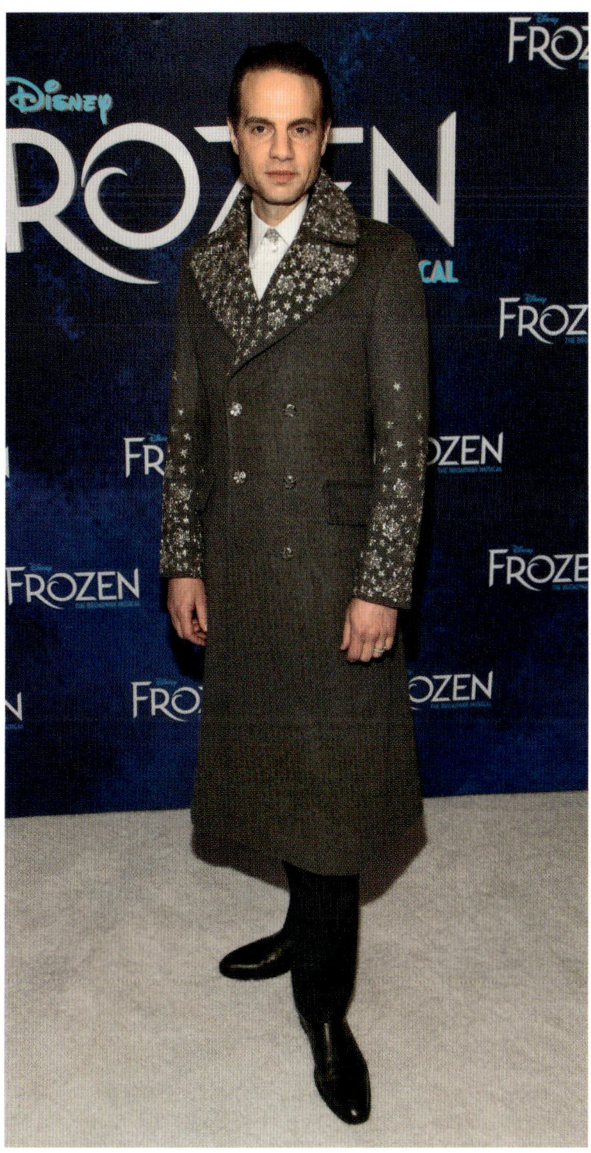

Producer Jordan Roth wears Zac Posen's *Frozen*-inspired coat to a Broadway premiere.

filled with memes of the actress as Belle before the Oscars ceremony even started. It wasn't a coincidence: Louis Vuitton created the gown to fulfill Vikander's childhood fantasy. "I think if you would've asked five-year-old Alicia what her biggest dream was, it was probably to be Belle in *Beauty and the Beast*," Vikander said of the look on the red carpet.

The magic of a Disney Princess gown is perfect for an important event, whether it's a celebrity attending the Oscars or a Disney fan walking down the aisle at their wedding. For many, it's the realization of a dream. "When you're growing up, your ideals about fantasy or glamour start in a Disney movie," says Posen, who also designed a *Frozen*-themed men's jacket for the musical's Broadway premiere. "That level of fantasy and dream is something that gets embedded into people's aspirations and their artistry. That's true of a great movie character, but with something that's drawn and animated, it can be even stronger."

DISNEYBOUNDING

Couture isn't necessary to emulate Disney Princess style. While the characters' original looks often involve ballgowns and unique outfits, items the average person might not wear on a daily basis, there's a way to evoke a costume without actually wearing one: DisneyBounding. DisneyBound, or bounding, involves creating an outfit inspired by your favorite character in a casual way—unlike cosplay, which is a costume. The trend was started by blogger Leslie Kay over a decade ago. A longtime fan of Disney, Kay got the idea when she saw a dress on now-defunct fashion website Polyvore and realized it looked like something Rapunzel might wear to the mall. She created an everyday look for the princess on her Tumblr page, and within weeks, it had gone viral, with fans begging Kay to do more characters.

"It's not an original concept," Kay explains. "We've all seen the fashion magazines like, 'Get the look.' But if you don't relate to celebrities or you don't feel seen when you're looking in those fashion magazines, you may not feel like that's for you. But you can see your favorite Disney Princesses or characters and want to emulate their style in that same sort of way."

Unlike cosplay, DisneyBound allows for more flexibility from its wearer because it's everyday clothes. Anyone can DisneyBound as any character, regardless of gender, and it can be as simplistic or elaborate as one wants. It relies on color-blocking and silhouette, particularly with a character like Ariel or Belle, and there are no props or wigs involved. Instead, Kay encourages creative use of accessories, like a dragon purse for Mulan or a frying pan necklace for Rapunzel. "One of the best parts of DisneyBounding is that looking like the character is not a requirement," Kay noted in her 2020 book *DisneyBound: Dress Disney and Make It Fashion*. "It's all about expressing your love for the character through fashion."

While many DisneyBounders have embraced bounding when visiting the Disney parks, the trend has spread beyond a day at Disneyland. Many bounders showcase their best looks at *run*Disney events like the Disney Princess Half Marathon Weekend, or even at their high school proms. It's a form of empowerment, allowing fans to find a sense of self-confidence by channeling a favorite princess in an everyday setting.

"It's hard not to love the concept of fairy tales and royalty," Kay says. "Of course you want to live a fairy tale, and when you go to the Disney parks, you are living this fairy tale. Each princess represents something different and it's hard to find somebody who doesn't relate to at least one of the princesses in one way or another. They're magical, so when you dress up like them, you get to live their lives and experience their magic for yourself."

An example of DisneyBounding, a style approach that was created by Leslie Kay.

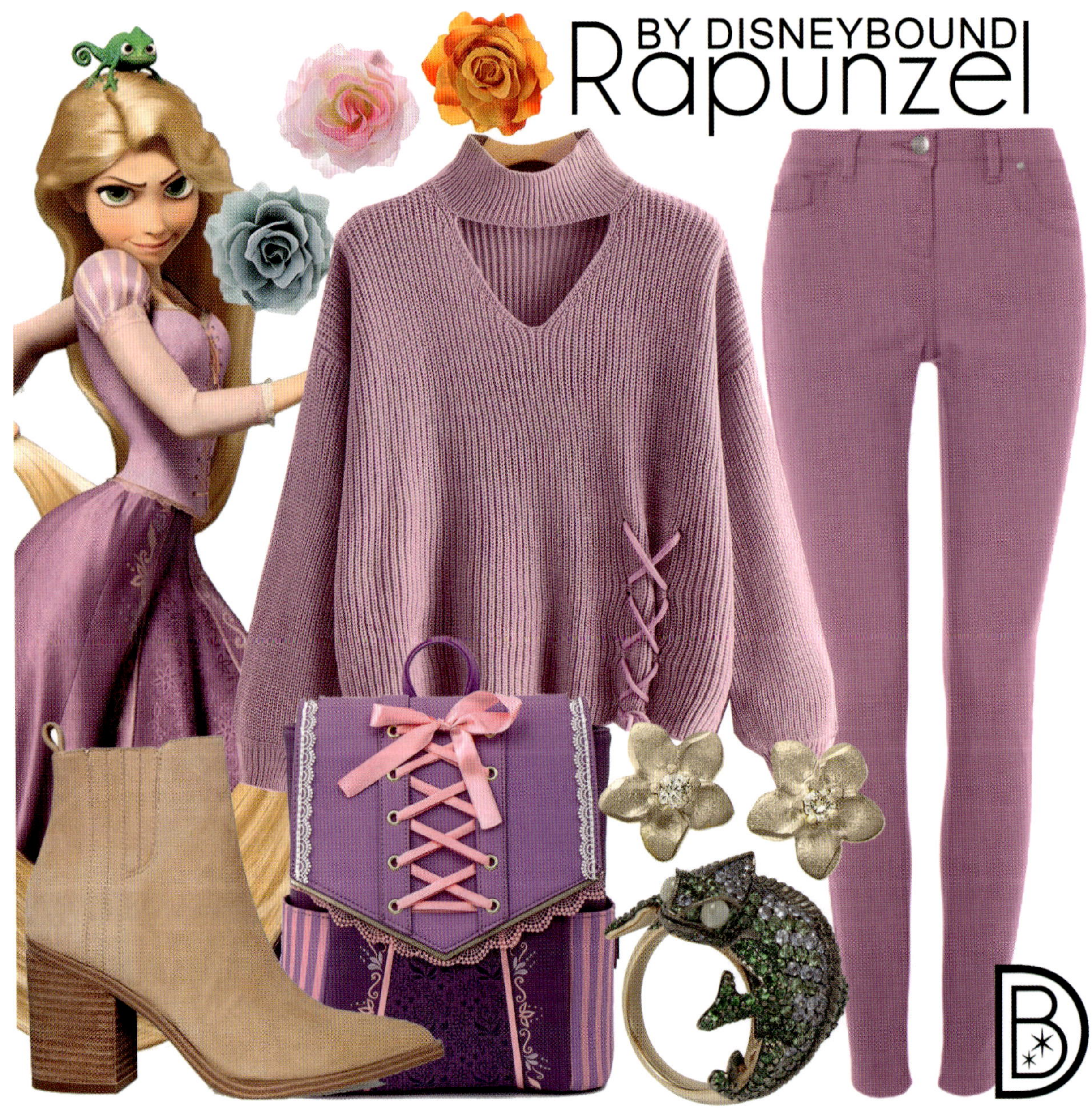

Halloween Costumes

Halloween costumes have been part of the Disney brand since the very beginning. The Wornova Manufacturing Company made Mickey and Minnie costumes as early as 1932. Wornova also made cardboard Snow White masks in 1938, but the first complete *Snow White and the Seven Dwarfs* Halloween costume came from A.S. Fishbach, a New York company that made character costumes and masks from 1938 to 1942. Kay Kamen's 1938-1939 Walt Disney Character Merchandise catalogue previewed the costumes, suggesting Snow White and her pals would be "the life of the thousands of children's masquerade parties this year." The costumes came in a range of sizes, and could be purchased as a complete look or just as a mask.

In 1942, the Ben Cooper Company joined as a costume licensee. The company, known for their disposable silkscreened costumes paired with masks, was popular for Halloween looks through the 1960s and tapped into a market of fans who wanted to dress up as their favorite characters. In 1950, Ben Cooper released a boxset, as part of their Spotlite collection, that included a Cinderella dress, crown, and mask, and sold at department stores such as Montgomery Ward for $1.98. Along with Cinderella, costume sets for other characters in the film, including Lucifer the cat, the Fairy Godmother, Gus the mouse, and the Prince were also available. In addition, Ben Cooper sold costumes of Aurora for *Sleeping Beauty*.

The Halloween tradition of dressing in costume to go trick-or-treating has gone in and out of favor over the decades, particularly for adults, but the 1980s saw a resurgence of Disney fans of all ages donning costumes of their favorite characters, both store-bought and homemade. Since *The Little Mermaid*, Disney licensees have created and sold replica looks of each Disney Princess—now with more of a focus on their actual film costume rather than an interpretation. Today, it's easy to find the perfect Halloween costume for a Disney Princess, whether you want to embody Snow White or go on an adventure as Moana.

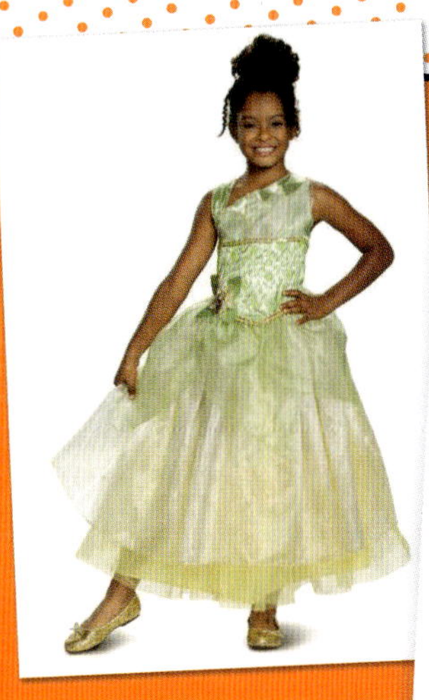

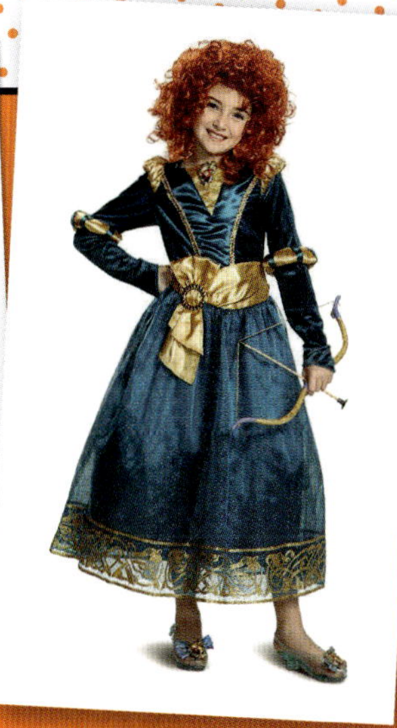

Disney Princess Halloween costumes have been popular since the release of *Snow White and the Seven Dwarfs*.

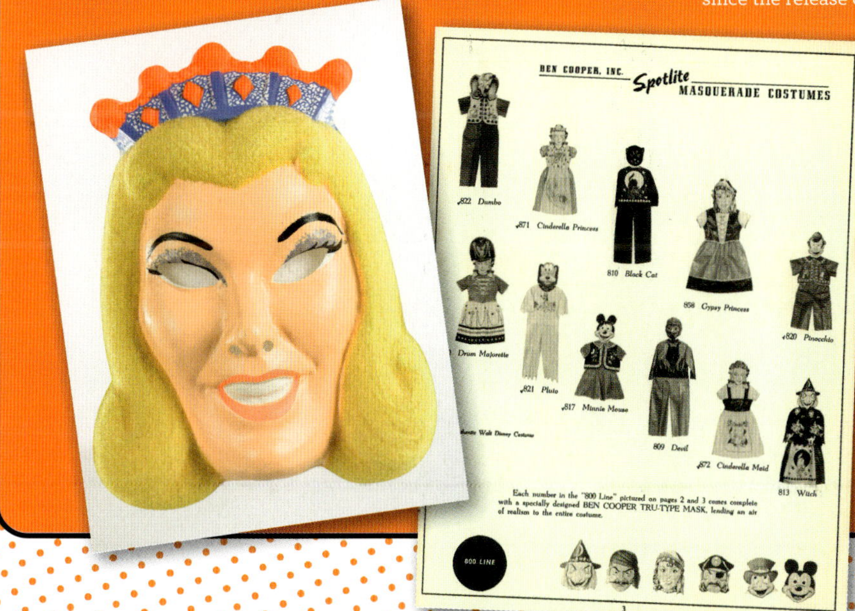

BEN COOPER, INC. Spotlite MASQUERADE COSTUMES

822 Dumbo

871 Cinderella Princess

810 Black Cat

858 Gypsy Princess

820 Pinocchio

Drum Majorette

821 Pluto

817 Minnie Mouse

809 Devil

872 Cinderella Maid

813 Witch

Each number in the "800 Line" pictured on pages 2 and 3 comes complete with a specially designed BEN COOPER TRU-TYPE MASK, lending an air of realism to the entire costume.

800 LINE

3

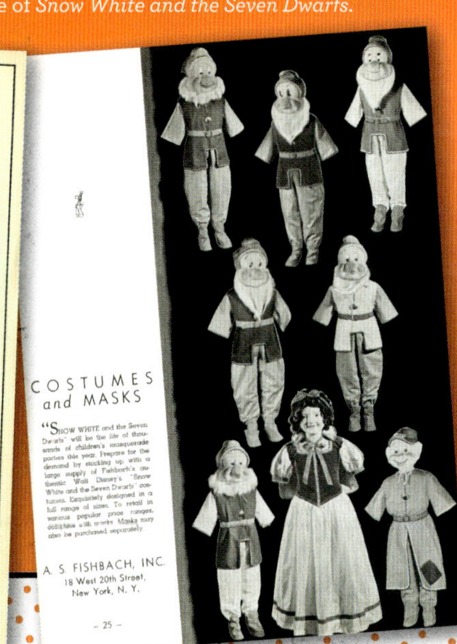

COSTUMES and MASKS

"SNOW WHITE and the Seven Dwarfs" will be the life of thousands of children's masquerade parties this year. Prepare for the demand by stocking up with a large supply of Fishbach's authentic Walt Disney's "Snow White and the Seven Dwarfs" costumes. Exquisitely designed in a full range of sizes. To retail in various popular price ranges, [illegible] Masks may also be purchased separately.

A. S. FISHBACH, INC.
18 West 20th Street,
New York, N. Y.

– 25 –

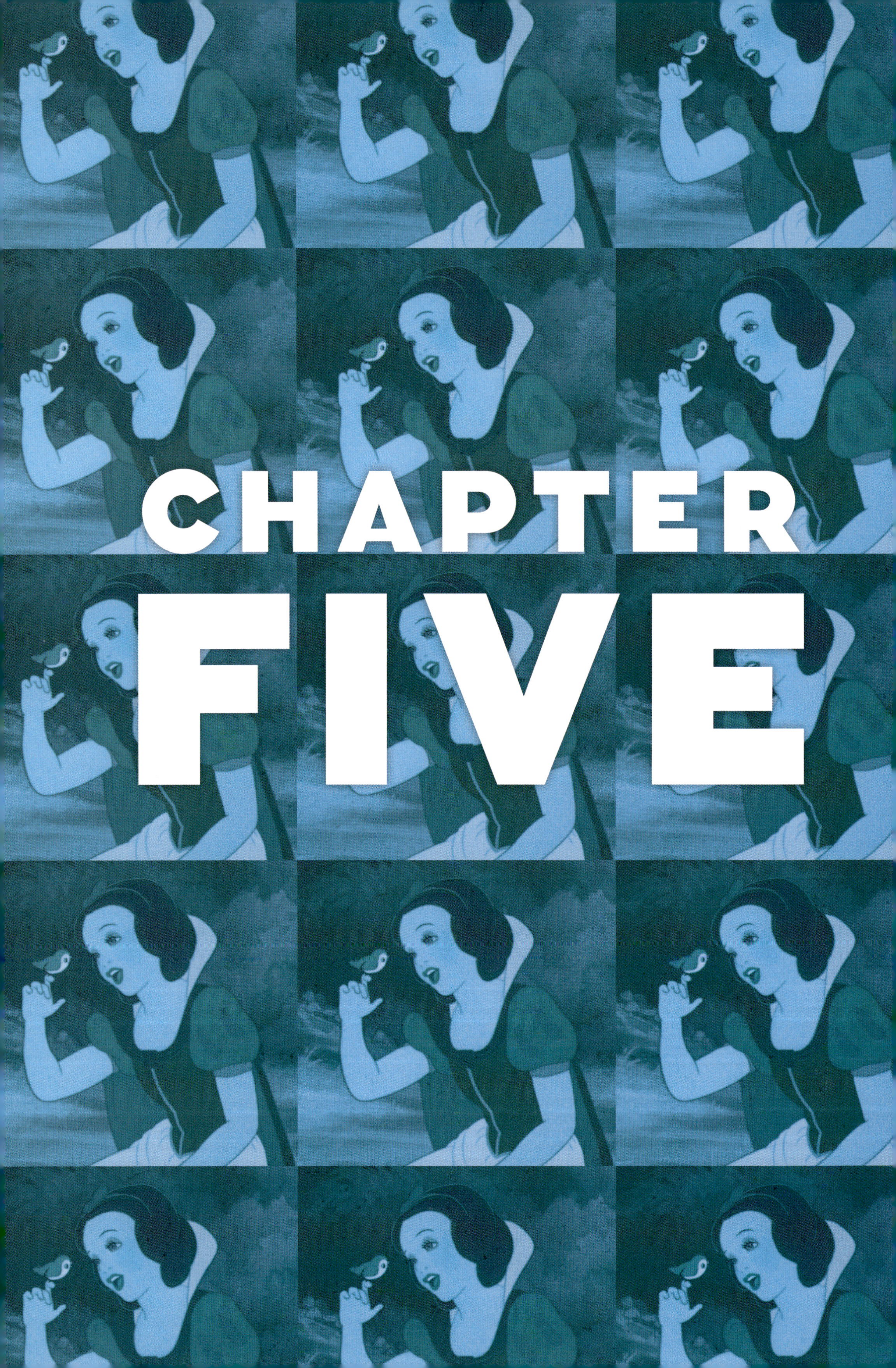

CHAPTER FIVE

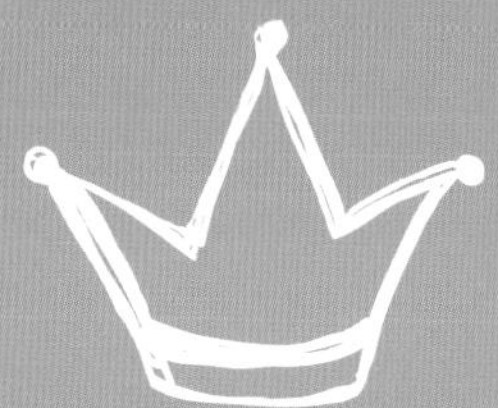

WITH A SONG AND A SMILE

MUSIC

Music has always been a central component of Walt Disney's films, ever since his early Mickey Mouse's debut animated short, *Steamboat Willie* (1928). Walt knew that music could provide a backdrop to his stories, helping viewers to better understand the characters' emotions and development. And through the years, the music of Disney films has proven to be not just entertaining, but essential. The songs in a movie like *Snow White and the Seven Dwarfs* or *The Little Mermaid* drive the narrative forward and offer insight into how the characters feel. And because these songs resonate so strongly with the audiences, it's easy to bring them into our own lives as inspiration.

“Disney songs are like heirlooms,” explains Randy Thornton, Supervising Producer and Music Historian at Walt Disney Records. “They’re handed down from generation to generation. Parents want to share their childhood with their own kids, and it’s become part of our culture. Nobody has a song catalogue like Disney does. It’s almost a genre in and of itself.”

While music is important in all Disney animated films, whether it’s with big, colorful musical moments or a carefully crafted instrumental score, it’s particularly essential in a Disney Princess story. Because Walt Disney Animation Studios, and its composers, often structures its films like Broadway musicals, there are recurring elements in each animated story that harken back to the stage. For instance, most musicals feature a moment early in the story when the lead character describes her aspirations in a song, as Snow White does in “I’m Wishing.” Howard Ashman, who wrote many of the lyrics for the iconic Disney songs during the period known as the “Disney Renaissance,” called this the “I want” song.

“The leading lady sits down on something and sings about what she wants in life,” Ashman explained in archival footage featured in the Disney documentary *Waking Sleeping Beauty* (2010). “And the audience falls in love with her and then roots for her to get it for the rest of the night.” If you look back, almost all of the Disney Princesses have that moment, when they clearly express what they want—the cornerstone of their musical journeys.

“In our films, we’re putting forth a worldview and a journey people can identify with, and it’s irrelevant whether it’s a Disney Princess or a Disney prince or anyone else,” Menken reflects. “It’s about the empowerment of the human spirit. The real significance of Disney Princesses is the yearning that is within young people who might feel disempowered or not heard.”

The magical songs from the Disney Princess films have traveled out into the world over the years, making their way onto soundtracks and compilations, into the Disney parks, to Broadway, and beyond. Musicians have covered them and DJs have remixed them. They’re a key part of many fans’ Disney-themed weddings. And as the princesses sing about their hopes and dreams, they evoke our dreams as well, whether we want to be part of another world, explore the great unknown, or simply find someone to love.

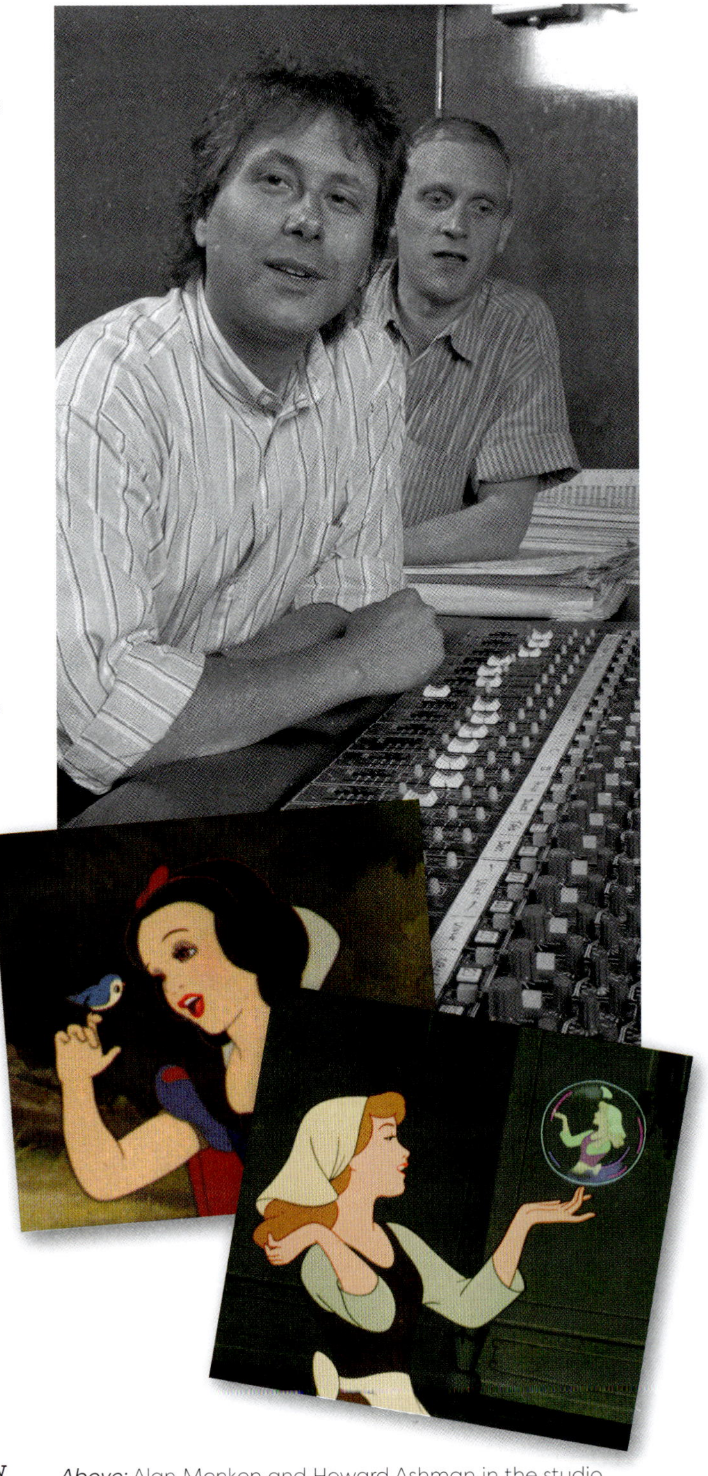

Above: Alan Menken and Howard Ashman in the studio, working on *The Little Mermaid*. *Insets:* Snow White sings a hopeful tune, and Cinderella puts her wishes into song.

MUSIC AND ANIMATION

Before Walt ventured into feature-length animation with *Snow White and the Seven Dwarfs*, Disney's original music numbers were created by sheer necessity. The studio didn't have a library of songs to draw from like other film studios, so many of Walt Disney's early animated works used classical music or songs available in the public domain. The studio's first original musical hit, "Who's Afraid of the Big Bad Wolf?," was written by Disney Legend Frank Churchill for the animated short *Three Little Pigs* in 1933. The song was a massive success at the time (and has since been performed by everyone from Duke Ellington to Barbra Streisand to LL Cool J), proving that audiences were as compelled by the music as they were by the animation.

As Walt was developing *Snow White*, he knew the story would be best presented as an animated musical feature. "I don't think there was ever any doubt in Walt's mind about making *Snow White and the Seven Dwarfs* as a musical," says Disney music historian Greg Ehrbar. "There were too many advantages to enhancing the storytelling, capturing the audience's emotions, and carrying the popularity of the film beyond the theater."

Like many of Disney's animated features, *Snow White*'s music reflected what musical styles were popular at the time, and that included the operetta. Most operettas in the 1930s were based on fairy tales, and the songs for *Snow White*, written by Frank Churchill and Larry Morey, embraced that aesthetic. Walt himself gave final approval over the musical numbers. In fact, it was Walt's idea for the film to contain a song called "Some Day My Prince Will Come," which voice actress Adriana Caselotti sang.

"One of Walt's suggestions in one of his early outlines for the movie was he thought that there really should be a song called 'Some Day My Prince Will Come,'" explains J.B. Kaufman, author of *The Fairest One of All: The Making of Walt Disney's Snow White*. "So, of course,

Snow White and the Seven Dwarfs celebrate with a song and dance.

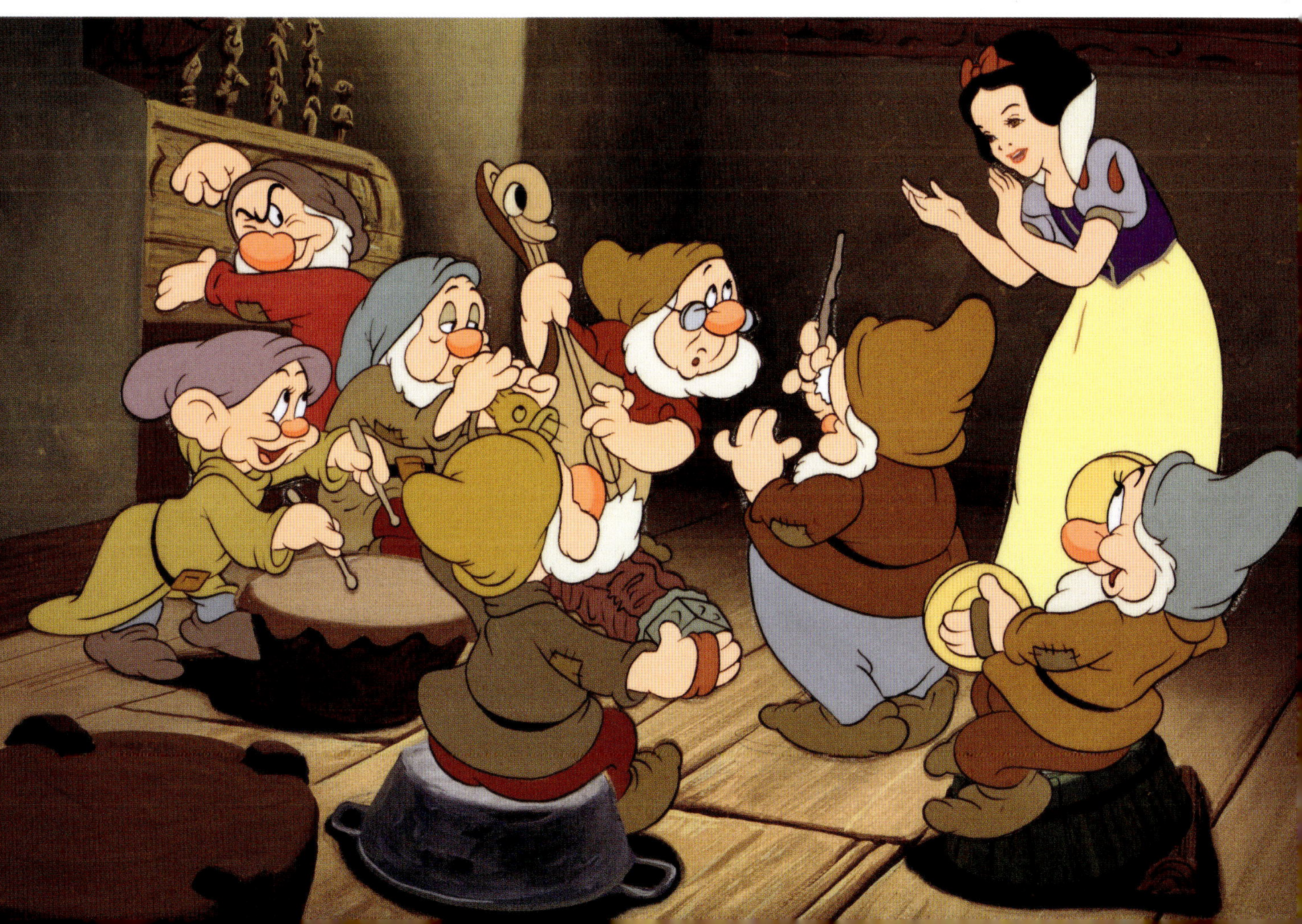

Churchill obliged. He came up with this melody, which ended up being a great song and an important part of the score, to this day."

But while the song-driven format of *Snow White* feels familiar to viewers today, in 1937 making an animated musical was an unusual endeavor. Each song fit the story inextricably, like in a popular stage musical, and Walt recognized the potential of the songs to act as promotional jingles for the movie. The songs were carried out of the theater with the viewer after the credits rolled, easy to hum or sing in one's head. "It was that little piece of the film that you could relive and it was yours," Thornton notes. "The music was the one thing you were able to take away instantly."

The recorded music of *Snow White and the Seven Dwarfs* was released as the first commercially available film soundtrack in 1938 via RCA Victor. The eleven-track collection, titled *Songs from Walt Disney's Snow White and the Seven Dwarfs (with the Same Characters and Sound Effects as in the Film of That Title)* and featured on three 78rpm singles sold in a package. It was extremely popular, with the songs played regularly on the radio. It was no wonder the film was nominated for Best Musical Score at the Academy Awards later that year. Back then, there was also no such thing as home video, so soundtracks were the best way for fans to relive their favorite film moments at home.

"The impact of the score of *Snow White* is not be underestimated," says historian Stacia Martin. "Those songs were massive, and not thought of as children's music. Those were Top 40 hit parade songs that everybody loved."

As Walt continued making animated features, he stuck with the tried-and-true musical format. He was so determined to get the music of *Cinderella* (1950) right, he enlisted Tin Pan Alley songwriters Mack David, Al Hoffman, and Jerry Livingston to pen the songs, including "Bibbidi-Bobbidi-Boo." Voice actress Ilene Woods performed "A Dream is a Wish Your Heart Makes," evoking Disney's earlier hit

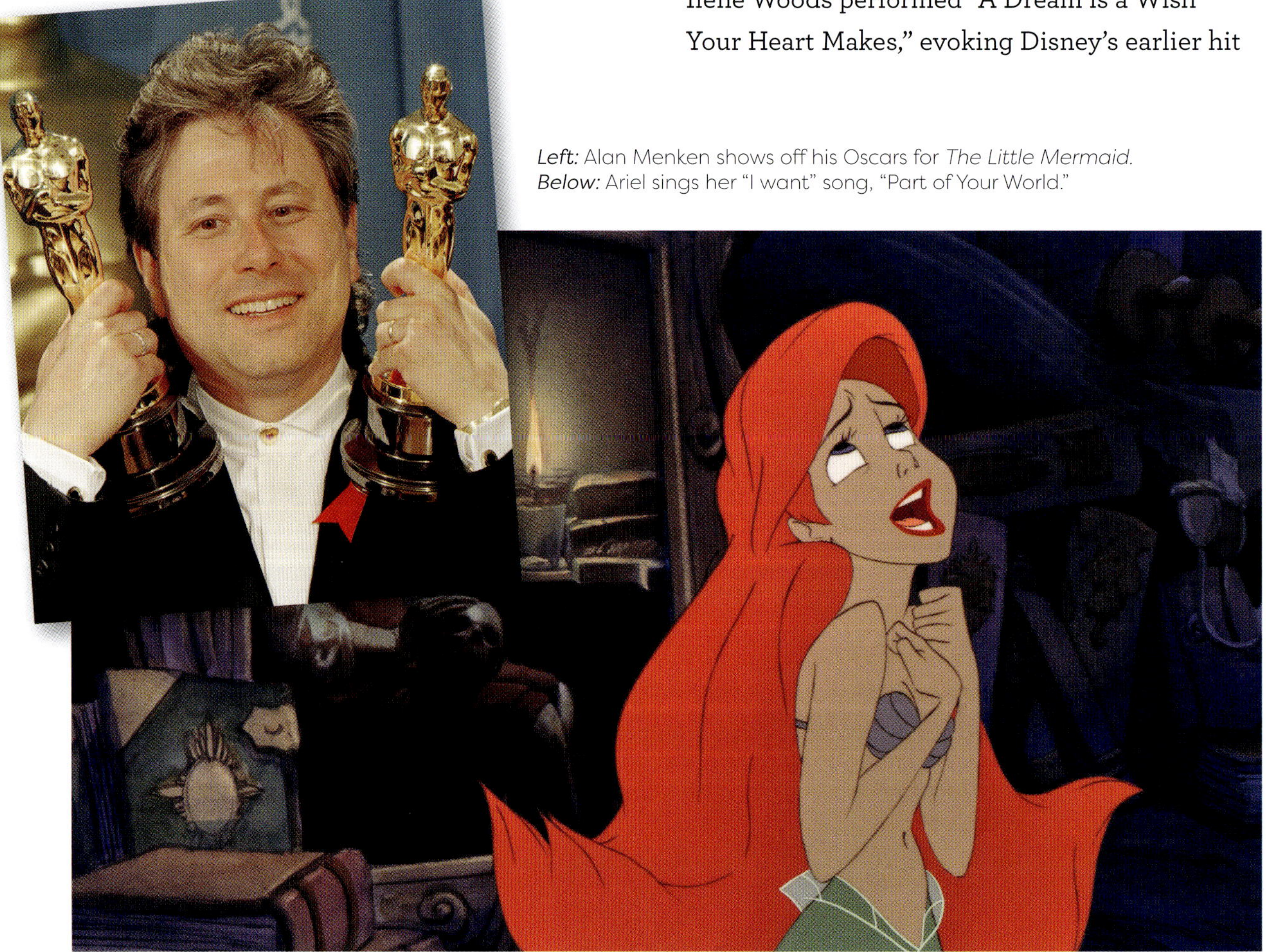

Left: Alan Menken shows off his Oscars for *The Little Mermaid.*
Below: Ariel sings her "I want" song, "Part of Your World."

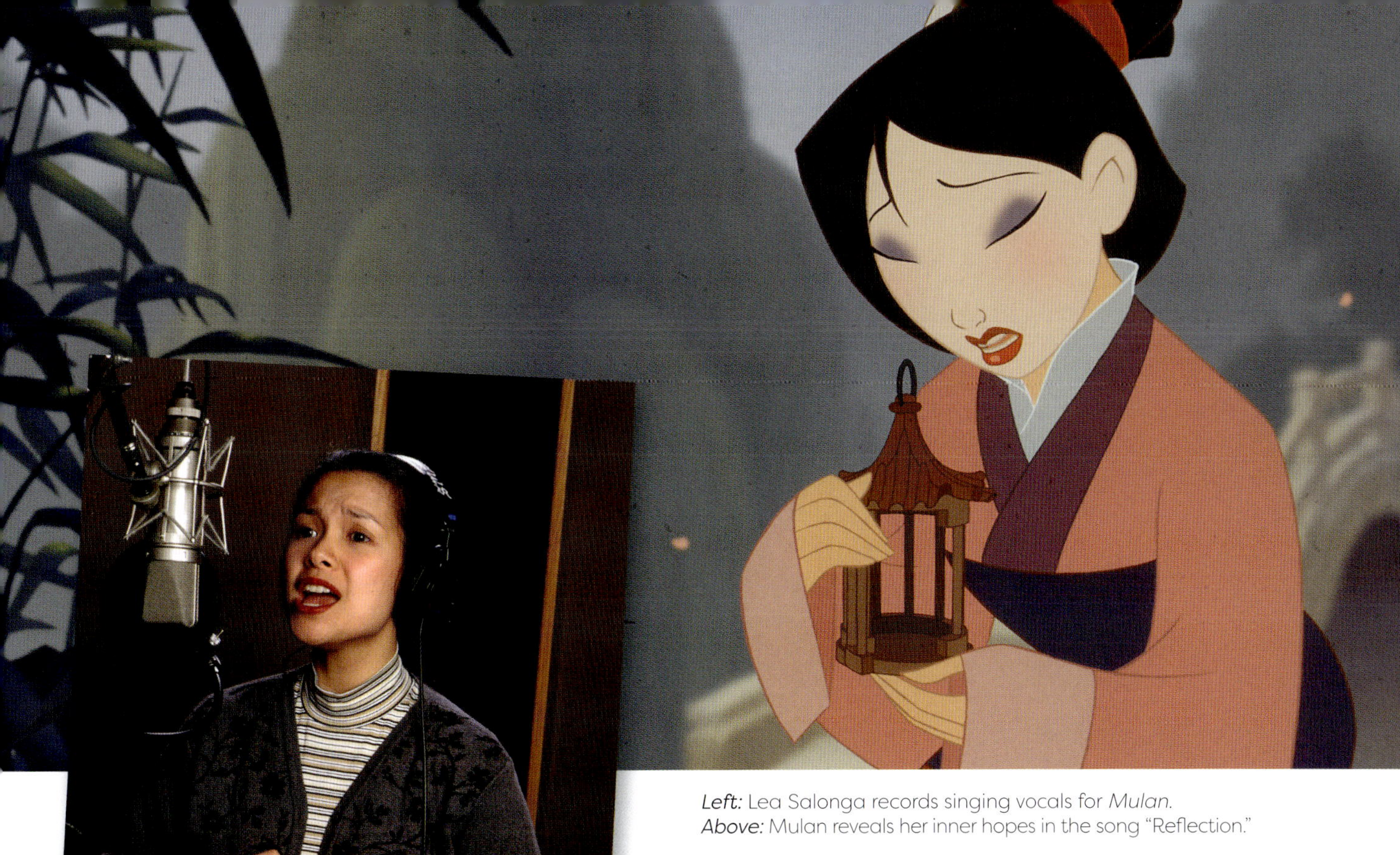

Left: Lea Salonga records singing vocals for *Mulan*.
Above: Mulan reveals her inner hopes in the song "Reflection."

"When You Wish Upon a Star" from *Pinocchio* (1940). *Sleeping Beauty* (1959), released nearly a decade after *Cinderella*, had a more classical tone, with George Bruns's score inspired by Peter Tchaikovsky's *Sleeping Beauty Ballet*. Its most iconic song was "Once Upon a Dream," sung by voice actress Mary Costa.

It was the era known as the "Disney Renaissance," however, that really solidified Disney's connection to the Broadway musical structure. Lyricist Howard Ashman and composer Alan Menken had success on Broadway with *Little Shop of Horrors* in the early 1980s, and were brought in during the production of *The Little Mermaid* to write the music. That collaboration ended up being transformative. Ashman and Menken were responsible for the film's award-winning hits, including "Under the Sea" and "Kiss the Girl," and went on to craft the songs for *Beauty and the Beast* and *Aladdin*. The two brought both a whimsy and a sense of emotional gravity to the songs, which captivated audiences. It was an interesting moment in pop culture, when animated musicals dominated the screens but actual stage musicals were much less popular.

"Homegrown American musicals were really not doing all that well in the '80s," explains charts expert Chris Molanphy. "The '90s weren't much better. Live humans breaking into song was, for about a twenty-year period, considered sort of uncool. However, in the middle of that period, if an animated character broke into song, it was fine with us."

Ashman tragically died of AIDS in 1991 at the age of forty, leaving behind an important legacy that carries on today. Menken teamed up with lyricist Tim Rice to finish *Aladdin*, and has since written the songs for *Pocahontas* and *Tangled*, as well as new songs for Broadway productions of Disney films like *The Little Mermaid* and *Aladdin*. He also worked on several of the live-action princess adaptations, including *Beauty and the Beast*, *Aladdin*, and *The Little Mermaid*.

"Howard was a genius, one of the greatest talents of our generation in terms of musical theater and songs and music being used in

“Let it Go”

There is perhaps no recent song that has impacted pop culture with such force as “Let It Go.” The memorable and powerful *Frozen* anthem spent thirty-three weeks in the Billboard Hot 100 and was the fifth best-selling song of 2014, eventually winning the Oscar for Best Original Song. The film’s composers Kristen Anderson-Lopez and Robert Lopez wanted to create a showstopping, transformative moment for Elsa, voiced by Idina Menzel. The songwriting team was inspired by singers like Tori Amos, Aimee Mann, Sara Bareilles, and Adele, as well as the woman behind Elsa. “Idina herself was an inspiration too—her voice is so iconic, and we were trying to write for it,” Lopez told Billboard. “She captures both the fragile vulnerability and the surging raw power that we wanted the song to have.”

After the filmmakers heard “Let It Go,” they made some adaptations to both the story and the character of Elsa, who was originally the film’s antagonist. “We got a new perspective,” explains *Frozen* director and writer Jennifer Lee. “We thought, ‘Let’s see what that moment is just for her to be alone with her powers for the first time and let them out.’ It just changed everything. We finally said, ‘She’s not the villain. She’s us. She’s trapped. She’s misunderstood.’ That song was the exhilarating moment of her rebelling against it.”

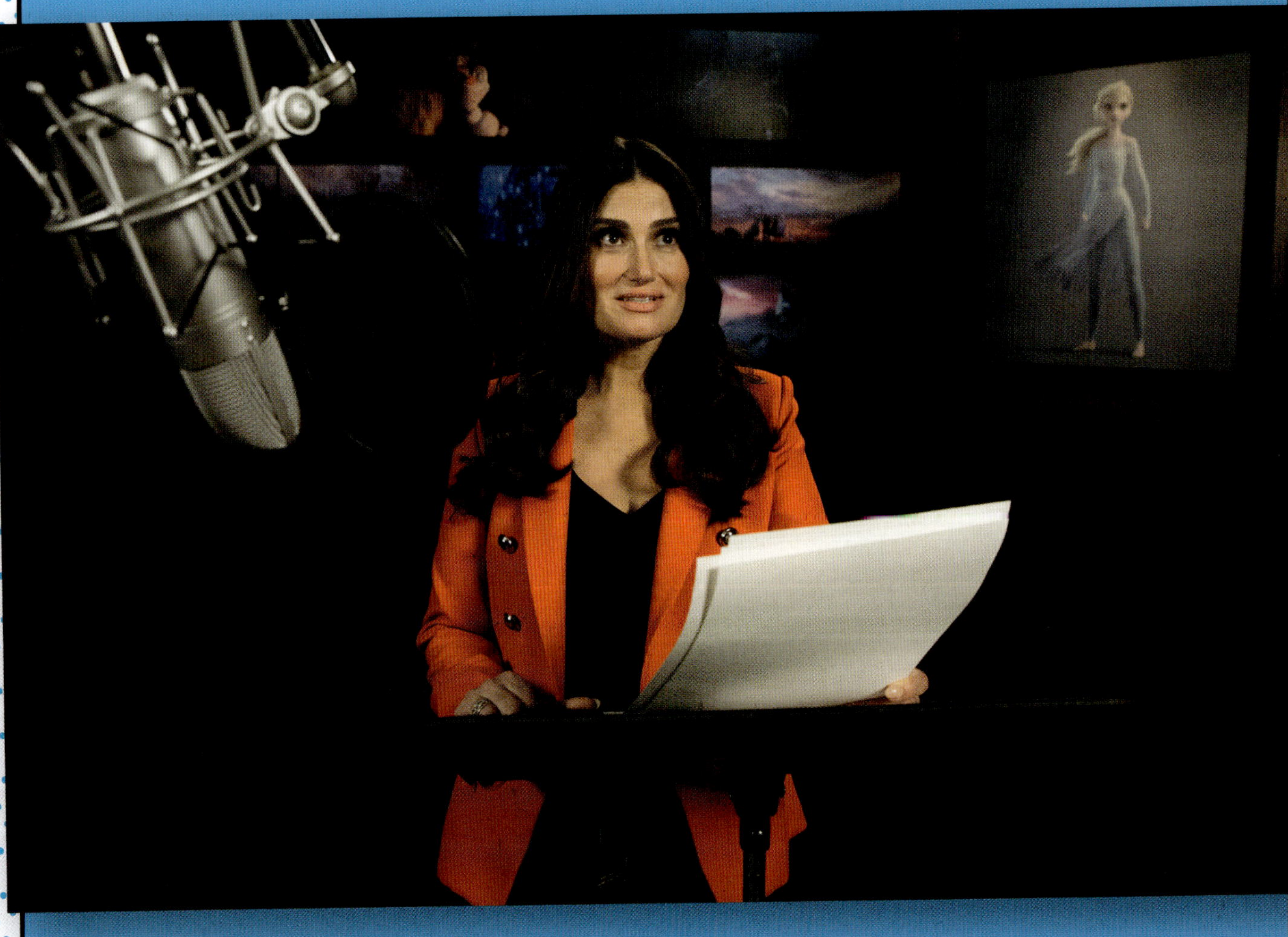

As the voice of Elsa, Idina Menzel was one of the inspirations for *Frozen*’s iconic tune “Let It Go.”

films," Menken says, crediting Ashman for the musical legacy that came out of the Disney films in the 1990s. "He was a really brilliant storyteller. One thing he understood is that a Disney Princess is no different than any of us. In a sense, we are all the Disney Princesses—a person with a passion, a desire, a dream, an obstacle to overcome, and a journey to go through that we can identify with."

Because Disney songs are so linked with pop music, Walt Disney Animation Studios always tapped the most current songwriters to be involved in the stories. For *Moana*, the filmmakers brought Lin-Manuel Miranda onboard to write songs alongside Mark Mancina and Opetaia Foa'i. The film's "I want" song, "How Far I'll Go," is one of the most memorable Disney Princess songs to date. It took the songwriters a few tries to get it right, eventually landing on the evocative anthem that sees Moana questioning why the ocean is calling to her.

"One of the most difficult things about it is really knowing what it is that your character wants," explains *Moana* producer Osnat Shurer. "You need to find a place in the storytelling where the emotion has built so high that you have to break into song, and you want to hint at what the character needs because it's not the same as what the character wants. Saying 'How far can I go? I want to go beyond the horizon. I want to go beyond what I know.'—who among us hasn't felt that?"

Songs like "How Far I'll Go" and "Part of Your World" act as a shorthand for the storytellers, as well as points of connection for the audience. They bring viewers along on the emotional journey of the film, and Walt Disney Animation Studios is where that unbreakable connection between animation and song started. Without these melodies, viewers wouldn't feel quite as immersed in the princesses' fairy-tale worlds. "Music is the ultimate storytelling tool and Walt realized that from the start," Martin confirms. "Despite the power of animation and visuals, it was music that could tie emotions to imagery."

SOUNDTRACKS AND COMPILATIONS

As Walt Disney Animation Studios released more animated musical features, there was an increasing appetite to bring the songs home. The early soundtracks were released on RCA Victor, but in 1956, Walt established Disneyland Records. The label was a place to release new soundtracks and compilations, but there was also a secondary goal, to revive and rerelease some of the older film scores. Walt hired producer and Disney Legend Salvador "Tutti" Camarata as music director, and Camarata created new versions of the soundtracks to several films, including *Cinderella* (1950). Instead of simply including the original

Film soundtracks and read-along books have been popular since the time of early Disney animated films, including *Snow White and the Seven Dwarfs*.

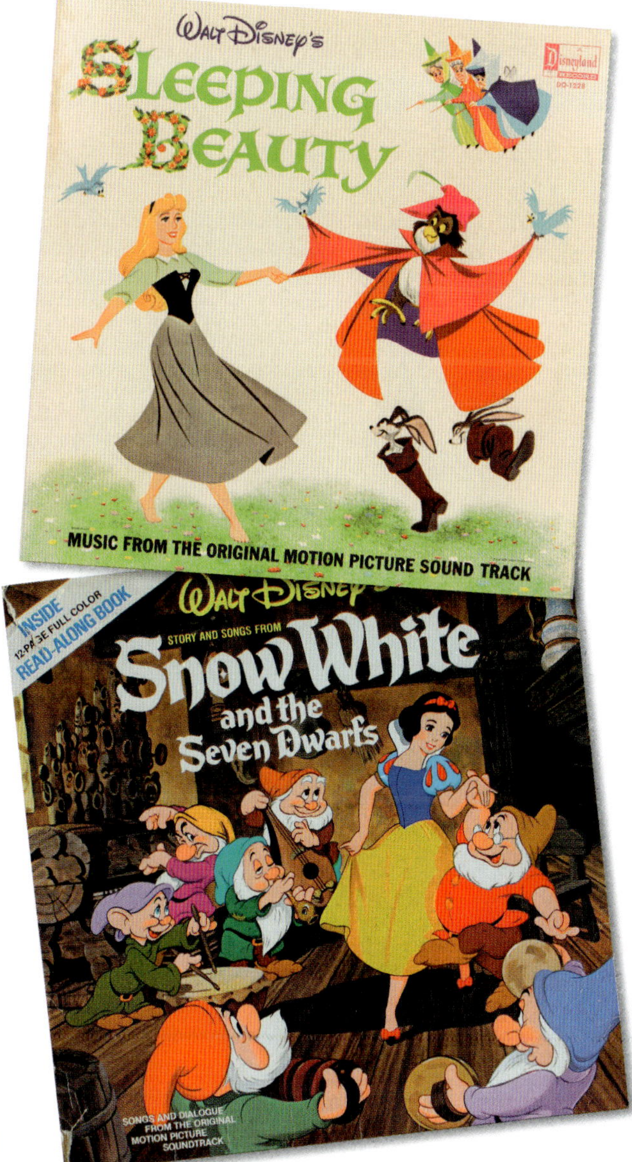

recorded songs, Camarata brought in the film score and dialogue, building a more immersive experience of the original animation.

"This way, you could hear the motion picture rather than see it," Camarata said. "It was probably one of the first times that soundtracks had been approached in this way. When starting a new record label, you want an identity and Disney's best identity was its animated classics."

That legacy carries on today at Walt Disney Records (the label was renamed in 1988). Randy Thornton joined the label in 1987 and has spent the past few decades restoring the old soundtracks and scores using new technology. *Walt Disney Records: The Legacy Collection* launched in 2014, on CD, with a new version of *The Lion King*'s soundtrack, and includes expansive reissues of the songs from *The Little Mermaid, Cinderella,* and *Pocahontas.* There's no definitive version of any Disney film soundtrack because they keep evolving generation after generation. "The cool thing with Disney is they made so many variations of each album—and there are so many to still be reissued," Ehrbar notes. "So there is an enormous wealth of wonderful versions to discover."

In the past few decades, soundtracks to Disney animated films, as well as the live-action adaptations, have included pop versions of the musical numbers—many of which have been mega-hits on the charts. "Beauty and the Beast," written by Ashman and Menken, was recorded as a duet by Celine Dion and Peabo Bryson for the film's soundtrack. It went to No. 9 in the Billboard Hot 100, which ranks radio pop songs. The following year, Bryson joined Regina Belle for a single version of "A Whole New World" from *Aladdin,* which was so popular it knocked Whitney Houston's "I Will Always Love You" off the No. 1 spot on the Billboard Hot 100. Similarly, Vanessa Williams's take on "Colors of the Wind" from *Pocahontas,* landed in the Top 5, while Disney Legend Christina Aguilera's "Reflection" from *Mulan,* helped launch her singing career after she left the *Mickey Mouse Club.* More recently, everyone from Lana Del Rey to Ariana Grande have been part of the Disney soundtracks, offering pop-inclined versions of the classic tunes.

Compilations, too, have been a way for artists to share their own interpretation of the songs, from 2006's *Disney Princess: The Ultimate Song Collection* to *Princess Disneymania* in 2008. There have been opportunities for musicians to get creative, too. In 2010, American accordion player Buckwheat Zydeco was inspired by the musical world of *The Princess and the Frog* for his album *Bayou Boogie.* It's clear there's an endless appetite for Disney Princess music, in whatever form it takes. "It's a cliché, but the Disney songs are the soundtrack of our lives," says Ehrbar. "The songs keep playing even after the movie ends or the album is over."

TAKING IT TO BROADWAY

While it may feel like Disney's stories have always been a part of Broadway, big stage interpretations of films like *Beauty and the Beast* (1991) and *Aladdin* (1992) only date back to the 1990s. However, there is a history of actors performing the beloved animated stories on stage much earlier. In 1979, director Frank Wagner staged a version of *Snow White and the Seven Dwarfs* at Radio City Music Hall starring Mary Jo Salerno and Anne Francine. Based on composer Frank Churchill's original music with a book and additional lyrics by Joe Cook, the stage adaptation made its way to New York City by way of The Muny theater in St. Louis. The production ran for 106 performances, and a televised version aired on HBO in 1980.

There was a real demand for stage renditions of the beloved films, which were produced in the Disney parks in the years before former Disney CEO Michael Eisner gave Broadway the green light. When *Beauty and the Beast* opened in movie theaters on November 22, 1991, a thirty-minute stage version premiered at Disney's Hollywood Studios Park the same day, with its

May I Have This Dance?

What's music without a little dancing? A Disney Princess is light on her feet, whether she has a prince or an owl as her partner. The magic of the dance sequence dates back to *Snow White and the Seven Dwarfs*, when Walt Disney was fascinated with the idea of a scene in which Snow White and her prince would dance through the clouds. The studio's artists created sketches and storyboards for the elaborate, dreamlike sequence, but the idea was ultimately cut from the finished film. Walt returned to the concept in *Cinderella*, but it wasn't until *Sleeping Beauty* that the animation team was able to send the hero off into the sky with her prince.

Years later, Walt Disney Animation Studios achieved an even greater technical and visual feat with the ballroom scene in *Beauty and the Beast*. After decades of hand-drawn animation, the film became the one of the first to use the CAPS system, which allowed the animators to scan drawings into a computer system and color them digitally. That gave the filmmakers the ability to manipulate the elements of a scene to allow for greater freedom of movement and staging in animation, which was key in creating the emotionally wrought waltz between Belle and the Beast. The scene swells with emotion and mood as Mrs. Potts sings the titular song, though ultimately, it's the sweeping camera movement, a dance in itself, that conveys the strength of the characters' connection.

Those aren't the only iconic dance scenes to feature a Disney Princess: Ariel tests out her human legs dancing with Prince Eric, Aurora spins through the forest with a cape-clad owl, Rapunzel urges the villagers to pick up their feet in the castle square, and Tiana twirls around her own restaurant, Tiana's Palace. It's about moving to the music, but also so much more.

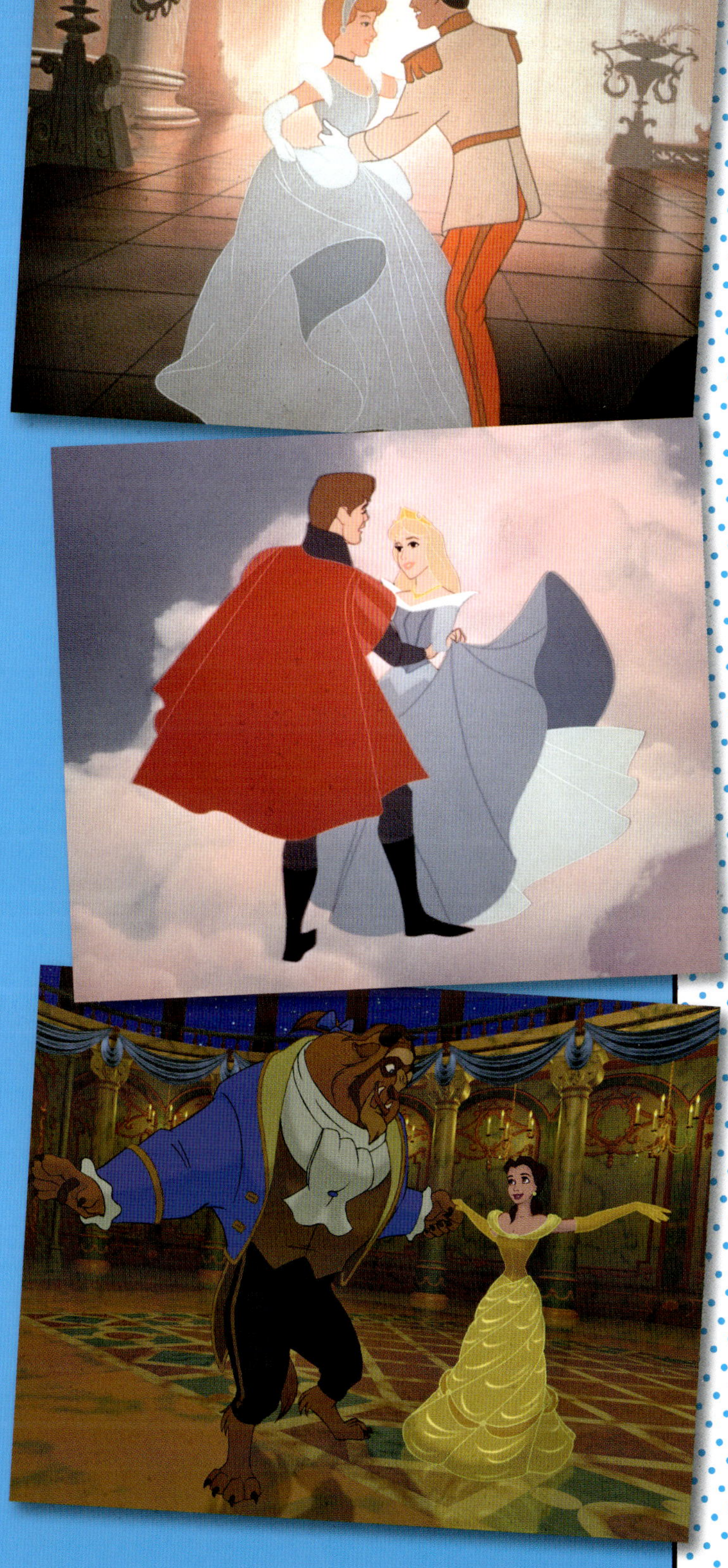

Memorable dance sequences in *Cinderella*, *Sleeping Beauty*, and *Beauty and the Beast*.

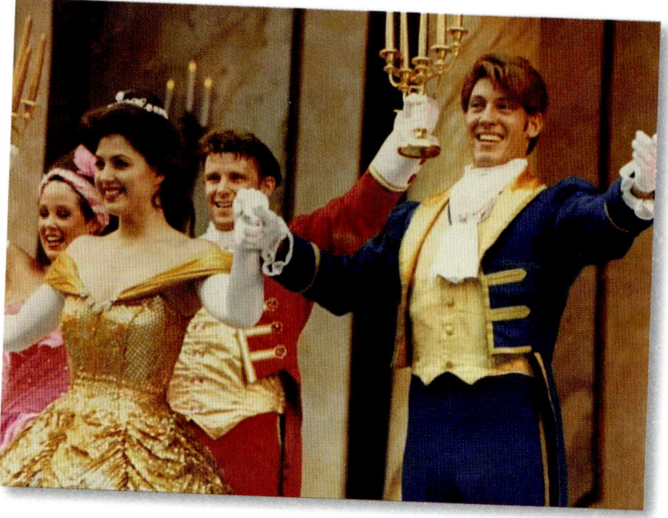

Andrea Canny as Belle in *Beauty and the Beast Live*.

cast performing five shows a day for park guests. This park-exclusive show, dubbed *Beauty and the Beast Live*, was directed by Judy Lawrence and choreographed by Robbie Mackey, and was staged as a revue, opening with a lively rendition of "Be Our Guest." Andrea Canny was one of two actresses who took turns playing Belle in the Disney World production, and Canny embodied the role for nearly five years.

"The very best part of being a princess, in my mind, was being able to have a positive effect on people who needed a little joy in their life and a little magic," Canny remembers of performing as Belle. "Disney has an innate magic to it, added to people thinking princesses are magical, and then you have somebody up onstage actually singing and looking people in the eyes—that is the bridge. It builds a bridge between the fans and the animated stories."

In 1992, Canny flew to New York City with Galen Fott, who played Gaston, and Paula Pell, who played Mrs. Potts. The actors joined Paige O'Hara and Jerry Orbach to perform a concert-style showcase at the Waldorf Astoria, where Michael Eisner was being honored with the Gold Medal award. They sang several songs from *Beauty and the Beast*, and Fott sang a duet of "A Whole New World" with Lea Salonga for the audience to preview Disney's next film, *Aladdin*. It was so successful that by the time the actors got backstage after the show, Eisner was already there, proclaiming that he was finally ready for Broadway.

"There were a lot of perks that came with being a princess," Canny says. "It was an exciting time to be part of that particular gig where it was

Several of the Disney stage and movie actors gathered at the Waldorf Astoria for a showcase performance to honor Michael Eisner. From left to right: Gaston stage actor Galen Fott, stage actor Darin DePaul, Belle voice actress Paige O'Hara, Lumiere voice actor Jerry Orbach, Jasmine voice actress (singing) Lea Salonga, stage actress Paula Pell, and Belle stage actress Andrea Canny.

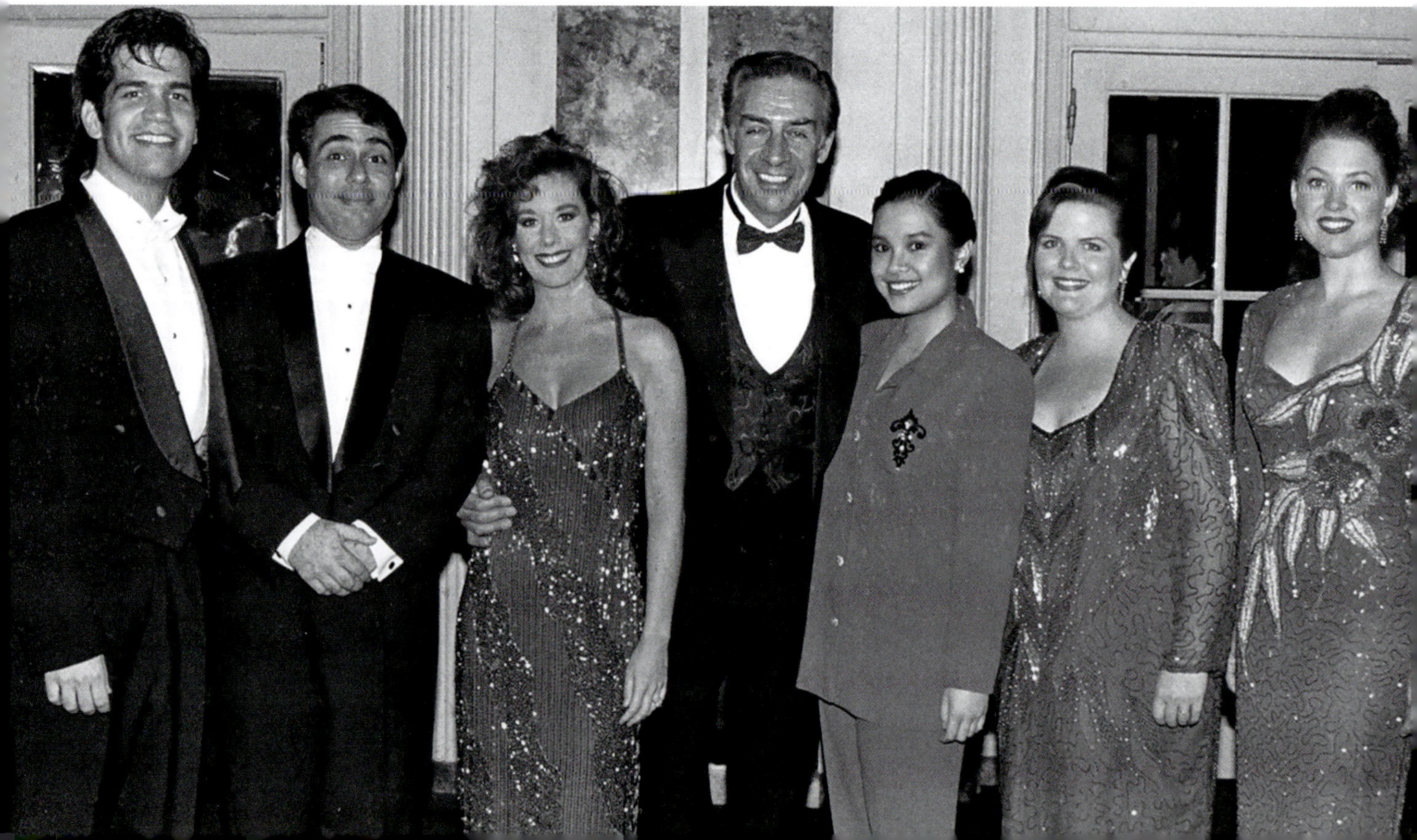

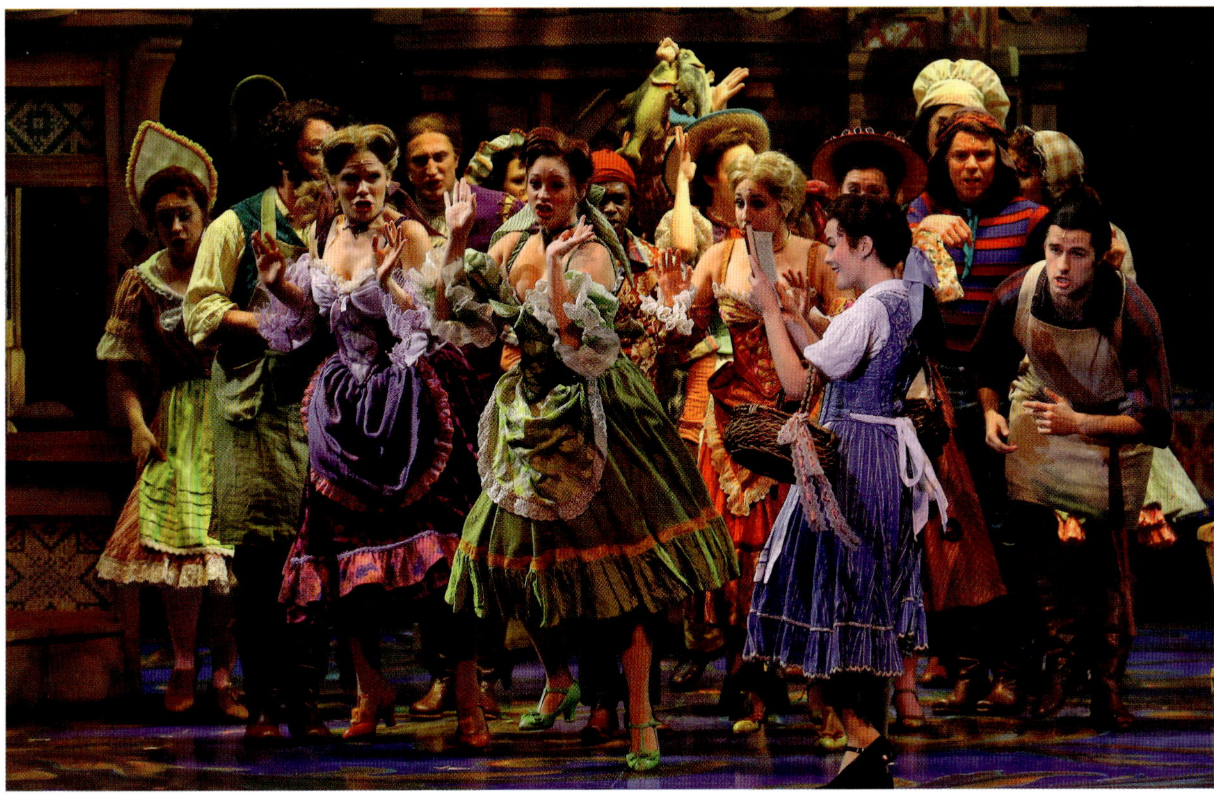

A musical number from the Broadway production of *Beauty and the Beast*.

the moment when Eisner was like 'Let's change the face of Broadway.'"

After getting the okay from Eisner, director Robert Jess Roth took the helm, working to bring the magic of *Beauty and the Beast* to the stage. The film's screenwriter Linda Woolverton returned to pen the musical's book, and Alan Menken and Tim Rice wrote six new songs to augment the production. While the stage show remained faithful to the beloved film, Woolverton wanted to use the opportunity to give the audience more insight into Belle.

"Being able to do the stage play was such a gift because I could expand Belle's character," Woolverton says. "I could expand the relationship between Belle and the Beast more, which allowed her to become more dimensional. We could understand more about her. It was a wonderful opportunity to deepen Belle, and deepen the Beast as well."

Beauty and the Beast opened on Broadway at the Palace Theatre on April 18, 1994, with Susan Egan as Belle. While critics were skeptical of Disney's arrival on Broadway, fans were not. "We didn't get good reviews, but the audience came and they came and they came," Woolverton says. "It moved from one theater in Times Square to another and they still came. They came for thirteen years."

Beauty and the Beast played on Broadway until 2007, with 5,464 performances in total. It was nominated for nine Tony Awards and had several national U.S. tours, with the production appearing on stages in dozens of U.S. and international cities. It reopened in the U.K. in the fall of 2021 in a reimagined format, using new theatrical staging technology. The musical proved that Disney would have a legacy on the stage as well as on the screen.

Beauty and the Beast was followed by stage adaptations of *The Lion King*, which opened in 1997, and an international run of *The Hunchback of Notre Dame*, in 1999. There were discussions of a possible stage version of *The Little Mermaid*, but it took many years to find the right approach, even though a musical show called "Voyage of the Little Mermaid" had been running in Disney's Hollywood Studios at Walt Disney World since 1992.

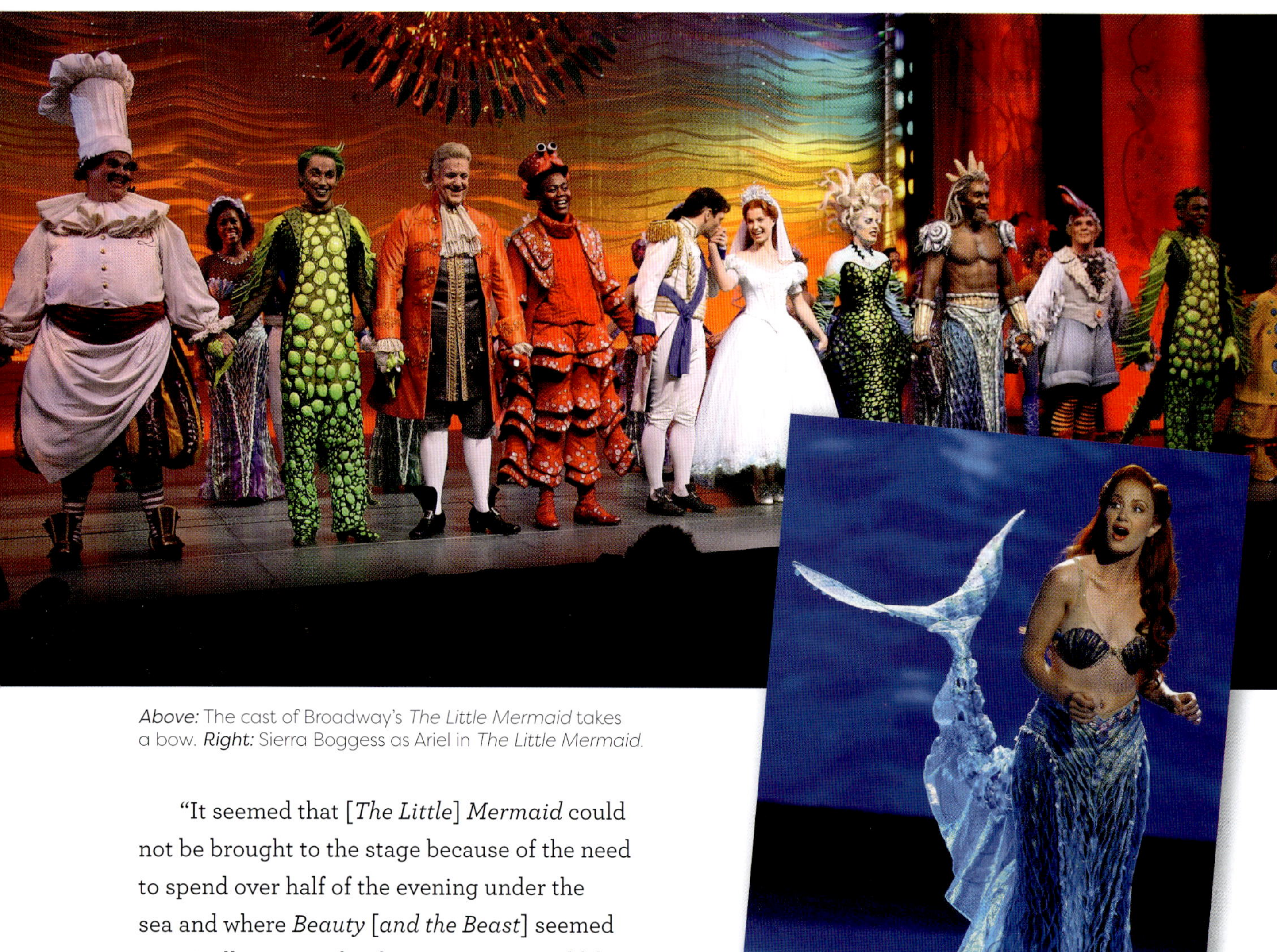

Above: The cast of Broadway's *The Little Mermaid* takes a bow. *Right:* Sierra Boggess as Ariel in *The Little Mermaid.*

"It seemed that [*The Little*] *Mermaid* could not be brought to the stage because of the need to spend over half of the evening under the sea and where *Beauty* [*and the Beast*] seemed practically written for the stage, *Mermaid* felt much more limited to its conception as an animated film," Menken wrote in *The Little Mermaid: A Broadway Musical.* "Then came the day when Tom Schumacher brought up the topic of developing our baby for Broadway. Would I commence the process of expanding the story and score for the stage, in hopes that a more avant-garde approach might help solve the physical staging challenges? Yes!"

Making it work came down to director Francesca Zambello's vision, which was to not get obsessed with making the characters appear to be swimming. One of the most important things for Zambello was to give the character of Ariel even more agency, particularly in the climactic battle scene with Ursula. Playwright Doug Wright wanted to ensure Ariel was both familiar to audiences and more developed than in the film. "There were several things I wanted do with the stage version," Wright noted. "One of those was to make it clear that Ariel's longing is not so much for the prince, but for a world in which she feels truly realized on her own terms, and it's important that she voice those aspirations before she even meets a prince. Her ambitions are bigger than any one man."

Actress Sierra Boggess was cast as Ariel and rehearsals began in the spring of 2007 at New York City's 42nd Street Studios. Menken and lyricist Glenn Slater gave Ariel a new "I want" song, "The World Above," which helped flesh out the character's desires. The songwriter also wanted to engage the now-older fans of the original film with new additions to the story.

"You want to keep the Disney Princess a Disney Princess, on one hand," Menken explains. "On the other hand, you want that to broaden the perception of who she is." He adds, "The little girls or young boys who are watching these movies now are teenagers or adults. And you want a sense of their childhood in it and you want something that also gives the audience more of a worldview. You look for something that could be both a family experience and a date experience."

The Little Mermaid opened on January 10, 2008 at the Lunt-Fontanne Theatre in New York, and ran until August 2009, captivating audiences with its spectacular underwater scenes. It proved that an adaptation of a Disney animation film didn't have to be an exact recreation; it could capture the essence using a more surreal visual aesthetic. Similarly, the Broadway production *Aladdin*, which opened New Amsterdam Theatre in New York City on March 20, 2014, embraced bold colors and wild spectacle.

Aladdin wasn't initially intended to make the journey to Broadway, although Disney Theatrical Productions had created an hour-long version for schoolkids, titled *Aladdin Jr.* Writer Chad Beguelin also wrote a forty-five-minute musical show for Disney California Adventure Park, which opened in January of 2003. But when Schumacher decided to adapt the film into a two-act amateur production with the help of Beguelin and Menken, they realized the story had real stage potential. Menken brought in several songs he'd written with Ashman for the original movie but didn't get used, and also wrote several new ones with Beguelin. The musical was first staged in Seattle in 2011 with Courtney Reed as Jasmine.

On March 22, 2018, *Frozen* joined the Broadway legacy as a stage musical with music and lyrics by Kristen Anderson-Lopez and

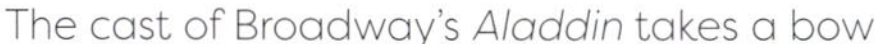
The cast of Broadway's *Aladdin* takes a bow.

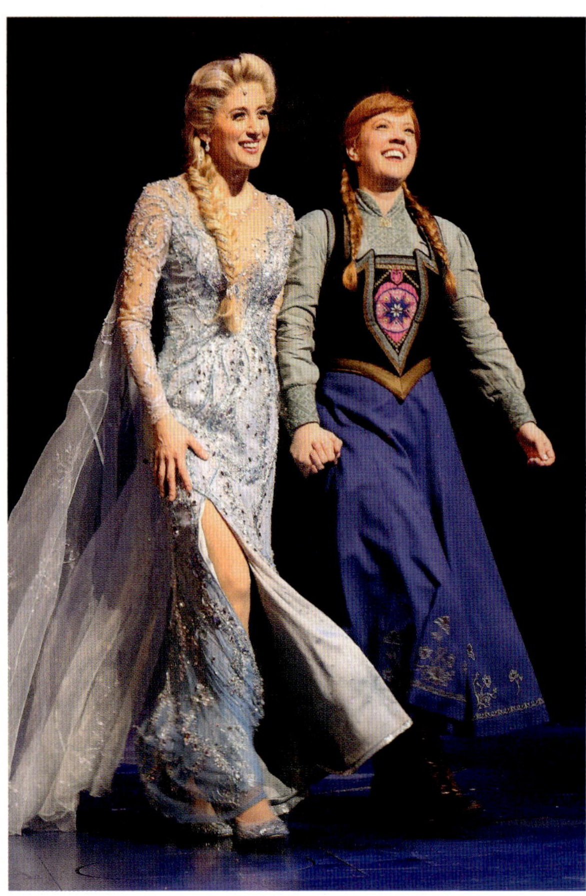

Actors Caissie Levy as Elsa and Patti Murin as Anna on opening night of the Broadway production of *Frozen* in 2018.

Robert Lopez, and book by Jennifer Lee. Disney Theatrical Productions had begun developing the musical before the film was even released, but the producers took their time to ensure it could be a sophisticated take on the animated story with compelling design elements. The show opened at the St. James Theatre on March 22, 2018, taking a deeper dive into Anna and Elsa's psyches. New songs were written to give audiences an insight into Elsa and her past, and Lee wanted to ensure that the character didn't feel emotionally distant, especially from the back of a Broadway theater.

"We were able to really open up these vulnerable moments and give the sisters more time together that allowed Elsa to confess what her childhood felt like," says Lee. "My favorite thing was adding a reprise of 'Let It Go' at the end where Elsa sings to Anna, 'The magic one is you.' I just sob every time because she recognizes it was Anna's love and the power of her perseverance that actually saved everyone."

COVERS AND REVISIONS

A good song lends itself to reinterpretation, whether it's a cover version, a remix, or a complete reworking of an entire movie soundtrack. And thanks to the pop inclinations of Disney musical numbers, lots of artists have offered their interpretations over the years. For instance, "Part of Your World" has been covered by everyone from Miley Cyrus to Bruno Mars to Faith Hill. Even unlikely singers like Sinéad O'Connor have taken on a Disney Princess tune—the musician covered "Someday My Prince Will Come" on 1988 tribute album *Stay Awake: Various Interpretations of Music from Vintage Disney Films*, produced by Hal Willner for A&M Records. Numerous jazz musicians, from Miles Davis to Herbie Hancock to Chick Corea, have been attracted to the *Snow White* classic as well. And it's clear why: If you grow up loving a song, why wouldn't you want to sing it yourself in your own way?

The Internet and YouTube has also helped to disseminate the Disney Princess cover songs. YouTube star Traci Hines has been singing the songs of *The Little Mermaid* since she was young, and continues to keep Menken and Ashman's classic tunes in her repertoire. She has created several music videos covering Disney Princess songs, including "Part of Your World," but she's also written and sung original songs inspired by the characters. In 2021, Hines tapped an international group of singers and cosplayers to film "Princess Hangout," an upbeat original song featuring all twelve Disney Princesses, as well as Tinker Bell, Anna, and Elsa. The video acted as a fundraiser for charity Campaign One At A Time, as well as a moment of hopeful connection for fans feeling isolated during the pandemic.

"I have been so blessed to meet such an incredible community through my work," says Hines, who feels the core message of Disney and Disney music is to follow your heart. "I always say, I started YouTube to get discovered as a

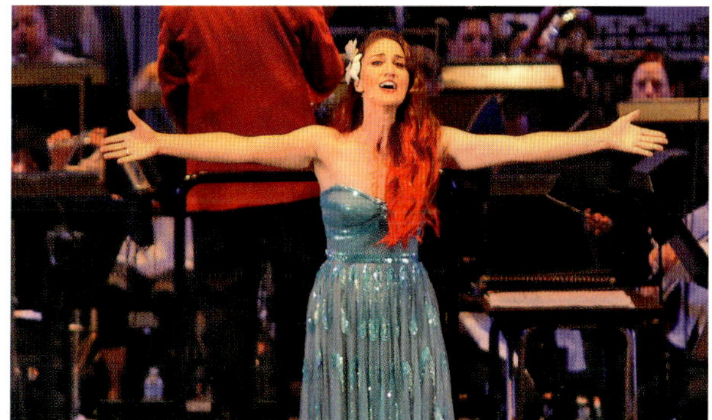

Above: Sara Bareilles in *The Little Mermaid* at the Hollywood Bowl in 2016. *Below:* Jodi Benson and Auli'i Cravalho backstage at *Disney Presents The Little Mermaid Live!*.

pop artist, but in the end what happened was so much better: I found my community."

The songs of Disney have such vast reach that they've been the subject of several live productions beyond the Disney parks and Broadway. In the summer of 2016, following a successful staging of *Tim Burton's The Nightmare Before Christmas*, producer and director Richard Kraft had the idea to put on an interpretation of *The Little Mermaid* (1989) at the Hollywood Bowl in Los Angeles. Instead of involving the original cast members, as he had with *The Nightmare Before Christmas*, Kraft envisioned the show as a celebration by singers who loved the film and its music. He cast Sara Bareilles as Ariel and tapped a seventy-one-piece orchestra to back the actors, who performed each music number live while the animated movie played in the background. Because Kraft wanted to give Ariel more to do, he added four songs from the Broadway production. He also brought Menken onstage as a guest performer. "Because I'm a fan, I put everything through a fan perspective," Kraft says. "I just thought, 'What could be the most cool?'"

Kraft enlisted a company called Mousetrap to create new digital projections for the show, inspired by the Disney parks' projections. The director met with animators to design original visuals that would enhance the animation and bring the iconic space of the Hollywood Bowl into the performance. For Kraft, it was about recontextualizing a favorite film, rather than simply staging it. The performances of *The Little Mermaid* were so captivating, in fact, that Kraft immediately embarked on a rendition of *Beauty and the Beast* (1991) in the summer of 2018, reframing the show with an Art Deco visual style to match the Hollywood Bowl's architecture.

"To me, there's no reason to do it as you expect to see it," the director notes, adding, "I didn't make *The Little Mermaid* and *Beauty and the Beast,* and none of the people I'm working with did. We're all celebrating somebody's else's accomplishment."

The Hollywood Bowl staged *The Little Mermaid* again in the spring of 2019, and took things even further that fall with a televised version on ABC. Titled *The Wonderful World of Disney Presents The Little Mermaid Live!*, the spectacular was filmed on a Disney soundstage, with Kraft putting *Moana*'s Auli'i Cravalho in the lead role. The elaborately staged musical numbers were interwoven into the animated film, offering audiences a never-before-seen hybrid experience that paid tribute to the original music.

For Kraft, these productions have revealed an essential truth about Disney music. "The songs, I think, were never written as contemporary songs," the director says. "A song from 1984 sounds like a song from 1984. A song from a Disney animated film from 1984 is not using the language of that period. They're already set in another musical vernacular that does not date it. Because the songs are never in style, they can never go out of style. You start with music that has a timeless quality to it."

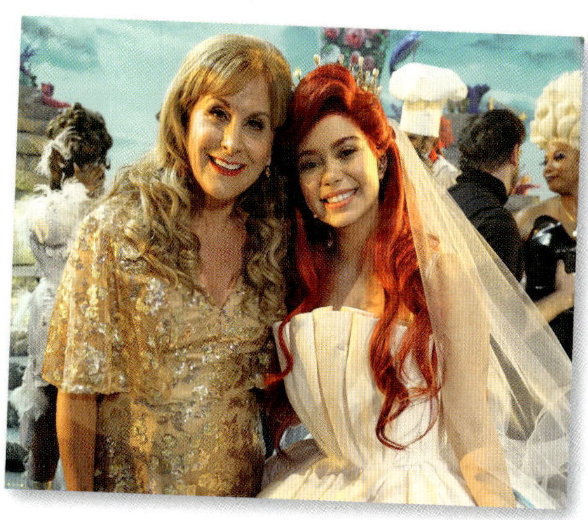

CHAPTER SIX

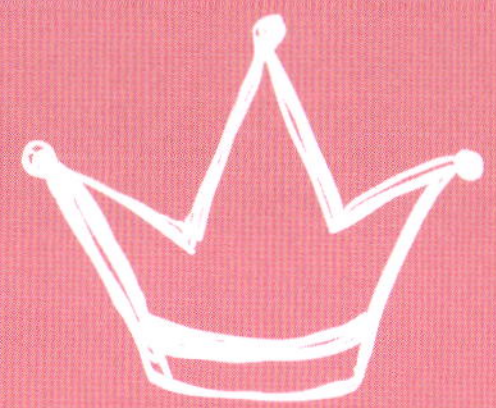

BE OUR GUEST

PARKS, RESORTS, AND CRUISE SHIPS

Walt Disney realized his dream of opening a theme park on July 17, 1955, when Disneyland swung open its gates and lowered its castle drawbridge in Anaheim, California. Walt called the park "a source of joy and inspiration to all the world," as half of the entire American population watched a live television broadcast of Disneyland's big day. He'd conceived of a theme park years before, but it wasn't until 1953, a few years after the success of *Cinderella*, that Walt was able to purchase a large enough piece of land and tap his studio artists to help design it. The concept was to create a place where adults and children could let go of their everyday lives. "I don't want the public to see the world they live in while they're in the park," Walt explained of his vision. "I want them to feel they're in another world."

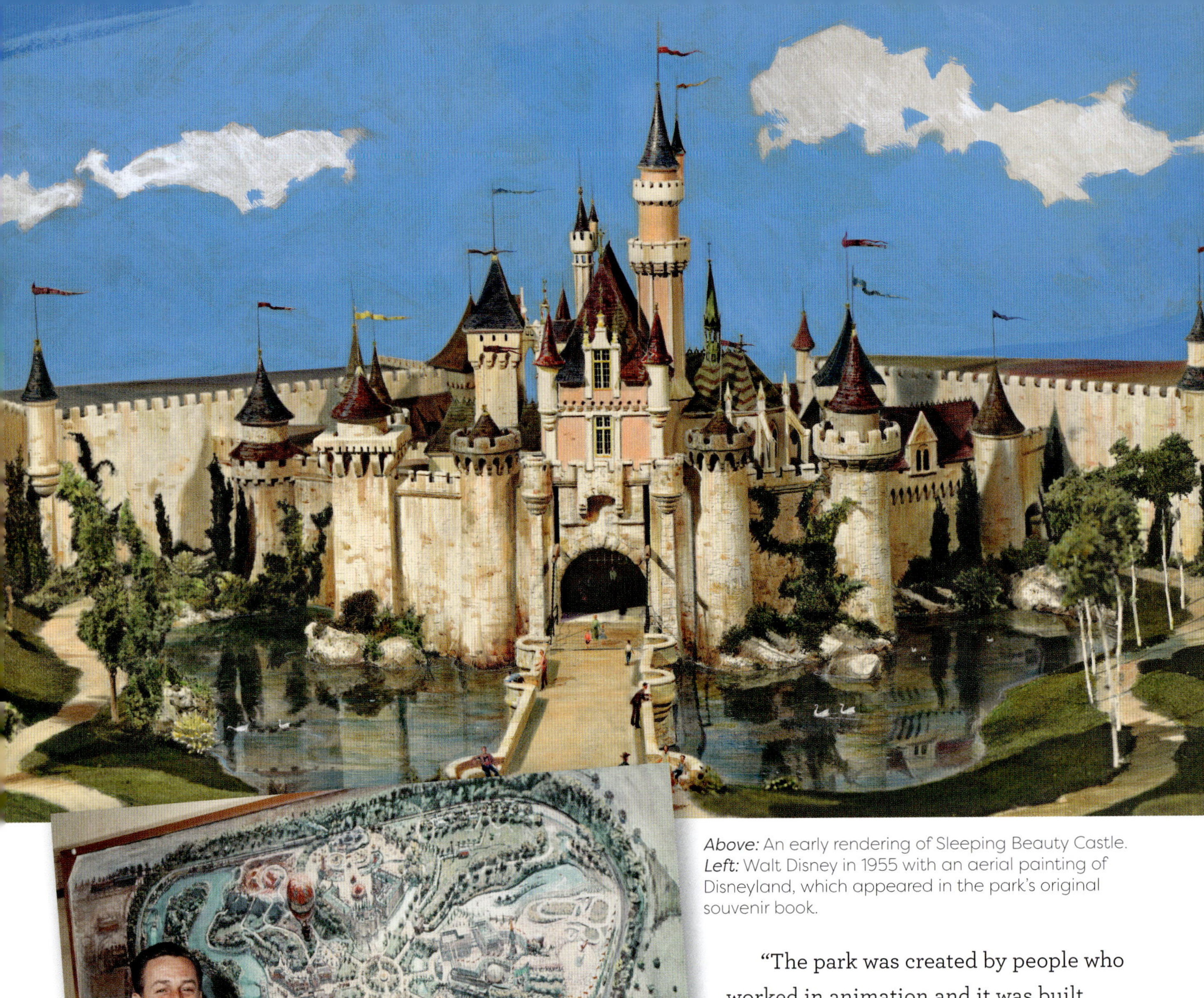

Above: An early rendering of Sleeping Beauty Castle. *Left:* Walt Disney in 1955 with an aerial painting of Disneyland, which appeared in the park's original souvenir book.

Herb Ryman, an artist and future Disney Legend, helped Walt capture his vision on paper, drafting Disneyland's first aerial view design in 1953—which included a fairy-tale castle. The Disneyland experience was planned to combine familiar characters, like the Disney Princesses, with magical lands and compelling attractions. It had a cinematic design, with each area of the park telling a different story. Disneyland was the first theme park to bring that immersive experience of being on a narrative journey to guests in the real world.

"The park was created by people who worked in animation and it was built by people who worked in film, so it's always been a reflection of American cinema and American pop art," explains Todd Martens, a Los Angeles-based journalist who has written extensively about Disneyland. "I've always seen it as a movie set. If you walk onto Main Street, it's like the curtain lifting on a movie screen and then you're in this romantic, magical film. The goal is to allow you to be the star of that film."

The entrance to Disneyland led guests directly into Main Street, U.S.A., a charming series of stores and attractions partly inspired by Walt's hometown of Marceline, Missouri. From there, the park extended into several different lands—Fantasyland, Frontierland, Adventureland, and Tomorrowland—with the fantastical Sleeping Beauty Castle in the middle, to welcome visitors. The park, of

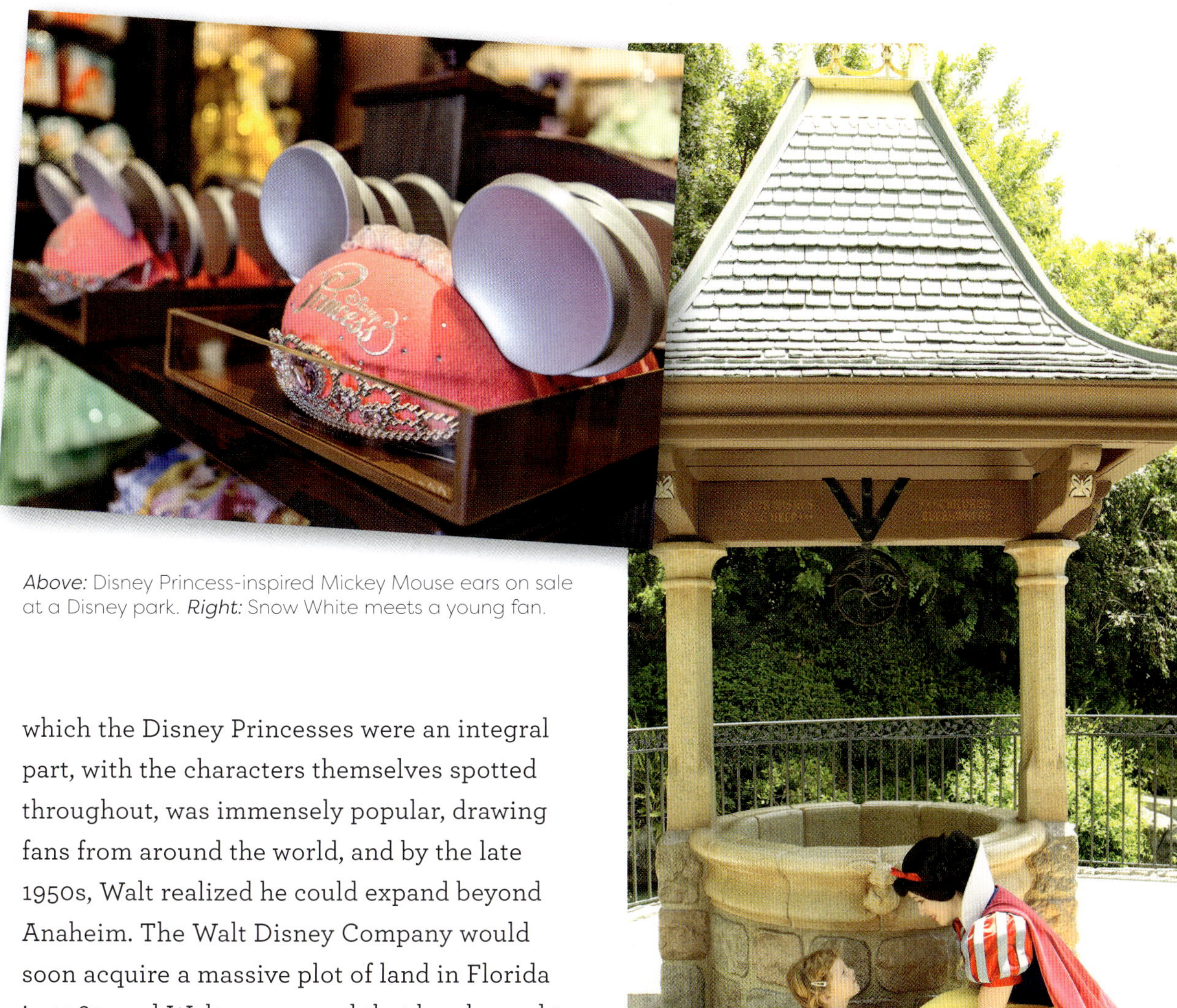

Above: Disney Princess-inspired Mickey Mouse ears on sale at a Disney park. ***Right:*** Snow White meets a young fan.

which the Disney Princesses were an integral part, with the characters themselves spotted throughout, was immensely popular, drawing fans from around the world, and by the late 1950s, Walt realized he could expand beyond Anaheim. The Walt Disney Company would soon acquire a massive plot of land in Florida in 1965, and Walt announced that he planned to open a second park there, which would become the Walt Disney World Resort. Although Walt died before the resort could be completed, his brother, Roy O. Disney, carried forward his vision, with the Magic Kingdom opening on October 1, 1971. In the years since, Disney theme parks have opened in Tokyo, Paris, Hong Kong, and Shanghai.

The Disney theme parks have also expanded into immersive resorts, such as Aulani, A Disney Resort & Spa in Ko Olina, Hawai'i, and onto cruise ships with Disney Cruise Line. All of these destinations are continually improving facets of the Disney experience, offering guests a way to live out their dreams and leave their troubles behind. Walt never saw Disneyland as a finished destination—he knew that it would grow and change with the times. "Disneyland will never be completed," Walt said once. "It will continue to grow as long as there is imagination left in the world."

That's the mindset that guides the Disney parks today, with the Imagineers—the designers and creators of the parks—always looking to the future for the next great attraction or experience. "We're such prolific storytellers and there's so much material we have, so taking advantage of opportunities to give our guests wide-ranging experiences is something we believe Walt would have endorsed," explains Imagineer Charita Carter, a senior producer at Walt Disney Imagineering. "We want to do things that are brand new. Walt was constantly going beyond guests' expectations, and I think that's something that would still be very important to him."

A CASTLE FOR EVERY PARK

Many of the Disney theme parks are known for their central storybook castles. Ever since Sleeping Beauty Castle was constructed as a focal point for Disneyland, guests often expect their park experience will center around a royal chateau. "One thing he insisted upon was that there be a very, very conspicuous castle," Imagineer Herbert Ryman recalled of Walt's vision for Disneyland. "Because the castle is going to be the symbol of this whole place."

Inspired by the nineteenth century German castle Neuschwanstein, as well as illustrator and Disney Legend Eyvind Earle's artwork from the original animated film, Ryman designed Sleeping Beauty Castle as the entrance to Fantasyland. Imagineers used a design trick called forced perspective that allowed the seventy-seven-foot castle to tower upwards in the eye of the viewer. There was some discussion about which animated princess's castle would be used, but ultimately Walt decided on *Sleeping Beauty*—which wouldn't be released in theaters for another four years. The animated classic was still in its early stages of development when Disneyland opened, which meant guests got a glimpse of the story, via the castle, long before they'd properly met Aurora. It was a clever way to market the film, as well as a point of connection for guests.

"The castle became intricately connected with Disney as a brand because of Disneyland," explains Dr. Sabrina Mittermeier, who researches American cultural history and has written extensively about the Disney parks. "It became the icon, surpassing Mickey Mouse—when you think Disney, those are the two things you think about. And when you see the castle, you also think 'princess'. It's the thing you see first when you enter the park. In Disney Imagineering speak, it's a 'weenie,' which means it's a visual magnet that also helps you orient yourself. It's about symbolism more than anything."

Sleeping Beauty Castle welcomes guests into Disneyland.

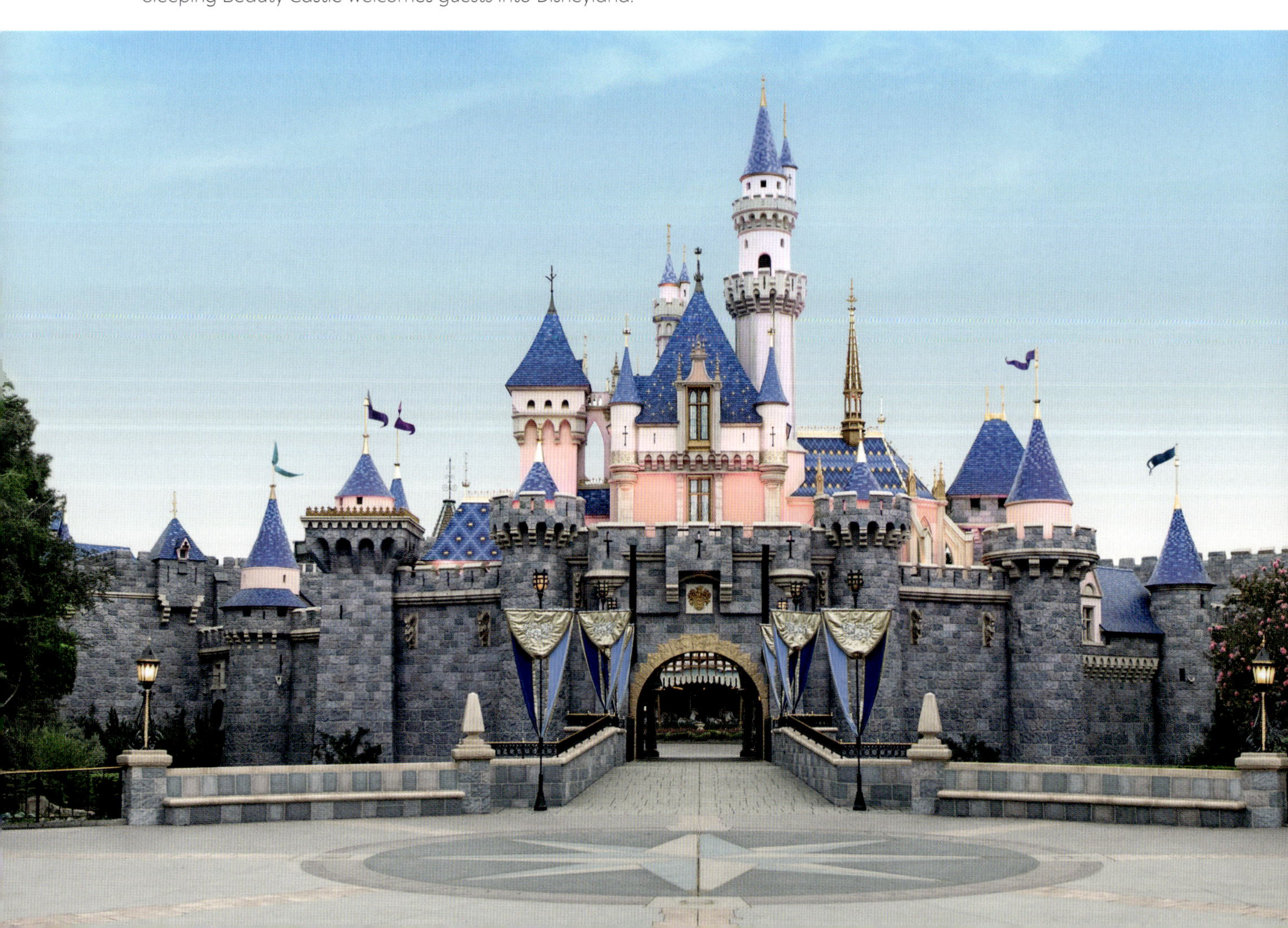

In late April 1957, Disneyland unveiled the *Sleeping Beauty Castle Walkthrough*, an exhibition featuring Earle's artwork and miniature dioramas from the upcoming film. Famed film star Shirley Temple joined Walt for a ribbon-cutting ceremony, with Temple wearing a regal cape and crown to mark the occasion. The walkthrough remains, although it's been updated with more modern technology. Sleeping Beauty Castle was a marvel, but Walt was determined to go even bigger on his next construction.

Instead of simply replicating Sleeping Beauty Castle for the Magic Kingdom at Walt Disney World, which opened in 1971, the Imagineers looked to *Cinderella* for inspiration. Cinderella Castle, also designed with the help of Ryman along with Imagineer and Disney Legend Marty Sklar, stood at 189 feet tall, more than twice the size of its Disneyland counterpart. It featured handmade glass mosaics, which told Cinderella's rags-to-riches tale, and in recent years it's been home to Cinderella's Royal Table (originally known as King Stefan's Banquet Hall), which offers fairy-tale dining for guests.

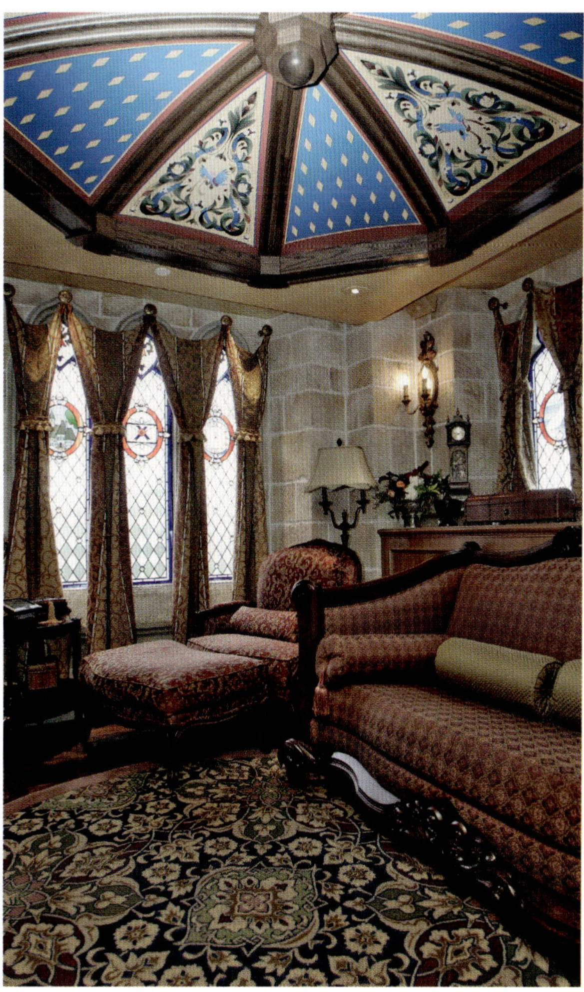

The luxurious Cinderella Castle Suite at at the Magic Kingdom at Walt Disney World.

While Sleeping Beauty Castle was never really intended as an interior space, Cinderella Castle has a secret: Cinderella Castle Suite sometimes welcomes overnight guests. The suite, designed after a seventeenth century French chateau, is occasionally used for promotional giveaways or invited VIPs, and it's gained a cultlike status among fans. Those who have gotten to spend the night as a guest of Cinderella include Tom Cruise and his daughter Suri, Kevin Jonas and his wife Danielle, and Mariah Carey.

As each new Disney park has opened, each castle has been an opportunity to explore further storytelling. Tokyo Disneyland has its own version of Cinderella Castle, while Disneyland Paris boasts Le Château de la Belle au Bois Dormant, a riff on the original Sleeping Beauty Castle that evokes the real-world castles of France's Loire Valley. Impressive details, like a dragon in the dungeon and tiny gold snails on the turret, help the castle feel like its own interpretation of the Sleeping Beauty story. It was designed by Imagineer Tom Morris, who incorporated elements of Earle's artwork with features of French castles like Mont St. Michel and Chambord. Morris wanted it to have a "déjà vu quality while also looking like a fantasy, something that came from a storybook and a Walt Disney film."

When Shanghai Disneyland opened in 2016, the Imagineers took a different approach. The Enchanted Storybook Castle, the tallest castle in a Disney park at 197 feet high, was the first to represent all of the Disney Princesses, as well as Elsa and Anna from *Frozen*. While the Enchanted Storybook Castle was inspired by Renaissance architecture, Imagineer Douglas Rogers, who was the production designer on *Tangled*, also

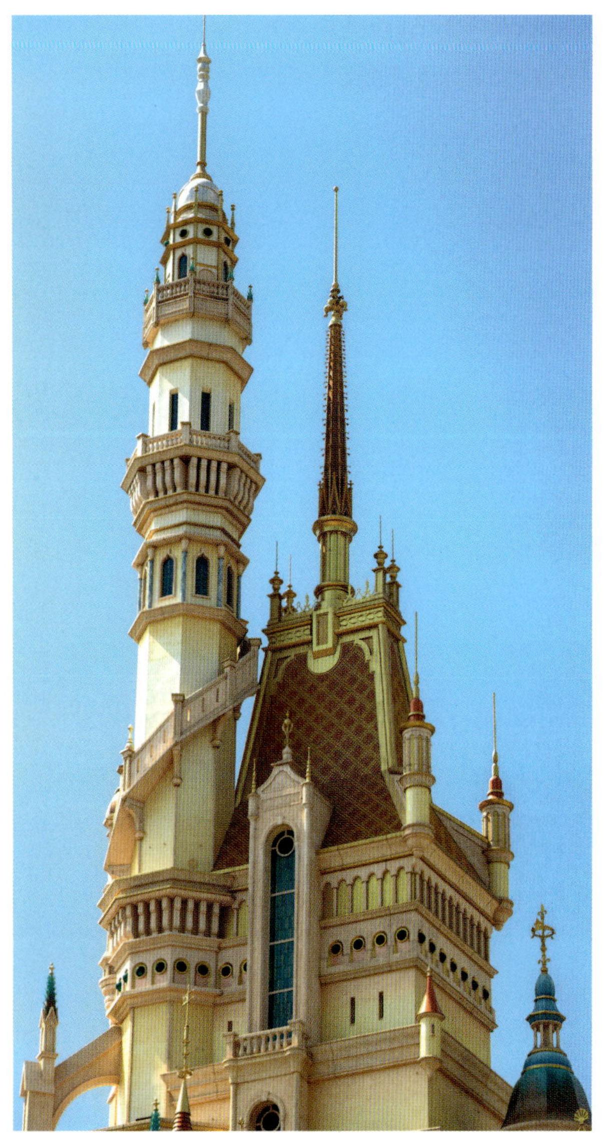

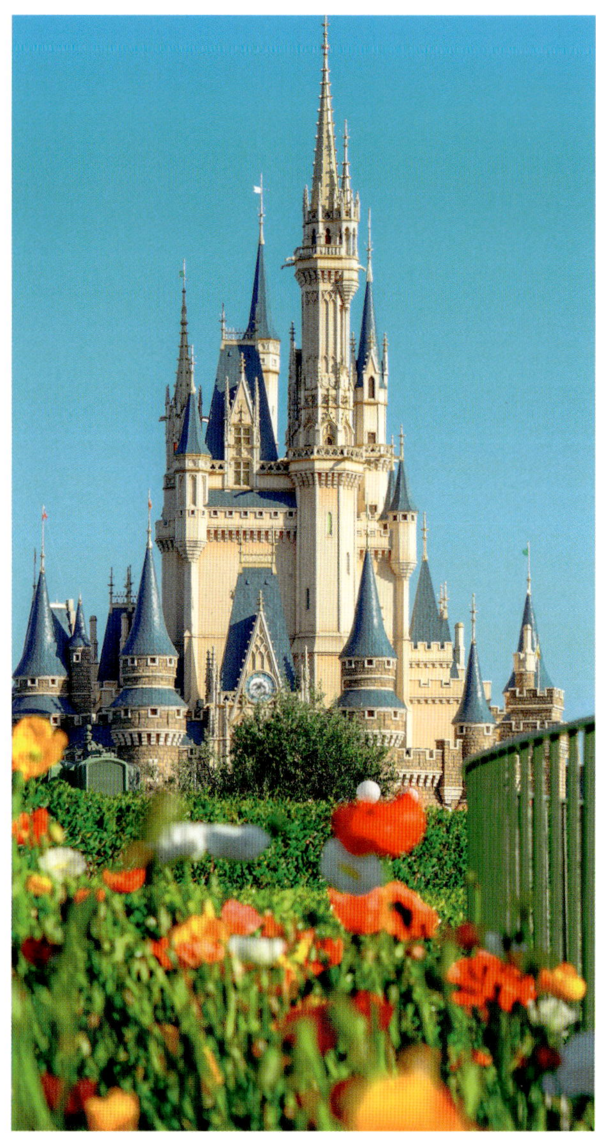

Above (left): The Castle of Magical Dreams at Hong Kong Disneyland. *Above (right):* Cinderella Castle at Tokyo Disneyland. *Below:* A stained glass window in Hong Kong Disneyland's Castle of Magical Dreams.

brought in elements of Chinese culture, topping the structure with a golden peony. The idea was that all of the Disney Princesses lived in the castle, which also includes a boat ride attraction, as well as the Bibbidi Bobbidi Boutique, the Royal Banquet Hall restaurant, and, of course, princess meet-and-greets.

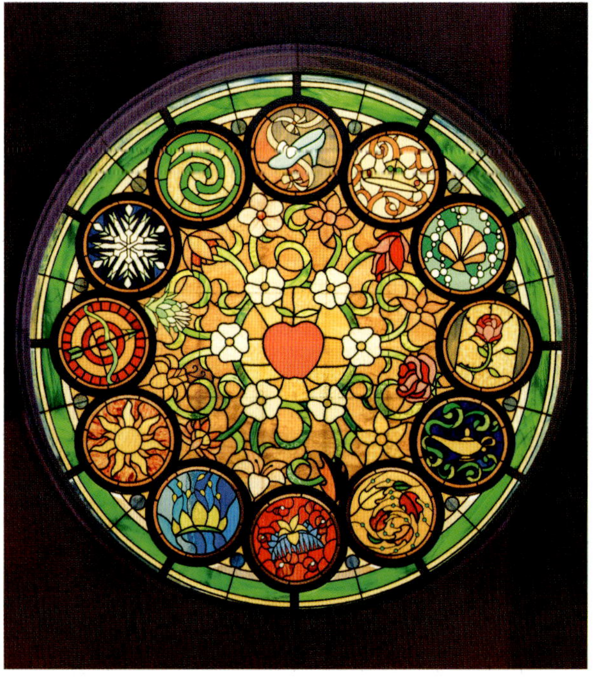

Inspired by the Enchanted Storybook Castle, Bob Weis, President of Walt Disney Imagineering, who recently took on a new role as Global Imagineering Ambassador, proposed renovating Sleeping Beauty Castle at Hong Kong Disneyland, originally built for the park's opening in 2005. He wanted the castle to have its own spirit and grand scale. Without closing the park, the Imagineers transformed the structure into the Castle of Magical Dreams, which opened in 2020. Inspired by the varied stories of the Disney Princesses and *Frozen* queens, each of the castle's thirteen turrets was built to embody a different hero, featuring all twelve princesses, plus Elsa and Anna. The designers used colors and symbols to represent the characters' distinct personalities.

While the earlier castles were inspired by European castles, the Castle of Magical Dreams embraces a broader array of architectural styles and cultures. The castle celebrates different parts of the world, rather than one princess or one location. "Our stories continue to grow, and we get to learn about different cultures around the world," Hilcia Pena, a senior architect at Walt Disney Imagineering, told *CNN*. "So how do we put that into the buildings and stories we try to tell?"

While Walt may have viewed his original theme park castle as a way for guests to stay oriented, the structures have evolved in their meaning for guests over the years. The castles are some of the most Instagrammed places in the entire world, and hundreds of marriage proposals have been staged in front of them. Disney's Fairy Tale Weddings & Honeymoons will even help guests plan that perfect moment.

"Over the past thirty years, we've seen our couples take literal inspiration from Disney Princesses and evolve to embrace the characteristics of the modern fairy tale," says Korri McFann, Marketing Director for Disney's Fairy Tale Weddings & Honeymoons. "From a sense of adventure, to romance, or fantasy, what we've always known is that no two love stories are the same and every couple's fairy tale is unique. Today, more than ever, couples have the ability to curate their own fairy tale. Taking influences from the Disney Princesses they know and love, they create a wedding experience that matches their dream."

A bride arrives by fairy-tale coach to Cinderella Castle at the Magic Kingdom at Walt Disney World.

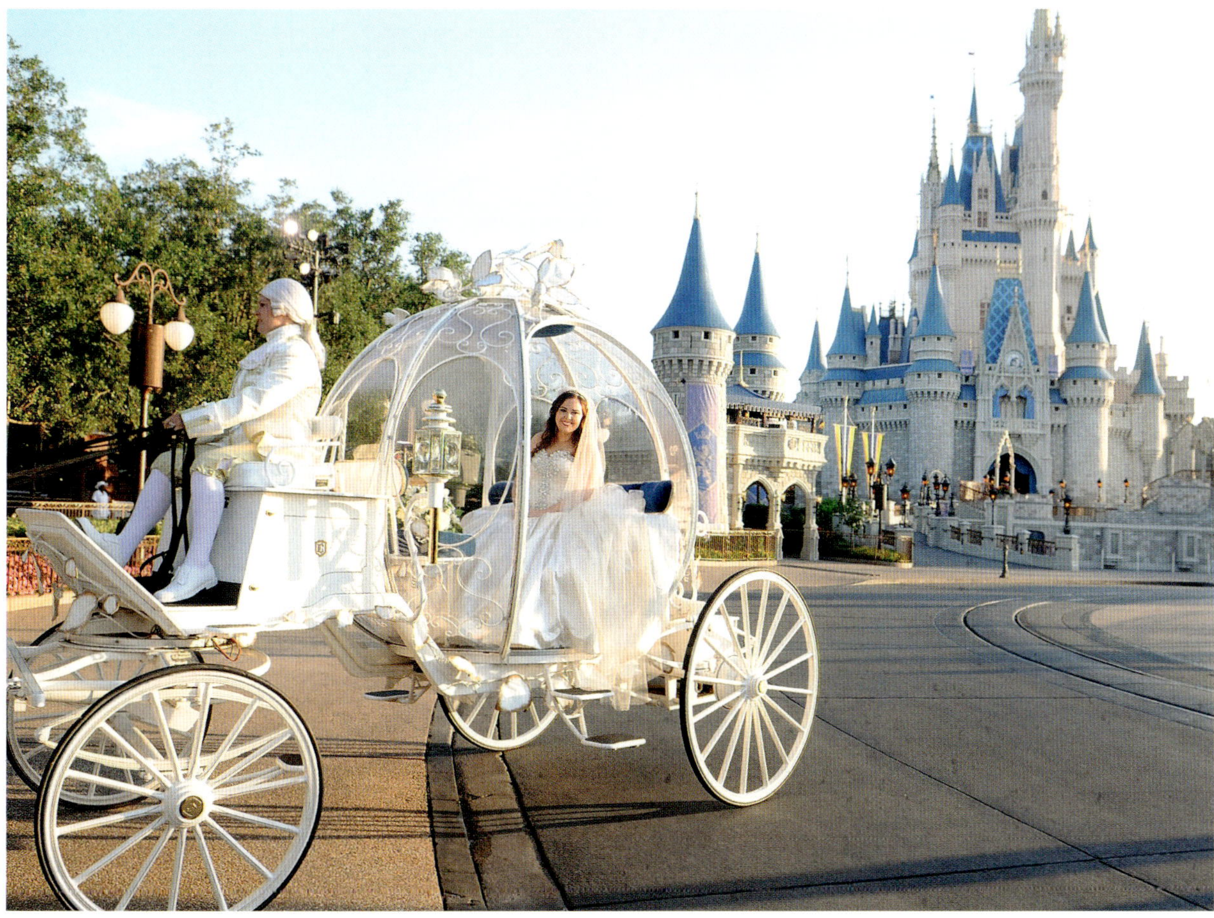

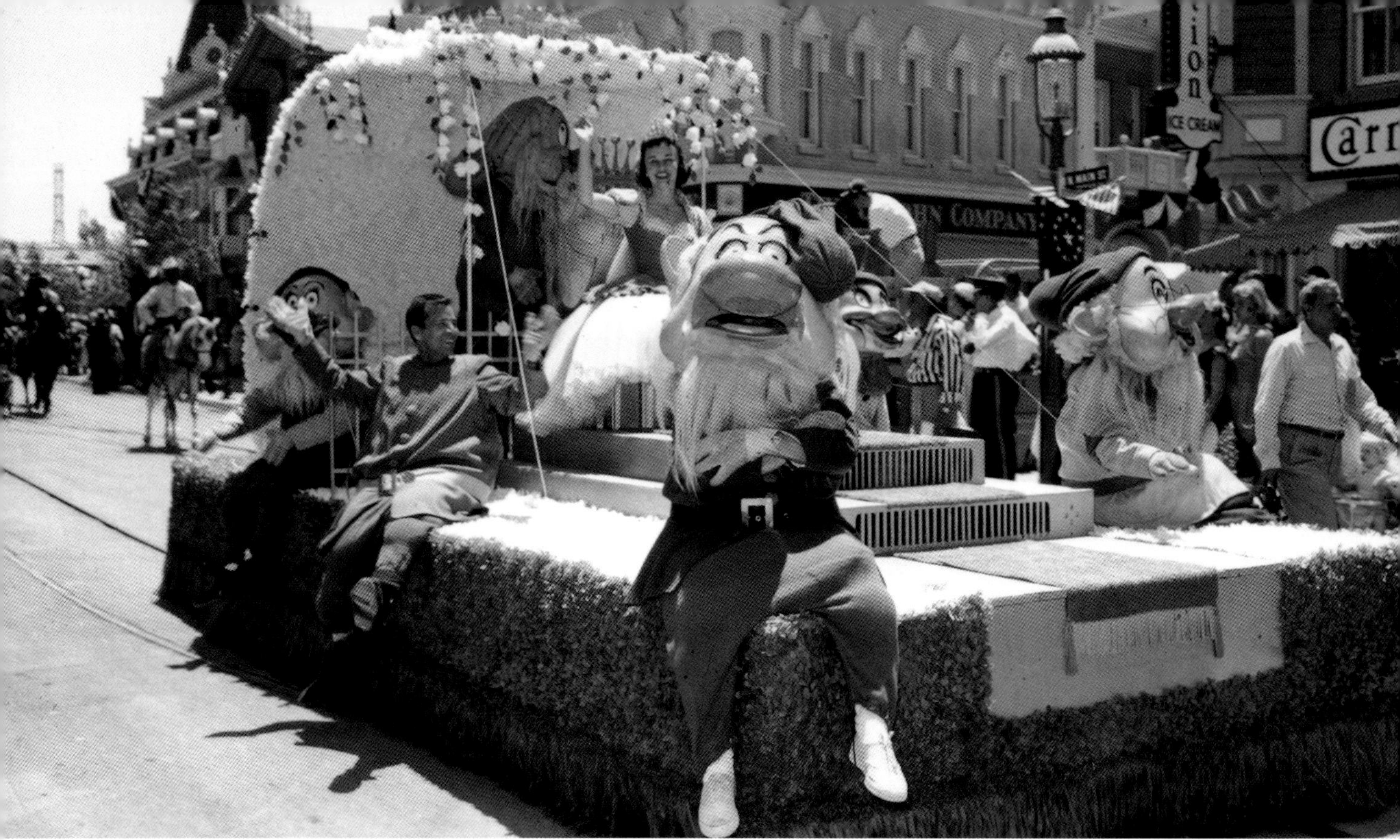

Above: JoAnn Dean Killingsworth as Snow White on the opening day of Disneyland. *Opposite (from top):* Snow White, Pocahontas, Cinderella, Ariel, Merida, and Rapunzel in the Disney parks.

MEET THE CHARACTERS

Even before Disneyland opened in 1955, Walt's characters made appearances to promote Disney films. Mickey, Minnie, and the Seven Dwarfs attended the premiere of *Snow White and the Seven Dwarfs* in 1937. In 1949, the traveling Ice Capades show featured its first program that included Disney characters, with Donna Atwood and Bobby Specht playing Snow White and Prince Charming as they skated across the ice. The script for the Ice Capades show stuck closely to the animated film, replicating the dialogue almost word for word. Two years later, the Ice Capades performed a version of *Cinderella,* and Atwood and Specht returned as Cinderella and her prince. Mickey Mouse and Minnie Mouse also appeared, skating in the Ice Capades of the early 1950s.

Some of those early Ice Capades characters even made their way to Disneyland and were there for the big opening day in 1955, although the festivities also included new looks for the characters, too. Snow White, in a new costume, appeared on a float for the televised opening day parade. The princess was portrayed by JoAnn Dean Killingsworth, who became the first person to play Snow White at Disneyland for the parade, which also included Cinderella and the Seven Dwarfs. The Disney characters didn't exist just in the parks either. Snow White and her pals appeared at the 1964-1965 New York World's Fair alongside Mickey Mouse, Goofy, Pinocchio, the Mad Hatter, Alice, and more.

Since the early years of Disneyland, character interaction in the Disney parks has been a key feature of the guest experience. Disney characters appear in all of the parks worldwide, as well as in many of the resorts and on Disney Cruise Line, both at meet-and-greet locations, at character dining experiences, and in shows. The goal is always the same: for the fan to become involved with the character in a moment of interactive magic. The Disney Princesses, as well as the *Frozen* queens, also feature in many Disney parks parades, which further enhances the magic of seeing a favorite character close up.

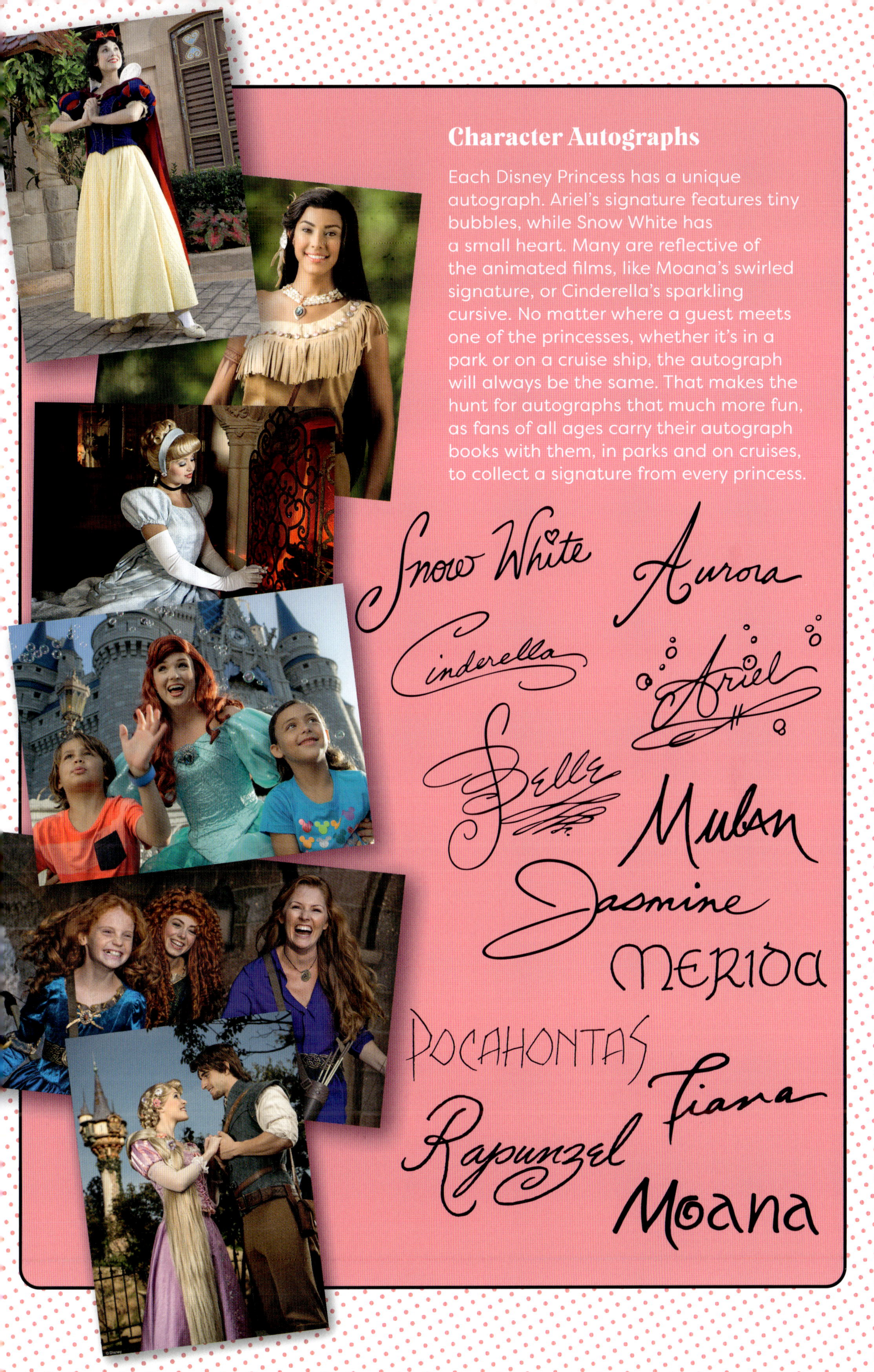

Character Autographs

Each Disney Princess has a unique autograph. Ariel's signature features tiny bubbles, while Snow White has a small heart. Many are reflective of the animated films, like Moana's swirled signature, or Cinderella's sparkling cursive. No matter where a guest meets one of the princesses, whether it's in a park or on a cruise ship, the autograph will always be the same. That makes the hunt for autographs that much more fun, as fans of all ages carry their autograph books with them, in parks and on cruises, to collect a signature from every princess.

RESORTS AND CRUISES

The Disney experience has always encompassed far more than the films themselves, as evidenced by the popularity of the Disney parks. Disney Cruise Line, founded in 1995, brought Disney's storytelling magic to the high seas, and Aulani, A Disney Resort & Spa, opened in 2011 in O'ahu, with the resort's overall design led by Walt Disney Imagineering. To be a true Disney fan often means living a Disney lifestyle, especially in one's leisure time, and the Disney Princesses have been part of that journey all along.

Many of the princesses appear onboard Disney Cruise Line ships, offering meet-and-greets and photo opportunities for guests, but their royal presence goes far beyond that. Several of the Disney Princess films have been adapted into live musical shows, which are performed on the cruises, including *Tangled: The Musical* and *Disney's Aladdin – A Musical Spectacular*. Elsa and Anna also appear in *Frozen, A Musical Spectacular*, a Broadway-style musical show that features both live actors and puppetry. The princesses in the cruise stage shows get their own version of the costumes, differing from those in the Disney parks.

Sarah Cubbage designed the costumes for *Beauty and the Beast*, which debuted in the Walt Disney Theatre on the *Disney Dream* ship in 2017. The production drew its inspiration from the live-action film, as well as the original animated classic, and Cubbage created more than 1,000 costume pieces for the seventy-minute show, including Belle's yellow gown.

"I've of course been inspired by the iconic Disney characters and also by the luscious costume designs in the film," Cubbage explained in an interview. "I've also really been inspired by the period, by exploring and researching what French country provincial wear is for peasants in the eighteenth century." She added, "The animated version of *Beauty and the Beast* is iconic, but of course it is flat by nature of the animation. Because the live-action film exists, it gives us license and leeway to delve into the texture."

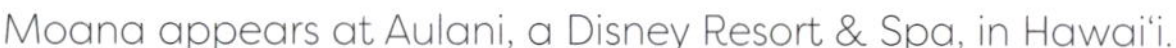
Moana appears at Aulani, a Disney Resort & Spa, in Hawai'i.

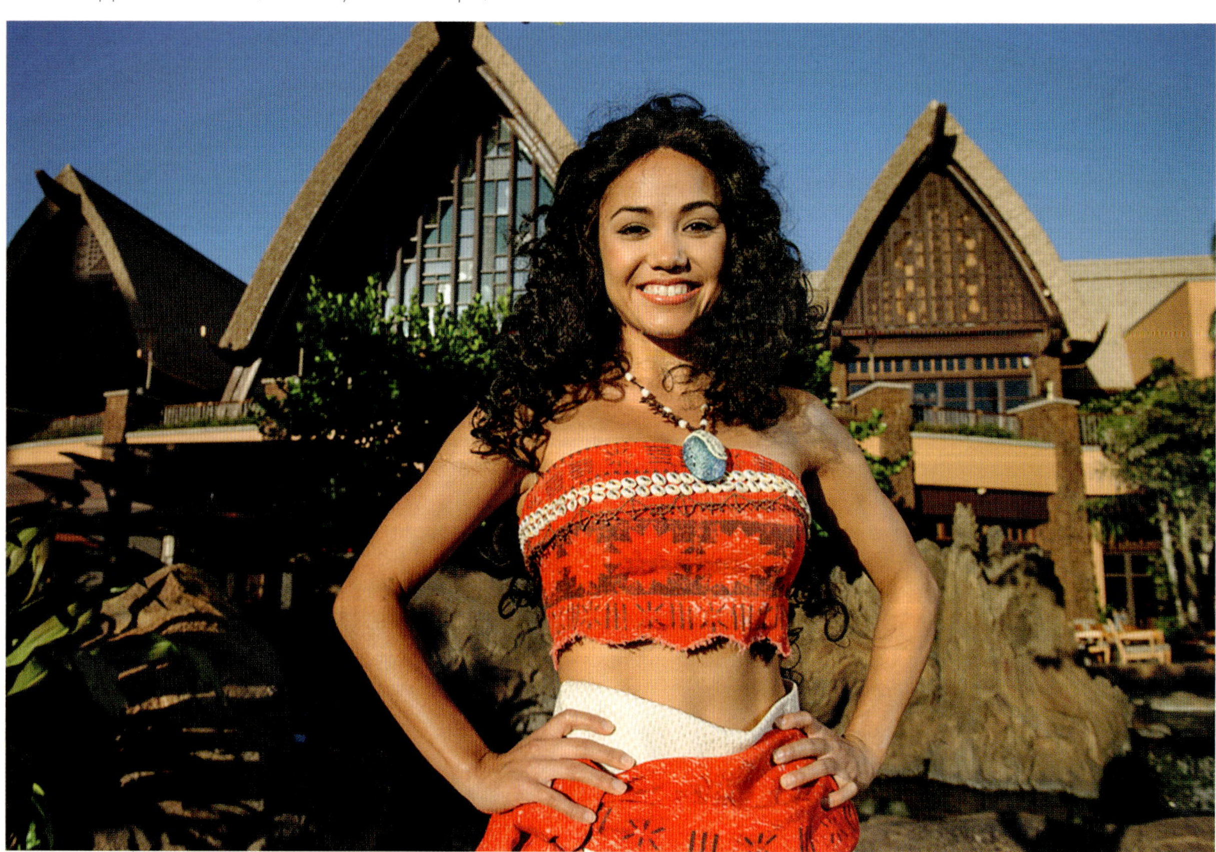

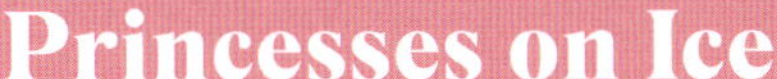

Princesses on Ice

Disney On Ice, created for its skating shows in 1981, similarly uses classic Disney characters and stories to expand fans' experiences. Today, Disney On Ice offers vibrant shows that tour the country, much like those early Ice Capades shows. Each year's show features a different theme, which have included "Princess Wishes" and "Princesses & Heroes." The shows, creatively overseen by Disney Theatrical, are yet another way the storytelling magic of the Disney Princesses captivates fans outside of the theaters.

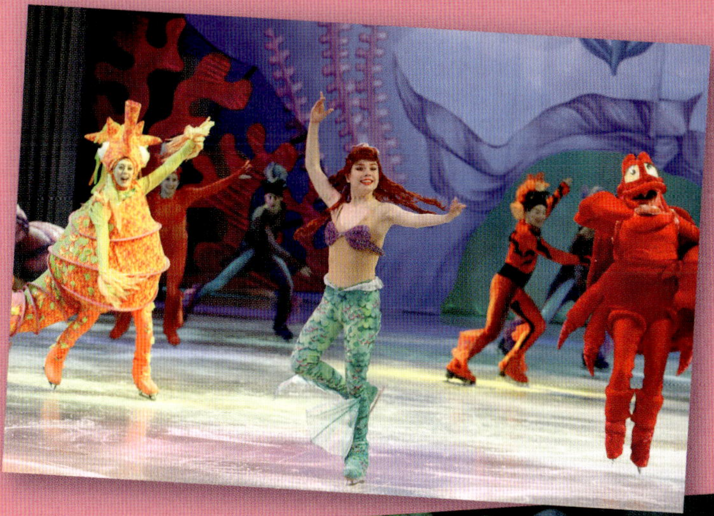

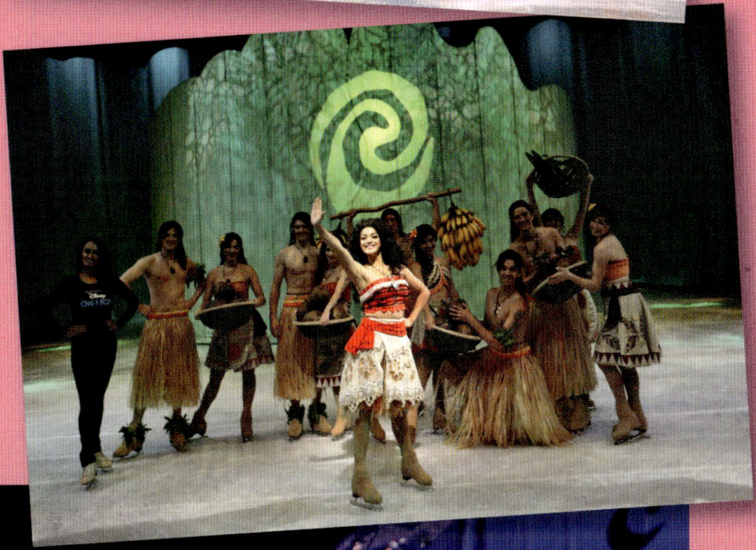

Actors bring the Disney Princesses and *Frozen* queens to life on skates for Disney On Ice.

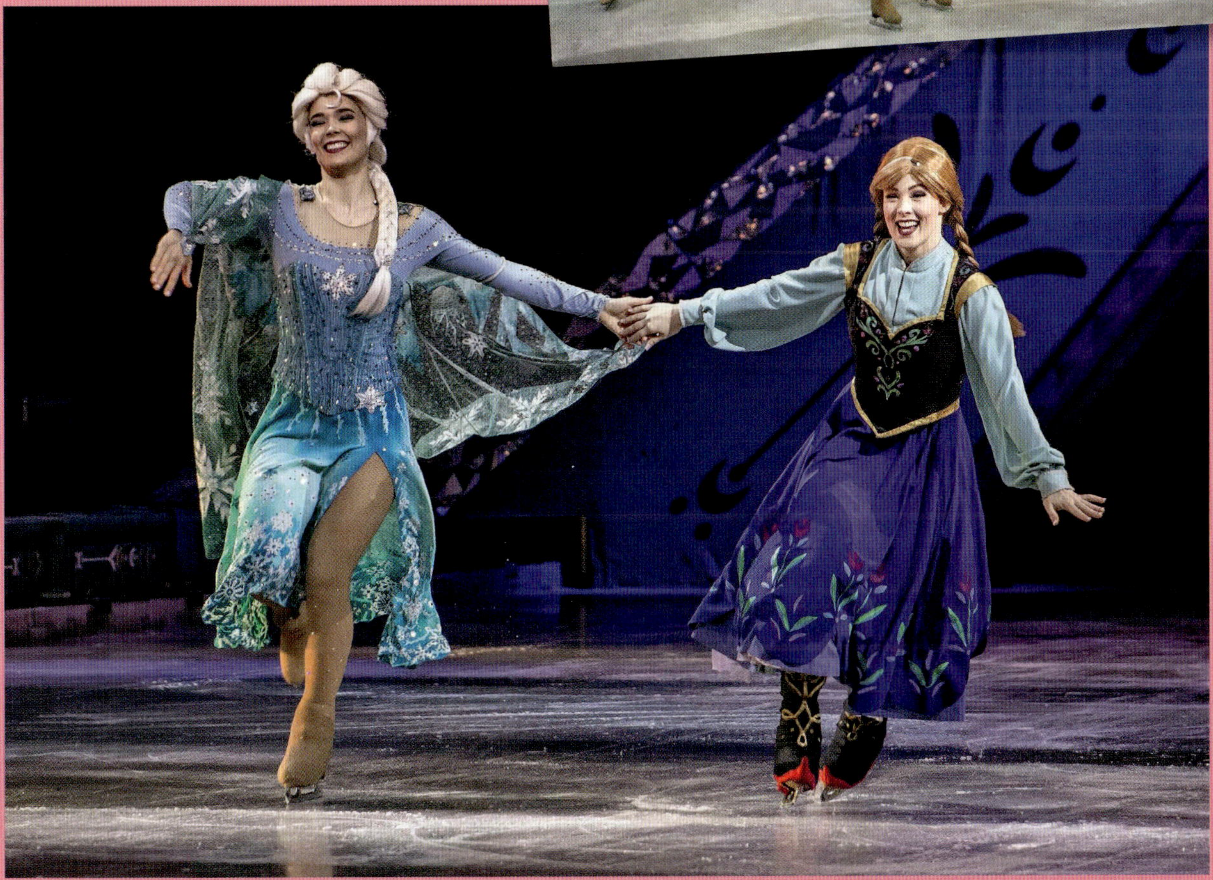

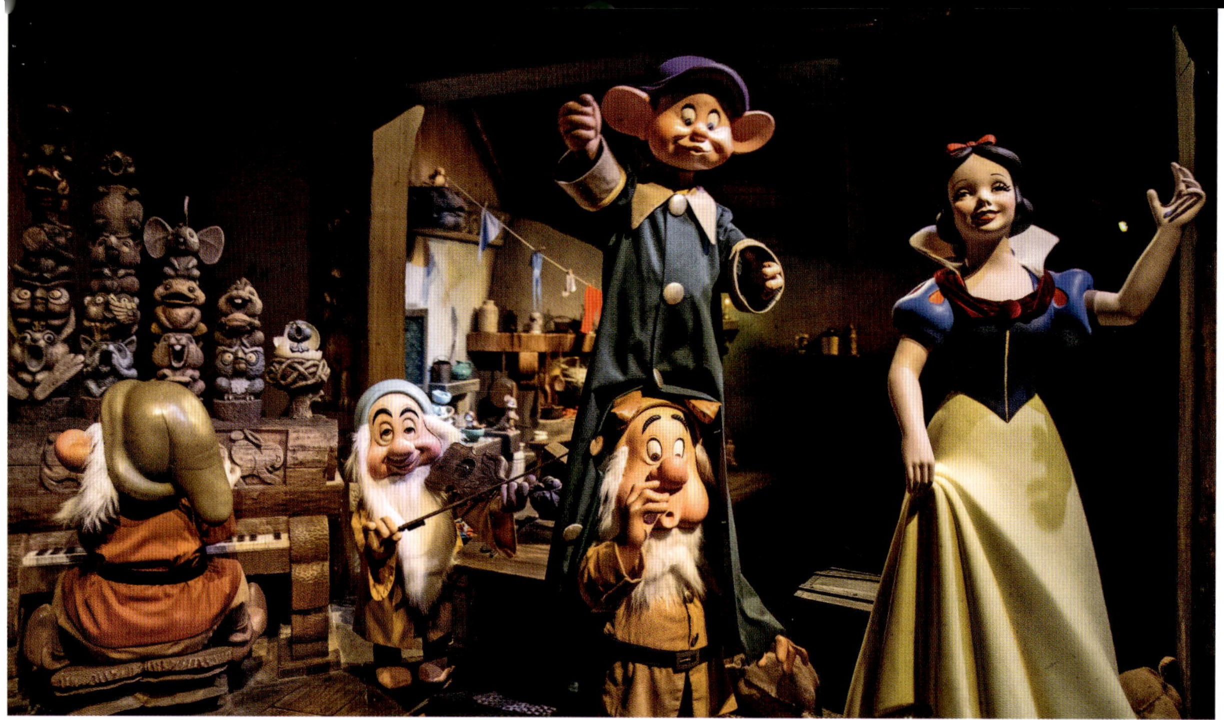

A scene in one of Disneyland's famous attractions, *Snow White's Enchanted Wish*.

Many of Disney's offerings are tailored to families, a sentiment that is found throughout Aulani, too. While the resort has welcomed guests since before the release of *Moana*, Moana's Pacific Island-inspired story has been a great fit for the resort ever since. The wayfinder princess appears at the resort, which was designed with details that celebrate its location in Hawai'i. As in *Moana*, Hawaiian culture also emphasizes embracing a connection with the water. It's also proof that a Disney Princess experience doesn't have to include a traditional fairy-tale castle or a long ballgown. There's magic everywhere, from the shores of Hawai'i to the open seas of the Disney Cruise Line to the gates of Disneyland.

THE EVER-EVOLVING PARKS

Walt's notion that Disneyland would never be finished is still part of the Disney parks' philosophy. When Disneyland opened in 1955, it wasn't as expansive as it is today. But one attraction that has been around since the beginning is the Fantasyland attraction *Snow White and Her Adventures*, now known as *Snow White's Enchanted Wish*. Originally, the attraction offered visitors an opportunity to ride through a series of set pieces from *Snow White and the Seven Dwarfs*. Designed by Disney Legends Claude Coats and Ken Anderson, the intention was to immerse guests in Snow White's story by taking on the role of the princess as she journeys through the dark forest, the gem mines, and past the witch's caldron. Snow White herself wasn't visible as part of the attraction, much to guests' dismay, and the Imagineers later added a Snow White figure into the experience. Disneyland's first park map encouraged visitors to "take the Snow White ride and meet the Seven Dwarfs, the Wicked Witch, who will offer you a poisoned apple, and all the other characters of this immortal classic."

The attraction has evolved over the years, shifting to reflect the desires of the guests. It was redesigned in 1983 as *Snow White's Scary Adventures*, and in 2020 Imagineers decided to renovate the attraction once again using new audio and visual technologies. *Snow White's Enchanted Wish* opened on April 30, 2021, the same day that Disneyland allowed guests to return following its closure due to the COVID-19 pandemic. The story remains, but many of the details have changed, including the addition of a figure of Snow White, who dances with

Dopey. At the end of the attraction, Snow White is presented playing with her animal friends, as well as being kissed by the prince.

"We didn't want to change the story," Imagineer Kim Irvine told the *Los Angeles Times*. "The old photograph at the end was her sitting sidesaddle on the horse with the prince leading her to the castle. That's too much of a 'he saved her' story. She has such a charm about her when she sings and talks to the animals. Her animals are her pals. That's why we moved her with the animals, and she's looking at you like, 'It's all good now.' He's over in the distance, waiting on a woman."

A similarly modern update is in the works for *Splash Mountain* at Disneyland and Magic Kingdom. The water attraction, which features a scream-inducing flume drop, opened in 1989 at Disneyland. While the excitement continued to engage guests, Imagineers felt it was time for a more contemporary take featuring a favorite Disney Princess.

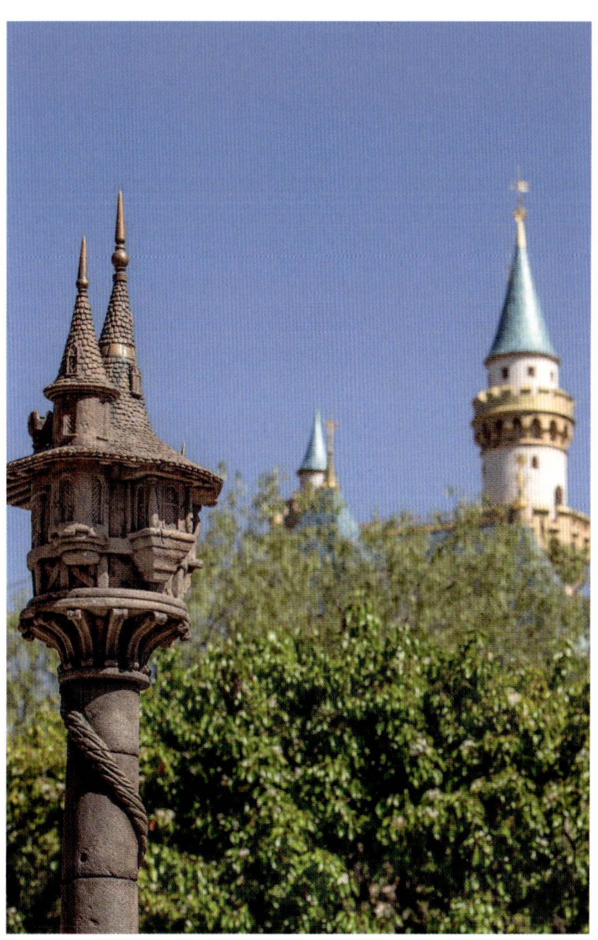

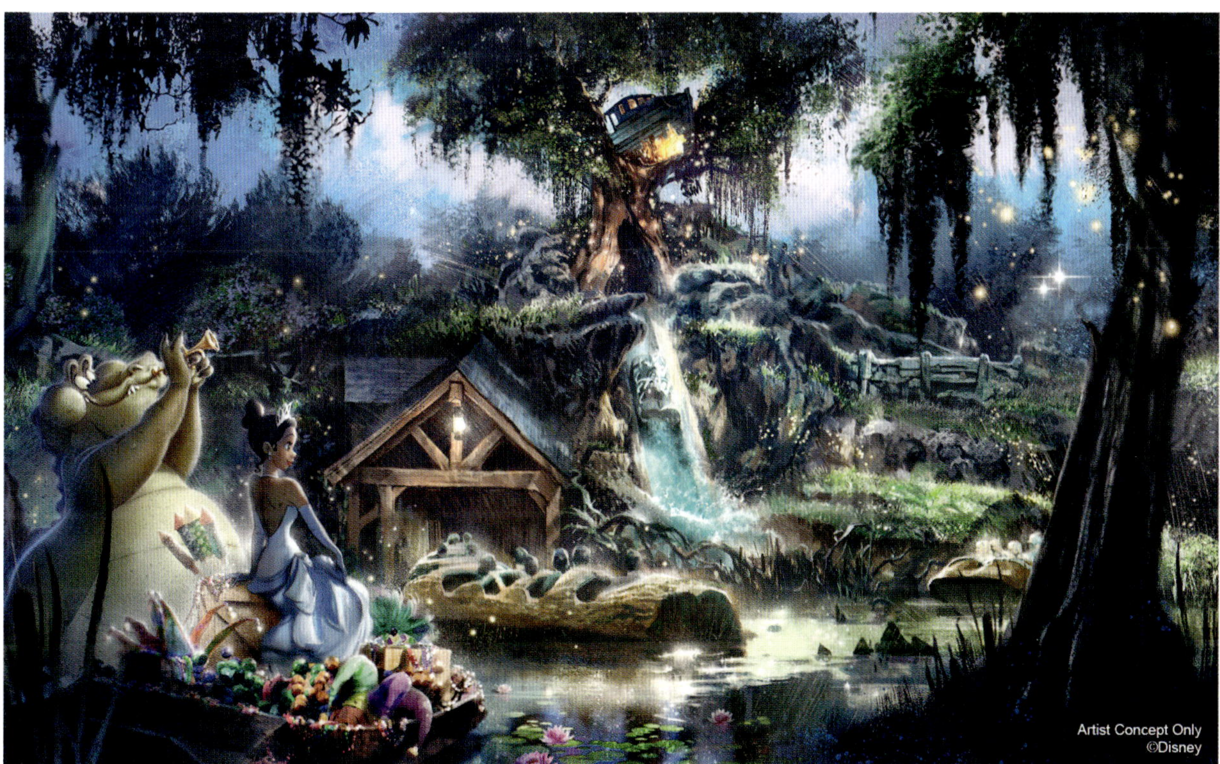

Above: Rapunzel's Tower at Magic Kingdom. *Below:* Concept art for the new Tiana attraction at the Disney parks.

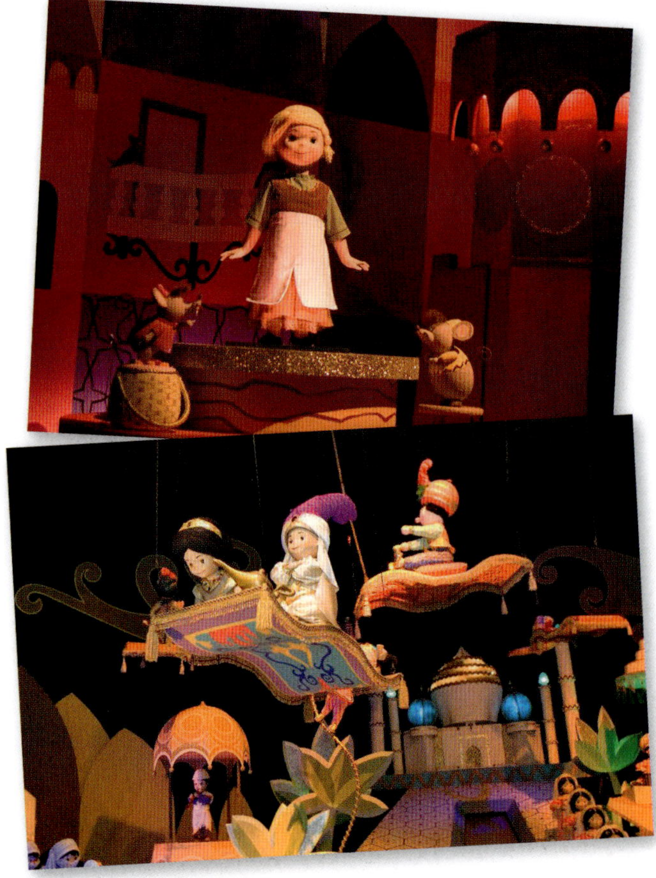

The Disney Princess characters join the fun as part of the Disney Parks' iconic attraction *"it's a small world."*

"There are a number of factors that led to where we are currently with wanting to reimagine *Splash Mountain,*" explains Imagineer Charita Carter, who is at the helm of the reimagining. "This was a good opportunity to be more culturally relevant. We're often looking at our classic attractions for opportunities to bring them into the twenty-first century with the way we execute our stories. Technology has changed so much and as a result of that, Imagineering has developed all kinds of techniques that are fairly new that allow us to present our stories in ways that guests have not experienced yet. We're really excited about being able to go into the attraction and bring Tiana to the park. We are creating this attraction for everyone, but we also think it will speak to a lot of audience members who may not feel like we have directly spoken to them."

Tiana's journey through the bayou will retain the flume aspect of the classic attraction while incorporating new techniques to make the experience feel more immersive. The story picks up where *The Princess and the Frog* ended. It's a next chapter for Tiana and her pals. "As Imagineers, we're always excited to tell unique stories from the Disney films our guests love so much," Carter notes. "We want to be able to immerse our guests in a journey that lets her story go forward."

As time goes on, the Imagineers aim to create a perfect balance between nostalgia and relevance in the Disney parks. That has included enhancing Sleeping Beauty Castle in 2019, and incorporating Anna and Elsa into the Norway Pavilion at EPCOT with the *Frozen Ever After* attraction. Rapunzel's Tower and her village were added to Magic Kingdom during an expansion in 2013, as well as to Fantasy Faire at Disneyland the same year. In addition, Magic Kingdom welcomed the *Seven Dwarfs Mine Train* in 2014.

Not all of the updates have been quite so obvious, however. In 2008, the Imagineers refurbished the attraction *"it's a small world,"* adding 29 additional, well-known Disney characters, created in the attraction's iconic style, including several Disney Princesses. Each additional character was placed in an area of the ride that corresponds to the native land of its story, staying true to the characters' original designs. "We tried to choose our very special classics, the ones that will live on for years and years," Irvine explained. "And we chose dolls that actually fit in lands that already existed in small world. So you have a Cinderella in France and Alice In Wonderland in England and a Mulan in China."

The Disney parks have a long legacy, which correlates with the animated films. Some recent impressive anniversaries include Walt Disney World's 50th anniversary on October 1, 2021, and Disneyland Paris's 30th anniversary in 2022. The parks are destinations for guests of all ages and interests, including adults, who visit for special dress-up events like Halloween celebrations. Many fans also unofficially celebrate "Dapper Day," where they don upscale attire. The magic of the parks—and their princesses—lives on in the spirit of Walt's original vision.

Run Like a Princess

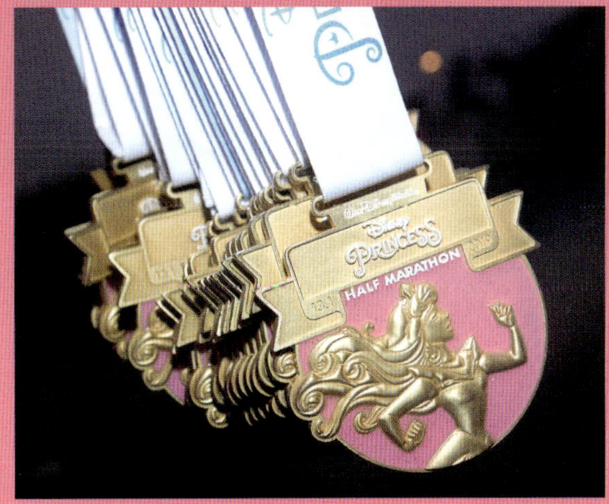

Not all princesses wear glass slippers. Some wear running shoes. The Disney Princess Half Marathon Weekend, put on by *run*Disney, has become a popular event at Walt Disney World since 2009. Part of the Walt Disney World Marathon, launched by *run*Disney in 1994, the female-focused event was created to celebrate personal accomplishment while also promoting a healthy lifestyle. Since then, it has become one of the world's largest race weekends geared toward women, drawing up to 60,000 fans, spectators, and runners from around the world. Runners are encouraged to channel their inner Disney Princess and to have fun with their race day attire, whether that means wearing official Princess Half Marathon merchandise or a unique costume.

The aim is to encourage women to push their limits. "Just like Disney Princesses, runners are on a journey to change their destinies for the better through setting goals, being active, and overcoming obstacles," says Faron Kelley, Vice President of *run*Disney. "From the time they begin training, they are pursuing their own story of personal triumph. The Disney Princess Half Marathon Weekend brings together people of all ages and backgrounds to embrace their inner princess and push their limits, and this supportive environment empowers and inspires them to achieve their dreams."

The race takes a slightly different route through Walt Disney World each year, with the organizers methodically planning out each stage for a one-of-a-kind marathon experience. At the end, there are medals for the runners, which emphasize the traits of the Disney Princesses.

"We recognize the importance of the race medal to every runner who steps on our course, and we put a lot of detail into the design and creation of this coveted prize each runner is training to receive," Kelley explains. "Ultimately, we want to tell a story throughout our races, and the medals are the final chapter of that story."

Racers embrace the princess spirit at the Disney Princess Half Marathon Weekend.

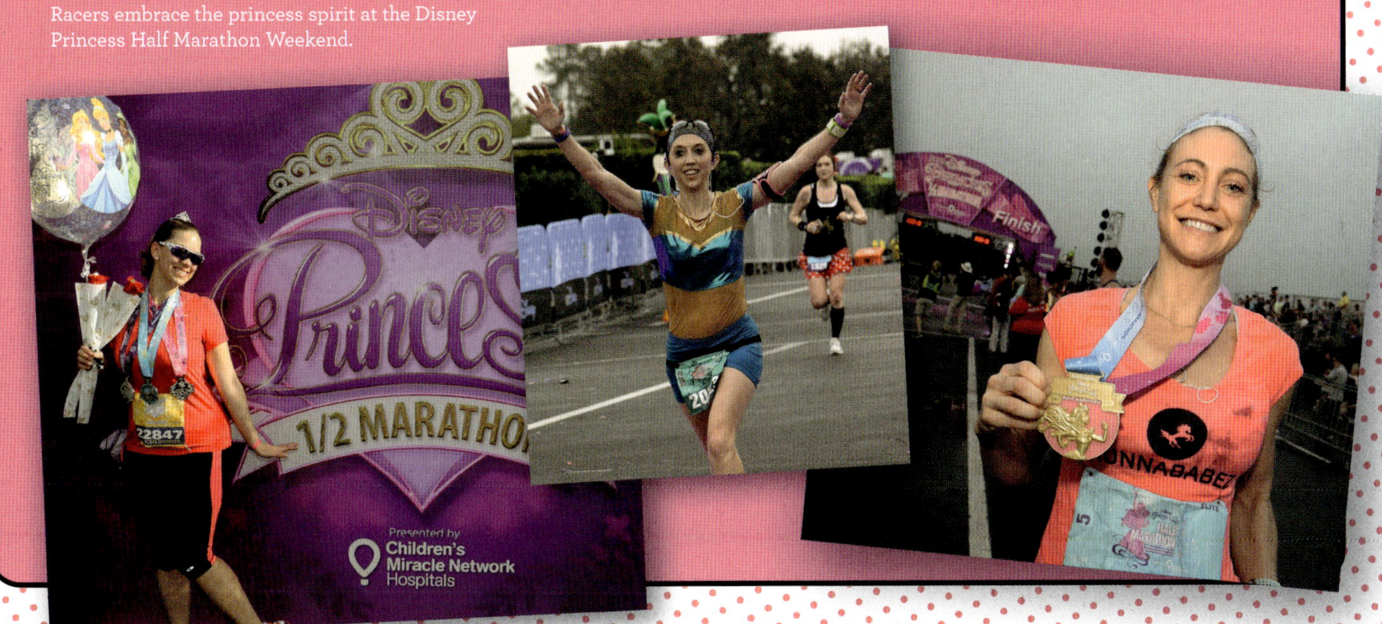

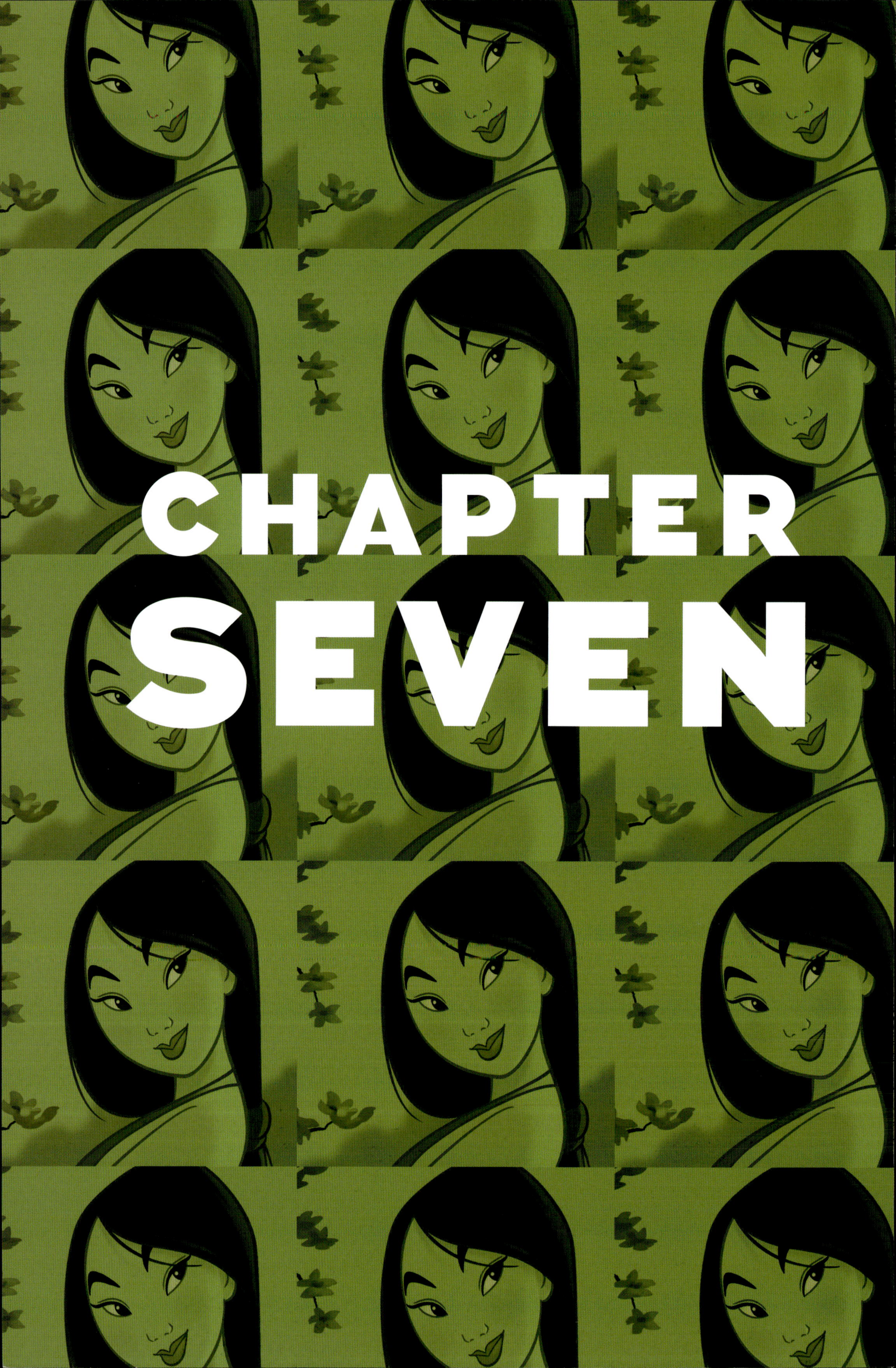

CHAPTER SEVEN

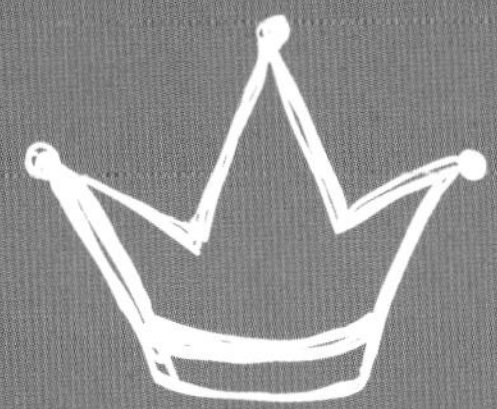

REFLECTION

FANDOM, COSPLAY, AND ART

Over its now century-long history, Disney's stories, characters, and parks have captivated audiences around the world, from all ages, genders, backgrounds, and creeds. There's a favorite character for everyone, no matter who you are. And to be able to dream yourself into that favorite Disney Princess is especially powerful. For many Disney fans, cosplay, or costumed play, offers an opportunity to embody the courage, kindness, and love of a Disney Princess, whether it's at a convention or at home on social media. For others, it's all about Disney Princess memes and fan art that's shared millions of times on social media.

"Something Disney has been really good at is keeping adults interested," explains Dr. Rebecca Williams, senior lecturer at the University of South Wales, who studies fandom. "You don't grow out of it in a way people would expect. Fandom and being a fan of Disney is now a lot more visible than it was ten or fifteen years ago because of social media. The Disney aesthetic and the princess aesthetic suit a platform like Instagram really well."

There are many ways for fans to showcase their enthusiasm, but the goal is always about self-expression—and, connecting with other fans. Ever since Disney released *Steamboat Willie*, fans have found ways of finding each other. The original Mickey Mouse Club was a movie theater program, which launched at the Fox Dome Theater in Ocean Park, California, on January 11, 1929. In order to attend, audience members had to officially join the fan club by enrolling at their local box office. Members attended Saturday meetings, at which Mickey Mouse cartoons were screened for the kids. There were even Mickey-themed bands and Mickey Mouse credos were recited.

"At the very beginning, the Mickey Mouse Club of the 1930s was very successful, being a children's theater club that spread across the United States from 1930-35 with great enthusiasm," explains Libby Spatz. "At its peak in 1932, with over one million members, they exceeded the membership of the Boy Scout and Girl Scout clubs combined."

While the original Mickey Mouse Club was short-lived, the legacy of coming together around a shared love of Disney had begun. More recently, in 2009, Disney created D23: The Official Disney Fan Club, a membership-based club that hosts the biannual D23 Expo, bringing together thousands of fans at the Anaheim Convention Center. The number of participants has grown tremendously since it started, and by 2019, the convention was bringing in fans from all fifty states, as well as forty different countries. At D23 Expo, cosplay is not only allowed, it's highly encouraged. There have been a number of special Disney Princess moments at the D23 Expo convention through the years as well, ranging from the induction of several voice actresses as Disney Legends in 2011 to the

1930s Mickey Mouse Club paraphernalia, including text of the organizations's theme song and official club button.

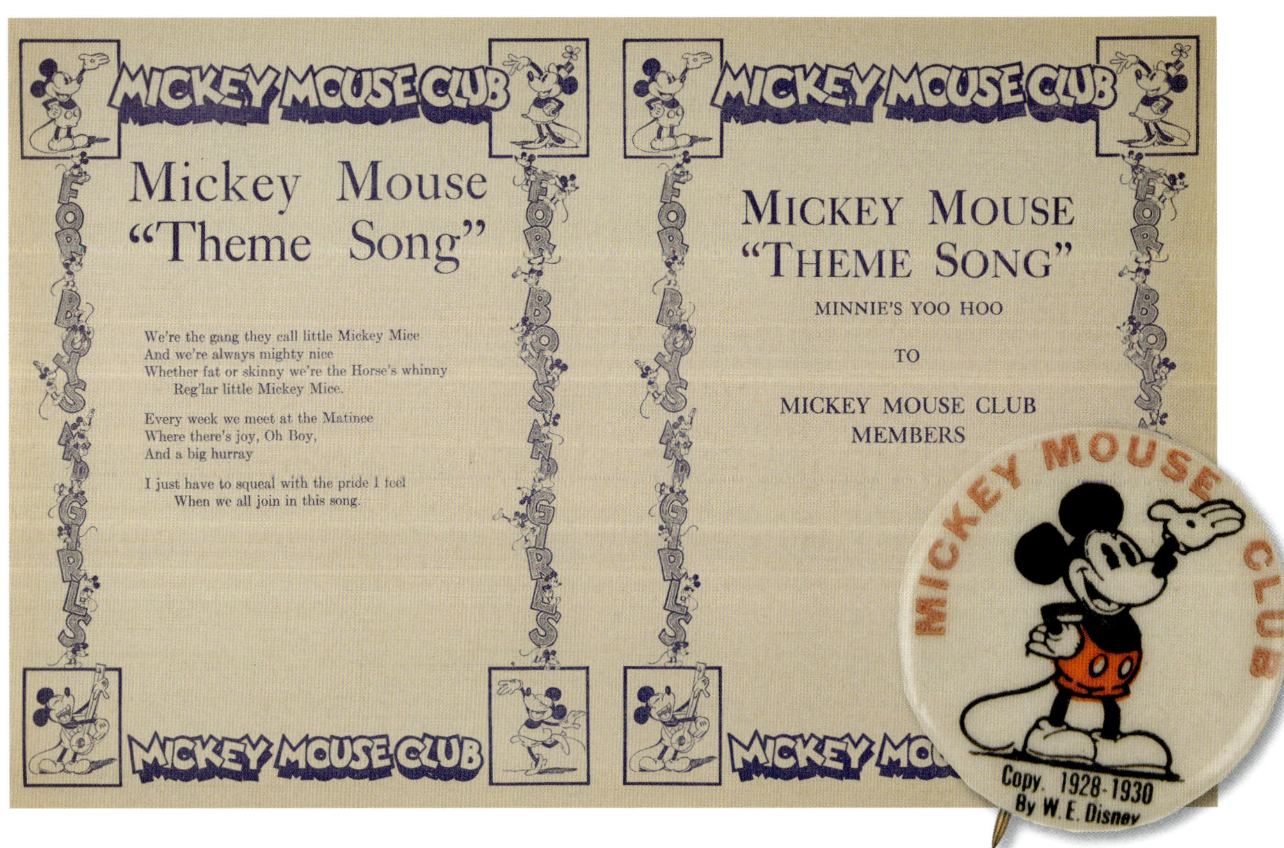

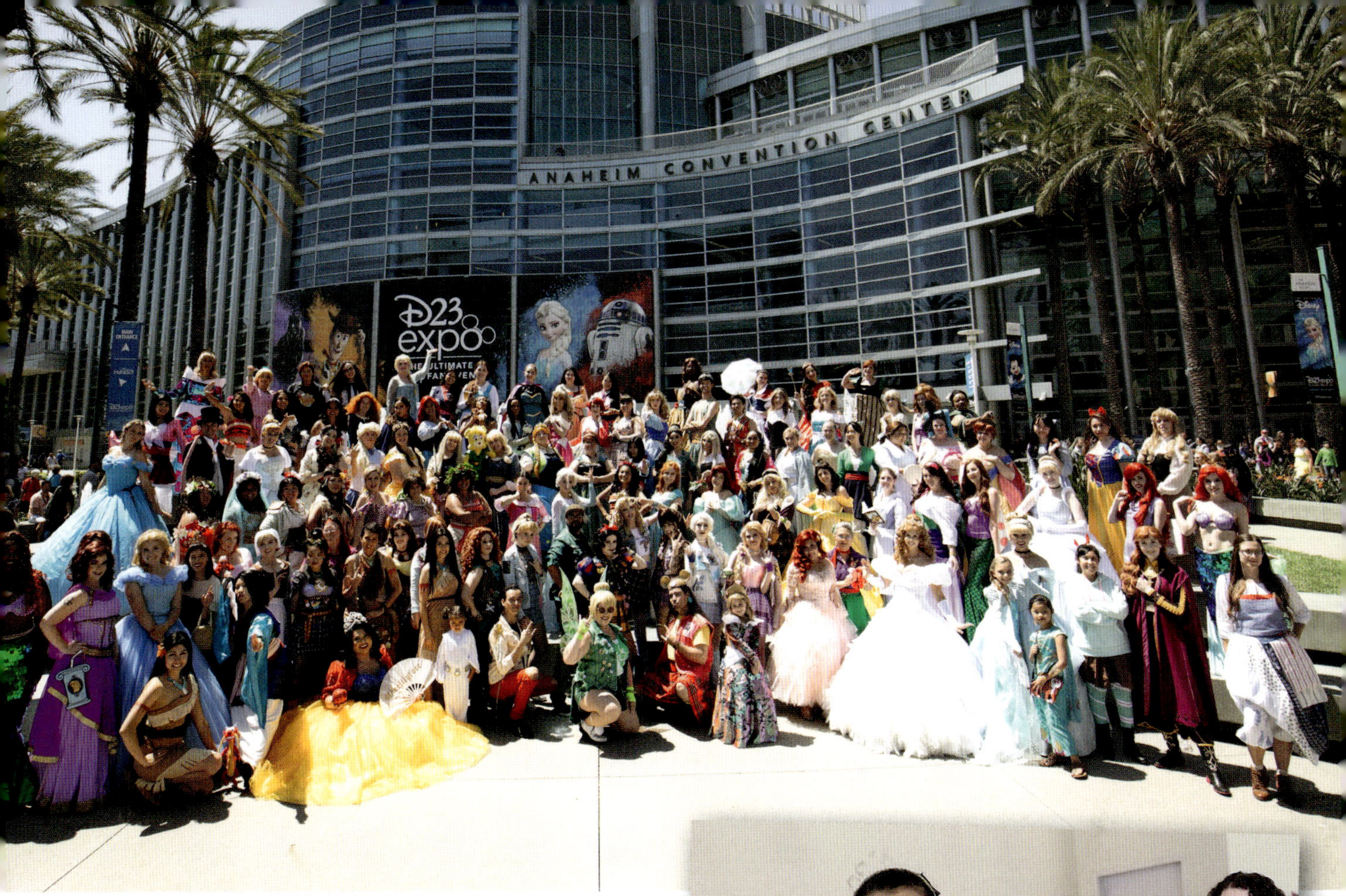

Above: Disney Princess cosplayers join forces at the D23 Expo.
Right: A cosplayer as Tiana.

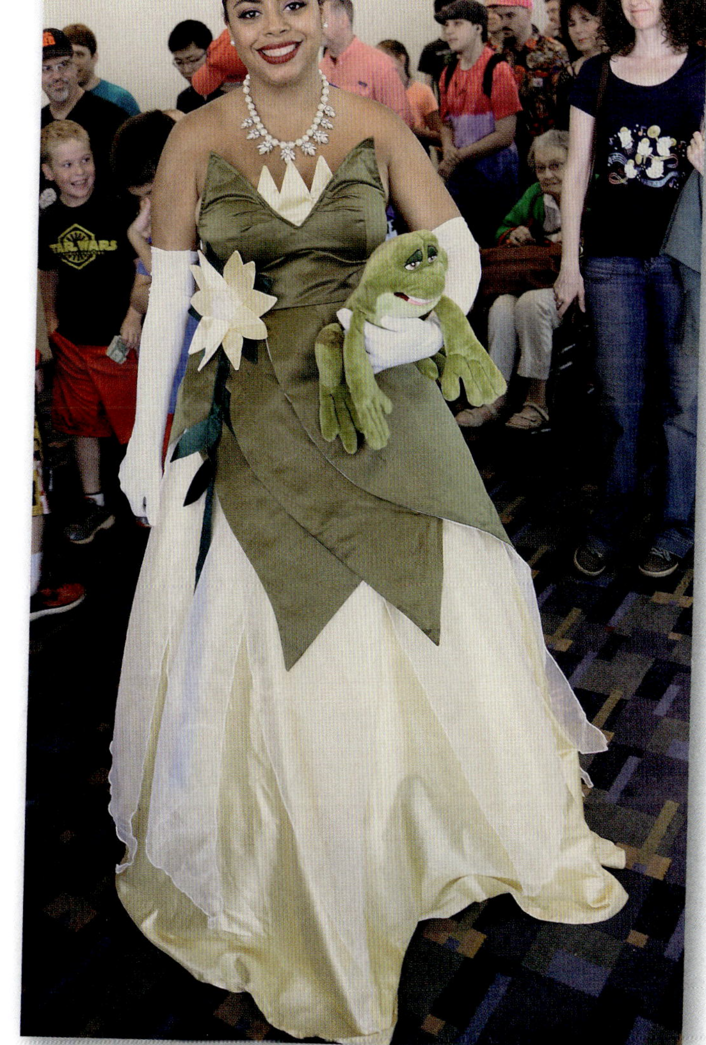

Disney Princess voice talent coming together in support of *Ralph Breaks the Internet* in 2017.

Similar to other famous fan conventions, like San Diego Comic-Con or Dragon Con, D23 Expo is a place to come together over a shared love of characters, however that might manifest itself. "D23 and the D23 Expos are all about providing the ultimate fan experience," notes Michael Vargo, Vice President of D23. "It's about how to connect and encourage community. You could be a lover of Disney, Pixar, Star Wars, Marvel or even the Muppets, or any combination of them, and still have this shared connection with all the other fans."

There are endless ways to share your love for a film or a character, and it's often the most creative efforts that take hold of our collective consciousness. The Disney Princesses and their stories have boundless possibilities for reinterpretation and tribute. Audiences infuse new life in the princesses every day, celebrating everything we love about them through genuine expression.

BECOMING THE CHARACTERS

While cosplay has become more mainstream over the past two decades, thanks to Instagram and other social media, the practice has technically been around for centuries. People have long enjoyed masquerade parties, where guests don elaborate costumes based on historical or literary figures. Science fiction conventions in the 1930s and 1940s saw some attendees dressed as futuristic beings, although at that time, the ensembles were seen as ordinary costumes rather than part of a specific fan tradition—a key element of cosplay. As conventions grew more popular, both in the U.S. and around the world, particularly in the 1970s, so did dressing in theme. The term "cosplay" was officially coined in Japan in 1984, and now refers to the act of dressing up as a fictional character from a movie, TV show, book, or video game.

To a casual observer, cosplay can seem like the simple act of putting on a costume. But to devoted cosplayers, it goes far beyond that. It's about embodying someone else, not just replicating their appearance with clothes, wigs, and makeup, which means cosplay is as much a mental experience as a physical one. "I get to be someone else but also myself at the same time," explains Annika Wilson, who frequently cosplays as Rapunzel and Elsa. "Doing it has increased my confidence immensely, as I was quite shy and introverted when I was younger."

Cosplay is also a way of augmenting the reality of a person's own life. "In some ways, it is a form of escapism," says Bethany Marx, who has designed and sewn numerous Disney Princess cosplay outfits, as well as

Cosplayers give Disney characters a punk rock spin.

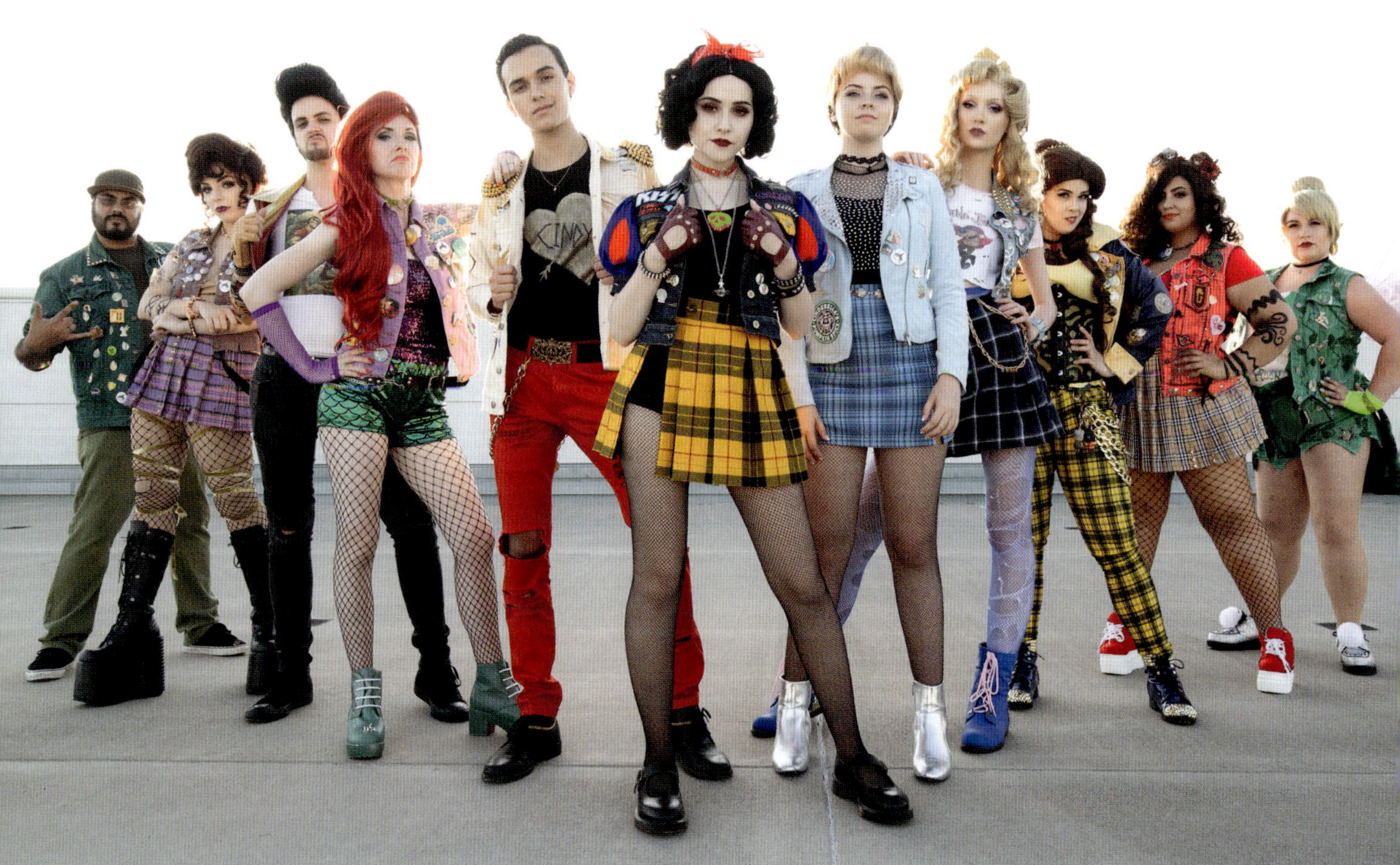

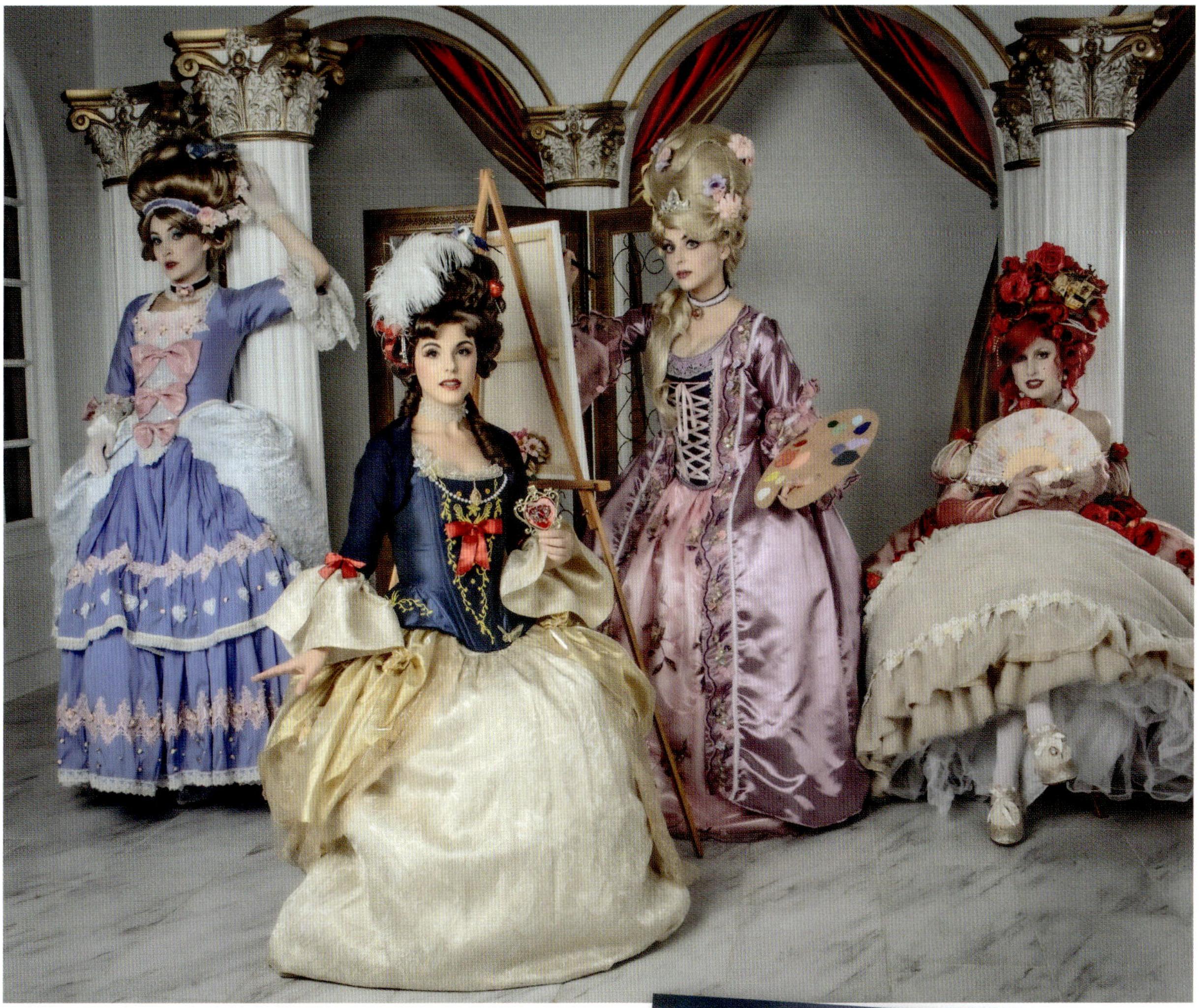

Above: Amber Arden and friends as Rococo Disney Princesses. *Right:* Snow White meets *Star Wars* in a mash-up cosplay by Amber Arden.

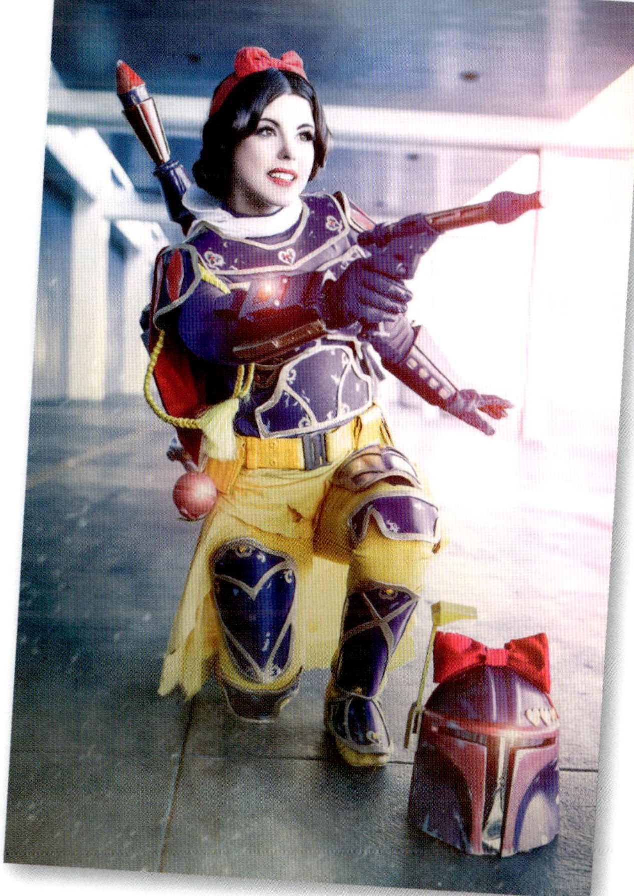

Anna and Elsa. "Human beings have a long history of using fantasy thinking, not only to creatively solve our problems, but also to help us dissociate from difficult things in our lives. Disney Princesses are generally hard working—but they are also dreamers—and they find a way to make those dreams reality."

For Amber Arden, cosplay isn't just a hobby. She's created an entire career out of cosplaying Snow White. Arden, who studied costume design and fashion history in college, began learning to create her own princess looks after being dubbed "Snow White" by friends for her cheerful demeanor. She now collaborates with other cosplayers on group cosplays, and found new opportunities, such as modeling for clothing site Her Universe. But most importantly, it brings

A Glass Arm for Cinderella

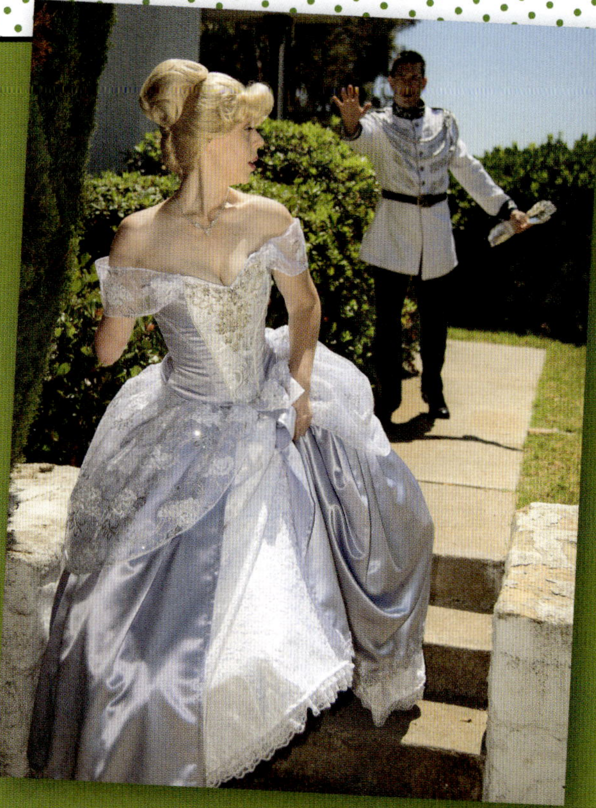

Cinderella's glass slipper is surely one of the most iconic shoes in history, recognizable throughout fairy-tale lore. But what if Cinderella's Fairy Godmother had given her a glass arm instead of a glass slipper? Cosplayer Mandy Pursley, who was born with a "limb difference," as she calls it, imagined a new narrative for the princess when her daughter was studying the original story at school. "We were talking about how this fairy tale had been adapted by so many different cultures to make it their own and I thought, 'How can I make this Cinderella story my own too?'" Pursley says. "I had this idea: 'What if she trades out her glass slippers for a glass arm instead?' I had to bring that to life."

Pursley, who sews her own cosplay costumes one-handed, took on the challenge. First, she designed and created Cinderella's blue gown herself. Then, she connected with artist Gilbert Lozano, who had previously worked for the Disney parks, asking him to build the glass arm, which is actually made of resin. The gown took Pursley sixty hours to sew. "With Cinderella, I wanted to make the gown look magical, so I went all-out on the fabrics and the lace and the sequins and the beading because I wanted it to be perfect," she explains. "That's one thing that separates it from being just a costume into cosplay. Making it this real adaptation from the screen into the real world." A photo of her Cinderella cosplay went viral almost immediately, leading Pursley to be invited onto *The Kelly Clarkson Show* to share her story. Pursley also won the Judge's Choice Award at the 2020 Comic-Con Masquerade, which was held virtually.

For Pursley, cosplay is an opportunity to expand on what it means to be a princess and what a princess can look like. She's added a version of Snow White to her repertoire, revealing that a princess can be the fairest one of all exactly as she is. "I was part of a wave of people who were beginning to realize cosplay was more than just dressing up as a character," Pursley says. "We can bring parts of ourselves into these characters. That's helped to change how inclusive cosplay is overall."

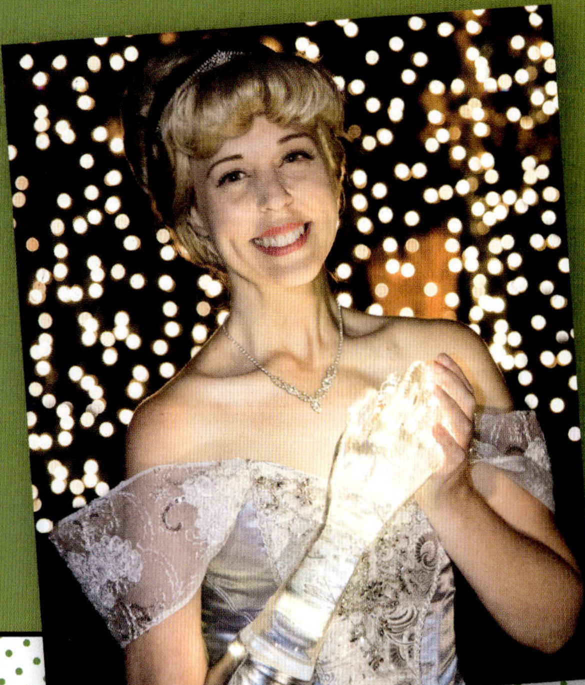

Mandy Pursley gives Cinderella a fresh spin with a glass arm instead of a glass slipper.

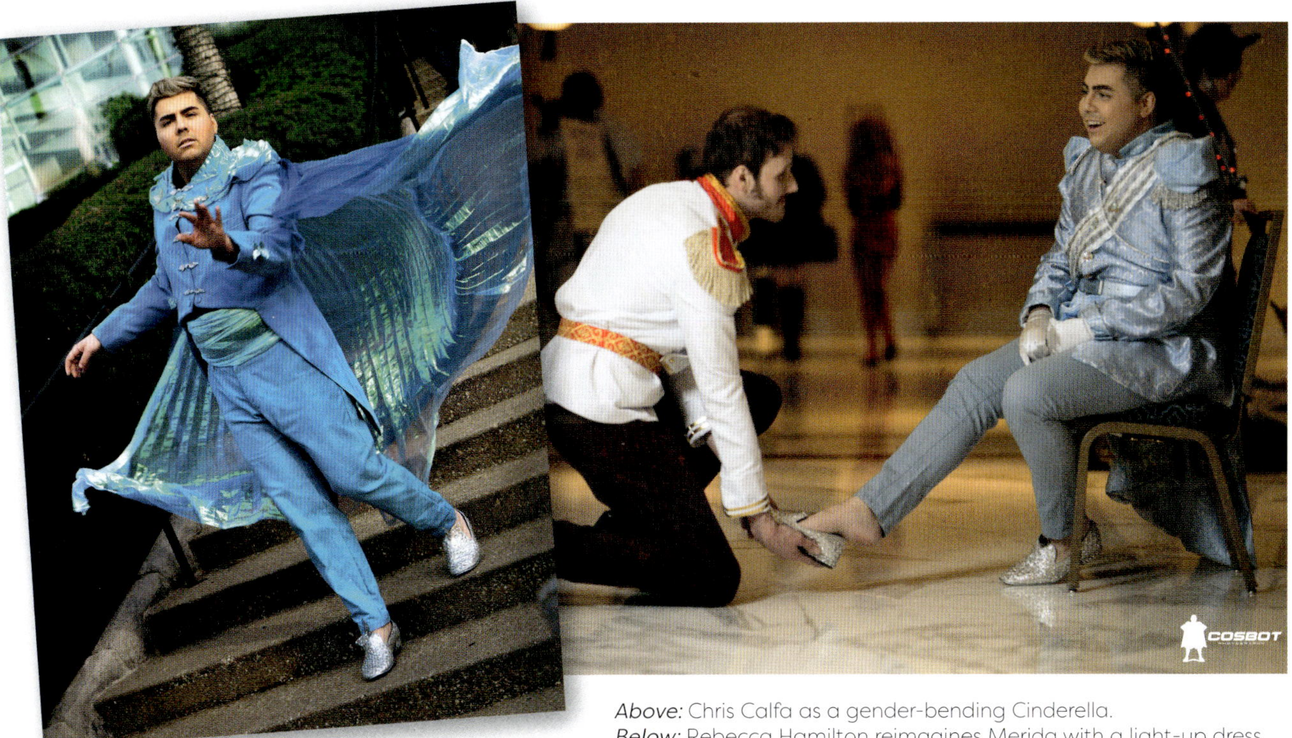

Above: Chris Calfa as a gender-bending Cinderella.
Below: Rebecca Hamilton reimagines Merida with a light-up dress.

Arden together with fellow fans. "Like they said in *Field of Dreams,* 'If you build it, they will come,' Arden says. "We Disney cosplayers are all huge Disney fans and you can connect quite quickly when you see another Disney cosplayer as you will probably both geek out."

While some cosplay purists feel that the artform is about recreating a character from head to toe, cosplay is evolving into a more inclusive practice. Over time, the cosplay world has begun to welcome all types of people. Williams explains that, traditionally, fan conventions were seen as masculine spaces, but that has shifted. "The idea that you could cosplay a princess and it could be good and it could be seen as belonging in that kind of space is really interesting," Williams notes. "Ninety-nine percent of the time it's adult women who are engaging in it, although I have seen men cosplaying as Disney Princesses as well."

The magic of cosplay means that everyone gets to have their own version of a character. Chris Calfa, who goes by Princess Chris, has designed masculine costumed versions of Rapunzel, Ariel, and Snow White to cosplay the characters. "Everyone has a different take on what these women would look like as men," Calfa says. "I've seen them interpreted so many different ways and it's wonderful when people can feel like themselves in a character

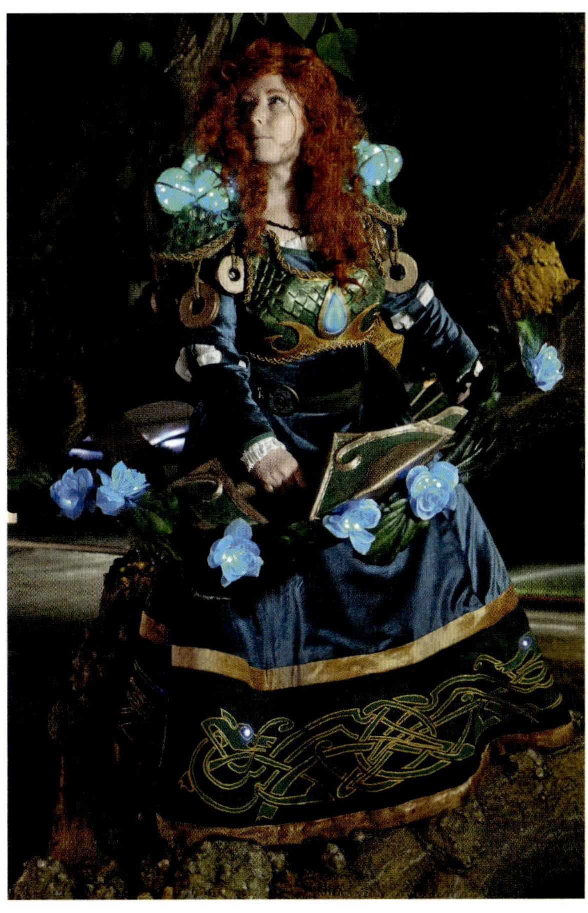

Mousequerade at D23 Expo

Creating an amazing cosplay outfit is quite an achievement. But winning an official award for doing so brings that achievement to a whole new level. As D23 Expo began to grow, it became clear to the organizers that the fans' dedication for arriving in costume should be celebrated. So, in 2013, the organizers launched a costume contest, which was later rebranded as the D23 *Mousequerade*. It's now a signature offering of the D23 Expo experience, with any fan eligible to enter. The categories shift at each incarnation of the convention and numerous celebrities have appeared as judges, including actors Yvette Nicole Brown, Zendaya, and Alfonso Ribeiro, Her Universe founder Ashley Eckstein, and *Once Upon a Time* costume designer Eduardo Castro. Contestants, who can enter solo or in a group, are judged on craftsmanship, quality, concept and design, showmanship, and stage presence.

Over the years, the winners have been impressive. "We've seen some incredible, detailed, creative costumes where the fans put so much effort into creating and into interpreting their favorite characters," says Michael Vargo, vice president of D23. "They plan months and months ahead of time in creating their costumes." While some *Mousequerade* categories look for exact recreations of the characters, others lend themselves to more imaginative interpretations. In 2019, a group of fans presented "Mad Princess Party," where the Disney Princesses transformed into Disneyland's spinning teacups onstage. That group won the award for Best Cast of Characters. Earlier, in 2017, Kaytie Metcalf entered her original costume "This is Not the Dwarf You're Looking For," a mash-up of Snow White and a Star Wars Jedi, complete with a tiny BB-8 in a Dopey hat. The crowd cheered her adventurous version of a sci-fi Disney Princess and her Dwarf-robot pal.

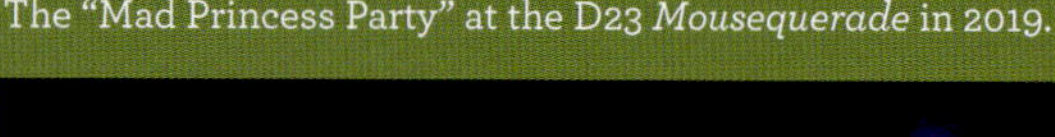

The "Mad Princess Party" at the D23 *Mousequerade* in 2019.

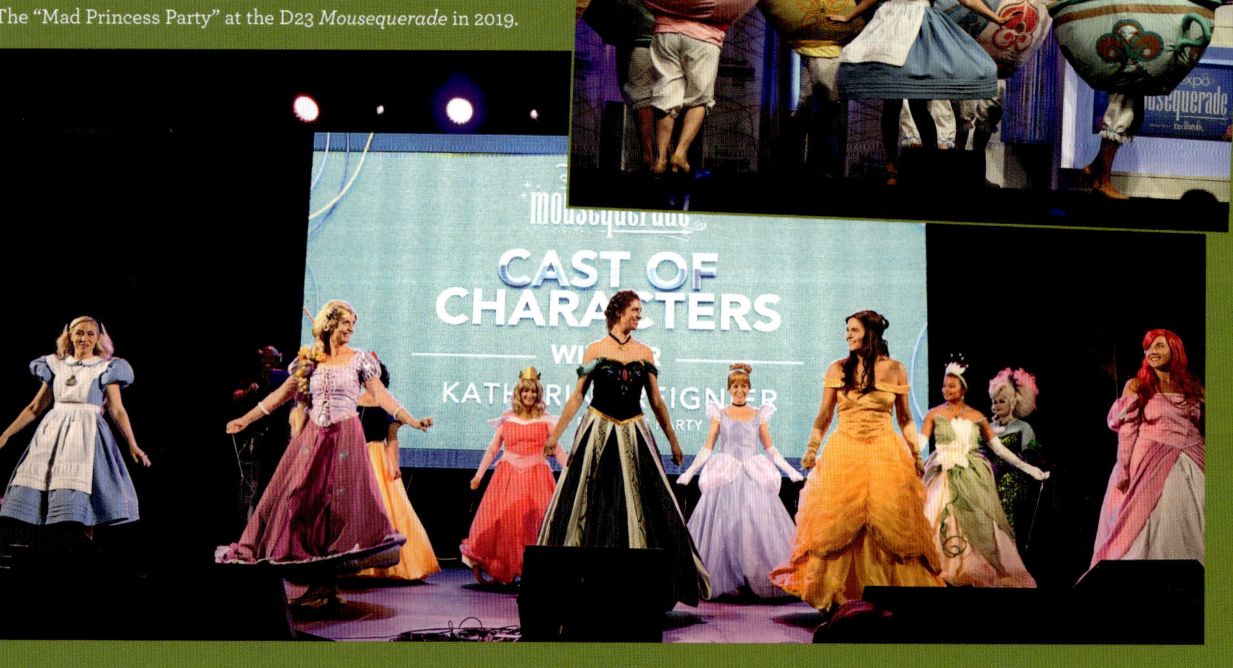

who is not the same gender as they are. Most people are excited to see something as unique as male Cinderella or female Aladdin even. I think gender-bending opens a lot of eyes and possibilities."

There are character mash-ups, like Rebecca Hamilton choosing to reimagine Princess Merida as a Wildhammer dwarf from Azeroth in *World of Warcraft*, creating an elaborate, light-up combination of the two for the BlizzCon gaming convention. There are also takes on class and race. Photographer Symone Seven reinterpreted the Disney Princesses in a 2020 art series she based on live-action film posters. She was largely inspired by Brandy and Whitney Houston's 1997 film *Rodgers & Hammerstein's Cinderella*. "Seeing a brown girl that looked like me be treated like royalty meant the world to me," Seven remembers. "I wanted to recreate that moment for little brown girls now who may not have known about the 1997 film." In the images, Seven cosplays the various princesses herself. "I love that cosplay allows anyone to be who they want to be," she notes. "Cosplay allows me the freedom to break through any barriers—racial, political, socio-economic."

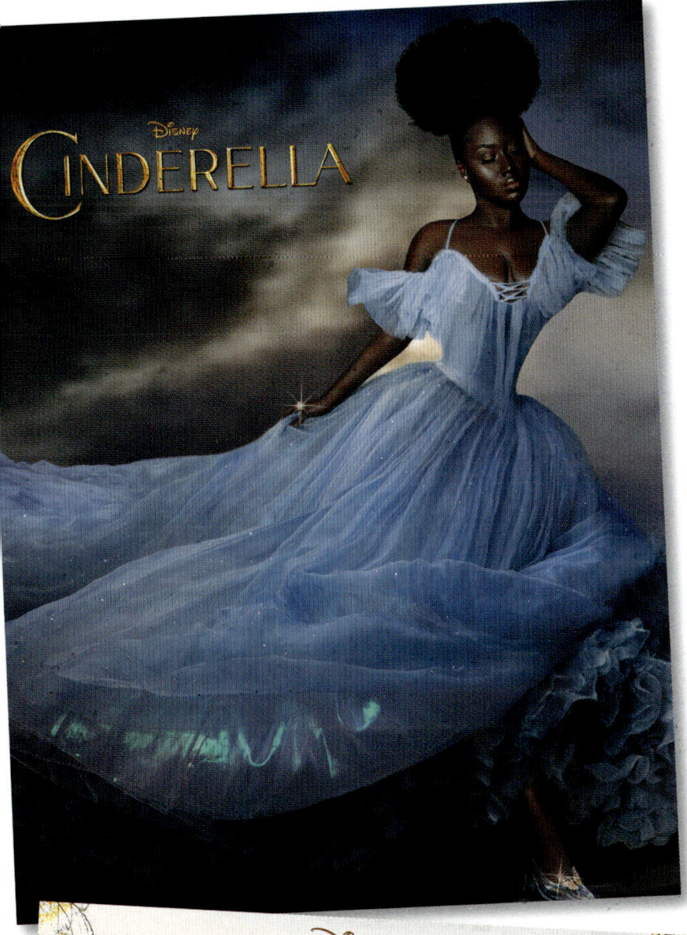

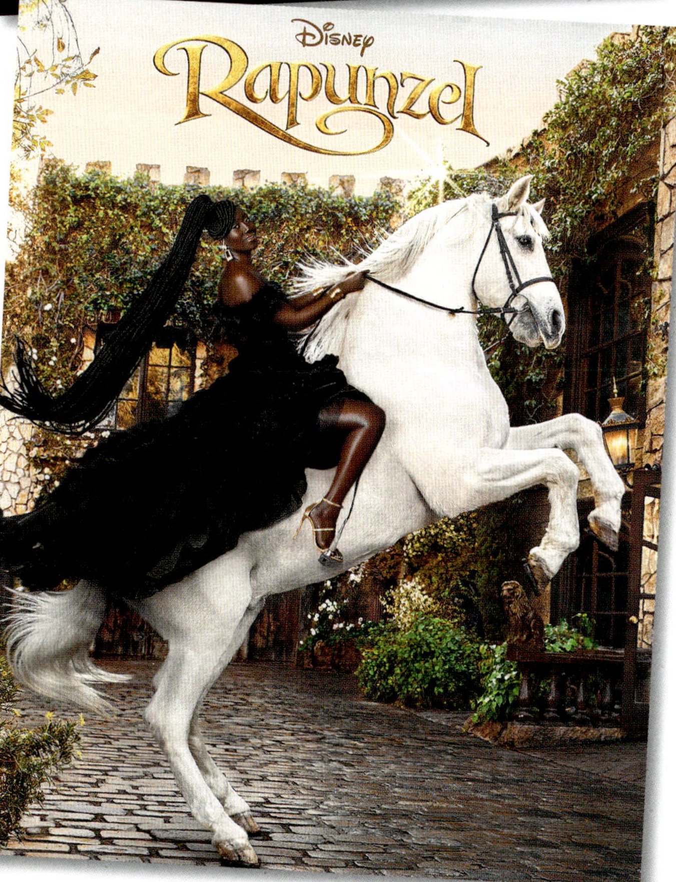

Photographer Symone Seven reinterprets Cinderella and Rapunzel.

TRIBUTES AND REINTERPRETATIONS

Classic characters and stories, many of which get handed down for generations, are ripe for reinterpretation. Because we have an established familiarity with the Disney Princesses, it's easy to create new, unofficial narratives or visual aesthetics for them to live in, whether it's a sincere portrayal or a loving parody. There's fan fiction, fan art, memes, YouTube skits, and more, all of which offer slightly different variations of these beloved characters and their well-known attributes.

For Amy Mebberson, transforming the princesses into a series of comics, "Pocket

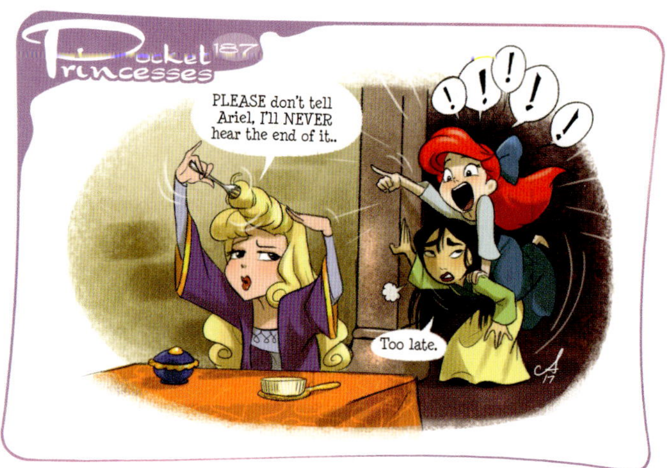

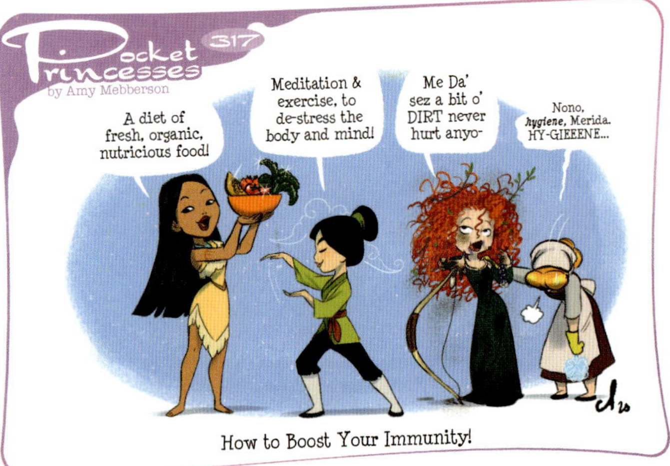

Princesses," was a way to emphasize aspects of the characters' personalities. "I started drawing the princesses being funny and finding the comedy in their personalities," says Mebberson, who began creating the comics while working for Disney Animation in Australia. Her early drawings appeared on popular fan art site Deviant Art in the mid-2000s and soon went viral. "People quickly engaged with the comics because a bit of self-parody is always relatable," she notes.

While Mebberson continues to release a weekly edition of "Pocket Princesses," which now lives on Instagram, she was also tapped to write official Disney Princess comics for publisher Joe Books in 2016. The all-ages comic showcases the princesses as everyday humans, giving fans an opportunity to experience them in new ways. "The princesses are not just figureheads," Mebberson says. "They are characters who have stories." She adds, "The princesses can show you the whole gamut of what it means to be a woman.

Above: Amy Mebberson's "Pocket Princesses" comic.
Below: Two Hipster Ariel memes created by Braden Graeber.

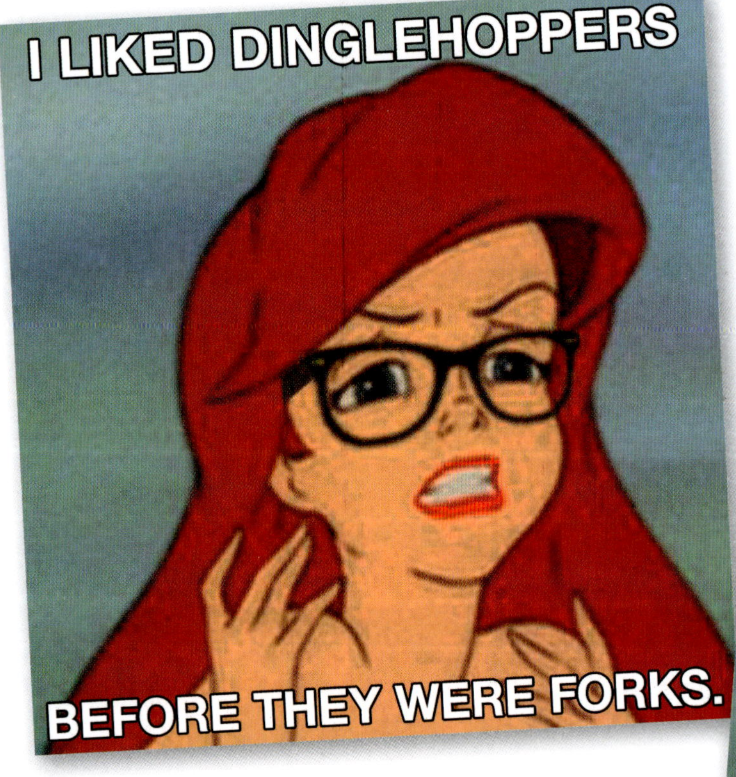

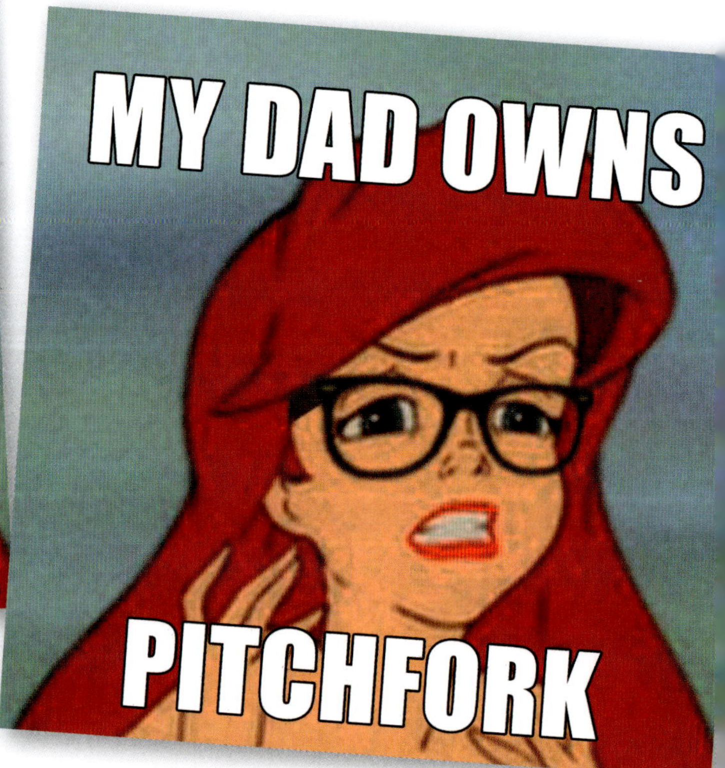

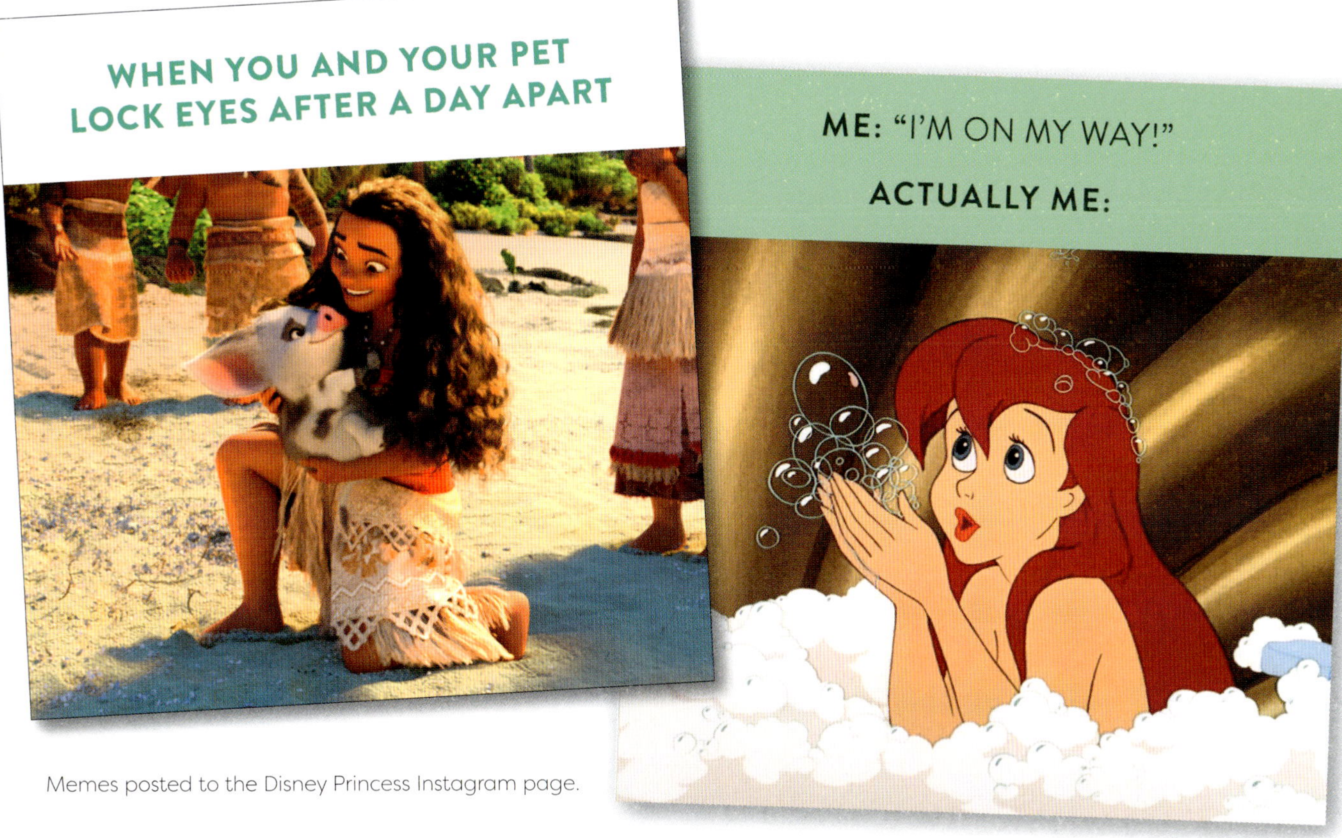

Memes posted to the Disney Princess Instagram page.

She can be kind and like to nurture, and she can be intelligent and an explorer."

Scrolling through Instagram, fans can find literally thousands of reinterpretations of the Disney Princesses. The characters have been reimagined in hundreds of different ways by fans who want to pay tribute to the original designs and animation.

For Braden Graeber, Ariel was the perfect vessel to articulate how millennials often reject the status quo. In February of 2011, Graeber began posting hand-drawn memes of Ariel wearing thick black glasses with clever lines like "My dad owns Pitchfork" and "I want to be where the people are... so I can judge them." This version of Ariel was dubbed "Little Hipster Mermaid," a.k.a. Hipster Ariel, and has become one of the most iconic Disney Princess memes to ever hit the Internet.

Ironically, Graeber didn't intend to create a meme. At the time, he was attending the Art Center College of Design in Pasadena, California, and decided to Photoshop glasses on Ariel, a character Graeber related to because they share red hair. After posting it to Tumblr, the image went viral and Graeber began to imagine what else Hipster Ariel might be into.

"Looking at Ariel in the tortoise shell glasses, I started to think about all the ways her character overlapped with the hipster archetype," Graeber explains. "Ariel wants out of her mainstream world. Ariel has a cave of thrifted objects. Ariel is friends with Scottish pop band Belle and Sebastian. Ariel is from 1989, so she's in the prime millennial hipster demographic."

As the meme took off, so did the copycat version. Graeber confirms that you can tell his originals from the alternative versions because he used the Helvetica typeface, which was a joke about the Hipster Mermaid being too cool for the font "Arial." Since then, fans have cosplayed Hipster Ariel and even created spin-offs, like Hipster Belle. While Graeber doesn't continue to create Ariel memes, he recognizes how his concept brought the Internet together over a collective idea. "I think Ariel hit a sweet spot in terms of timing in that she was a character from the childhood of a generation just becoming adults,"

Fit for a Princess

Home is where the heart is, but it can also be filled with magic. For some Disney fans, creating themed rooms or Disney Princess-inspired home décor is a way to surround themselves with the love of fairy tales. Kelsey Hermanson has attracted a massive online following for her whimsical Disney house, which has rooms designed after *The Little Mermaid*, *Tangled*, and *Aladdin*. She's not alone, either. While there are plenty of official Disney home goods available to buy, many adult fans DIY their way to a princess bedroom or library.

Hermanson started decorating her home in Disney style because of her family's love for the parks. She now has ten rooms with different Disney themes, including a *Cinderella*-inspired master bedroom. "I have a huge amount of respect for the Imagineers and people that work for Disney," she explains. "I admire the details and heart that they put into the parks. I wanted to create a bit of that magic in my home, as well."

She's done a lot of the work herself, using items she's been creating and collecting for the past decade. "I have created banners for our Rapunzel room and hand-painted lanterns," Hermanson notes. "I also created a large bubble installation for our *Cinderella* bedroom with images from the film." She adds, "Living in our Disney house provides a source of inspiration and imagination. It's also a wonderful home for my two daughters to grow up in."

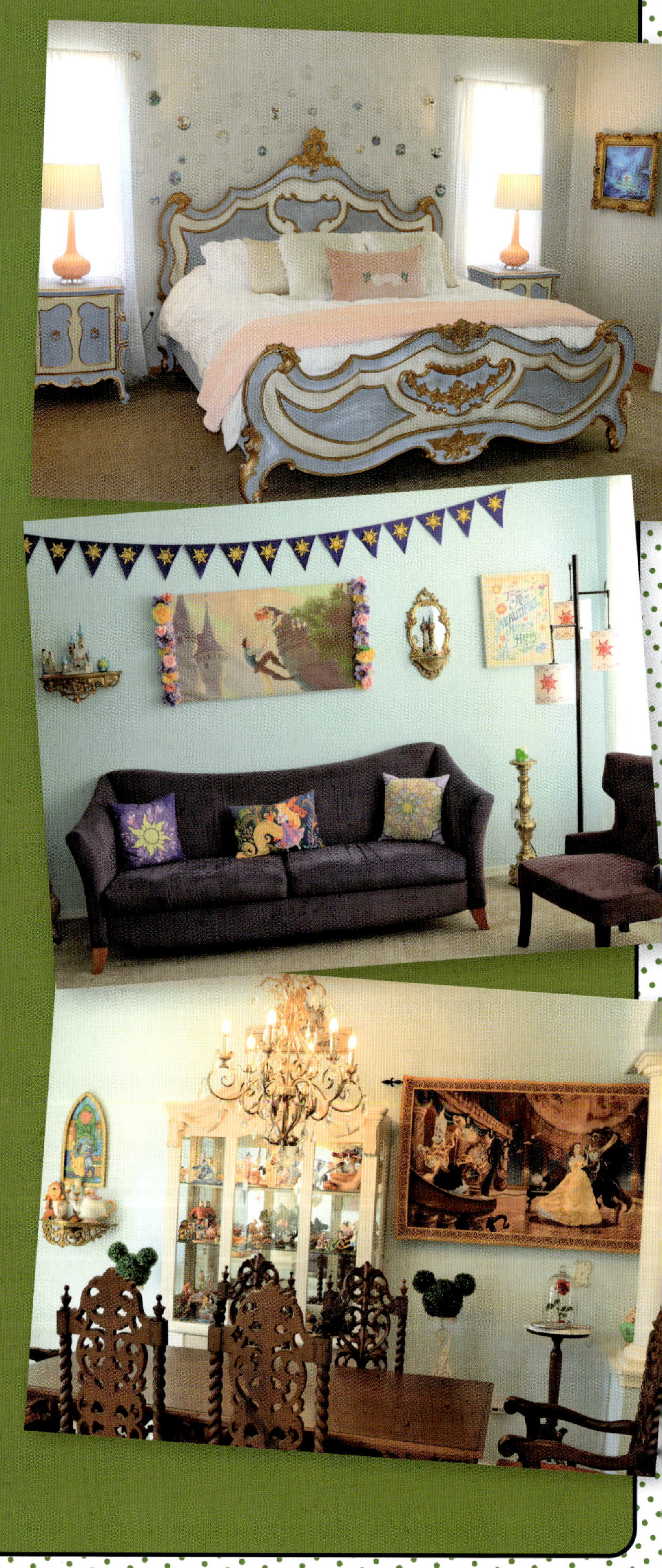

Right: Disney Princess-inspired interior design, created by Disney fan Kelsey Hermanson.

he notes. "Her character and desire to be part of a world of her own was loaded with understood meaning and ripe for remixing by millennials finally coming into a real world of their own."

Hipster Ariel isn't the only Disney Princess meme, and in fact the characters are often reimagined in various scenarios or used to convey fans' feelings about everything from Mondays to their obsession with pets. The princesses have been modernized, put on the cover of *Vogue*, made into emojis, drawn as characters from other movies, and even been the subject of memes about Zoom fatigue. The memes work because the Disney Princesses are so ingrained into pop culture that they don't require any explanation.

"Disney is such a part of American culture, and world culture," explains Matt Schimkowitz, Senior Editor of "Know Your Meme." "You can just use them and people know exactly what is meant by the image. You can take Cinderella and change her around a little bit because everyone knows Cinderella. That leads to a community of people who also know and understand Cinderella."

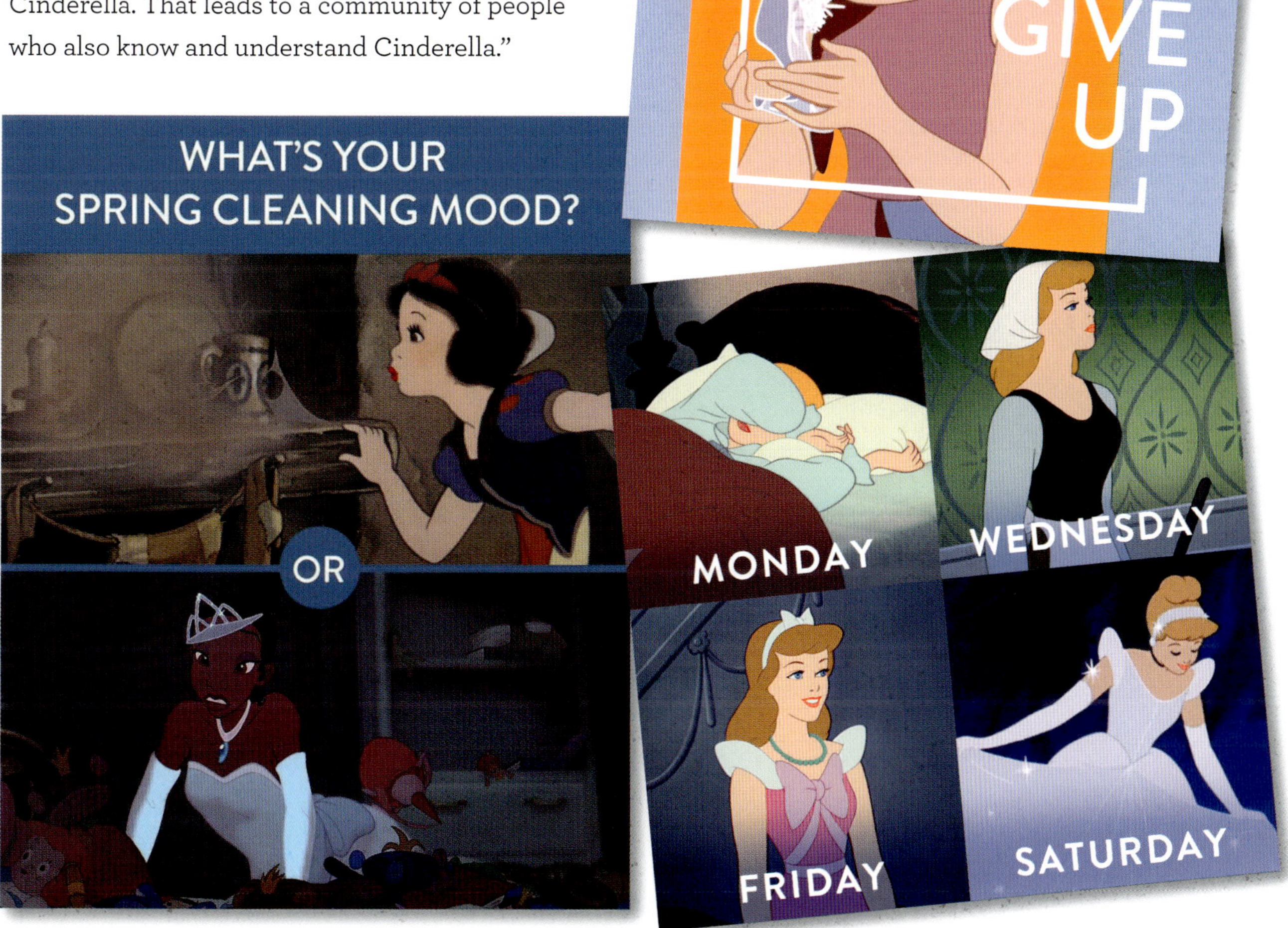

Above and Right: Examples of Disney Princess memes.

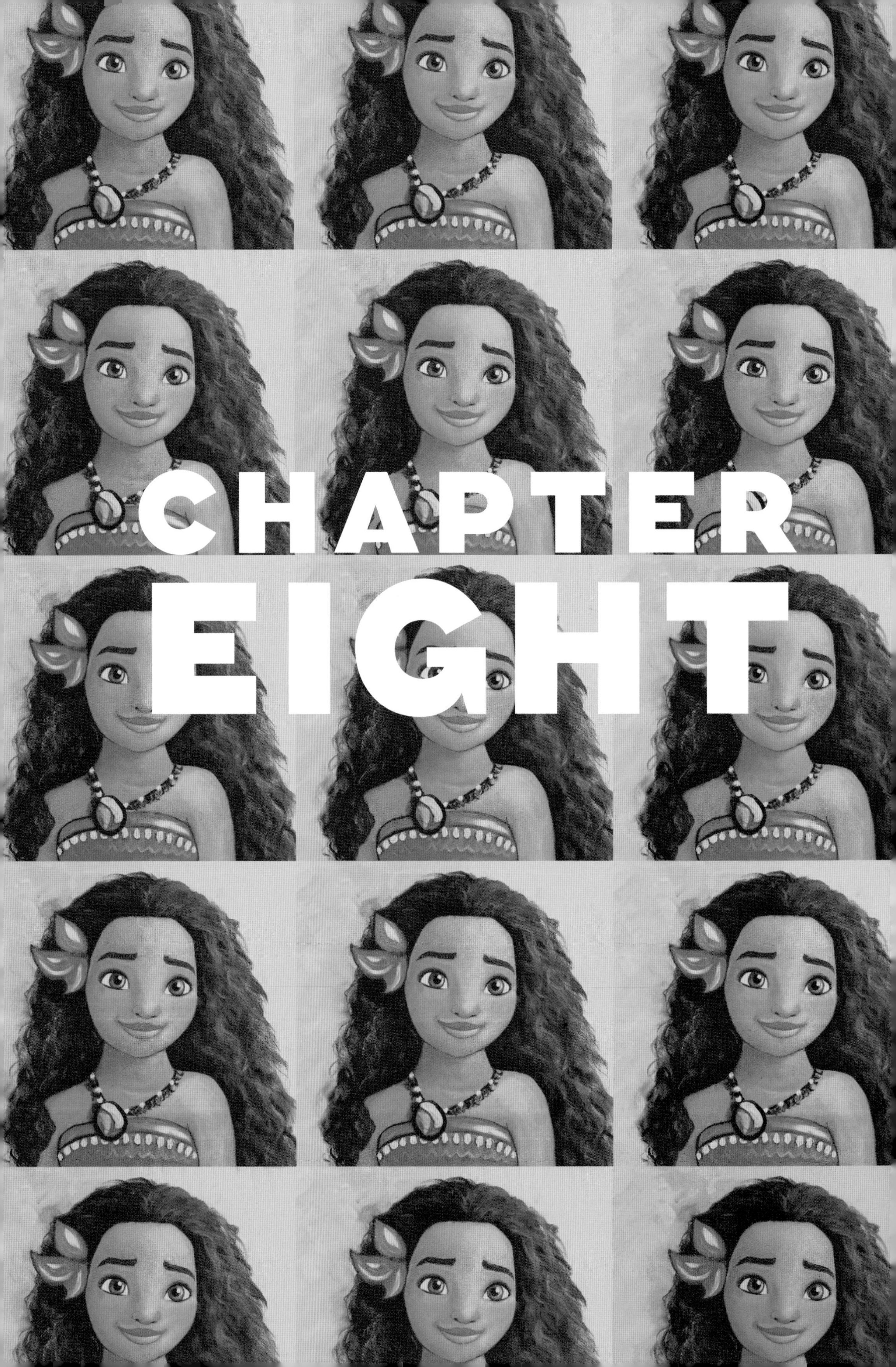

CHAPTER EIGHT

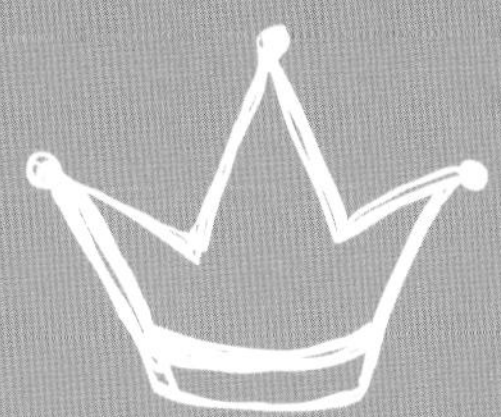

HOW FAR I'LL GO

GIRL POWER

What we see in entertainment matters. When an empowered character appears onscreen, their strength ripples out into the world. Over the course of Disney's decades-long history, the company has created some of the most influential onscreen characters in the world, and their impact can't be underestimated. Courageous, kind-hearted, empowered characters like Cinderella, Ariel, Mulan, and Moana have affected millions of people around the world. Those characters' qualities and actions inspire us, teach us positive values, and encourage us to follow our own dreams.

"With the reach we have, particularly to young minds, I think we have a responsibility to not just reflect the moment we're in, but to help create the next moment we're going to be in," says *Moana* producer Osnat Shurer. "We're part of culture in a significant way. We create new stories and those stories reverberate. That's an opportunity and a huge responsibility, especially as we create strong female characters on the screen."

Each Disney Princess embodies unique traits and brings with her a tangible influence over her fans. Disney has reflected those positive traits in their girl power campaigns, like Dream Big, Princess and the Ultimate Princess Celebration, and the impact of the characters can be felt everywhere from exercise classes to chefs' kitchens. In their individual ways, the characters remind us that we can be anything we want to be and we can rise above any challenge to get there.

"I utterly believe in the power of storytelling to change the world," says *Beauty and the Beast* (1991) screenwriter Linda Woolverton. "That's the whole point: We're changing the culture through storytelling. You're enlightening and shining a light. If little girls see somebody like Belle it becomes, 'Oh, it's okay not to pretend to be less smart than I am. It's okay to really like reading. It's okay to be an intellectual.'"

Many of the voice talent and the live-action film actresses have become living embodiments of the spirit and traits of their respective characters as well. It's been especially powerful to see the diversity of recent films, as the Disney Princesses have become reflections of cultures from all over the world.

"I'm so proud of how diverse our cast is," *Aladdin* actress Naomi Scott said after the film's release in 2019. "For me growing up, Jasmine was my [favorite] princess, probably because I saw myself in her. She was someone that I could play." She added, "I think, ultimately for young kids, seeing themselves in a character is really powerful. Even if they don't get the nuanced, small things, they probably do pick it up subconsciously. For me, I think that's beautiful."

The Disney Princesses also represent the possibilities of feminism, as do the actresses who have played them. In 2014, Emma Watson stood before the United Nations in New York and gave an impassioned speech about her HeForShe

Below: Bell walks through town reading her book in *Beauty and the Beast*.
Inset: Linda Woolverton, the screenwriter for *Beauty and the Beast*.

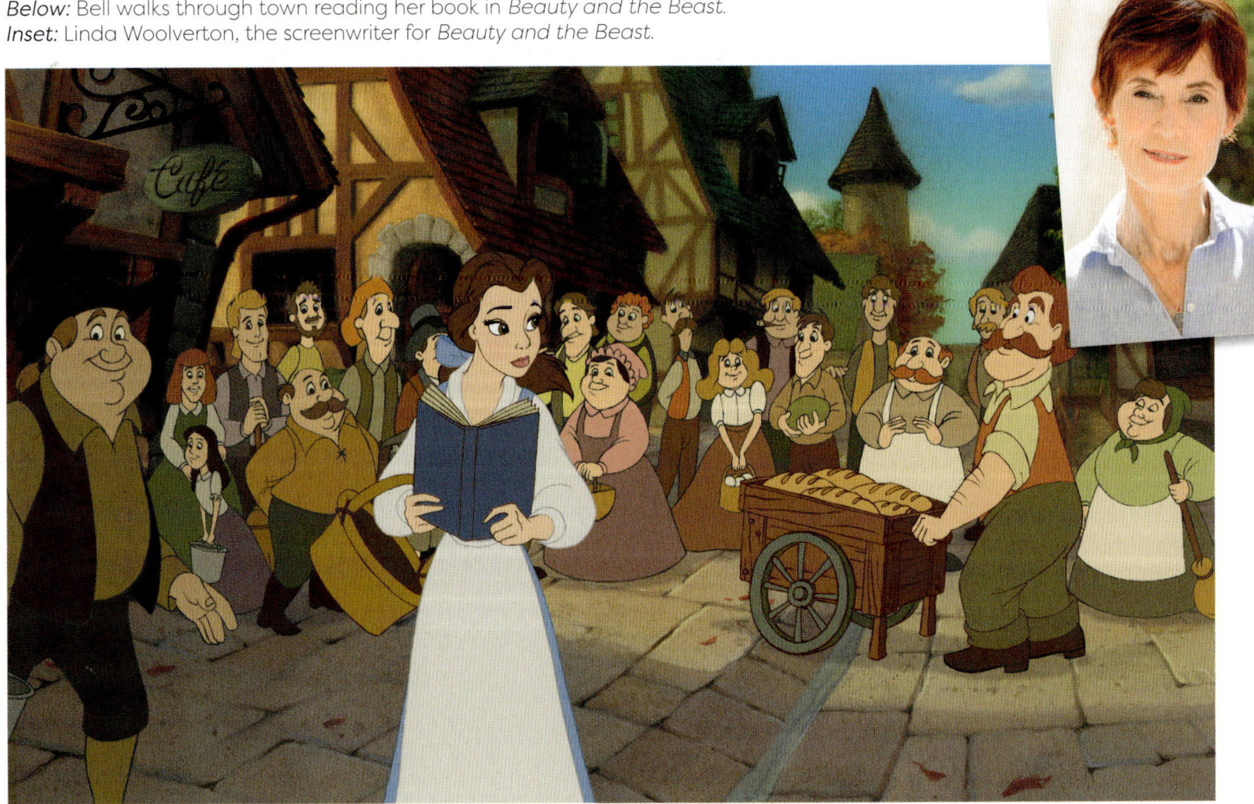

campaign, an alliance launched by the actress to create global solidarity around gender inequality. Watson, who was cast as Belle the following year, spoke about the importance of encouraging men to be advocates for gender equality and why feminism simply means allowing all genders access to the same rights.

That sense of equality is represented in many Disney films. True feminism means that an individual can be whatever they want to be, unrestricted by any societal mores or pressures. Women can be fierce warriors or gentle homemakers, and both are equally valid expressions of self. No one character has to represent everyone, which is why it's so amazing that there's a Disney Princess—or a *Frozen* queen—for everyone.

"The earlier princesses were a little more reactive to their situations and the more recent ones were more proactive," explains animator Kira Lehtomaki. "But I think both sets of stories are useful to us. Every princess has a dream and a goal, and sometimes they are proactive in going out and getting it, and other times they need a little help along the way. I didn't get to where I'm at here at Disney without help from other people. Depending on the moment in your life, maybe you need that Fairy Godmother to come help you. And then other times you need to take charge and fearlessly go for your dreams."

Like Lehtomaki, many of the women behind the scenes at Disney Animation can point to a Disney Princess for inspiration. And as Walt Disney Animation Studios looks to the future, there's a real awareness of how much the company's uplifting stories, memorable characters, and magical worlds matter. At both Walt Disney Animation Studios and The Walt Disney Studios, each filmmaker aims to create authentic tales rooted in cultures from across the globe, with a diverse, inclusive group of performers onscreen and an equally diverse, inclusive group of artists and storytellers working behind the scenes.

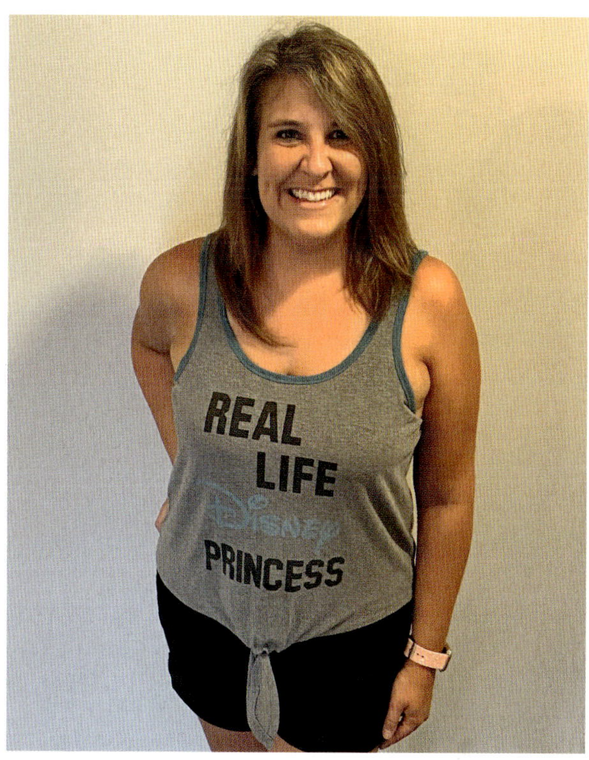

Disney Princess merchandise encourages fans to find their inner hero.

The emphasis on embracing fairy tales and folk stories from around the world is reflected in films such as *Raya and the Last Dragon* (2021) and *Encanto* (2021). There are endless fantastical narratives that can be woven through animation and live-action film, and Disney filmmakers are known for their careful research and consideration for other cultures. For viewers, the films offer new experiences and encourage a sense of empathy toward others, beginning in childhood, since the Disney films are often the first point of exposure that children experience to cultures outside their own families.

"Films have such a strong impact on our culture in general, and Disney films especially have such a strong impact because they're reaching young kids and families who watch these stories over and over again," says Jessica Julius, Vice President, Creative Development at Walt Disney Animation Studios. "The reason they resonate is because they are complex and interesting characters. To see those characters over and over has a really important impact on what people think women and girls can do and be and achieve. It's the idea: If you can see it, you can be it."

#DREAMBIGPRINCESS

Disney's Dream Big, Princess campaign launched in 2016 and aimed to bring the Disney Princess stories front and center, inspiring kids to realize their full potential. The initial campaign ran over the course of a year, with new themes each month, and Walt Disney Animation Studios Chief Creative Officer Jennifer Lee helped kick off the festivities by sharing a heart-warming letter about how much Cinderella has helped her overcome her own challenges. "Cinderella was a dreamer, herself, which I loved," Lee wrote. "But what inspired me most about her was her kindness in the face of adversity. Cinderella was a part of my earliest memories, but she was also there for me in middle school, when I was bullied very badly... Cinderella went on to a better life and left the bullying and meanness behind. She gave me the courage to remain true to myself and believe that one day I'd be able to leave the bullying and meanness behind. And I did just that."

It's a sentiment that continues to ring true for Lee. "Cinderella persevered when all the things she loved most were taken from her," Lee says. "And she persevered by having a strength and a dream in her heart and this feeling of 'If I stay true to myself, I can find a way through this.' She does and she's rewarded for it. She's not rewarded because she met the prince—she's rewarded because she's a wonderful person."

These positive attributes are important in understanding how the Disney Princesses inspire us every day. During the Dream Big, Princess campaign, each princess embraced a positive motto, like "Don't Judge a Book By Its Cover" for Belle and "Make a Dream Real" for Tiana, to emphasize what makes the individual princesses so special. And while each has her own unique qualities, they also share a common resilience and an ability to triumph over adversity in order to make their dreams come true. In its messaging, Dream Big, Princess underscored the idea that these fictional

A post created for the official Disney Princess Instagram page.

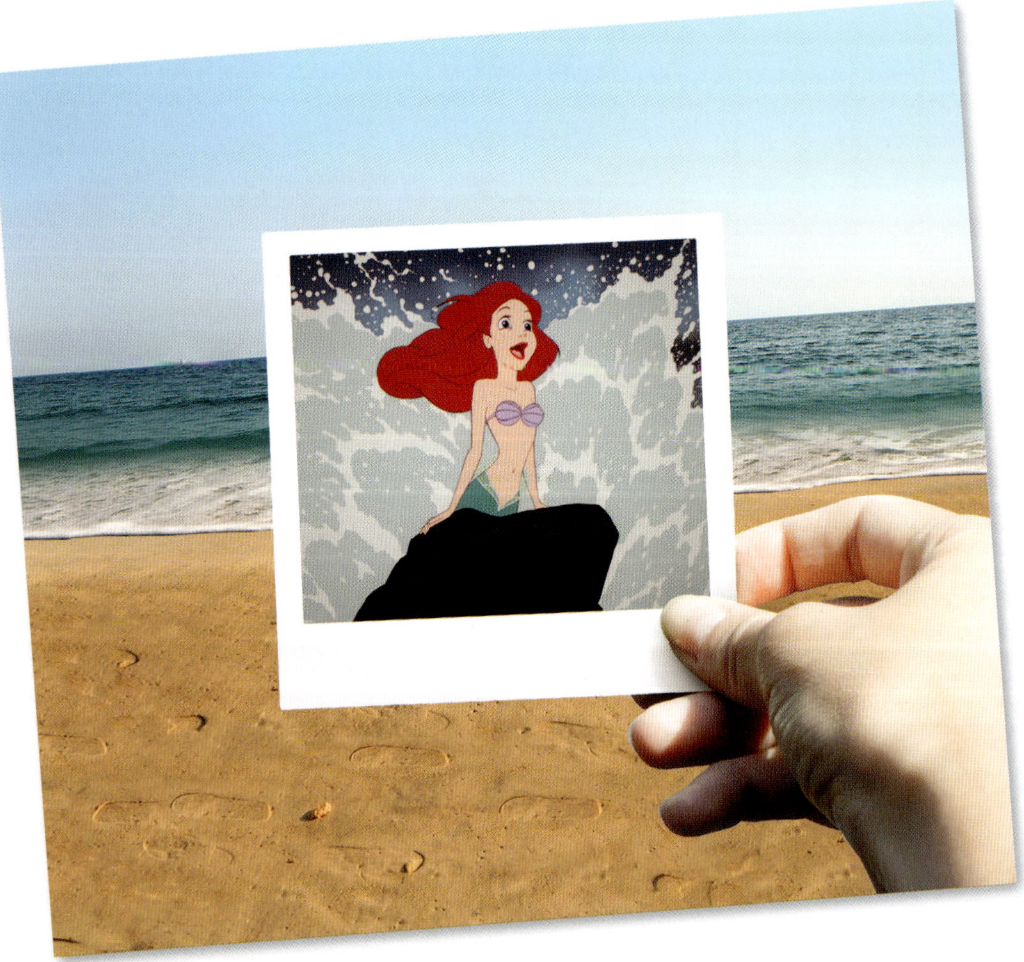

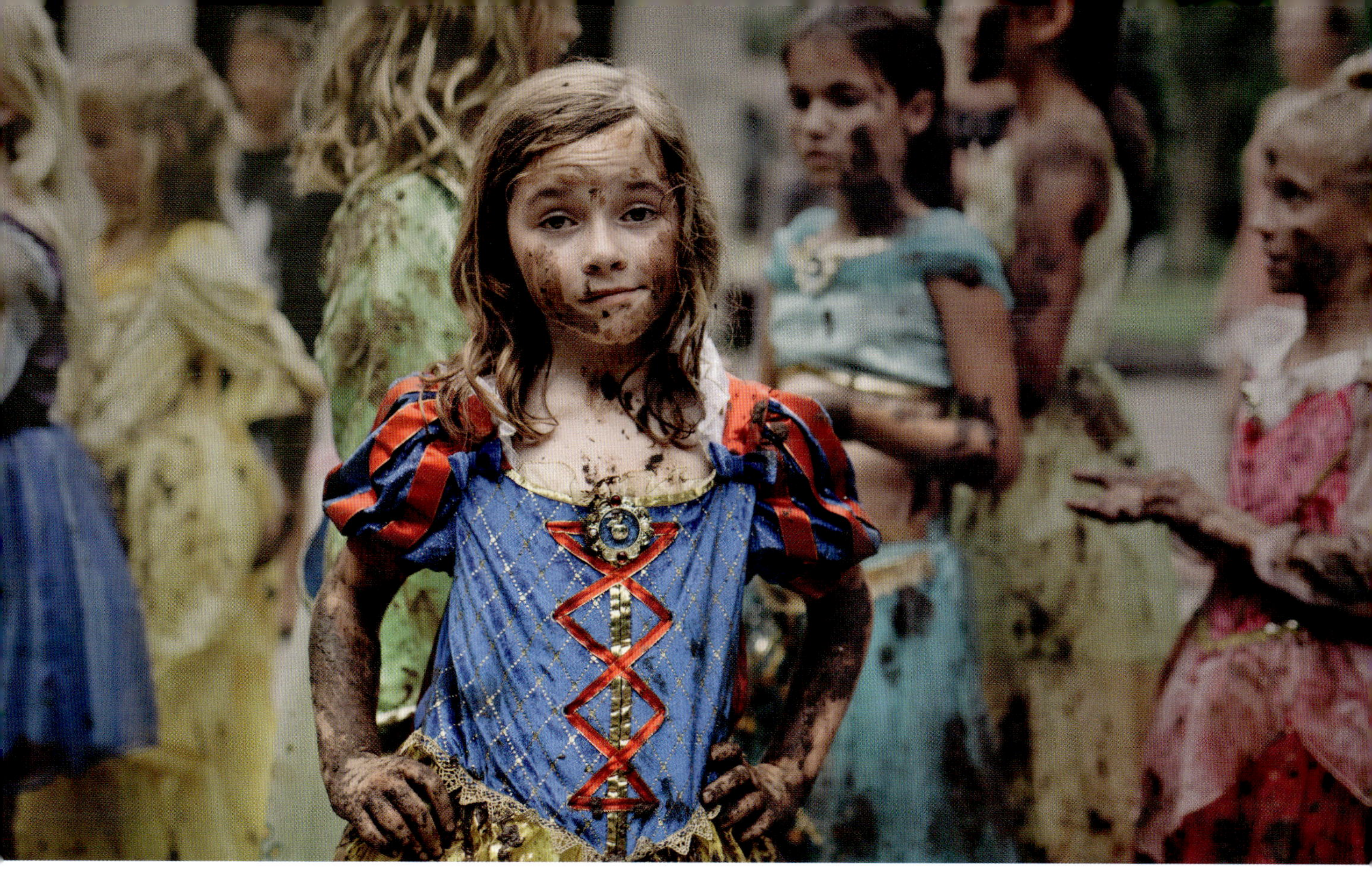

Photographer Kate T. Parker captures a muddy soccer team dressed in Disney Princess gowns.

characters can help real-world people feel more determined in their own lives. The tagline emphasized Lee's own experience: "For every girl who dreams big, there's a princess who shows her it's possible."

The official Disney Princess YouTube channel and Instagram page emerged alongside the Dream Big, Princess campaign in 2016. The social media team wanted to ensure that each princess had her own voice on Instagram with inspirational memes and art. Original artwork, memes, and inspirational posts were created to coincide with Dream Big, Princess. "The goal of the campaign was to make sure fans were recognizing our princess characters as these empowered heroes with their own dreams and adventures," explains Sean Reed, Social Media Manager at The Walt Disney Company. "But it was also to showcase new young girls who were becoming fans of the franchise so they could also pursue their dreams and see these characters as these modern role models. So it was character-driven, and then we wanted the audience to see that in themselves."

In 2017, Dream Big, Princess continued with an added emphasis on real-world role models. The campaign helped to create a three-month exhibition for the United Nations Headquarters' New York City lobby in partnership with UN Foundation's Girl Up initiative and UNICEF. By showcasing inspirational imagery of women and girls overcoming adversity, the exhibition presented positive, uplifting figures who embraced the spirit of the Disney Princesses. It featured photographs by female photographers from around the world, including Ami Vitale, Theresa Balderas, and Lulu Liao. In one image, by Kate T. Parker, nine-year-old Alice Parker wears Snow White's iconic dress while covered in mud on a soccer field. In the background, her teammates wear costumes from the other Disney Princesses, including Aurora and Jasmine. "The Blasters are all about teamwork and toughness and don't let anything, not even a little mud, get in their way," the caption noted of the team.

In 2018, Dream Big, Princess took the campaign a step further. Disney enlisted twenty-one aspiring young filmmakers to direct digital shorts highlighting the stories of female trailblazers to inspire the next generation to follow their own dreams. The shorts spotlighted

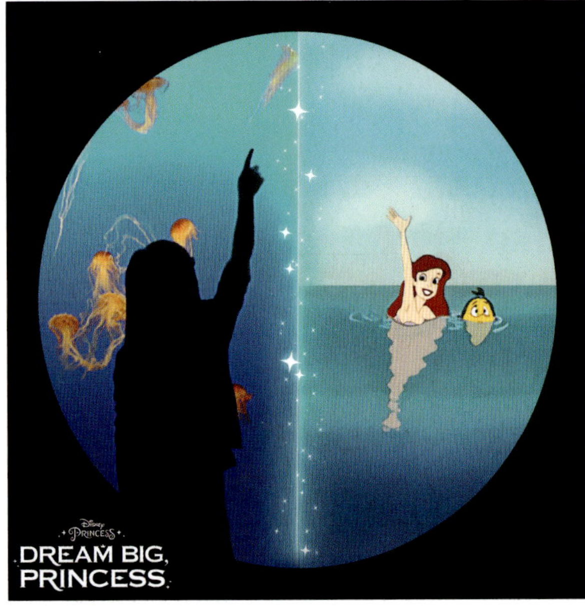

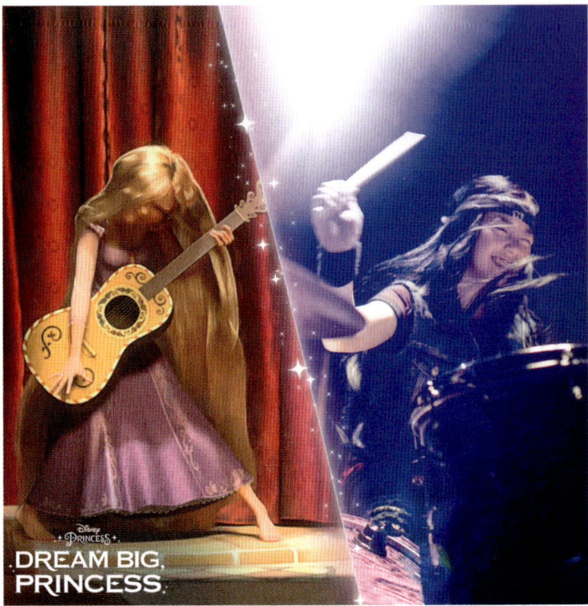

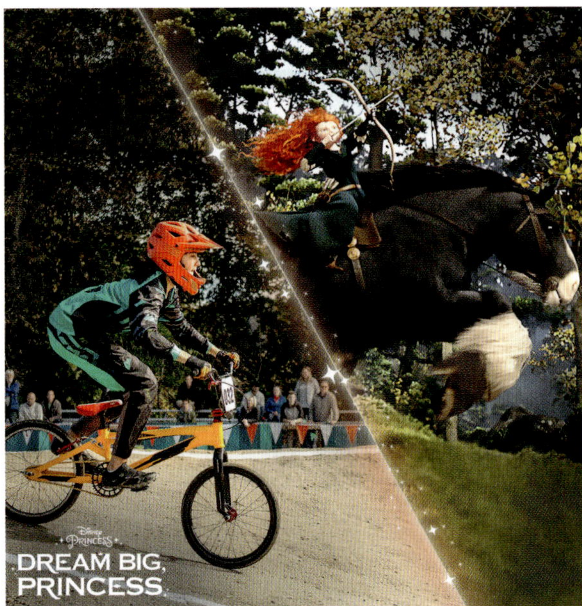

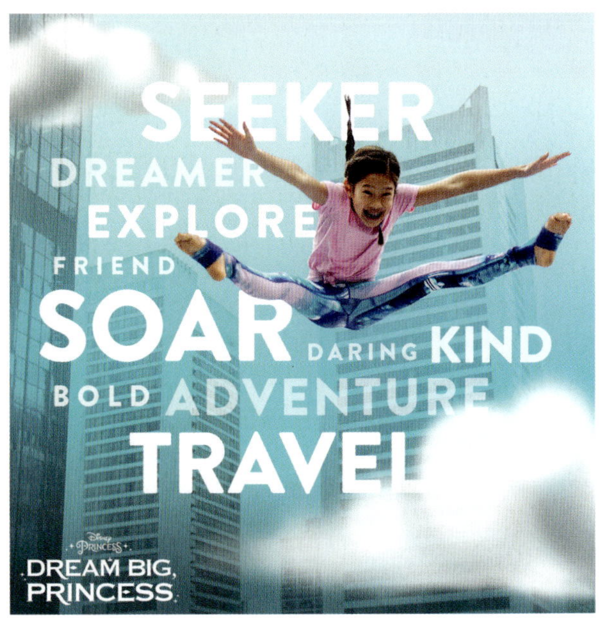

Inspirational social media posts created for the Dream Big, Princess campaign.

everyone from Jennifer Lee herself to actress Emily Blunt to ABC anchor Robin Roberts to Kathleen Kennedy, President of Lucasfilm. Dubbed the #DreamBigPrincess series, the inspiring clips were a strong reminder that seeing the success of one woman can help encourage the future success of another. "There's a line in *Mary Poppins* where she says anything is possible, even the impossible," Blunt explained in a press release. "I think that really symbolizes what dreaming big is all about, the idea if you want something big enough that the universe is going to conspire to give it to you."

It's clear the Disney Princesses can represent big ideas and encourage real-world change. They can also provide moments of hope during challenging times. In 2021, as the world was grappling with the pandemic, Disney launched the Ultimate Princess Celebration, a year-long event spotlighting the courage and kindness of the Disney heroes. The celebration, which also included Anna and Elsa, kicked off with a new anthem from Brandy, singer and star of *Rodgers & Hammerstein's Cinderella*, titled "Starting Now," a reminder of what we can take from each hero to find success on our own journeys.

REAL-WORLD IMPACT

The protagonist of a fairy tale or legend often has an underdog quality, which is why they feel so relatable in the real world. "The lead character in a fairy tale is traditionally perceived as weak," says Charles Solomon, author of several books about the Disney Princess films. "Through intelligence and courage and imagination, they overcome a stronger foe. These are characters children can identify with because they often feel powerless when faced by stronger people and rules they don't understand." It's no wonder that the Disney Princesses, who embody that intelligence, courage, and imagination, have helped people around the world surmount great obstacles.

The Disney filmmakers have heard from hundreds of fans about how their stories have gotten them through challenges and hardships. The films and the characters have given fans a reason to stay alive, they've encouraged them to change careers or learn a new skill, and they've

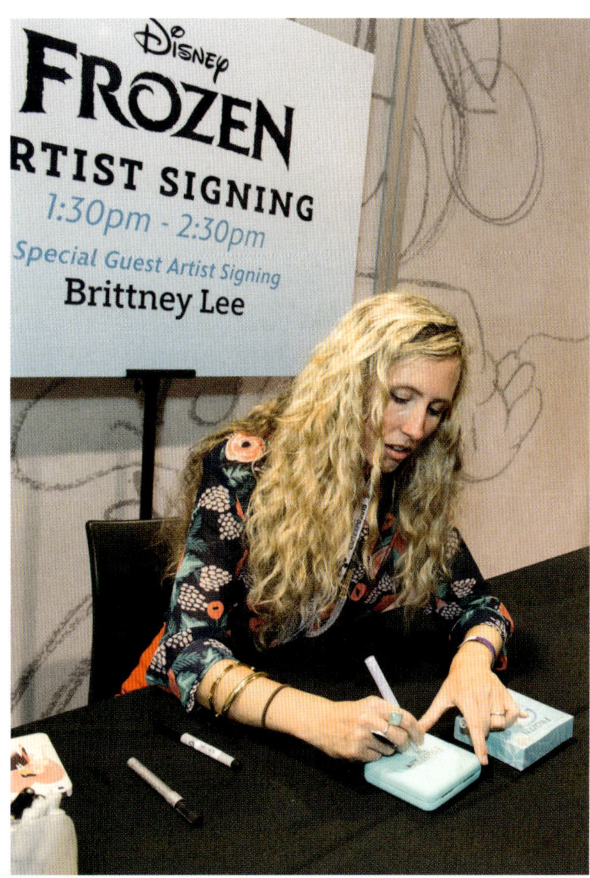

Above: Animator and artist Brittney Lee signs autographs at D23 Expo in 2015. *Below:* Paige O'Hara poses with her paintings of Belle.

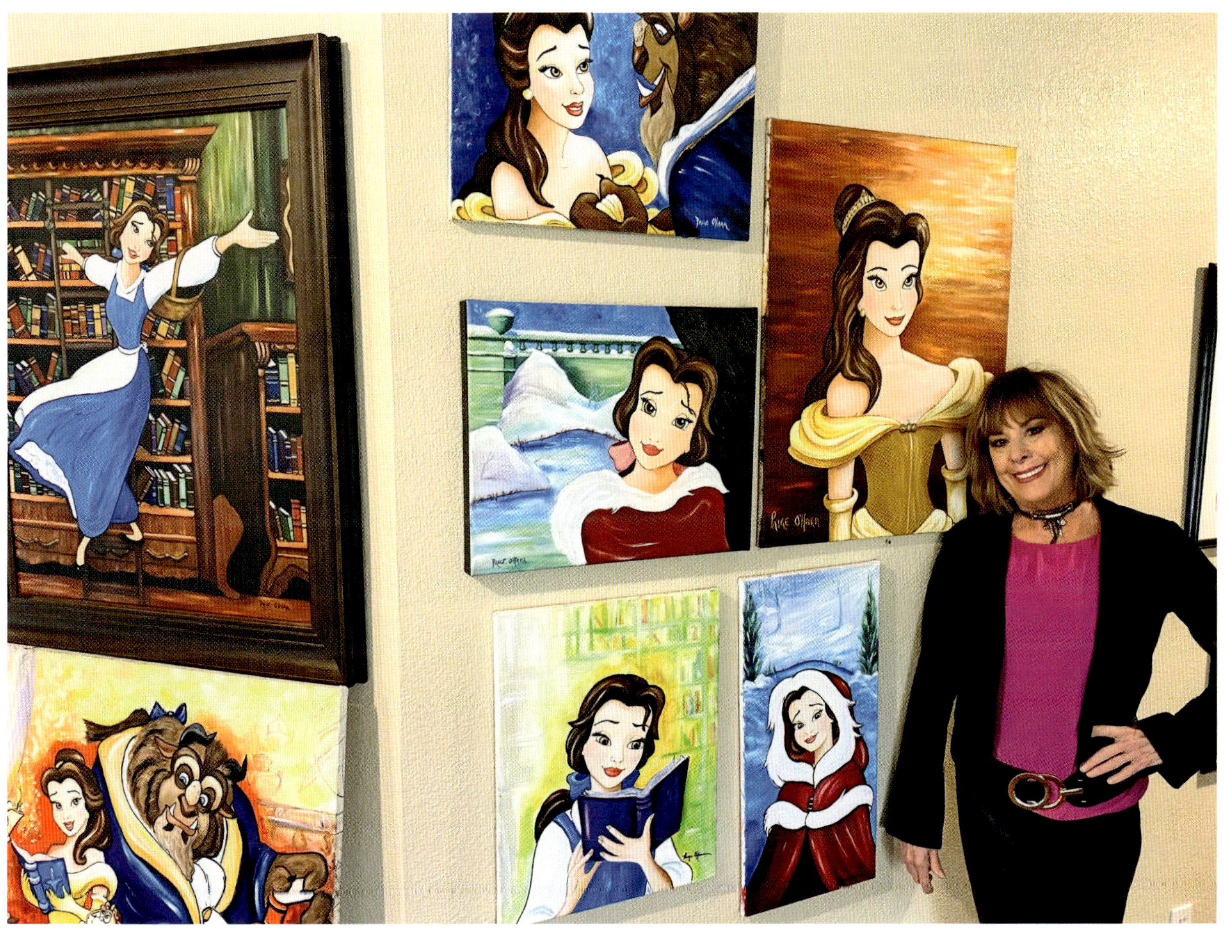

provided a literal soundtrack of empowerment. "I know our films have an impact from the outpouring of love I've received from working on the film," says *Frozen* visual development artist Brittney Lee. "I go yearly to conventions like Comic-Con and people always show up in their homemade gowns and tell me how these characters have saved their lives."

The voice actresses experience this impact regularly, both at in-person events and via social media. Each can point to interactions that reveal just how impactful the Disney Princesses have been on fans. "So many times, I've met fans who say Belle made them feel accepted for who they are," recalls Paige O'Hara, who has been inspired herself to paint the Disney Princesses in vibrant artwork. "One of the children I met could barely speak, but she handed me this letter and it was very articulate. She said, 'Because of Belle, I'm going to be a writer.' Things like that happen all the time. It's so incredibly humbling and inspiring to me that this character can do that and affect people that way."

Jodi Benson has had a similar experience. "I hear these stories all the time," she says. "How children learn to speak by watching our film. How children feel like they belong because of Ariel. How they've learned how to speak English from our film. How the only thing that comforts a cancer patient or burn victims during their treatments is by watching our film. People have made such a connection to Ariel that it's unfathomable to me. I'm just a small piece of that puzzle. That's the part I take very seriously and I'm very honored to be a tiny part of a person's story of their life."

It's that life-affirming magic that the Disney Princesses bring to Make-A-Wish. Disney has helped Make-A-Wish grant wishes since 1980, granting over 450,000 wishes from around the world. In the United States, Make-A-Wish often brings children with critical illnesses, who are between the ages of two and a half and eighteen years old, to both Walt Disney World and Disneyland to meet the princesses.

"For wish kids, the carefree days of childhood really tend to get replaced with doctors' visits and unplanned hospital stays and uncomfortable procedures," says Shaina Reeser, Director of Entertainment and Sports Relations at Make-A-Wish, who facilitates any wish that involves meeting a celebrity—which includes the Disney Princesses. "The difficulties of living with a critical illness can take a real physical and emotional toll. Staying positive and optimistic really requires strength and courage—traits the Disney Princesses possess. Wish kids learn to tap into the fearless leader inside themselves when they have a chance to watch the Disney Princesses in action. It's a way to escape and hope and look forward to their future. They can start to envision what the rest of their lives can look like."

Each wish is unique to the child and Make-A-Wish sends their volunteers to complete a process called "wish discovery," where they can learn about the child's interests, dreams, and favorite princess. The most recent Disney Princesses, like Moana, and the *Frozen* queens tend to be the most popular, but there's an ongoing love for all of the princess heroes. Make-A-Wish is also concerned with being inclusive. In 2020, the organization granted a wish for María, a six-year-old being treated for leukemia. Because María only spoke Spanish, Make-A-Wish arranged a virtual royal visit from a Spanish-speaking Belle. Afterwards, María said to her mom, "Did you see that Belle is like me? That we are the same, she speaks Spanish like me." "Those little details are really essential for having the most impact for the child," Reeser says. "That's the incredible kind of impact that this personalization can have for the kids."

Wishes aren't the only way the Disney Princesses help children in their times of need. In 2021, to coincide with the Ultimate Princess Celebration, Disney collaborated with the Starlight Children's Foundation to create the first ever line of Disney Princess-themed hospital gowns and pants to help inspire courage and empowerment in kids during hospital stays. The brightly colored

A Friend Like Me

No one can expect to achieve their dreams alone, especially if the path ahead is challenging. That's why each Disney Princess has always been given a friend (or two) to help her along the way. And in watching these friendships bloom, we can learn to embrace cooperation, empathy, and kindness ourselves. Over the years, the filmmakers have used animal sidekicks to showcase the power of camaraderie. Some, like Ariel's fish pal Flounder in *The Little Mermaid*, can speak, while others, like Hei Hei, the wacky chicken in *Moana*, are more silent companions.

"They're a safe character you can confide in and tell your true feelings to and you know they're not going to betray you," explains *Moana* animator Kira Lehtomaki. "Sometimes the Disney Princesses find themselves alone and needing to overcome certain obstacles by themselves. Yet if they have their furry friend with them, they've got a partner. It gives them an outlet to share their feelings. And for us, as audience members, it's a window into what's going on inside their heads."

While Disney fans may not have their own tigers at home, like Jasmine has Rajah, these furry companions remind us that we can't succeed on our journeys without the spirit of friendship. They also reveal that a real hero is not only courageous, but empathetic and kind as well. These animal sidekicks make the Disney Princesses—and those inspired by them at home—that much stronger.

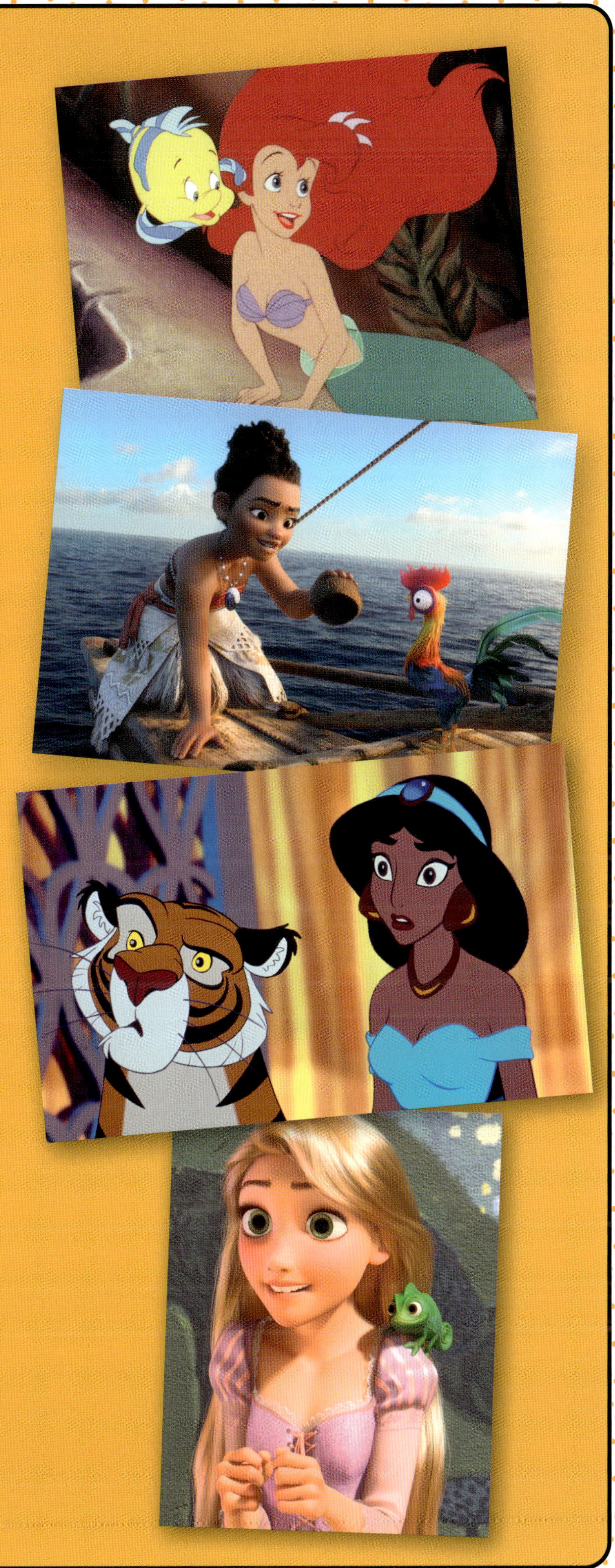

Each Disney Princess has an animal pal or two, from tigers to chameleons.

Becoming a Chef

It would be impossible to watch *The Princess and the Frog* and not walk away craving a delicious, sugary beignet. But many fans have also been inspired to learn to make their own. Tiana's dream of becoming a chef and owning her own restaurant has translated to the real world. Disney has released several cookbooks based on Tiana's recipes, including *The Princess and the Frog: Tiana's Cookbook: Recipes for Kids.* Books like *Disney Princess Baking* and *Disney Cookbook: The Cookbook on the Dishes Based on the Famous Disney Movies* have also encouraged film fans to embrace their inner chef.

Gabrielle Williams, a chef and baker from Georgia, took things a step further. Her popular TikTok page went viral for Williams's recreation of iconic dishes from Disney films, like Aurora's drooping birthday cake and Mushu's breakfast from *Mulan.* Her first-ever post was, of course, Tiana's beignets. "What I love most about cooking and baking these dishes is being able to bring the foods that I've wanted since I was a child to life," Williams told BuzzFeed. "It's an incredible feeling. Disney is such a passion of mine, and it warms my heart so much every time I recreate a new dish. There's also no greater feeling than when people thank me for helping them relive their childhood, and giving them a safe place to go on the Internet."

Like Tiana, Williams wants to inspire other to follow in her footsteps. "I hope people see how far I've come in such a short amount of time, and realize that they can do it too," she said. "With just a little perseverance, passion, and determination, they can make their dreams come true."

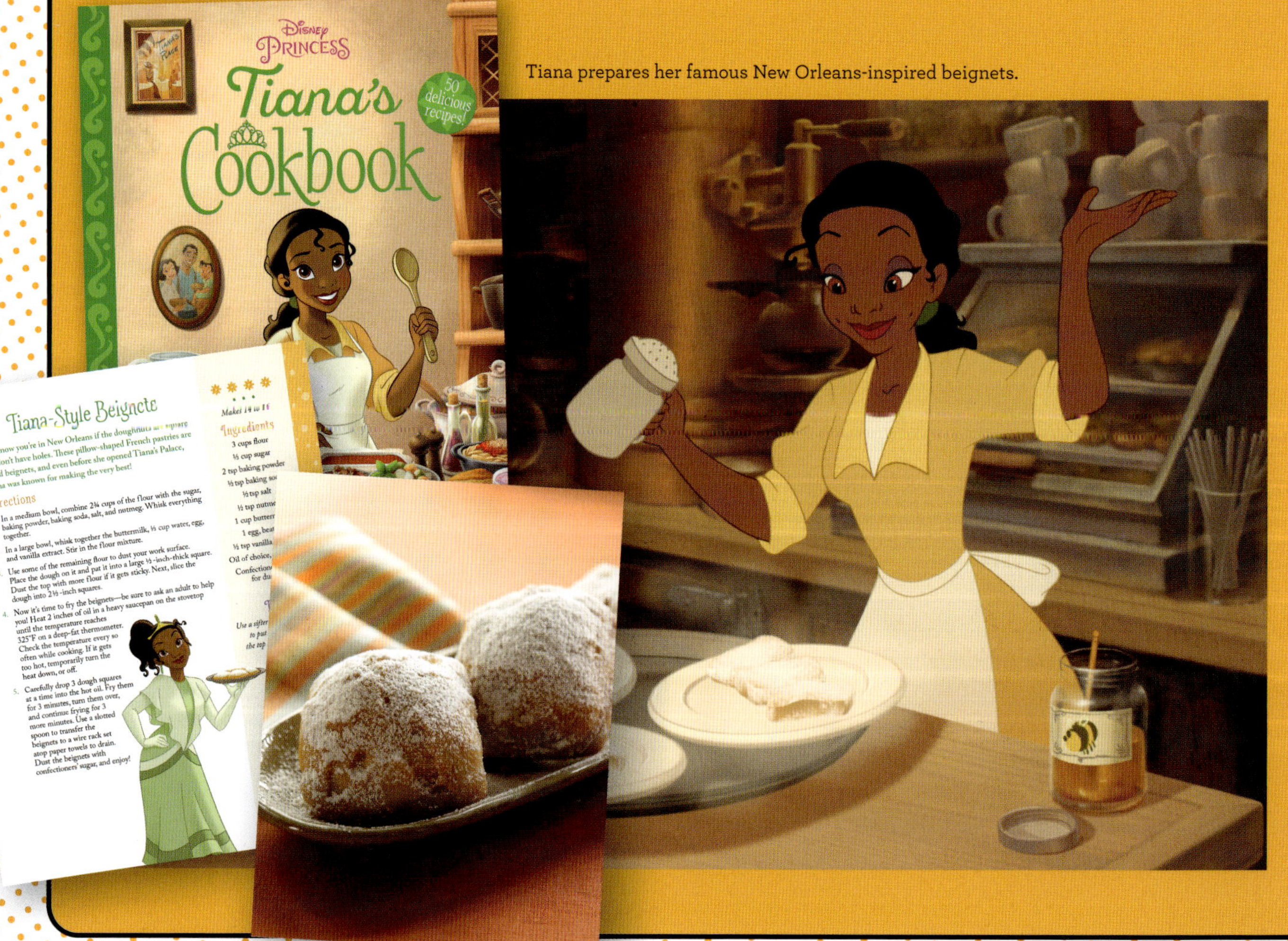

Tiana prepares her famous New Orleans-inspired beignets.

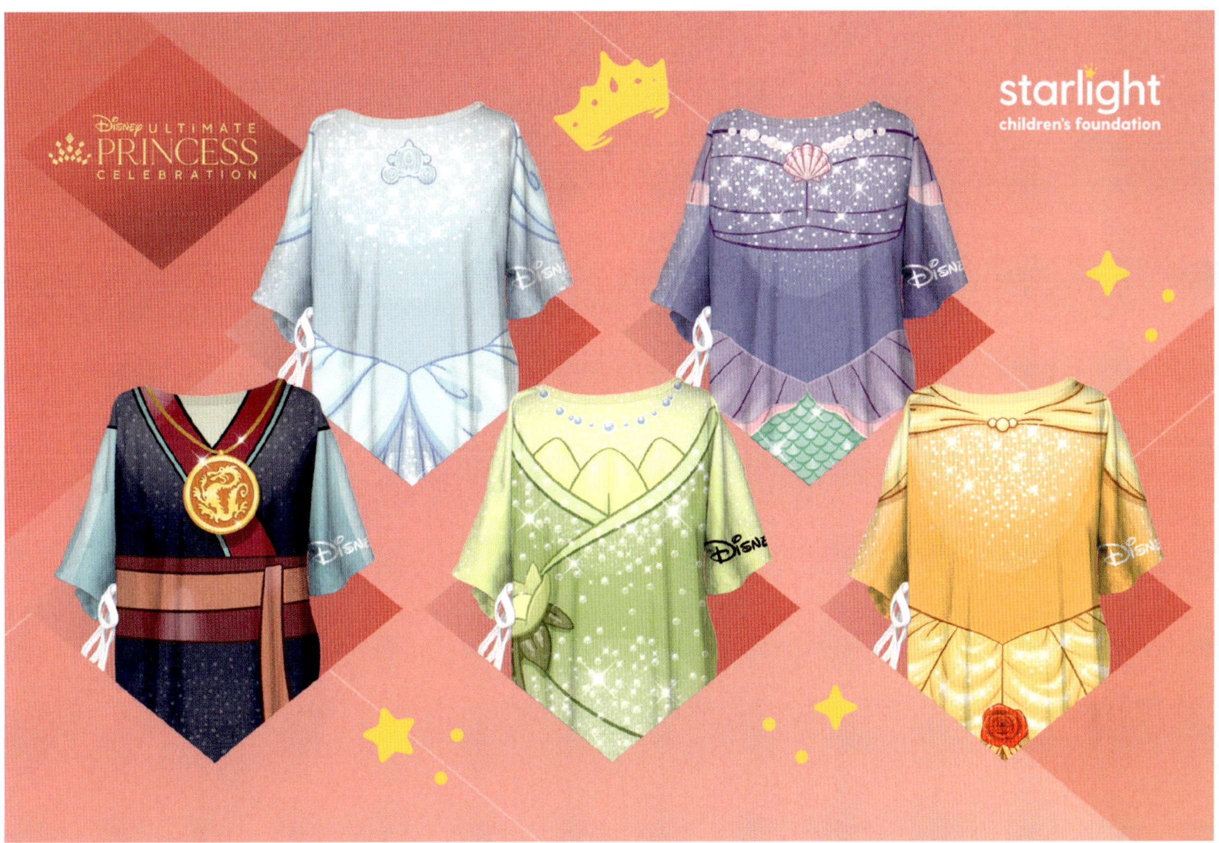

Starlight Children's Foundation designed a line of Disney Princess-themed hospital gowns and pants.

gowns, donated to hospitals around the U.S., included Mulan, Tiana, Belle, Cinderella, and Ariel, as well as Elsa and Anna from *Frozen*. "For many hospitalized kids, one of the most stressful moments during their hospital journey is when they take off their own clothes and put on a hospital gown," Adam Garone, CEO of Starlight Children's Foundation, said. "We've seen how Disney-themed Starlight Hospital Gowns have transformed this moment—bringing smiles when these kids need them the most."

Auli'i Cravalho also experienced the real-world magic of the Disney films after the release of *Moana*. After voicing *Moana* for the English-language version of the film, Cravalho rerecorded her lines and songs in Hawaiian. The new version, which marked the first time a Disney film was dubbed in Hawaiian, was given for free to every accredited school in Hawai'i in 2018. Cravalho, who credits *Moana*'s emphasis on preserving nature for her desire to study Environmental Science at Columbia University, is grateful for the experience.

"I loved working on the 'Ōlelo Hawai'i [Hawaiian language] version because I felt like there was suddenly so much more to learn about my own character and the lines that I was saying," the actress remembers. "It was really beautiful to have it premiere in Hawai'i and to watch it in Hawaiian and to have my cousins, who are in Hawaiian immersion school, where they learn math and science in Hawaiian, see it with me. 'Ōlelo Hawai'i is a dying language—it was forbidden to be spoken for generations across Hawai'i—so to know that our film is being used as a perpetuating force for the language and to keep it alive was my proudest achievement for *Moana*."

YOU CAN BE IT

Walt Disney famously hired numerous women in the early years of the studio. The Ink & Paint department, which was tasked with outlining and coloring the animation cels, was largely female back in the days of *Snow White and the Seven Dwarfs*. Artist and Disney Legend Mary Blair was instrumental in creating early visuals for *Cinderella*. Alice Davis, Disney Legend and wife of animator Marc Davis, not only help to design the *"it's a small world"* attraction, but also made Aurora's Briar Rose costume for the live-action model who shot reference footage used by the animators.

Since then, the number of women becoming storytellers, directors, animators, and artists at Walt Disney Animation Studios has dramatically increased. And while all of them have arrived at Disney via different paths, many of these women—and some men—can point to a Disney Princess who helped them get there.

Brittney Lee, visual development artist on *Frozen* and *Frozen 2*, points to seeing Ariel in *The Little Mermaid* as her moment of recognition. "At six, I don't think I'd ever seen a character who so thoroughly had a want," Lee remembers. "She wanted something and she was going to do anything to get it. She was so determined and had so much agency. I realized I could find the things I wanted to do and work really hard to get there. That was hugely inspiring and impactful for me."

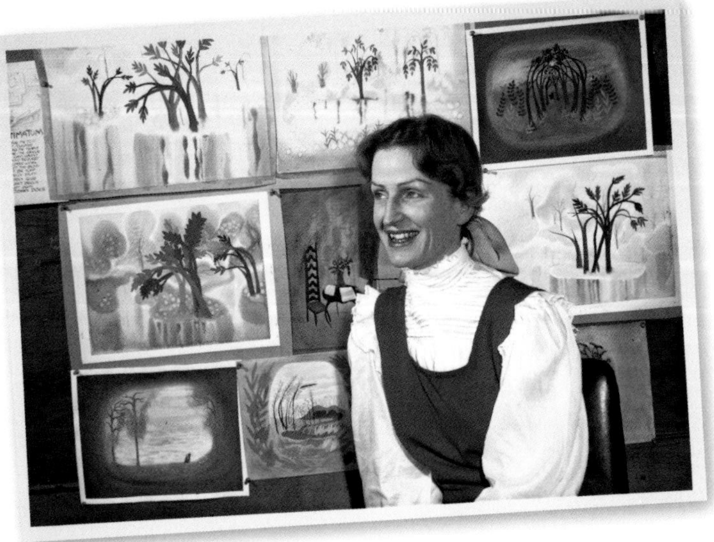

Left: Artist Mary Blair with her paintings.

For director Suzi Yoonessi, who, like Walt, is creating an animated film based on a fairy tale her grandmother told her as a child, seeing Jasmine in *Aladdin* made a huge impression. It was the first time she had ever seen her Persian culture reflected onscreen. "Jasmine gave me a moment of such pride in my heritage and my culture," Yoonessi says. "And especially being from upstate New York, in the suburbs of Buffalo where there was little diversity, it showed me there was a whole world out there that was filled with all these different shades of brown. That, for me, was a defining moment in terms of the princesses and their power. The Disney Princesses were my superheroes. They gave me the values I want to embody in my life and in the way I interact with people. They taught me kindness, they taught me heart, and they taught me patience."

It isn't just the women behind the scenes who've been inspired by the power of the Disney Princesses. The characters and what they represent have also been deeply meaningful to the men at Disney. Heroes like Ariel, who is an icon for many queer individuals, connect with people who feel marginalized by traditional society.

"I loved Ariel and Belle, and I wanted to be them," remembers Juan Pablo Reyes Lancaster Jones, a Senior Creative Executive at Walt Disney Animation Studios. "Ariel wanted to achieve her goals, her passions, and her dreams, the same as me. She was stuck in a place where she didn't fit in, which is relevant to many communities, including the LGBTQIA+ community. We should look at the characters not for their gender, but for their soul. They mean so much. The Disney Princesses made me feel like I fit in."

Having people with diverse backgrounds and experiences be part of the storytelling process definitely impacts the final films we see in theaters. It means the heroes are more grounded and more real, from the way they deal with their hair to their relationships as

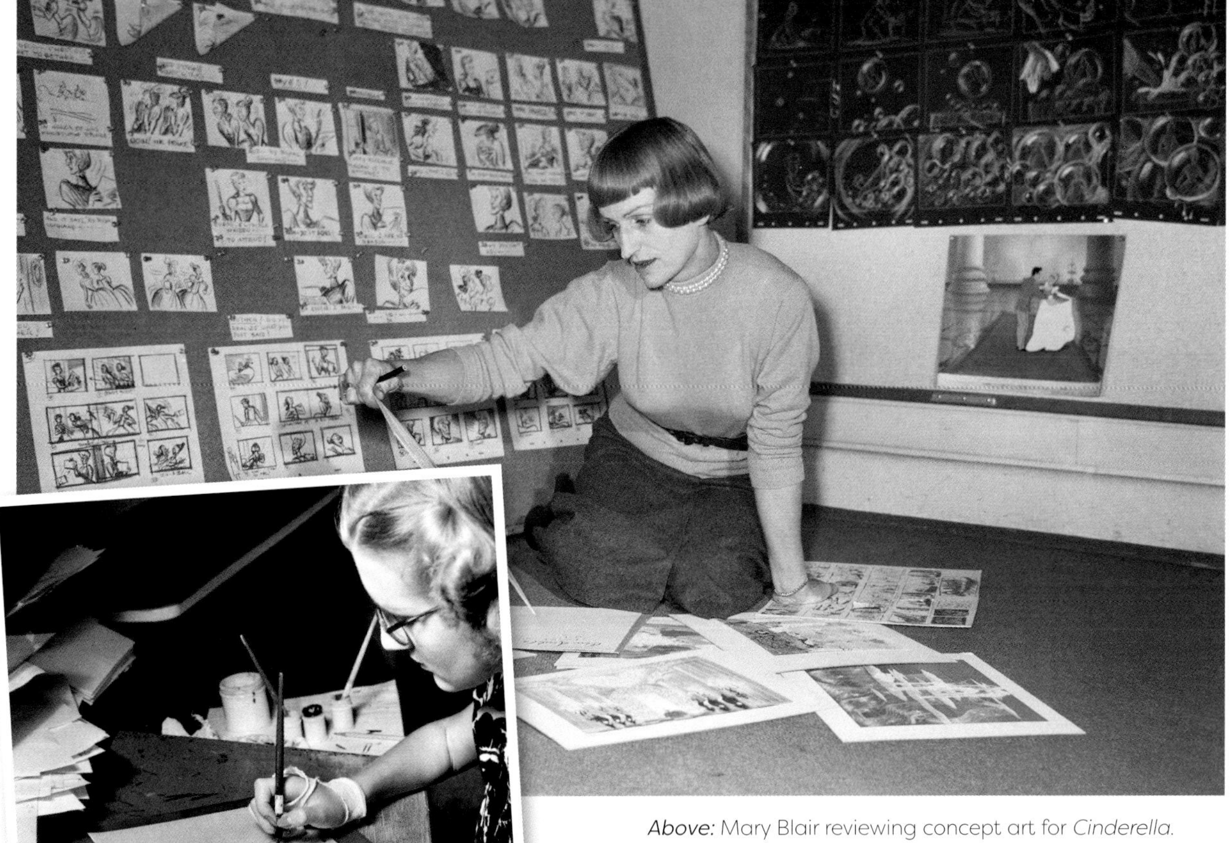

Above: Mary Blair reviewing concept art for *Cinderella*.
Left: Inker Fern Ahlstrand works on an outline of Snow White.

siblings to their fears and wants. "It's incredibly important to have people who identify with whatever you are portraying onscreen be intimately and meaningfully involved in the creation of our characters," Julius notes. "There's just an authenticity that comes with lived experience that you have."

"I hold strongly that the more women who are in the room now, the more of us who will be in the room in the future," Shurer adds. "We will make an effort to include each other and echo each other and amplify each other, and allow the voices to shift and to change. For me, being able to work on characters like Moana and like Raya, who are strong female heroes with flaws and have a journey to take and big lessons to learn and can fight, is important. All of those things reflect back and forth. We inspire the character on the screen and the character on the screen inspires us back."

Ever since *Snow White and the Seven Dwarfs* dazzled audiences in 1937, Walt Disney Animation Studios has continued to redefine the idea of what a princess can be. And it's not birth or marriage that makes her royal, it's who she is inside. From Snow White to Moana, we can see the evolution of those ideas, with each Disney Princess reflecting the culture and the time in which she was made. They embrace contemporary values, desires, and concerns, each hero representing hope and courage for her own generation of viewers. It's a lot of pressure on a fictional character, but also the reason they've endured for so long.

"No matter when they were written or animated or created, female characters carry a lot of responsibility," says Jennifer Lee. "Studies have shown they're judged more than male characters. People idealize them and they project themselves onto them. The ladies of Disney have stood up very well to that. These heroes are carrying responsibility for others. They carry the burdens of their society. Half the time they do it in big dresses and still pull it off. The Disney Princesses carry a lot of expectations, but at the end of the day they always inspire us."

AFTERWORD

KEEP ON BELIEVING

It's clear that the Disney Princesses are powerful icons, recognized and celebrated around the world. They bring us joy, hope, and inspiration, and reveal that even the most daunting of challenges can be met with courage and grace. Thanks to these onscreen heroes, our own inner strength and confidence can be unlocked.

"The Disney Princesses represent the best parts of ourselves," says voice actress Linda Larkin. "They show us the value of truth and kindness and integrity. They have to find their courage and their strength to challenge the forces against them. What we see is when they do that with this pure heart, with their truth and integrity at the forefront, they triumph over the forces holding them down. If you follow that goodness and that truth, and use your values and your integrity, you too will succeed."

From Snow White to Moana, the princesses have each made an indelible mark on pop culture. They've inspired how we dress, how we communicate with each other, how we see ourselves, and what sort of people we want to be. The characters hold our hands, encourage us forward, and remind us that all you really need is a dream. Like the Disney Princesses, whatever we can imagine is possible, if we just keep on believing.

Opposite: A concept painting of Pocahontas as she's embraced by the spirit of Grandmother Willow, by Disney artist Vance Gerry.

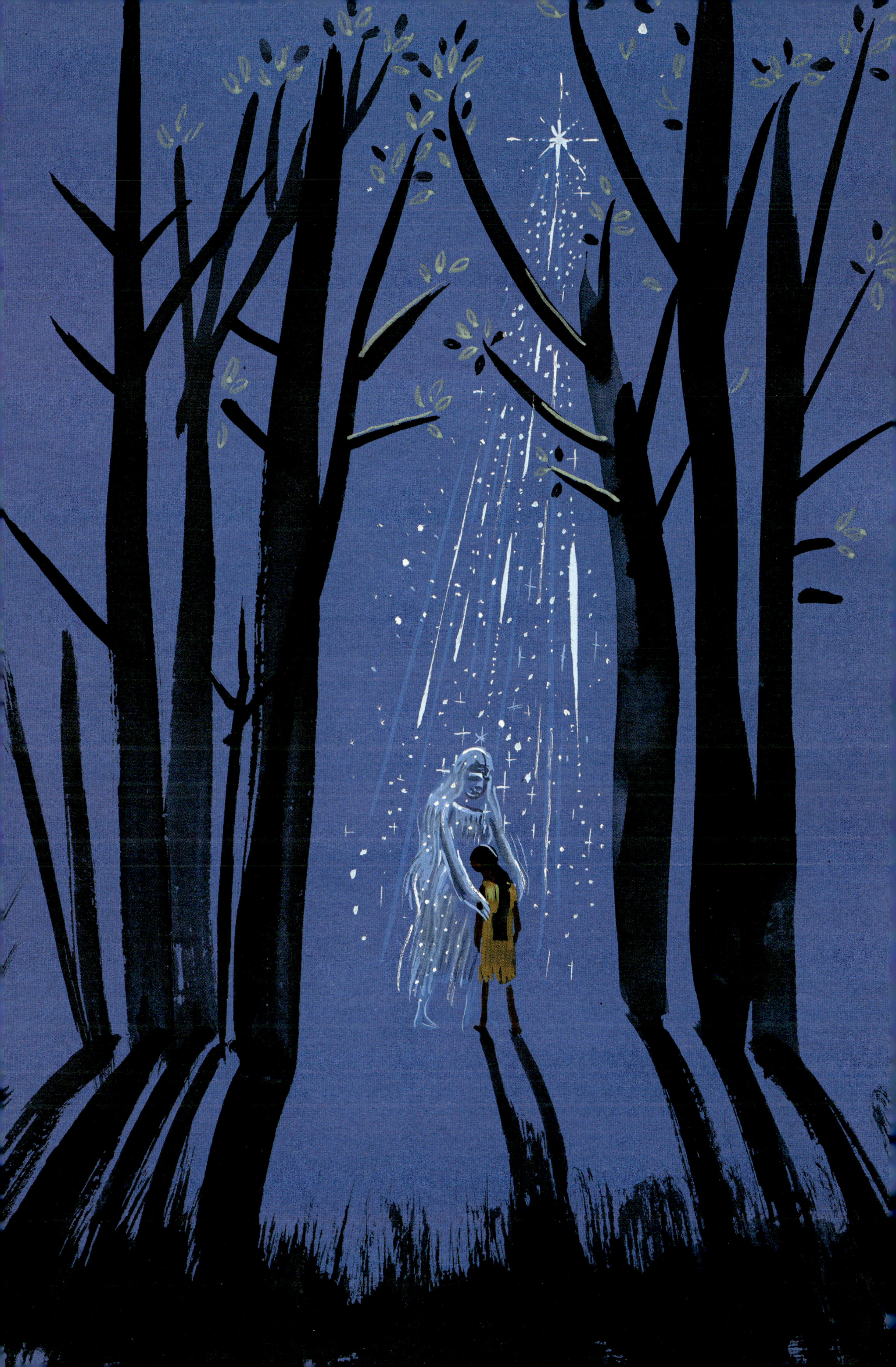

ACKNOWLEDGMENTS

As every Disney Princess knows, an adventure is always more fun with help along the way. This book was a deeply collaborative effort and I couldn't have done it without the expertise, wisdom, and knowledge of dozens of people.

First and foremost, thank you to my editor Laura Hitchcock, who will hereby be known as my Fairy Godmother. Thank you to Delia Greve and Haley Stocking at becker&mayer, to Julie Alissi, our fearless photo researcher, and to Kim Winscher, who designed this beautiful book. Thank you to Holly P. Rice, Lauren Burniac, Krista Wong, and Eugene Paraszczuk at Disney Publishing—I quite literally could not have written this book without you. Thank you to Kevin Kern, Nicole Carroll, Michael Buckhoff, and Rebecca Cline at the Walt Disney Archives for fact-checking every detail and finding images of obscure Disney Princess memorabilia. Thank you to Jill Breznican, a fountain of knowledge about the Disney Princesses, and to Libby Spatz for sharing incredible historical details.

I'm deeply grateful to everyone who gave me their time to be interviewed for this book. Each of you—and there were nearly sixty—made its pages better. Immense thanks to Jodi Benson, Linda Larkin, Irene Bedard, Auli'i Cravalho, Paige O'Hara, Jennifer Lee, Sean Bailey, Alan Menken, Dave Pacheco, Stacia Martin, Greg Ehrbar, Andi Cochrane, Linda Woolverton, Osnat Shurer, Alyssa Moon, Jessica Julius, J.B. Kaufman, Mark Henn, Roy Conli, Byron Howard, Todd Martens, Tracey Mollet, Charles Solomon, Brittney Lee, Kira Lehtomaki, Becky Bresee, Josie Trinidad, Edward Kitis, Adam Horowitz, Elaine Carovilla, Karen Torpey, Lauren Preston, Bethan Holt, Law Roach, Zac Posen, Leslie Kay, Andrea Canny, Chris Molanphy, Charita Carter, Faron Kelley, Randy Thornton, Richard Kraft, Sabrina Mittermeier, Amy Mebberson, Sherri Stoner, Rebecca Williams, Braden Graeber, Suzi Yoonessi, Michael Vargo, Juan Pablo Reyes, Matt Schimkowitz, Sean Reed, Shaina Reeser, and to all of the amazing cosplayers and fan artists who shared their work.

A special thank you to the staff of the BFI Reuben Library in London, who dug out book after book for me, in the midst of a pandemic. I can't wait for this one to join your shelves.

Finally, thank you to Alan Light, Michael Bourret, and Mandy Rodgers for your additional support. Thank you to my parents, who raised me on an endless stream of Disney VHS tapes and let me dress up like a princess for most of my childhood. And, most importantly, thank you to Dominic, my own personal version of a Disney prince.

ABOUT THE AUTHOR

Emily Zemler is a freelance writer and journalist based in London. She is a frequent contributor to the *Los Angeles Times* and *Rolling Stone*, among other prestigious outlets. Emily is the coauthor of *A Sick Life*, with TLC's Tionne "T-Boz" Watkins, and the author of *The Art and Making of Aladdin*. Her favorite Disney Princess is Ariel.

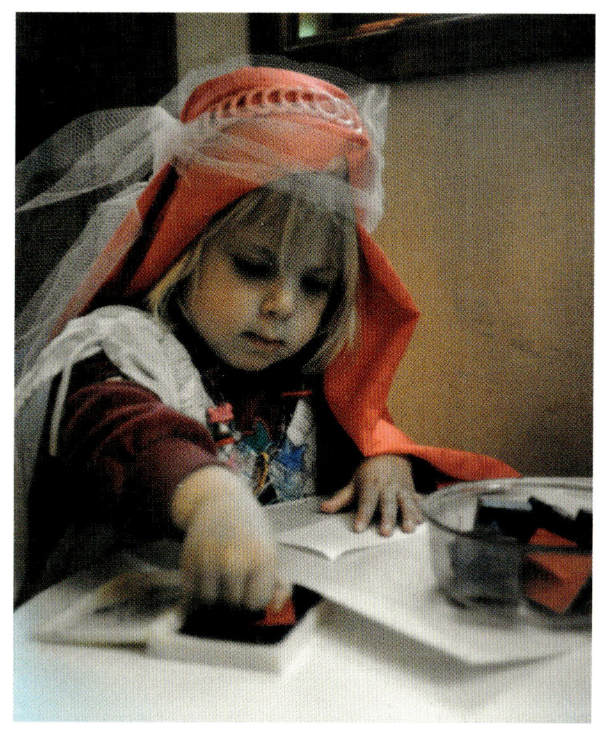

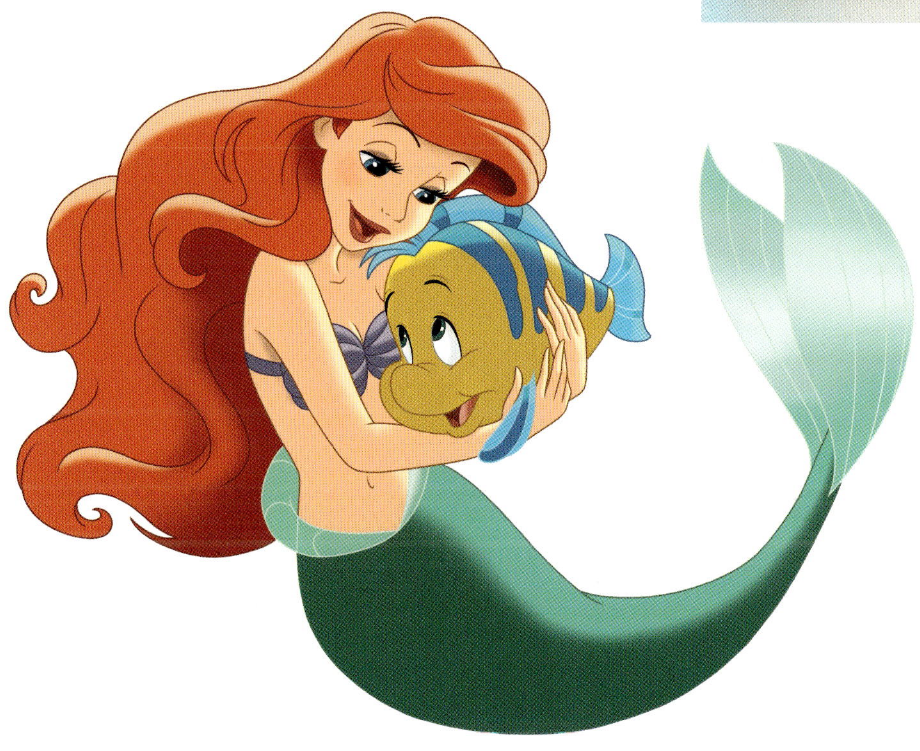

DISNEY PRINCESS MOVIE, TV SERIES, AND BROADWAY MUSICAL TIMELINE

1937
Snow White and the Seven Dwarfs
Princess: Snow White

1950
Cinderella
Princess: Cinderella

1959
Sleeping Beauty
Princess: Aurora

1989
The Little Mermaid
Princess: Ariel

1991
Beauty and the Beast
Princess: Belle

1992
Aladdin
Princess: Jasmine

1992–1995
The Little Mermaid (TV series)
Princess: Ariel

1993
Full House (TV episode "The House Meets the Mouse")
Princesses: Snow White, Cinderella, Jasmine

1994
The Return of Jafar
Princess: Jasmine

1994–2007
Beauty and the Beast (Broadway musical)
Princess: Belle

1995
Pocahontas
Princess: Pocahontas

1995–1996
Sing Me a Story: with Belle (TV series)
Princess: Belle

1996
The Hunchback of Notre Dame
Princess: Belle (Easter egg walkthrough cameo in "Out There")

1996
Aladdin and the King of Thieves
Princess: Jasmine

1997
Beauty and the Beast: The Enchanted Christmas
Princess: Belle

1998
Mulan
Princess: Mulan

1998
Beauty and the Beast: Belle's Magical World
Princess: Belle

1998
Pocahontas II: Journey to a New World
Princess: Pocahontas

1999
Belle's Tales of Friendship
Princess: Belle

2000
The Little Mermaid II: Return to the Sea
Princess: Ariel

2001–2003
Disney's House of Mouse (TV series)
Princesses: Snow White, Cinderella, Aurora, Ariel, Belle, Jasmine, Pocahontas, Mulan

2001
Mickey's Magical Christmas: Snowed in at the House of Mouse
Princesses: Snow White, Cinderella, Ariel, Belle, Jasmine

2002
Cinderella II: Dreams Come True
Princess: Cinderella

2005
Mulan II
Princess: Mulan

2007
Cinderella III: A Twist in Time
Princess: Cinderella

2007
Disney Princess Enchanted Tales: Follow Your Dreams
Princesses: Aurora, Jasmine

2008-2009
***The Little Mermaid* (Broadway musical)**
Princess: Ariel

2008
The Little Mermaid: Ariel's Beginning
Princess: Ariel

2009
The Princess and the Frog
Princess: Tiana

2010
Tangled
Princess: Rapunzel

2011-2018
***Once Upon a Time* (TV series)**
Princesses: Snow White, Cinderella, Aurora, Ariel, Belle, Jasmine, Mulan, Tiana, Rapunzel, Merida

2012
Sofia the First: Once Upon a Princess
Princess: Cinderella

2012
Brave
Princess: Merida

2012
Tangled: Ever After
Princess: Rapunzel

2013-2018
***Sofia the First* (TV series)**
Princesses: Snow White, Cinderella, Aurora, Ariel, Belle, Jasmine, Mulan, Tiana, Rapunzel, Merida

2014
Maleficent
Princess: Aurora

2014-Present
***Aladdin* (Broadway musical)**
Princess: Jasmine

2015
***Cinderella* (live-action)**
Princess: Cinderella

2015
Descendants
Princess: Belle

2016
Moana
Princess: Moana

2017
***Beauty and the Beast* (live-action)**
Princess: Belle

2017
Tangled: Before Ever After
Princess: Rapunzel

2017
Descendants 2
Princess: Belle

2017-2020
Rapunzel's Tangled Adventure
Princess: Rapunzel

2019
***Aladdin* (live-action)**
Princess: Jasmine

2019
Maleficent: Mistress of Evil
Princess: Aurora

2019
Descendants 3
Princess: Belle

2020
***Mulan* (live-action)**
Princess: Mulan

2023
***The Little Mermaid* (live-action)**
Princess: Ariel

To Be Announced
***Tiana* (Disney+ TV series)**
Princess: Tiana

To Be Announced
***Moana* (Disney+ TV series)**
Princess: Moana

SOURCES

PRINT AND INTERNET SOURCES

"A Conversation With Ruthie Davis." *aafaglobal.org*. Web.

Allan, Robin. *Walt Disney and Europe: European Influences on the Animated Feature Films of Walt Disney*. Indiana University Press, 2000.

Bailey, Alyssa. "Stuart Vevers On Disney X Coach's A Dark Fairy Tale Collection And Designing With Selena Gomez." *ELLE*. 14 Mar. 2018. Web.

Behlmer, Rudy. *America's Favourite Movies: Behind the Scenes*. Frederick Ungar, 1982.

Berman, Eliza. "Why Disney Decided to Make Moana the Ultimate Anti-Princess." *TIME*. 1 Sept. 2016.

Billboard Charts. *Billboard.com*. Web.

Blasberg, Derek. "Cover Story: Emma Watson, Rebel Belle." *Vanity Fair*. Mar. 2017.

Brandon, Elissaveta M. "Hong Kong Disneyland's new castle is an architectural vision of diversity." *CNN*. 3 Apr. 2021. Web.

Bueno, Annette. "Even Alicia Vikander Agrees Her Gorgeous Oscars Dress Looks Like Princess Belle." *ET Online*. 28 Feb. 2016. Web.

Canemaker, John. *Walt Disney's Nine Old Men and the Art of Animation*. Disney Editions, 2001.

Cerone, Daniel. "'Jafar': New Journeys to Profitland?: Videos: Industry experts predict Disney's sequel to 'Aladdin' will wind up among the all-time top sellers." *Los Angeles Times*. 20 May 1994.

Chanel, Sunny. "This Is the Real Person Who Was the Inspiration for The Little Mermaid." *Brit + Co*. 21 Mar. 2018. Web.

Cochran, Jason. "Pocahontas Needed an Ethnic Look." *Entertainment Weekly*. 16 Jun. 1995.

"Disney Legends: Alice Davis." *D23.com*. Web.

"Disney Legends: Kay Kamen." *D23.com*. Web.

"Disney Legends: Tutti Camarata." *D23.com*. Web.

Disney Parks Blog. *disneyparks.disney.go.com*. Web.

Docter, Pete and Christopher Merritt. *Marc Davis in His Own Words: Imagineering the Disney Theme Parks*. Disney Editions, 2019.

Editors of Canterbury Classics. *Disney: The Little Mermaid*. Canterbury Classics, 2022.

Finch, Christopher. *The Art of Walt Disney: From Mickey Mouse to the Magic Kingdoms*. Harry N. Abrams, Inc., 1973.

Fleming, Mike Jr. "Sean Bailey On How Disney's Live-Action Division Found Its 'Beauty And The Beast' Mojo." *Deadline*. 21 Mar. 2017. Web.

Glancy, Mark and John Sedgwick. "Cinemagoing in the United States in the Mid-1930s." *Going to the Movies: A Personal Journey Through Four Decades of Modern Film*. Bantam Dell Publishing Group, 2001.

Graham, Bill. "Animation Director Glen Keane Exclusive Interview." *Collider.com*. 22 Nov. 2010. Web.

Heinrich, Shelby. "This Woman Has Gone Mega-Viral For Recreating Foods From Disney Movies, And They're Completely Spot-On." *BuzzFeed*. 1 Jul. 2021. Web.

Hill, Jim. "How Glen Keane & Mark Henn Turned Some of Disney's Most Popular Princesses into Toddlers." *Jim Hill Media*. 11 Apr. 2012. Web.

"A History of Disney Theatrical's Productions." *Variety*. 22 Nov. 2013. Web.

Internet Movie Database. *imdb.com*. Web.

Johnston, Ollie, and Frank Thomas. *The Illusion of Life: Disney Animation*. New York: Hyperion, 1981.

Julius, Jessica. *The Art of Frozen 2*. Chronicle Books, 2019.

Julius, Jessica and Maggie Malone. *The Art of Moana*. Chronicle Books, 2016.

Julius, Jessica. *The Art of Ralph Breaks the Internet*. Chronicle Books, 2018.

Kaufman, J.B. *The Fairest One Of All: The Making of Walt Disney's Snow White & the Seven Dwarfs*. Aurum Press Ltd, 2012.

Kay, Leslie. *DisneyBound: Dress Disney and Make It Fashion*. Disney Editions, 2020.

Know Your Meme: Internet Meme Database. *knowyourmeme.com*. Web.

Krentcil, Faran. "Christopher Kane On His New 'Beauty And The Beast'-Inspired Collection." *ELLE*. 14 Mar. 2017. Web.

Kurtti, Jeff, Rebecca Cline, and the Staff of the Walt Disney Archives. *The Art of Disney Costuming*. Disney Editions, 2019.

Kurtti, Jeff and Bruce Gordon. *The Art of Disneyland*. Disney Editions, 2017.

Kurtii, Jeff. *The Art of Mulan*. Hyperion, 1998.

Kurtti, Jeff. *The Art of Tangled*. Chronicle Books, 2010.

Kurtti, Jeff. *The Art of The Princess and the Frog*. Chronicle Books, 2009.

Lassell, Michael. *Aladdin: A Whole New World—The Road To Broadway and Beyond*. Disney Editions, 2017.

Lassell, Michael. *The Little Mermaid: A Broadway Musical: From the Deep Blue Sea to the Great White Way*. Disney Editions, 2009.

Lee, Jennifer. "Dream Big." *thewaltdisneycompany.com*. 11 Feb. 2016. Web.

Lerew, Jenny. *The Art of Brave*. Chronicle Books, 2012.

"Louboutin Takes On Cinderella." *ELLE UK*. 6 Jul. 2012. Web.

Loughrey, Clarisse. "Aladdin star Naomi Scott: 'For women, a lot of the time we have to work twice as hard.'" *Independent*. 16 May 2019.

Maloney, Alison. "WOULD YOU DATE HIM? Disney-obsessed man, 25, has spent THOUSANDS on his collection of over 50 princess dolls." *The Sun*. 28 Jul. 2016. Web.

Maltin, Leonard. *The Disney Films, Fourth Edition*. Disney Editions, 2000.

Martens, Todd. "Disneyland's Snow White ride makeover: How critics underestimate the timeless princess." *Los Angeles Times*. 26 May 2021.

Mollet, Tracey L. *Once Upon an American Dream: A Cultural History of the Disney Fairy Tale*. Palgrave Macmillan, 2020.

Munsey, Cecil. *Disneyana: Walt Disney Collectibles*. Hawthorn Books, 1974.

Okwodu, Janelle. "A First Look at Christopher Kane's Collaboration With Disney for Beauty and the Beast." *Vogue.com.* 13 Mar. 2017. Web.

"Once Upon a Dream: The History of Sleeping Beauty Castle." *waltdisney.org.* 19 Dec. 2018. Web.

Potter, Courtney. "Reflecting on Mulan with Director Niki Caro and Star Yifei Liu." *D23.com.* 31 Aug. 2020. Web.

Radish, Christina. "'Beauty and the Beast': Emma Watson, Dan Stevens, Luke Evans, and Josh Gad on the Fairytale Film." *Collider.com.* 15 Mar. 2017. Web.

Radish, Christina. "'Ralph Breaks the Internet' Creatives on Princesses and the 'Oh My Disney' Sequence." *Collider.com.* 25 Oct. 2018. Web.

Rebello, Stephen. *The Art of Pocahontas.* Disney Editions, 1995.

Smalle, Will. "How One Man's Eureka Moment Earns Disney $3bn a Year." *BBC.* 24 Dec. 2018. Web.

"Snow White Film to Influence All Styles, Accessories." *The Decatur Daily Review.* 25 Dec. 1937.

Solomon, Charles. *The Art of Disney's Frozen.* Chronicle Books, 2013.

Solomon, Charles. *A Wish Your Heart Makes: From the Grimm Brothers' Aschenputtel to Disney's Cinderella.* Disney Editions, 2015.

Solomon, Charles. *Once Upon a Dream: From Perrault's Sleeping Beauty to Disney's Maleficent.* Disney Editions, 2014.

Solomon, Charles. *Tale As Old As Time: The Art and Making of Beauty and the Beast.* Disney Editions, 2017.

Solomon, Charles. *The Disney Princess: A Celebration of Art and Creativity.* Chronicle Books, 2020.

Solomon, Charles. *The Disney That Never Was.* Little, Brown and Company, 1996.

Solomon, Charles. *Enchanted Drawings: The History of Animation.* Random House Value Publishing, 1994.

"Talking Disney's Descendants with Kenny Ortega." *D23.com.* Web.

Thomas, Bob. *Disney's The Art of Animation.* Hyperion, 1991.

Tracy, Joe. "An Inside Look at the Original Beauty and the Beast." *Digital Media FX Magazine.* Web.

Tumbusch, Tom. *Tomart's Illustrated Disneyana.* Gazelle Book Services Ltd., 1990.

"Walt's Quotes." *D23.com.* Web.

Weiss, Josh. "'We're Taking It Somewhere New': Niki Caro & Mandy Walker Break Down Disney's 'Mulan' Remake." *Forbes.* 3 Sept. 2020. Web.

Woerner, Meredith. "How the new 'Beauty and the Beast' empowers Belle's inner feminist with books, not boys." *Los Angeles Times.* 16 Mar. 2017.

Zemler, Emily. *The Art and Making of Aladdin.* Insight Editions, 2019.

VIDEO AND AUDIO SOURCES

"Audio Commentary." *Snow White and the Seven Dwarfs Platinum Edition DVD*. Walt Disney Animation Studios, 2001.

"Alice in Wonderland (March 18, 1951)." *The Fred Waring Show*, 1951.

"Emma Watson at the HeForShe Campaign 2014 - Official UN Video." *United Nations*.

"Galen Fott as Gaston with Paige O'Hara as Belle, 1992." *Galen Fott*.

"Galen Fott singing 'A Whole New World' with Lea Salonga, 1992." *Galen Fott*.

Garner, Bob and Pete Schuermann. *Disneyland: Secrets, Stories And Magic Of The Happiest Place On Earth*. Walt Disney Home Entertainment, 2007.

Hahn, Don. *Howard*. The Walt Disney Studios, 2018.

Hahn, Don. *Waking Sleeping Beauty*. The Walt Disney Studios, 2010.

Iwerks, Leslie. *The Imagineering Story*. Disney+, 2019.

"Making Of 'L'histoire d'un soulier' par Christian Louboutin." *Cinderella* Diamond Edition DVD. Walt Disney Animation Studios, 2012.

"María's Royal Wish with a Little Help from Princess Belle | Make-A-Wish® & Disney." *Make-A-Wish America*.

Molanphy, Chris. "Hit Parade: The Lullaby of Broadway Edition." *Slate*. 28 Jun. 2019. Podcast.

Volk-Weiss, Brian. "The Castles." *Behind the Attraction*. Disney+, 2021.

"Walt Disney Family Museum's Happily Ever After Hours (Tom Morris)." 17 Jun. 2020.

Concept artwork for the upcoming Tiana attraction at the Disney parks.

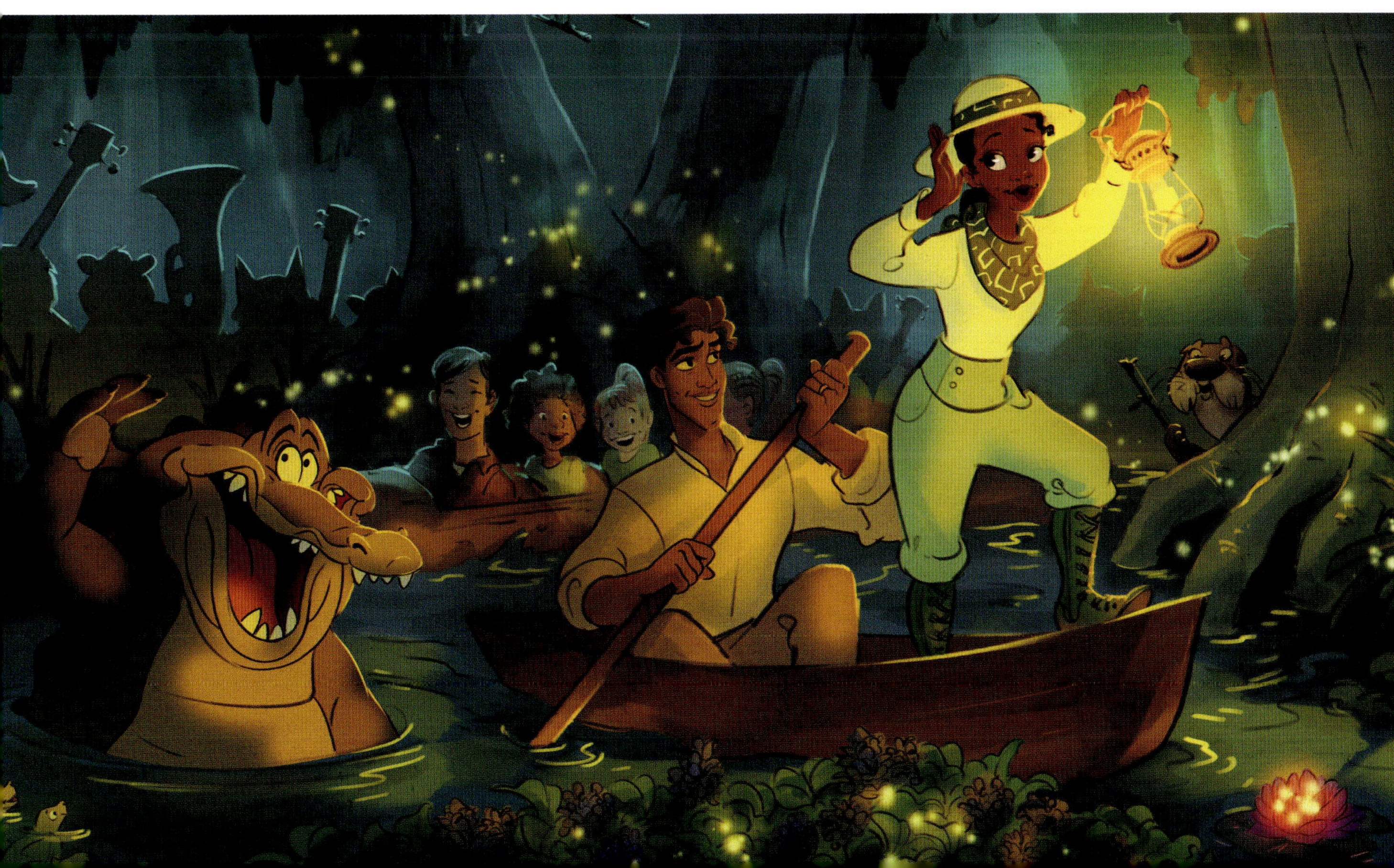

IMAGE CREDITS

Every effort has been made to trace copyright holders. If any unintentional omission has been made, Epic Ink, as an imprint of The Quarto Group, would be pleased to add appropriate acknowledgments in future editions.

Unless otherwise noted below, all images are copyright to The Walt Disney Company. © Disney Enterprises.

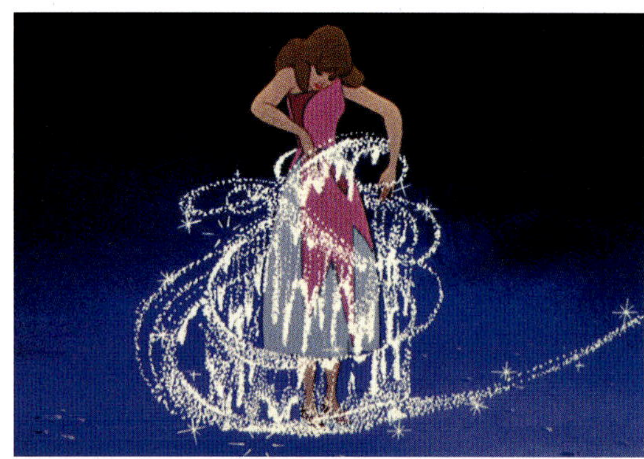

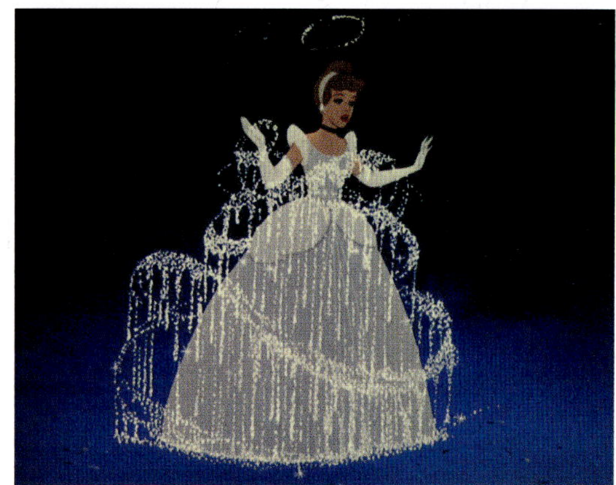

Page 18 (bottom left) AF Archive/Alamy Stock Photo; (bottom right) Collection Christophel/Alamy Stock Photo

Page 19 Bettmann/Getty Images

Page 21 (bottom left) History and Art Collection/Alamy Stock Photo

Page 24 (bottom center) IFTN/United Archives GmbH/Alamy Stock Photo

Page 27 (bottom right) Michael Ochs Archives/Moviepix/Getty Images

Page 31 (bottom left) Album/Alamy Stock Photo; (bottom right) PictureLux /The Hollywood Archive/Alamy Stock Photo

Page 34 (bottom middle) Courtesy of Mark Henn

Page 38 (bottom right) Lebrecht Music & Arts/ Alamy Stock Photo

Page 43 (bottom left) Cheryl Gerber/AP Photo; (bottom right) S. Bukley/Shutterstock

Page 46 (center) The Picture Art Collection/ Alamy Stock Photo; (center right) Barry King/FilmMagic/Getty Images; (bottom) James Lavrakas

Page 49 (bottom) History and Art Collection/ Alamy Stock Photo

Page 70 Walt Disney Pictures /Album/Alamy Stock Photo

Page 74 (top) Honor Goss; (bottom right) Heritage Auctions, HA.com

Page 75 (right) Hake's Auctions

Page 76 (left) Hake's Auctions; (right) Courtesy David Pacheco TWDC

Page 77 (top) Pook and Pook, Inc.; (bottom) Hakes Auctions

Page 78 (top) Honor Goss

Page 79 Courtesy of Hasbro

Page 81 (top to bottom) Hake's Auctions; (left) Enio fotografia/Shutterstock; (right) Andrew Twort/Alamy Stock Photo; Barcroft Media/I Hasbro

Page 83 LEGO

Page 88 Courtesy David Pacheco, TWDC

Page 93 (top, two) Funko, LLC.; (bottom) Kendri Rodriguez/Barcroft Media/Getty Images

Page 96 (bottom) Stuart Ramson/AP Photo

Page 98 (top) PictureLux/The Hollywood Archive/Alamy Stock Photo; (bottom) Interfoto/Alamy Stock Photo;

Page 99 (top) Everett Collection; (bottom) Anwar Hussein/Hulton Archive/Getty Images

Page 101 (top) Bettmann/Getty Images

Page 103 (top to bottom) Foc Kan/WireImage/Getty Images, Brian Jannsen/Alamy Stock Photo, Dominique Charriau/WireImage/Getty Images

Page 104 (top) Alexander Image/Shutterstock.com; (bottom) Paolo Sebastian

Page 105 (top, right Frozen bag) Courtesy of H&M, (all others) Courtesy of Coach

Page 106 Snow White Collection by Bésame Cosmetics; (inset) Cinderella Collection by Bésame Cosmetics

Page 107 (top left) Timothy A. Clary/AFP/Getty Images; (top right) Courtesy Matin Maulawizada; (center) Dan MacMedan/WireImage/Getty Images; (bottom) Kurt Krieger/Corbis /Getty Images

Page 109, 110 (left) Karwai Tang/WireImage/Getty Images

Page 110 (right) Sky Cinema/Shutterstock.com

Page 111 Jason Smith/Everett Collection/Alamy Live News

Page 118 (top) NewsBase/AP Photo

Page 121 (bottom) Blueee/Alamy Stock Photo

Page 124 (top) Courtesy Andrea Canny, (bottom) Courtesy Andrea Canny, Galen Fott

Page 125 Volkan Furuncu/Anadolu Agency/Getty Images

Page 126 (top) Andrew H. Walker/Getty Images; (bottom) Gary Hershorn/Reuters/Alamy Stock Photo

Page 127 Walter McBride/Wire Image/Getty Images

Page 128 Bruce Glikas/WireImage/Getty Images

Page 129 (top) Randall Michelson/Rmpix.com; (bottom) Eric McCandless/Getty Images

Page 135 Robert Sullivan/AFP/Getty Image

Page 136 (top right) Parinya Suwanitch/Alamy Stock Photo

Page 137 Gerardo Mora/Getty Images

Page 141 (top to bottom) Agencia El Universal/Berenice Fregoso/EELG/AP Images, Agencia El Universal/Alejandra Leyva/MAR/AP Images, Agencia El Universal/Yadín Xolalpa/EELG/AP Images

Page 142 Jay L. Clendenin/Los Angeles Times/Getty Images

Page 145 (top) Phelan M. Ebenhack/AP Images; (bottom left) "She Did It!" by Perfectance is licensed under CC BY-NC-SA 2.0; (center and right) Phelan M. Ebenhack/AP Images

Page 149 (top) LA/Getty Images; (bottom) Shannon Finney/Getty Images

Page 150 The Walt Disney Company/Image Group

Page 151 (top and bottom) Mike Saffels

Page 152 (top and bottom) Kelly Anderson

Page 153 (top left) Noel Whitmire; (top right) CosBot Photography; (bottom) Albert Ng

Page 155 (top and bottom) Symone Seven

Page 156 (top, two) Pocket Princesses ©Amy Mebberson. Reproduced with Permission; (bottom, two) Braden Graber

Page 158 (all) Kelsey Hermanson

Page 160 Courtesy of Paige O'Hara

Page 162 (inset) Courtesy of Linda Woolverton

Page 163 Mandy Rodgers

Page 165 Kate T. Parker/INSTITUTE

Page 167 (top) Walt Disney Television/Image Group LA/Getty Images; (bottom) Michael Piontek

Page 177 (top) Luann Waldrep

INDEX

*Page numbers in italics indicate illustrations.

20,000 Leagues Under the Sea, 56

A

Academy Awards, 109, 110–111, 118, *118*, 120
Adele, 120
Aguilera, Christina, 122
Aladdin, 29, 33–35, *33*, *34*, 57, 69–70, *69*, 80, 119, 122, 124, 127, *127*, 155, 158, 162, 172
Aladdin – A Musical Spectacular, 140
Aladdin and the King of Thieves, *57*, 59
Aladdin: The Return of Jafar, 57, *57*
Aladdin Jr., 127
Alcott, Louisa May, 29
Alice Comedies, 16
Alice in Wonderland, 23, 56, 144
Allure Bridals, 108
Amos, Tori, 120
Andersen, Hans Christian, 25, 52
Anderson, Ken, 142
Anderson-Lopez, Kristen, 120, 127
Andrews, Mark, 48
Animation Research Library, 83, 99
Anna, 52, 53, *53*, 62, *83*, 85, 87, 106, 128, 135, 137, 140, 144, 151, 166, 171
Arden, Amber, 151, *151*, 153
Ariel, 8–9, *9*, 10, 15, *25*, *26*, 27, *27*, 28–29, *28*, 40, 41, *41*, *59*, 60, 61, 62, 71, 79–80, *79*, 84, 87, 95, 97, *99*, 108, 112, *118*, 123, 126, *126*, 129, 138, 139, *139*, 153, 157, *157*, 159, 161, 168, 169, *169*, 171, 172
Armour Star Jubilee Ham, 76, *76*
"The Art of Animation" exhibit, 92
The Art Corner shop, 89, 92
"The Art of Disney" stamp series, 88
A.S. Fishbach company, 113
Ashman, Howard, 28, 29, *32*, 116, *116*, 119, 122, 128
Atwood, Donna, 138
Aulani, A Disney Resort & Spa, 133, 140, *140*, 142
Aurora, 10, 14, 23, 24, *24*, 41, *41*, 55, *61*, 62, 65, 66, *66*, 79, 97, 99–100, *99*, 106, 108, *110*, 113, 123, 134, 165, 170, 172
autographs, 139, *139*

B

Bailey, Halle, 71
Bailey, Sean, 11, 56–57, *56*, 71
Balderas, Theresa, 165
The Ballad of Mulan poem, 70–71
Ball, Lucille, 101
Bambi, 16, 20
Bareilles, Sara, 120, 129, *129*
Baxter, James, 30, 32
Beauty and the Beast, 15, 29–32, *30*, *31*, *32*, *56*, 60, 63, *63*, 68–69, *68*, 80, *83*, 84, *90*, 97, 104, 110–111, 119, 122, 123, *123*, 124, 125, *125*, 126, 129, 140, 162
Beauty and The Beast: Belle's Quest game, 84
Beauty and the Beast Live, 124, *124*
"Beauty and the Beast" song, 122
Bedard, Irene, 36, 37, *37*
Before the Story series, 58
Beguelin, Chad, 127
Belle, 10, *10*, 29–32, *30*, *31*, *32*, 41, *41*, 56, *56*, 57, 62, *62*, 63, *63*, 64, 68, *68*, *83*, 84, 87, 93, 96, *96*, *107*, 108, 110–111, *110*, 112, 123, 124, *124*, 125, 140, 159, 162, 163, 164, *167*, 168, 171, 172
Belle, Regina, 122
Ben Cooper Company, 113
Benson, Jodi, 27, *27*, 28, 29, 62, *129*, 168
"Be Our Guest" song, 124
Bésame Cosmetics, 106
"Bibbidi-Bobbidi-Boo" song, 118
Bibbidi Bobbidi Boutique, 136
Blair, Mary, 21, 22, *22*, 172
Blunt, Emily, 166
Boggess, Sierra, 126, *126*
Bolger, Sarah, *61*
books, 58, *58*, 78, 170, *170*
Bove, Lorelay, *42*
Branagh, Kenneth, 57, 66, 67
Brandy, 166
Brave, 47–48, *48*, *49*
Bresee, Becky, 53
Breznican, Jill, 99, 100
Brinkley, Christie, *27*, 28
Broadway, 124–128, *124*, *125*, *126*, *127*, *128*
Brongniart, Palais, 103
Brown, Yvette Nicole, 154
Bruns, George, 119
Bryson, Peabo, 122
Buck, Chris, 52
Burger King, 80
Burton, Tim, 129

C

Calfa, Chris, 153, *153*, 155
Camarata, Salvador "Tutti," 121–122
Canny, Andrea, 124–125, *124*
CAPS system, 123
Cardi B, 107
Carey, Mariah, 135
Caro, Niki, 70, 71
Carovilla, Elaine, 81, 82, 84
Carter, Charita, 133, 144
Carthay Circle Theatre (Los Angeles), 19
Cartier company, 101
Caselotti, Adriana, *18*, 19, 117
Castle of Magical Dreams, 136–137, *136*
Castro, Eduardo, 63, 154
"Celebrate the Century" stamp series, 88

Champion, Marge, 18, *18*
Chanel company, 110, *110*
Chapman, Brenda, 47–48
Charles (prince), *99*, 100
Chase, Leah, 43, *43*, 44
Chen-Yi Chang, 38, *39*
Christian Dior, 98, *98*, 100
Chung, Jamie, *61*
Churchill, Frank, 117, 118, 122
Cinderella (character), 11, 21, *21*, 22, *22*, 23, *23*, 41, *41*, 44, 55, 56, 57, 58, *58*, 59, 60, 61, 63, *63*, 74, 78, *78*, 95, 98, 100, *100*, 102, 103, *103*, *106*, 107, *107*, 108, *108*, 109, 110, 113, *113*, *116*, *123*, 135, 138, 139, *139*, 159, *159*, 161, 171, *173*
Cinderella (film), 16, 20, 22–23, *20*, *21*, *22*, 53, 60, 63, *63*, 66–67, *67*, 78, *78*, 80, 84, 90, *91*, 98–100, 102, 103, *103*, 118, 121–122, 123, *123*, 135, 138, 144, 152, *152*, *153*, 155, *155*, 158, 164, 172, *173*
Cinderella II: Dreams Come True, *57*, 59, *59*
Cinderella III: A Twist in Time, 59
Cinderella Castle (Orlando), 42, 135, *135*, *137*
Cinderella Castle (Tokyo), 136, *136*
Cinderella (Rodgers & Hammerstein), 155, 166
Cinderella's Romantic Castle LEGO set, 84
Cinderella's Royal Table, 135
Clark, Marguerite, 16
Classic Dolls, 81
Clements, Ron, 25, 42, 80
Coach Outlet, 105
Coats, Claude, 142
Coats, Emma, 48
Colbert, Claudette, *18*, 19, 98
Colcombet company, 101
"Colors of the Wind" song, 122
Columbia company, 106
Condon, Bill, 68
Conli, Roy, 45, 47
cookbooks, 170, *170*
The Cookie Carnival, *16*, 19
Cook, Joe, 122
Corea, Chick, 128
Costa, Mary, *23*, 24, 119
Courvoisier gallery, 89
Cravalho, Auli'i, 50, 51, *51*, 129, *129*, 171
Cruise, Suri, 135
Cruise, Tom, 135
Cubbage, Sarah, 140
Cyrus, Miley, 128

D

D23 Expo, 148–149, *149*, 154, *154*, *167*
D23 Mousequerade, 154, *154*
D23: The Official Disney Fan Club, 148
dance, 18, 78, 98, *117*, 123, *123*, 142–143
Danes, Claire, 107, *107*
David, Mack, 118
Davis, Alice, 24, 172
Davis, Marc, *20*, 21, 22, 23, 24, 65, 172
Davis, Miles, 128
Davis, Ruthie, 106
Del Rey, Lana, 122
DePaul, Darin, *124*
Depp, Lily-Rose, 110, *110*
Descendants, 57, 64, *64*
Designer Daddy, 108
Diana (princess), *99*, 100
Dietrich, Marlene, 19
Dion, Celine, 122
Disneyana, 89, *89*, 92
Disneyana Collectibles Show and Sale, 92
Disneyana Fan Club, 92
Disneyana Shop, *89*, 92
Disneyana: Walt Disney Collectibles (Cecil Munsey), 92
Disney Animation Research Library, 83, 99
Disney Animator's Collection Dolls, 83
Disney Before the Story series, 58
DisneyBounding, 111–112, *112*
Disney California Adventure Park, 127
Disney Consumer Products, 41, 74, 80, 81, 96, 102
Disney Cruise Line, 133, 140
Disney Dream ship, 140
Disney Emoji Blitz game, 87, *87*
Disney Fairies series, 41
Disney Frozen Adventures game, 87
Disneyland, 25, 89, *89*, 92, *92*, 131–133, *132*, 134–135, *134*, 138, *138*, 142–143, *142*, 144, 168
Disneyland Hong Kong, 136, *136*
Disneyland Paris, 144
Disneyland Shanghai, 135–136
Disneyland Tokyo, 135, 136, *136*
Disneyland Records, 121
Disney, Lillian, 101
Disney Mirrorverse game, *86*, 87
Disney On Ice, 141, *141*
Disney Princess game, 84
Disney Princess: Enchanted Journey game, 85, 87
Disney Princess franchise, 41–42, *41*
Disney Princess Half Marathon Weekend, 145, *145*
Disney Princess Majestic Quest game, 87
Disney Princess: My Fairytale Adventure game, 87
"Disney Renaissance," 25, 40, 57, 100, 116, 119
Disney, Roy O., 16–17, 75, 133
Disney's Aladdin – A Musical Spectacular, 140
Disney's Fairy Tale Weddings & Honeymoons, 96, 108, *108*, 137, *137*
Disney's Hollywood Studios Park, 122, 125
Disney Sorcerer's Arena game, *86*, 87
Disney, Walt, *15*, 16–17, 19, 23, 25, 45, 56, 73, *74*, 75, 88, 115, 117, 118, 121, 131, 132, *132*, 133, 135
Disney World, 42, 92, 124, 125, 133, 135, *135*, 137, *137*, 143, *143*, 144, 145, 168
dolls, 74, 77, *77*, 78, 79, *79*, 81, *81*, 82, 83, 92, 93, *93*
Donald Duck, 19, 75
Dooky Chase's Restaurant (New Orleans), 43, *43*
"A Dream is a Wish Your Heart Makes" song, 118–119
#DreamBigPrincess series, 166
Dream Big, Princess campaign, 162, 164–166, *166*
Duck, Donald, 19, 75
Durran, Jacqueline, 63

E

Earle, Eyvind, 134
Eaton, Mary, 100
Eckstein, Ashley, 154

Egan, Susan, 125
Ehrbar, Greg, 117, 122
Eisner, Michael, 25, 122, 124–125
Ellington, Duke, 117
Elsa, 52, 53, *53*, 62, *83*, 84, 85, 87, *96*, 97, 106, 120, *120*, 128, *128*, 135, 137, 140, 144, 150, 151, 166, 171
Emmerich, Peter, 88
Emoji Blitz, 87, *87*
Encanto, 163
Enchanted Fine Jewelry, 106
Enchanted Storybook Castle, 135
Evan K. Shaw company, *74*, 78, *78*

F

The Fairest One of All: The Making of Walt Disney's Snow White (J.B. Kaufman), 117–118
Fanning, Elle, *65*, 66, *66*
Fantasia, 19
feminism, 29, 68–69, *68*, 162–163, *163*
Ferretti, Alberta, 102
Flounder, 169, *169*
Foa'i, Opetaia, 121
Fott, Galen, 124, *124*
The Fox and the Hound, 25
Francine, Anne, 122
The Fred Waring Show, 22–23
The Frog Prince (Brothers Grimm), 42
Frozen, 52–53, *52*, *53*, 58, 62, *83*, 84, 97, 105, 106, 111, *111*, 120, *120*, 127–128, 135, 137, 138, *141*, 163, 168, 172
Frozen 2, 53, *53*, 87, *96*, 106, 172
Frozen, A Musical Spectacular, 140
Frozen Ever After attraction, 144
Frozen Fever, 60
Funko dolls, 93, *93*

G

Gabriel, Mike, 36
games, 84–87, *84*, *85*, *86*, *87*
Garcia, Nephi, 108
Garone, Adam, 171
Gerry, Vance, *175*
Gerwig, Greta, 71
Gilmore, Jean, *35*
Girl Up initiative, 165
Givenchy, Hubert de, 100
Glancy, Mark, 19
Glee television series, 53, *53*
The Goddess of Spring, *16*, 19
Goldberg, Eric, 35
Gold Key comic books, 79
Gong Bell company, 79
Gooding, Ian, *42*
Goodwin, Ginnifer, *61*
Graeber, Braden, 157
Graham, Martha, 53
Grande, Ariana, 109, 122
The Great Mouse Detective, 25
Greno, Nathan, 45, *45*

H

Halloween costumes, 113, *113*
Hamilton, Alyson, *30*
Hamilton, Rebecca, *153*, 155
Hancock, Herbie, 128
Harlow, Jean, 98
Harrods department store, 102
Hasbro company, 81
Head, Edith, 100
HeForShe campaign, 163
Hei Hei, 169, *169*
Henn, Beth, 34, *34*
Henn, Mark, 30, 31, 32, 34, 38, 39–40, *40*, 44, 83, 100
Hepburn, Audrey, 31, 99, *99*
Hercules, 29, 36
Hermanson, Kelsey, 158, *158*
Hill, Faith, 128
Hines, Traci, 128–129
Hipster Ariel meme, 157, *157*, 159
Hirschfeld, Al, 34
Hoffman, Al, 118
Hollywood Bowl, 129, *129*
Holmes, Katie, 110, *110*
Holt, Bethan, 97
home décor, 158, *158*
Horowitz, Adam, 60, 62
hospital gowns and pants, 168, 171, *171*
Howard, Byron, 45, *45*
"How Far I'll Go" song, 121
Huffy company, 80
The Hunchback of Notre Dame, 29, 36, 125

I

Ice Capades, 138
Ideal Toy Company, 76
Imagineers, 133, 134, 135, 136, 140, 142, 143, 144
"I'm Wishing" song, 116
Ink & Paint department, 172
Instagram, 137, 148, 150, 156, 157, *157*, *164*, 165
interior design, 158, *158*
Irvine, Kim, 143, 144
"it's a small world" attraction, 144, *144*, 172
"I want" songs, 70, 116, *118*, 121, 126
"I Wonder" song, 104

J

James, Lily, *63*, 67, *67*
Jasmine, *11*, 29, 33–35, *34*, 41, *41*, 57, 69–70, *69*, 85, 87, 106, 127, 162, 165, 169, *169*, 172
JCPenney company, 102, *102*
Joe Books, 156
Johnston, Phil, 70
Jolie, Angelina, 65, *65*
Jonas, Danielle, 135
Jonas, Kevin, 135
Julius, Jessica, 53, 163, 173
The Jungle Book, 25

K

Kamen, Herman S. "Kay," 75, *75*, 78
Kamen, Kay, 101, 113

Kane, Christopher, 97, 104
Katzenberg, Jeffrey, 25
Kaufman, J.B., 117
Kay, Leslie, 111–112, *112*
Keane, Claire, 46, *46*
Keane, Glen, 27, 28, 29, *35*, 37, 45, 46, 60, 83
Keane, Linda, 28
Kelley, Faron, 145
Kelly, Grace, 21, *21*, 108
Kelly, Kirstie, *96*, 108
Kennedy, Kathleen, 166
Khan, Naeem, 102
Kidston, Cath, 105
Killingsworth, JoAnn Dean, 138, *138*
Kingdom Hearts game, *84*, 85, *85*
King Stefan's Banquet Hall. *See* Cinderella's Royal Table.
"Kirstie Kelly for Disney's Fairy Tale Weddings" collection, 108
"Kiss the Girl" song, 119
Kitsis, Edward, 11, 60, 62
Knickerbocker Toy Company, 76
Kraft, Richard, 129
Kroger's grocery stores, 76
Kuhn, Judy, 37, *37*

L

Lady and the Tramp, 23
Lancaster Jones, Juan Pablo Reyes, 172
Lapin-Kurley Kew Inc., 101
Larkin, Linda, 34, *34*, 57, 174
Larson, Eric, 22, *23*
Lawrence, Judy, 124
Le Château de la Belle au Bois Dormant, 135
Lee, Brittney, 53, *167*, 168, 172
Lee, Jennifer, 10–11, 52, 120, 128, 164, 166, 173
LEGO Disney Princess set, *83*, 84
Lehtomaki, Kira, 46, 100, 163, 169
Lelong fashion house, 101
"Let It Go" song, 53, 120, *120*, 128
Lhuillier, Monique, 102
Liao, Lulu, 165
The Lion King, 29, 36, 122, 125
The Little Mermaid, 8–9, *9*, 11, 25–29, *25*, *26*, 28, *28*, *29*, 32, 40, 71, 79, *79*, 80, 83, 90, *90*, 96, 98, *99*, 113, 115, *118*, 119, 122, 125–127, *126*, 128, 129, *129*, 158, *169*, 172
The Little Mermaid II: Return to the Sea, 59, *59*
The Little Mermaid III: Ariel's Beginning, 59
The Little Mermaid Live!, 129, *129*
The Little Mermaid television series, 59
Littledove, Shirley, *35*, 37
Little Golden Books, 58, 78
Little Town, 60
Little Women (Louisa May Alcott), 29
Lively, Blake, 107
Livingston, Jerry, 118
LL Cool J, 117
Lopez, Robert, 120, 128
Louboutin, Christian, 103, *103*
Louis Vuitton, 110–111
Lowe, Anne, 100
Lozano, Gilbert, 152
Lund, Dan, 53
Luske, Hamilton, 19

M

MacDonald, Alexander K., *37*
Macdonald, Kelly, 47
MacDougall, Tom, 70
Mackey, Robbie, 124
Madame Alexander company, 77, *77*, 79
"Mad Princess Party," 154, *154*
Magic Kingdom, 92, 133, 135, 137, 143, *143*, 144
The Mail Pilot, 88
Main Street, U.S.A., *89*, 92, *92*, 132
Make-A-Wish Foundation, 168
Maleficent, 64, 65–66, *65*, 85
Maleficent: Mistress of Evil, 66, *66*
Mancina, Mark, 121
Mann, Aimee, 120
Marchesa company, 102, 110
Mars, Bruno, 128
Marshall Field company, 101
Martens, Todd, 132
Martin, Stacia, 74, 78, 118
Marx, Bethany, 150–151
Mattel company, 81
McDonald's, 80, *80*
McFann, Korri, 137
Mebberson, Amy, 60, 155–156, *156*
memes, 11, 111, 147, 155, 157, *157*, 159, *159*, 165
Menendez, Mario, 93, *93*
Menken, Alan, 28, 29, 40, 70, *116*, *118*, 119, 122, 125, 126, 127, 128, 129
Menzel, Idina, 120, *120*
Merbabies, 25
Merida, 42, 47–48, *48*, 49, *49*, 61, 62, 80, 97, *138*, 139, *139*, *153*, 155
Metcalf, Kaytie, 154
Mickey Mouse, 19, 74, 75, 76, 88, 113, 115, *133*, 138, 148
Mickey Mouse Club, 81, 122, 148, *148*
Milano, Alyssa, 28
Miller, Ann, 101
Ming-Na Wen, 38, *38*, 39
Minnie Mouse, 113, 138
Miranda, Lin-Manuel, 121
Mittermeier, Sabrina, 134
Moana, 13, 15, 42, 48, 50–52, *50*, *51*, 60, 74, 80, *91*, 97, 100, 113, *113*, 121, 129, 139, *140*, 142, 161, 162, 168, 169, *169*, 171, 173
Molanphy, Chris, 119
Mollet, Tracey, 14
Montgomery Ward, 113
Mooney, Andy, 41
Moore, Mandy, 45, 46, *46*, 60, 62
Morey, Larry, 117
Morrison, Jennifer, *61*
Morris, Tom, 135
Mouse, Mickey, 19, 74, 75, 88, 113, 115, *133*, 138, 148
Mouse, Minnie, 113, 138
Mousetrap company, 129
movie posters, 90, *90–91*
Mulan, 11, 29, 36, 38–41, *38*, *39*, *40*, *41*, *56*, 57, *61*, 62, 70, *70*, 71, *71*, 87, *91*, 106, 112, *119*, 122, 144, 161, 170, 171
Mumolo, Annie, 60
Munsey, Cecil, 92
Mushu, 170
Music Land, 16
Musker, John, 25, 42, 43, 50

N

Natwick, Grim, 18, 19
Neilsen, Kay, *26*
Neuschwanstein castle, 134
"New Look" fashion, 98, *98*
New York World's Fair (1964–1965), 138
Nielsen, Kay, 25
"Nine Old Men," 22
novelizations, 58, *58*
Nyong'o, Lupita, *107*, 109

O

Obama, Barack, 42
Oceanic Story Trust, 14–15, 51
O'Connor, Sinéad, 128
Odie, Mama, 100
O'Hara, Paige, 31, *31*, 32, *32*, 124, *124*, *167*, 168
'Ōlelo Hawaii, 171
Oliver & Company, 25
"Once Upon a Dream" song, 119
Once Upon an American Dream: A Cultural History of the Disney Fairy Tale (Tracey Mollet), 14
Once Upon a Time television series, 11, 57, 60–62, *61*, *62*, 63, *63*, 154
Orbach, Jerry, 124, *124*
Oreb, Tom, 23
Ortega, Kenny, 64

P

Pacheco, Dave, 79, 82, 88, 97, 106
Packham, Jenny, 102
Pan, Peter, 98
Paquin fashion house, 101
Parker, Alice, 165, *165*
Parker, Kate T., 165, *165*
"Part of Your World" song, *118*, 121, 128
Pascal, *169*
Patou fashion house, 101
Pell, Paula, 124, *124*
Pena, Hilcia, 137
Perrault, Charles, 20, 67
Peter Pan, 23, 98
picture books, 58, *58*
Pinocchio, 19, 119
Pirates of the Caribbean: The Curse of the Black Pearl, 56
Pixar, 88
"A Place Called Slaughter Race" song, 70
Pocahontas, 29, 35–36, *35*, *36*, 37, *37*, 41, *41*, 80, 119, 122, 138, 139, *139*, *175*
"Pocket Princesses" comic series, 155–156, *156*
Posen, Zac, 96, 107, *107*, 109, 111, *111*
Powell, Sandy, 63, *63*, 103
Prada company, 109
Preston, Lauren, 85, 87
The Princess and the Frog, 42, 44, *44*, 60, 83, 122, 144, 170
The Princess and the Frog: Tiana's Cookbook: Recipes for Kids, 170, *170*
"Princess Hangout" song, 128
Pursley, Mandy, 152, *152*

R

Radio City Music Hall, 19, 122
Rajah, 169, *169*
Ralph Breaks the Internet, 70, 149
Rapunzel, 42, 45, *45*, 46, *46*, *47*, 60, *60*, 64, 80, 85, 87, 111, 112, 123, *138*, 139, *139*, *143*, 144, 150, 153, *155*, 158, *169*
Rapunzel's Tangled Adventure television series, 60
Rapunzel's Tower, *143*, 144
Ravin, Emilie de, 62, *62*
Raya and the Last Dragon, 163, 173
Red Riding Hood, 61, 76
Reed, Courtney, 127
Reed, Sean, 165
Reeser, Shaina, 168
"Reflection" song, *119*, 122
The Reluctant Dragon, 56
The Rescuers, 25
The Return of Jafar, 57, *57*
Ribeiro, Alfonso, 154
Ribon, Pamela, 70
Rice, Tim, 119, 125
Richard G. Krueger Company, 76, 77
Rider, Flynn, 45
Ritchie, Guy, 69
Ritchie, Robina, 34
Roach, Law, 109–110, *109*
Roberto Coin company, 106
Roberts, Robin, 166
Rogers, Douglas, 135–136
Roman Holiday (film), 24, 99, *99*, 100
Roque, Lazaro, 93, *93*
Rose, Anika Noni, *43*, 44
Roth, Jordan, *111*
Roth, Robert Jess, 125
Rumpelstiltskin, 62
runDisney events, 112, 145
Ryman, Herbert, 132, 134, 135

S

Saks Fifth Avenue, 102, *104*
Salerno, Mary Jo, 122
Salonga, Lea, 34, *38*, *119*, 124, *124*
Sanders, Chris, *30*, 40
Sanitone company, 102
San Souci, Robert D., 39
Sarg, Tony, 77
Schimkowitz, Matt, 159
Schneider, Peter, 36
Schumacher, Tom, 126, 127
Schwab, Bill, *42*
Scott, Naomi, 69–70, *69*, 162
Sebastian, Paolo, 104
Sedgwick, John, 19
Seiberling Latex Products Co., *74*, 75–76
Sephora company, 106
Seven Dwarfs Mine Train attraction, 144
Seven, Symone, 155, *155*
Shearmur, Alli, 67
Sheppard, Anna B., 66
Shimmer Doll line, 81

Shurer, Osnat, 50, 52, 60, 121, 162, 173
sidekicks, 169, *169*
Silly Symphony series, 16, *16*, 19, 25
Silverman, Sarah, 70
Simon & Schuster company, 58
Siriano, Christian, 107
Sklar, Marty, 135
Slater, Glenn, 126
Sleeping Beauty, 23, *23*, 65, 78–79, 90, *91*, 92, 99, 104, 105, 106, 113, 116, 119, *121*, 123, *123*, 134, 135
Sleeping Beauty Castle, 132, *132*, 134, *134*, 135, 144
Sleeping Beauty Castle (Hong Kong), 136
Smeed, Amy, 51
The Snow Queen (Hans Christian Andersen), 52
Snow White and Her Adventures attraction, 142
Snow White and the Seven Dwarfs, 10, 13, 14, *14*, *15*, 16–17, 19, *17*, 19, *19*, 20, 58, *58*, 61, 71, 74, *74*, 75–76, 77, *77*, *78*, 80, 81, 89, 90, *90*, 93, 98, 101, *101*, 102, *102*, *104*, 105, 106, 113, 115, 117–118, *117*, *121*, 122, 123, 128, 138, 172, 173
Snow White (character), 10, 14, *14*, *15*, 17, *17*, 18, *18*, 19, 20, 23, 41, *41*, 55, 61, *61*, 62, 71, 74, *75*, 76, 78, *78*, 81, *81*, 83, 85, 88, 97, 98, 101, 102, 105, 106, *106*, 113, *113*, 116, *116*, *133*, 138, *138*, *139*, 142, 143, *151*, 153, 154, 165, *165*, 173
Snow White board games, 77
Snow White household bleach, 76, *76*
Snow White's Enchanted Wish attraction, 142–143
Snow White's Scary Adventures attraction, 142
Sofia the First television series, 62, 64
Solomon, Charles, 167
"Someday My Prince Will Come" song, 117, 128
Sora, 85
Sorcerer's Arena game, *86*, 87
Sparkle Dolls, 81
Spatz, Libby, 76, 148
Specht, Bobby, 138
Splash Mountain attraction, 143–144
stamps, 88
Stanley, Helene, 21, *21*, 24
Starlight Children's Foundation, 168, 171, *171*
"Starting Now" song, 166
Star Wars, 19, *151*, 154
Steamboat Willie, 115
Steinem, Gloria, 69
Stoner, Sherri, 27, 28–29, *29*, 31
Stones, Tad, 57
Streisand, Barbra, 117
Stromberg, Robert, 66
Swan, Emma, 61, *61*, 62
Swift's Allsweet Margarine, 76
"The Swing" (Fragonard), *46*

T

Tales of Courage and Kindness, 58
Tangled, 45, *45*, 47, *82*, 100, 119, 158
Tangled: Before Ever After, *57*
Tangled Ever After, 60, *60*
Tangled: The Musical, 140
Tarzan, 29
Taylor, Elizabeth, 31, *31*
Tchaikovsky, Peter, 119
Tell-A-Tale Books, 78
"The Tempest" (John William Waterhouse), 49, *49*
Temple, Shirley, 19, *19*, 98, *98*, 135
Tenggren, Gustaf, 90
Theodoulou, Nick, 93
Thomas, Frank, 20, 21
Thornton, Randy, 116
Three Little Pigs, 16, 117
Tiana, 42–44, *42*, *43*, 60, 83, 95, 100, *100*, 123, *143*, 144, *149*, 157, 164, 170, *170*, 171
TikTok, 170
Time company, 102
Tinker Bell, 41, *41*, 128
Tomart's Illustrated Disneyana (Tom Tumbusch), 92
Tommy Hilfiger company, 109
TOMS Disney Collection shoes, 96
Tony Awards, 125
Torpey, Karen, 96, 102, 108
The Tortoise and the Hare, 16
Treasure Island, 56
Tumbusch, Tom, 75, 92–93

U

Ultimate Princess Celebration, 162, 168, 171
"Under the Sea" song, 119
U.S. Postal Service, 88

V

Valentino (designer), 102
Vanellope, 70
Vargo, Michael, 149
Vevers, Stuart, 105
video games, 84–87, *84*, *85*, *86*, *87*
Vikander, Alicia, *107*, 110–111
Villains stamp series, 88
Villeneuve, Gabrielle-Suzanne Barbot de, 29
Vitale, Ami, 165
Vivienne Westwood Couture, 107
"Voyage of the Little Mermaid" show, 125

W

Wagner, Frank, 122
Waking Sleeping Beauty, 116
Walker, Mandy, 71
Walt Disney Animation Studios, 14, 23, 36, 40, 42, 47, 53, 55, 57, 58, 79, 116, 121, 123, 163, 164, 172, 173
Walt Disney Character Merchandise catalogue, *89*, 113
Walt Disney Classics series, 80
Walt Disney Classics Collection, 92
Walt Disney Collectors Society, 92
Walt Disney Family Museum, 101
Walt Disney Imagineering, 133, 134, 135, 136, 140, 142, 143, 144
Walt Disney Masterpiece Collection, 80
Walt Disney Records, 122
Walt Disney World, 42, 92, 124, 125, 133, 135, *135*, 137, *137*, 143, *143*, 144, 145, 168
Walt Disney World Marathon, 145
Walt Disney World Resort, 133
Waterhouse, John William, 49

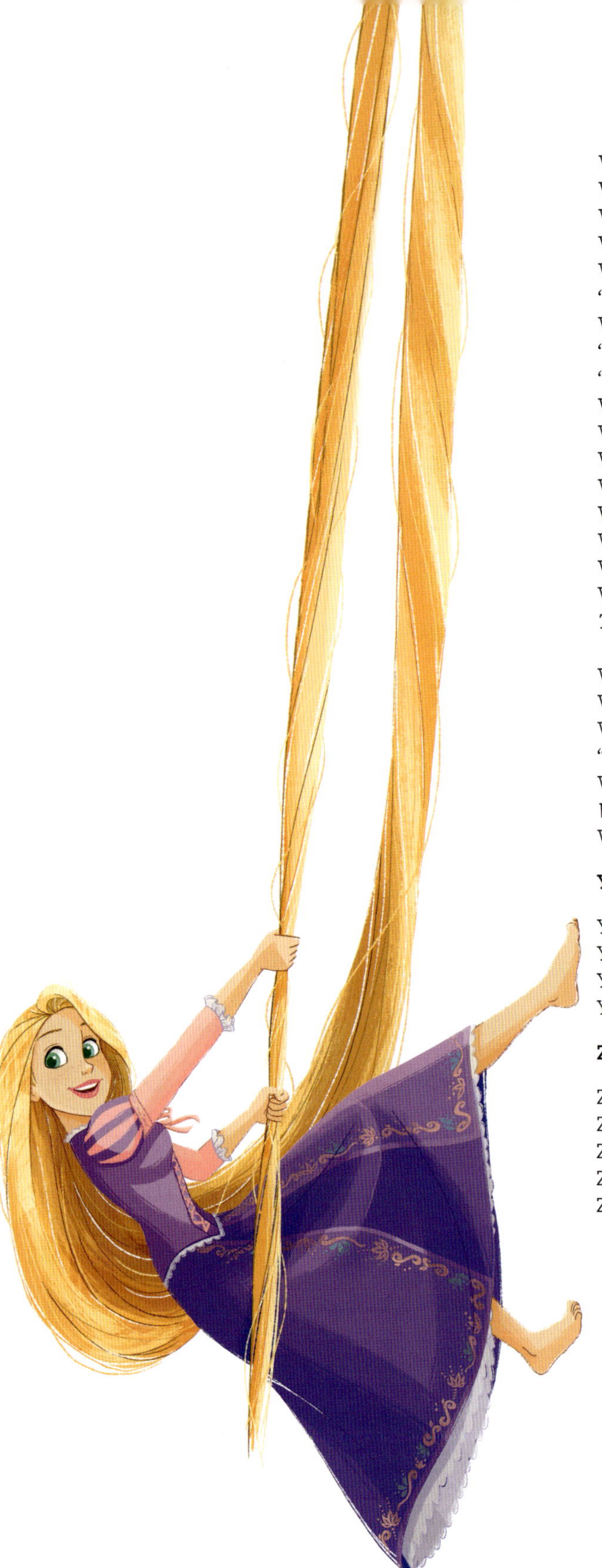

Watson, Emma, *56*, 63, *63*, 68, *68*, 162–163
Webb, Marc, 71
Weis, Bob, 136
Weitz, Chris, 66
Wells, Frank, 25
"When You Wish Upon a Star" song, 119
Whitedove, Debbie, *35*, 37
"A Whole New World" song, 122, 124
"Who's Afraid of the Big Bad Wolf?" song, 117
Wiig, Kristen, 60
Williams, Gabrielle, 170
Williams, Rebecca, 148, 153
Williams, Vanessa, 122
Willner, Hal, 128
Wilson, Annika, 150
Winfrey, Oprah, 43
Winter, Ariel, 62
The Wonderful World of Disney Presents The Little Mermaid Live!, 129, *129*
Wood, Natalie, 31, *31*
Woods, Ilene, *20*, *21*, 118
Woolverton, Linda, 15–16, 29–30, 33, 65, 125, 162, *162*
"The World Above" song, 126
Wornova Manufacturing Company, 113
Wreck-It Ralph, 70
Wright, Doug, 126

Y

Yifei, Liu, *70*, 71, *71*
Yoonessi, Suzi, 172
Young, Loretta, 98
YouTube, 84, 128, 155, 165

Z

Zambello, Francesca, 126
Zegler, Rachel, 71
Zemler, Emily, 10–11
Zendaya, 109–110, *109*, 154
Zydeco, Buckwheat, 122